# THE LAST LATRINE

## Richard Grainger

**MINERVA PRESS**
LONDON
MONTREUX   LOS ANGELES   SYDNEY

THE LAST LATRINE
Copyright © Richard Grainger 1997


All Rights Reserved

No part of this book may be reproduced in any form,
by photocopying or by any electronic or mechanical means,
including information storage or retrieval systems,
without permission in writing from both the copyright owner
and the publisher of this book.


ISBN 1 86106 775 5


First Published 1997 by
MINERVA PRESS
195 Knightsbridge
London SW7 1RE

2nd Impression 1998

Printed and bound in Great Britain by
Antony Rowe Ltd, Chippenham, Wiltshire

# THE LAST LATRINE

Profits from this book will be shared equally between
SeeAbility and The Everest Marathon Fund.


Acknowledgements to Rob Howard for the use of the photograph 'The
Early Birds at Tengboche'.

To my wife, Kirsty, whose task of being *here*
whilst I was *there*, was no less arduous than mine.

Also, thanks to all those who supported, encouraged
or humoured me in the pursuit of this goal; particularly Neil
Pocket, the staff and governors of St John's School, Sidmouth.

# *Foreword*

Every two years the Everest region of Nepal is invaded by a bunch of about one hundred lunatics who say that they have come to run a marathon in the foothills below Everest base camp. For the competitors the four week trip to Nepal is the culmination of at least a year's preparation and *angst*. They come with vastly different expectations and ambitions, ages and experience, temperaments and prejudices. But, by the day of the race itself, this group of unlikely bedfellows has been welded into a tightly knit group by illness, injury, endurance and suffering, culture shock and fear of what might happen in this harsh but majestic mountain environment. No one forgets the awe-inspiring scenery or the shared achievement of just being there.

Richard's account relates how he was affected and changed by this mountain adventure as life got harder and harsher at the top of the world. Yes, he was a moaner, determined not to be forced into the group mould, but that was partly his way of coping with the unknown and unexpected. At least he had a sense of humour and was able to laugh at his own shortcomings and misfortunes!

One of the main reasons for organising this extraordinary race is to raise money for the Everest Marathon Fund which supports education and health projects in rural Nepal. Over five races we have raised over one hundred and sixty thousand pounds, and that does not include the money which runners have raised for many other charities. For so many, the event becomes not only proof of athletic achievement, but also a chance of helping others less fortunate. For Richard, the pain of the experience was amply rewarded by the gain of being able to raise money for a day centre attended by his handicapped son Jake.

*Diana Penny Sherpani*
*Everest Race Organiser*
*Trustee Everest Marathon Fund*

# *Prologue*

## Thursday 28th October, 1993, 12.50 p.m.
## Somewhere in Dartmoor National Park, England

"What the bloody hell are we doing here?" I yelled to my companion, which was neither very helpful, nor particularly meaningful to her.

My companion, Floss, a six year old Border Collie bitch, had just disappeared into the third bog of indeterminable depth and consistency in as many minutes.

To a normally more white than black fastidious little dog, who has a daily conflict reconciling a loathing of being washed with a strong desire to experience the pleasures associated with getting covered in mud from nose to tail, this was a new experience.

Extricating herself from the bog, with fur so firmly plastered to her back that even a shake violent enough to cause her to overbalance would not shift, she eyed me with the kind of suspicion normally reserved for headmasters and council tax assessors.

Her mind, so used to unquestioning loyalty and go-anywhere devotion, was experiencing the same dark thoughts and questions as mine. This little dog, who had gamely accompanied me on all but a few of the two hundred and eighty-five miles of the Cornwall Coast path run over ten days in April '92, was well used to foul conditions, filthy weather, and paths suddenly ceasing to exist, or becoming rivers.

But this was different. This was Dartmoor.

The thing about Dartmoor, and why it is so very, very dangerous, is that you can virtually guarantee that the conditions you set out in will always be better than those you return in. Which is why it's always vitally important to tell someone where you intend going. Assuming of course that you know where you're going.

I neither know Dartmoor well nor possess proven navigational skills, so it was perhaps a curious decision to set out from Postbridge on what should have been a twelve mile training run. Curious, but not entirely without aforethought.

After discussion with the lady in the National Trust shop, I decided to run from Postbridge, and circumnavigate Fernworthy Forest and Reservoir as far as Assycombe Hill, where I would pick up a path bringing me back to the road and, ultimately, my starting point.

On paper it looked simple enough. "A good day's walking," she had enthused. "Should take five to six hours, at a steady pace. Just follow the river until it turns west, then head for Long Ridge. The path will take you through the forest, and you'll see the reservoir from there."

Within five minutes, we were lost. What she had omitted to say, was that the term 'path', contrary to what the map suggested, was a notional idea of where it may be possible to make forward progress somewhere between river, tor and bog, and as such had little real value in navigational terms.

Being a firm believer in holding the high ground, Floss and I headed for Stannon Tor, and made steady if unspectacular progress from White Ridge to Long Ridge, keeping the forest on our right.

Then two things happened.

First, the reasonable surface of mossy grass, which had been quite suitable for running, disappeared. Secondly, the forest, which was essential for navigation, also disappeared. The former was replaced with marshy, unpredictable little fields, inexplicably enclosed by dry stone walls which could only be traversed by elaborate but extremely unhelpful upright wooden styles. The latter had completely disappeared into the mist which had suddenly descended. Visibility was down to less than twenty yards.

Somewhere here was the path entering the forest that would have brought us to the reservoir, but we had scant hope of finding it as, due to the nature of the ground, it was impossible to run close enough to the perimeter of the forest to see it.

We had two choices. First, to turn back, try to find the river which we had abandoned in favour of the Tor, and follow it back to Postbridge. The second was to follow the perimeter of the forest to the reservoir, and either pick up the Two Moors Way, or head for Water Hill along Hurston Ridge, from where it should be possible to stumble across the road.

We chose the second course of action, as in the fog it would have been impossible to obtain an accurate compass bearing (even if I could use it properly), so there was no guarantee of finding the river. Although the former was undoubtedly the quicker route, we set off with the wind in our teeth, and the rain stinging our faces, running as close to the perimeter of the forest as the terrain would allow.

I cursed as I sank up to my waist on two occasions, and when, despite my dependable fell shoes, I slid thirty feet down a gully, coming to rest painfully on a concealed boulder.

Eventually, through the mist, we could see the reservoir, and knew that our ordeal should soon be at an end. We followed a good path, which joined a lane around the reservoir, and struck out across the moor again, confident of attaining the high ground which would take us back to the road.

My hands, feet and other parts of my body had by now lost all sensation, and despite having demolished a foul tasting but highly effective energy bar, and drunk most of my water, the puffy white clouds on the periphery of my vision told me that I was fairly close to exhaustion. This was a familiar and sinister warning sign, telling me of rapidly advancing dehydration.

Floss had had a Bonio, and didn't seem to be any the worse for wear. This was tolerable, as the road was only over the next ridge, and a steady trot of a couple of miles downhill to Postbridge and the van. It was also tolerable, as this was probably my last long training run before the Everest Marathon, after which it was extremely unlikely that I would ever do anything particularly athletic again. At least, for some considerable time.

So why then was the forest still on our right? I got out the compass which, to my horror, confirmed that we were heading west. We should have been heading due south.

There was nothing to do but continue. It was within fifteen minutes that the full horror of the situation dawned on me. Thankfully Floss was fairly oblivious to what was happening, or if she wasn't, she wasn't saying anything.

At first, I thought it was fatigue, but gradually it dawned on me that the evidence was irrefutable – we were passing landmarks which we had run past two hours ago. The final proof of this was when the fog lifted momentarily to reveal the path through the forest that we had looked for, leading to the reservoir.

I stopped, and sat down. I had never before felt so demoralised, so frustrated, so knackered and so alone. Throughout the run, we had not seen another living soul, sheep apart.

Later, I entered in my diary: "It was a foul run, and made me realise what a bleak and hell-like place Dartmoor is. Even the sheep looked depressed; small wonder with skeletons and bones picked clean by crows constantly littering the landscape.

If I was a sheep, I would consider slitting my throat with my hoof and having the predators pick my bones a preferable alternative to life, in this drab wilderness."

It was at this point that I realised that I wasn't enjoying this very much.

We were lost, although I knew exactly where we were. What mattered was that I hadn't a clue as to how to get back to where we had started from. We were at the furthest point from our start and destination. That meant it was at least another hour, even if we could get our bearings. That meant we would be well overdue, and my wife would assume the worst and call out the emergency services. That meant I would not only waste time and resources, but I would look a complete and utter moron, having only twenty-four hours ago appeared on Westcountry Television, being interviewed on Dartmoor.

I had talked dismissively about the perils of running in the world's highest marathon, and how training on Dartmoor was the perfect preparation. I had unintentionally implied that I was something of an authority on Dartmoor. I had stressed how important was "pushing back the boundaries of one's goals and horizons against the humdrum of everyday challenges".

I could hear the laughter now. "'Ere Elsie, did you see that bloke on TV last night? Talkin' about running down Everest, 'e was. On telly again tonight, 'e was. Got 'imself lost on Dartmoor, had to be flown to hospital by 'elicopter. 'Im and 'is dog. Poor little bugger! Talk about find 'is way down Everest, 'e couldn't find 'is way out of a wet paper bag!"

I was a complete failure. Perhaps, faced with failure, and the prospect of a long, tiring and hazardous journey back to safety, over unfamiliar country in poor weather conditions, when the body was too tired and the mind was too numb to make normal rational judgement... perhaps similar feelings of despair, frustration and even anger were felt by George Mallory, by Norton, Odell, Smythe, Evans and Bourdillon, among others, who had come so close to the goal that had eluded them all.

Only my goal was simply to get back to the car park.

Eventually, I got myself going. Exposure, and the onset of hypothermia was a mounting worry, as it had been on several occasions throughout the previous two months. I was wearing most of the minimum gear which I always carried in the event of injury (or getting lost), but if things got really bad I could seek shelter from the elements, and crawl into my bivvy bag.

I decided to retrace our steps to the reservoir, rather than continue to orbit the forest, look for the river or seek an alternative path through the forest. Twenty minutes later, we came to a wire fence, which I didn't remember previously crossing. There was something on the map which seemed to correspond to its whereabouts and, in desperation, we decided to follow it.

Half an hour later we were still following it.

And so it was here, at around 12.50 p.m., on that Thursday afternoon, when any flickering hopes of finding our way back were virtually extinguished, here, somewhere between hell and high water, that Floss emerged from a near watery grave and shook violently and decisively. It was here that she turned and looked at me, knee-deep in mud, a look that conveyed more disbelief than desperation, but echoed the question I had voiced: "What the bloody hell are we doing here?"

It was here, also, that perhaps I came to understand George Leigh Mallory's reply to the question of a young American journalist, who enquired as to why he wanted he risk his life attempting to climb Everest.

"Because it is there," came the reply, which currently has more common than mountaineering usage.

This was not the dismissive, flippant reply of a man haunted by failure thus far to achieve his dream, frustrated by petty officialdom, and irritated by the lack of interest in his American lecture tour. The calculated use of the word *there*, referred to the mystical quality of a goal to which he aspired, and indeed to which he gave his life. And, for all we know, he may well have achieved.

*There* referred to that holiest of grails, that most formidable of opponents that requires every last ounce of strength, guile and adrenalin. Just to survive. *There* represents the ultimate challenge, whether it be to learn to walk again after a serious accident, to overcome an illness, to climb Mount Everest, or to run the Everest Marathon.

It is the greatest effort, physical, mental, and perhaps even spiritual, that one can give at that particular time, and is the driving force behind one's existence. *There* overcomes the *how* and *why* and overrides the logic button.

As the poet Franz Wefel once put it: "For those who believe, no explanation is necessary; for those who do not believe, no explanation is possible."

And so for months Floss and I had been grinding out the miles, day after day, week after week, in all conditions, so as I would be prepared for going there. To be prepared to survive and complete the Everest Marathon was all that mattered. To meet the greatest physical challenge of my life.

But all this was a little hard to explain to Floss.

In any case, where we were right then, was *here*.

## *Epilogue of the Prologue*

Some fifteen minutes later the mist cleared, as we struggled to the top of Merripit Hill, and from there two very relieved pairs of eyes saw, beneath us, the road. With renewed vigour, we bounded down the hill, and jogged back to the van, some three hours after leaving it.

Thankfully, I managed to contact my wife before she raised the alarm.

Almost a month later, on the Khumbu Glacier, I was to ask myself the same question. It is my hope that, as I get older, I will perhaps get a little wiser. But that wisdom should not preclude perusing a goal, for no other reason than because it's *there*. This is what makes the here and now, however dull and humdrum, worthwhile.

Adventure is not purely the province of 'The Adventurer'. As an adventure, The Everest Marathon was unparalleled in my experience. This book is a candid and more often than not affectionate account of my month in Nepal, of which the 1993 Everest Marathon was but one day. The purpose of writing my story is to show that 'Joe Average', with a lot of determination, luck and support, can experience the thrill of a real adventure.

# Contents

| | |
|---|---|
| *Introduction* "Which One's Everest?" | xvii |
| "Running to the Top?" | 21 |
| "Dog Day in Dhaka" | 29 |
| "There's a One-Eyed Yellow Idol to the North of Kathmandu…" | 38 |
| The Road to Jiri and a Voice in the Dark: "Namaste! Give Me Pen, Give Me Bonbon!" | 60 |
| Mali to Bhandar, Farewell to the First Latrine | 82 |
| Bhandar to Sete: "Got to Keep the Loonies on the Path" | 106 |
| Sete to Junbesi: "These Shoes Aren't Made for Walking!" | 120 |
| Junbesi to Tragsindho La: "Everest? I Must Have Mist It!" | 140 |
| Tragsindho La to Lukla: "Stairway to Heaven or the Road to Hell?" | 154 |
| Lukla to Namche Bazaar: "Heaven Knows I'm Miserable Now!" | 170 |
| Namche Bazaar: "Introducing the Band" | 188 |

| | |
|---|---|
| The Road to Tengboche: "And Some Say That There Is No God!" | 227 |
| "High Plains Drifter": The Mad Axe-Woman of Dingboche | 253 |
| "Some Things Hurt More, Much More Than Cars and Girls" | 277 |
| "We All Have Wings, but Some of Us Don't Know Why" | 305 |
| "There's a Rat in the Kitchen, What Am I Gonna Do?" | 319 |
| The Race: "If You Fail, Whatever You Do Don't Blame the Weather" | 352 |
| Dysentery and Descent: "Show Me the Way to Go Home" | 379 |
| Kathmandu Revisited, and the End of an Adventure | 388 |
| *Epilogue*     "Great Four Weeks, but Great to Be Back" | 409 |

## Introduction
# "Which One's Everest?"

One morning towards the end of April 1993, a large brown envelope, bearing the postmark Windermere tumbled into my letterbox with an ominous plop.

I knew, before I had opened it, that my application to take part in the Everest Marathon had been accepted. My razor sharp investigative skills told me that the thickness and weight of its contents were indicative of more than a scant rejection.

Sure enough, as my eager and nervous hands tore away the brown wrapping, I knew that I was standing at the threshold of a dream.

"Dear Richard," I read, "I am writing to offer you a place in the 1993 Everest Marathon," the first sheet informed me. "As you can see," it continued, "there is an awful lot of literature to wade through."

And so there was...

Booking form, liability waiver, equipment order form, doctor's certificate, general information booklet, sample insurance certificate, Everest Marathon Fund leaflet, sponsorship forms, letter and questionnaire from press agent, visa application, flight details.

And so on...

Half an hour of intensive reading later, my dream was becoming a reality. An hour later, I had found the Liability Waiver, and the reality was becoming a nightmare.

*I, the undersigned* – it began – *do hereby* (solemnly, it may as well have said,) *declare*:
1) *I understand the hazards of travel in Nepal both by transport on poorly surfaced roads and by small aircraft in mountainous regions.* Small aircraft? I hate flying. In roomy safe jets, never mind dropping off cliffs in Skodas with wings driven by elastic bands. The only way

to entice me onto a plane is with large quantities of liquid anaesthetic inside.

2) *I understand the hazards of travel by foot in the foothills of the Himalayas with regard to general health, changeable weather conditions, poor trail conditions and insubstantial bridges.* Okay, so take plenty of Rennies, warm clothes, but what's that bit about dodgy bridges?

3) *I understand that:*

* *The Everest Marathon will begin at an altitude of 5,184 metres at Gorak Shep (Base Camp), and descend to 3,446 metres at Namche Bazaar; by running at this altitude I may suffer from altitude sickness* (AMS, which, if undetected, will develop into cerebral or pulmonary oedema, and is frequently fatal in as little as thirty to forty minutes, unless the victim is immediately evacuated to lower altitude);

* *temperatures may vary from −25C* (that cold?) *to +30C* (that hot?) *during the race;*

* *there are both steep descents and ascents,* (wait a minute, who said anything about going up?) *on the course;*

* *the course may be over ice, hard-packed snow, grass, gravel and sand;*

* (And, now for the best bit) *falling off the trail could result in severe injury or death.* (Good golly!) *Medical assistance may not be timely.* (Good golly, Miss Molly!)

And so it went on. I was being asked to sign my life away, Not just physically, but also commercially. *I grant full permission to the organisers and sponsors to use my name, photographs, video tapes, motion pictures, recordings, and any other record of my participation in this race for any publicity and promotional purposes without obligation or liability to me.* No royalties? Not even if we top the video charts? Not a penny.

"Is anyone in their right mind going to sign that?" I asked my wife.

"Would anyone in their right mind have applied for it in the first place?" she replied.

I looked at the picture postcard on the cover of the information booklet. It was the view from Kala Pattar across the Khumbu Glacier to Everest and Nuptse, taken by Rob Howard, the photo-journalist who would accompany the party.

It was awesome, and it was pretty. On a clear day, the blue of the sky and the white of the snow looked so beckoning, so intoxicating, so compelling. On a bad day, with gusts of up to eighty m.p.h. snow driving stinging your eyes and blinding you, with temperatures of below minus twenty degrees centigrade, it would be pretty awesome. Or so I imagined.

"By the way, which one's Everest?" I asked my wife.

She didn't know, either.

And so I signed the waiver and completed the booking form. I had a medical, and obtained a doctor's certificate pronouncing me to be physically fit but probably certifiable. I made my will, my wife made a will, and my dog considered making a will. I took out more life assurance.

Then I started serious training, just to be sure that my ageing body could still take it.

Despite my two long distance runs in 1992, during which I had run more than a marathon a day for an extended period, I do not enjoy running in crowds, and had never actually felt the desire or need to enter a marathon race. Throughout the early summer, training progressed well, and by early June I had reached peak fitness without sustaining injuries, which was my main concern. On consecutive Saturdays I competed in the Man v Horse v Bike Marathon (twenty-two miles plus four thousand feet ascent, multi-terrain), and the East Devon 'Midsummer Madness Dream Footpath Marathon', a tortuous event over at least twenty-eight miles and God knows how much ascent, over hill, dale, bog, valley and anything else the organiser could find, navigating by the sun, the moon and the stars.

Having, survived these – in particular the latter, and achieved more than respectable times, I satisfied myself that I could, in all probability, survive most things. I relaxed and introduced myself to my family for the summer.

My goals were simple – firstly to get to the start. Even extreme fitness is no guarantee that the body is able and willing to tolerate altitude. At the start of the race, there is less than half the oxygen in the air that is present at sea level.

Secondly, to complete the race. If I achieved the first, I felt confident of the second. Provided, of course, I could survive confrontations with dubious suspension bridges; herds of yaks made belligerent from centuries of being forced to carry the burdens and then be eaten by the indigenous population; snow, ice, ravines, not to mention the local gastronomic vagaries.

Thirdly, to complete the race as quickly as possible. It was, after all, a race, and whilst survival and completion would be very much to the fore in everyone's mind, I would be in the company of fifty-nine other highly competitive and experienced mountain runners from all around the world, and a further ten locals. But this was the least important. In previous races, there had been little correlation between fast marathon times, and a good performance in the Everest Marathon.

Then at the end of August, Floss, (unreasonably denied a visa to Nepal on the grounds that she might not agree with the locals' digestion), and I set out for hour after hour of pounding the hills of East Devon.

During September and October I trained hard, running between fifty and ninety miles per week, all off-road. By the time of our Dartmoor experience, I had had enough, and wanted to be on my way.

Mentally, I was also prepared. I was conscious that luck would play a vast part in my success or otherwise, and that I must be prepared for disappointment which would be beyond my control.

I was ready for anything.

Or so I thought. For, in all truth, I had no idea exactly what it was I had let myself in for.

# "Running to the Top?"

Everest was named in honour of Sir George Everest, the Surveyor General of India, who was the man most responsible for the Great Trigonometrical Survey. While Sir George did not approve of this on the grounds that his name could not be written in Hindi, and the natives could not pronounce it, at least we should be grateful that he was not called Ramsbottom.

Since 1953, six hundred people have climbed Mount Everest.

People have now even climbed Everest using thirteen different major routes. There are those who have hang-glided and skied down it. They have even ballooned over it. What else is there to do? Perhaps it was inevitable that sooner or later some nutter would come up with the idea of running down it.

Diana Penny Sherpani, the race organiser explains:

"In 1985, two Englishmen called Tony Hunt and Jan Turner were trekking in the Khumbu. They got to Namche Bazaar and they decided to hold an impromptu race, from Namche to Tengboche and back again. They scoured the lodges for unlikely volunteers, got twenty names, but only fourteen people turned up the next morning. That was the first event. They came home with the idea of running a marathon in the foothills of Everest. It took two years to get off the ground, and the first event was held in 1987."

Through Diana's British trekking agency, Bufo Ventures Ltd., runners were offered a month's package which was in every way similar to what they might expect from a normal trekking expedition.

In every way, except one.

On reaching Gorak Shep, at almost 17,500 feet, those who were declared 'fit' would run a full marathon of 26.2 miles, to finish in Namche Bazaar, the Sherpa capital, and only sizeable town in the Khumbu region.

However, from Gorak Shep to Namche is a mere twenty miles, and after examining several possibilities, such as running over the ridge above Pheriche and out towards Chhukung, it was decided to add a loop, out to Thamo and back to Namche. It was, after all, supposed to be the world's highest marathon, and not the suicide trip it might become if the weather suddenly deteriorated on the barren slopes over Dingboche.

Foremost in their thinking, was that runners who were in bad shape on reaching Namche could pull out, or be pulled out, after twenty miles. Sound logic, except that it is more than a little demoralising to reach Namche knowing that the winner is singing in the shower or sipping his first beer, and you have six of the toughest miles still to cover!

Having decided the course, it was measured using a Trumeter wheel, much to the amusement of the locals. At each teahouse where they stopped, children would take the wheel for a spin, thus adding on extra yards. This, of course, was accurately documented by the team of measurers! Trumeter advertises using the slogan, "Accurate site or building measurement and estimating." I can only conclude that there must have been more estimation than measurement! Most of the trail is so boulder-strewn or rock-stepped as to make accurate measurement impossible. But I have it on authority from Dave Blakeney, one of the guys who measured the course, also our group leader in '93, that it is a "good" 26.2 miles.

Nothing like this had been attempted before, although Richard and Adrian Crane had run the entire length of the Himalayan chain, some two thousand miles from Darjeeling to Rawalpindi, in 1983.

But the runners who took part in the 1987 Everest Marathon were not just pioneers taking part in a 'world first', they were also guinea pigs. The medical authorities, including Britain's leading high altitude expert, forecast dire consequences of running at this kind of altitude.

In 1984, the World's Highest Hash had tragically resulted in one runner dying and another in a coma caused by high altitude pulmonary oedema, where water builds up in the lungs and the victim literally drowns.

In the event, time allowed for acclimatisation, which is one of the more beneficial facets of the trek, appeared to have been sufficient, and there were no serious casualties as a result of Acute Mountain Sickness. All but three of the forty-five runners completed the race. In fact, despite a considerable amount of snow and ice on the upper section of the course, the race was an unqualified success. It had been two years in the planning, and every contingency seemed to have been covered.

Helicopters will not take off without advance payment, so sufficient money had been paid to the British Embassy and instructions given should an emergency arise. As winds frequently prevented helicopters reaching Pheriche, the closest that a helicopter could get was the helipad at Namche. In practice, it is frequently not possible to get even that far due to fog in the Kathmandu Valley.

There is little doubt that had there been major logistical problems or a fatality, the race would not have been repeated. However, Diana and her team had done their research well, and the gods of the mountains smiled kindly on them. It was so successful that it was decided to make it a biannual event. As one of aims of the marathon was "...to promote tourism and sensible trekking in Nepal which relies heavily on and is being seriously affected by tourism," the number of entrants for future events was restricted to sixty, with an additional ten Nepali runners.

And so the Everest Marathon was born.

\*

I could scarcely believe, on my return from Nepal, the local interest that the Everest marathon had generated. People who knew me and people who didn't know me alike, expressed interest and admiration for my completion of the marathon. Even a drunk who thankfully I didn't know from Adam, emerging from a bar in Sidmouth just before Christmas, gave his fairly jaundiced view of how the money might have been better spent.

Westcountry Television did a fairly humorous follow-up, and I managed to squeeze in a bit about wishing to return to live in Namche Bazaar, reinventing the toilet seat, and making a fortune.

Local radio stations demanded and got interviews, and all the major papers in the South-West did features on me. *The Express & Echo*, no doubt devoid of any news in the period between Christmas and New Year, devoted a double centre page spread to a spectacular view, taken from one of my slides, of the race course above Namche, with the Imja Khola a mile below.

Even the good old *Sidmouth Herald*, bless them, interrupted their coverage of the debate as to whether or not there should be an extension of the railings along the Esplanade, to print a full page of my account of the race. I gave them a choice of slides, and one of the ones they featured was of me standing above the Shyangboche airstrip with Everest and Lhotse in the background. In the photo I was bare-chested, and the caption below read: "Stripped to the waist, and ready for the greatest challenge of his life."

I was pretty sure that the following week's edition would feature letters of complaint to the editor about my flagrant breach of Nepali custom in failing to cover my torso. None appeared. The letter writing population of Sidmouth was too interested in its relentless campaign against dog shit in public parks to take issue. In my defence, it was 7.30 a.m., there was no one around, and we were pretty warm as a result of having just bashed up a steep four hundred metre climb for a view of Everest.

I was flattered, but a little perplexed by all the attention.

The previous April, I had run around the Cornwall coast path, some 285 miles in ten days, to raise five thousand pounds for the West of England School for Children with Little or No Sight. Our son Jake attends St David's House, the recently opened department for visually impaired children with additional handicaps. Jake was severely brain damaged following an operation when he was a few weeks old. He is now almost ten, and benefits from the superb facilities and the care and expertise of the staff at St. David's.

It was the least I could do to try and raise funds on their behalf. This was my first attempt at fundraising, and I am thankful that we set the target at no greater than five thousand pounds. It taught me that getting people to part with money, even for worthy causes, is infinitely more arduous than the months of training and the run itself.

Not that I would describe the latter as having been easy. The choice of season proved a bad decision, as the weather mostly fluctuated somewhere between foul and hideous, and the condition of the path, especially on the north coast, was less than suitable for running. Add to this the fact that two adults, one of whom snored loudly, shared a cramped caravan with a little dog with flatulence and terminal halitosis, who also snored, and you get the result that I was running between twenty-five and thirty miles a day on around two hours' sleep.

In all, it wasn't really very enjoyable, and when I completed the run at Cremyll, there was no elation, just a sense of relief that it was over, and a resolve not to do anything so stupid again.

But I was also peeved that the media had shown so little interest in the venture. Most of the papers squeezed something in, and I did an interview for Radio Cornwall one Sunday lunchtime, but in general TV and radio were onto something much bigger – the general election! I could not compete with that.

However, I couldn't help but feel that in the eyes of the media, my run did not have a vast amount of appeal. Thousands of people have been around the Cornwall coast path, and whether it's walked or run matters little. I was not out to establish a record, there were no particular 'nasties' that I was likely to contract by running as opposed to walking, and the danger of death or serious injury was not greatly increased either.

If I had fallen off a cliff, as I almost did on more than one occasion, it would suddenly have become very newsworthy.

The Everest Marathon, on the other hand, had a vast amount of media appeal. If nothing else, I was fortunate enough, from the publicity point of view, to be the only runner in the South-West. It was also a 'world event', with the seventy-two runners coming from some fifteen countries.

However, I also could not help feeling that the interest it stimulated was from a position of ignorance. After all, I had absolutely no idea what was involved when I had first heard of it.

Moreover, to use the name 'Everest' is something of a misnomer, however justifiable. The London Marathon is run through London, the Boston Marathon is run through Boston, but, hair-splitting as it may be, the Everest Marathon is not actually run on Mount Everest. Yet, to give it the name 'Everest', rather than, say, 'Khumbu', adds that touch of glamour, and accords it the reverence and mystique reserved for a concept so at odds with anything that even slightly deranged people would attempt, that it draws instant interest.

Everest is the world's ultimate mountain, and is synonymous with the ultimate in human daring and endeavour. 'Marathon' conjures an image of endurance, reserves of physical and mental strength, and determination. Put the two words together, embroider them on a T-shirt, walk into your local pub and, without saying a word, you attract attention.

"Did you really do that, or are you just wearing the T-shirt?"
"Did you run all the way to the top?"
"How far did you run?"
"Why did you do it?"
"Would you like to buy some raffle tickets?"

Questions. Many questions, most of which were similar to those I had asked, not that long ago.

\*

Since returning from Nepal, my almost fanatical interest in the Khumbu region and the history of Everest exploration and eventual conquest has prompted me to make several frivolous comparisons between myself and George Leigh Mallory.

Unfortunately, however, the attributes of character which we shared could hardly be described as our strongest points.

Like Mallory, I am something of a drifter. Most of my life has been shaped by the hand of destiny, rather than by strong convictions. Both of us shared the same technological ineptitude which is nowadays referred to as 'challenged'. Mallory attracted much ridicule by his inability to light a Primus stove on the 1921 reconnaissance expedition. Worse still, his placing of the photographic plates into the camera the wrong way round was almost certainly to cost him the deputy leadership of the 1922 expedition. He was summed up thus by A.R. Hinks, then secretary of the Royal Geographical Society: "…he seems to be a very innocent traveller, who can hardly be trusted to get his own luggage aboard." And worse was to come: "The failure of Bullock and Mallory to photograph anything is deplorable– they must be singularly unintelligent people not to learn the elements of the thing in a day or two."

I also managed to bring the worst out of state-of-the-art technology in 1993, which is well-documented later in this account.

Both of us, despite having literary illusions, drifted into teaching – a career for which we were both temperamentally unsuited.

Mallory and I were both married, had three small children and were about the same age, give or take a year, when we first visited the Everest region. Perhaps that's why we went.

We really should have known better.

And yet the most striking similarity is that both of us drifted into making that initial trip. Like me, Mallory had never consciously tried to shape the events of his life, and arrived on the 1921 expedition largely by chance.

In a manner not dissimilar it was quite by chance that I became a part of the 1993 Everest Marathon. But life is a question of chance, and there the frivolous comparisons between myself and Mallory must end.

It was in the early spring of 1992, shortly before my Cornwall run, that I first heard of the Everest Marathon. Dieter Loraine, a Royal Marine with two boys at my school had run the 1991 Marathon and had offered to give a lecture on his experiences to the school. At the time I was curious, but not sufficiently motivated to interrupt my preparations for Cornwall to attend the lecture. It wasn't until I heard how good the lecture had been, and shortly after met Dieter, now a good friend, that I knew I had missed something special.

One summer's afternoon, some months after my return from Cornwall, I again met Dieter and Denise, his wife, at the school Association Day. My enthusiasm for running projects was at an all-time low, but his description of his time in Nepal, and the race itself, persuaded me that this was a challenge I ought seriously to consider.

Of course I could consider it. I could even make enthusiastic noises about it. But I knew that there was absolutely no chance of taking part in it. The race took place at the end of November, and the entire trip was from 6th November to 4th December. By an unhappy coincidence, November is the one month when we do not have any school holiday. Not even a lousy half term week.

And so I consigned it to the back of my mind, and spent six days in July running from home to Land's End along the coast path with a twenty-five pound pack and a lightweight tent, just to see if it was the running or the weather and logistics that had made April so miserable.

208 miles, six days, one hour and twenty-five minutes later, I had regained my enthusiasm for long-distance running. A chest infection drove me into the luxury of bed and breakfasts after the third night, much to the amusement of my wife who, knowing how much I like comfort, had considered the whole project to be absurd in any case. Despite this, I collected a lot of happier memories and a diary full of illegible squiggles. But that's another story.

The rest of the summer I spent poring over maps of the Pyrenees, loosely planning a run for the summer of 1993 from west to east, either using the GR 10 or the more remote high mountain route.

A few months later, I was discussing my summer run with my headmaster, Neil Pockett.

"I suppose you'll want to have a crack at the Everest Marathon," he said. "I've asked Dieter to pass on the application form to you when he receives it."

Was he trying to get rid of me?

And so it went from there. The governors, much to the surprise of both Neil and myself, allowed me the time off with full pay, and, more importantly, Kirsty gave it her blessing.

Given a choice between running across the Pyrenees on my own, and running the Everest Marathon, she felt happier that, despite the dangers, I would be looked after by ten doctors, would be less likely to get lost, and would not have to trouble myself with any of the logistical arrangements.

Because, like George Leigh Mallory, I could hardly be trusted to "...get *my* own luggage aboard."

## Sunday 7th November

The waiting was finally over. Dieter dropped round with his good old "Berghaus Centurion" rucksack, which had seen an assortment of action in the Falklands as well as the Everest region, and imparted some final words of advice, such as, "drink the local beer, it's a lot cheaper!"

After a night in Windsor staying with friends, we left for Heathrow the following morning. I cannot ever remember feeling so full of excitement and nervous apprehension.

It was the beginning of an adventure, a journey into the unknown, which had less chance of the safe return of both myself and my possessions than a package trip to the moon.

# "Dog Day in Dhaka"

## Monday 8th November

Stepping out of the plane in Dhaka, I stepped into another world. It was the beginning of the sledge-hammering my naive cultural sensory system was about to receive; a pounding that Dieter's slides could only superficially prepare me for.

Having left England on a typically gloomy November morning, some eleven hours later, our fatigued senses were smacked by the extreme heat, noise and smell of a Dhaka Monday morning, as we began our reluctant eight hour stopover.

Bangladesh, and in particular Dhaka, is somewhere I would not wish to visit again. After a paltry breakfast in the restaurant, where the waiter first insulted us then tried to steal my pen (English waiters do not have the monopoly on this type of behaviour), we were offered a guided tour of the city.

Sightseeing was not at the top of my list of priorities after a sleepless night above the clouds, but it seemed a better alternative than hanging around the departure lounge in temperatures of twenty-five degrees plus, surrounded by armed guards.

\*

I had had a sleepless 'night' on the plane. To describe Biman Bangladesh as a 'luxury airline', would be a bit like according charitable status to 'Virgin'. However, as I loathe flying, I regard a good mark of an airline as one that gets you to your destination without diving into swamps or slamming you into the tarmac from thirty-five thousand feet. In this department Biman Bangladesh scored admirably, although I did feel a good deal happier upon learning that their planes were maintained by British Airways crew.

As one entered the plane, the frosty reception from the hostesses did much to convey the impression that they were doing us an enormous favour. This frostiness was consistent throughout the trip, and compounded by the Gestapo-like tactic of turning on the lights and distributing breakfast just as the film ended and darkness descended, when most people were drifting into a fitful but welcome sleep.

By our body clocks, it was approaching midnight.

My trip had not got off to the most auspicious start. Upon arriving at terminal three, we could find no trace of the Everest Marathon, which was more than a little alarming as Dieter had said that there would be banners all over the place. For an instant, we were filled with horror at the thought that the departure day may have been Saturday and not Sunday. It was with considerable relief to be reassured by the itinerary that we were at the right place at the correct time and, half an hour later, discovered that there was a lower tier in the terminal where our party was assembling.

After a tearful farewell, I began what is the key feature of travel to, from and throughout the Third World, namely, queuing. That meant that you got to know two people, the one in front and the one behind, fairly well. In front of me was Kevin Williams, a Londoner and a keen Rugby player, who would not be in my group and with whom I would have little to do throughout the trip. Behind me was another Williams, Joy, a policewoman from South Wales, who would be in my group, and with whom there would be a host of shared memories.

Eventually, we were permitted through to the departure lounge, and I had a couple of beers to steady the nerves. In the far corner there was a loud group of fellow runners who clearly knew each other well, and who were enjoying themselves. At the helm of the group was a rumbustious little man who constantly swigged from a water bottle as if he had just run to the airport from Outer Mongolia.

He got up, and strutted past me in his skin tight Lycra bottoms on his way to the toilet, doubtless to make room for further inputs of water.

He looked at me disapprovingly. "Well, we know what *you'll* be doing for the next four weeks," he said humourlessly.

"Yes, we do, don't we," I replied, equally humourlessly. I dislike people standing in judgement, particularly when my lifestyle has no bearing on them. I resolved to beat him in the race, or to die in the attempt.

Ironically, he was wrong. After the final night in Kathmandu, when things got a bit out of hand, I didn't feel like drinking for almost three weeks, not until after the race, which, for me, was something of a personal record.

Once on board the plane there was chaos. One of the leaders had decided that as we were a large group – there were almost a hundred of us – we should ignore the seat allocation and sit anywhere in a block. Unfortunately, this message had neither reached me nor the hostesses, and when I asked one of the latter to help me find my seat, it caused a considerable rumpus. The hostess disapproved of this skulduggery, and was on the point of insisting that we evacuate the plane and sit in the allocated seats. Several of the leaders made conciliatory noises, shot me black looks, and I sat down in the nearest available empty seat.

One leader in particular, whose decision it had been to replace the perfectly well-ordered system with chaos, took what resulted as a personal affront, and branded me as a rebel and potential trouble maker. Thankfully, I was not in his group.

'Oh well, I thought, reclining in my seat as we left miserable British skies behind us, and waiting for the drinks trolley to come round, 'talk about give a dog a bad name!'

There was, of course, no drinks trolley.

*

Outside the airport there were two ancient jalopies waiting to take us on the guided tour of the city. The first thing I noticed was the smell. Of all the senses which worked hard to comprehend the month that was to follow, it was Mr Smell who had to work the most overtime.

The Third World stinks.

The principal reason, is, of course, an almost total lack of sanitation which wouldn't even have been tolerated in Elizabethan England. There are many other associated reasons, such as pollution caused by exhaust emissions and the almost religious insistence that farm animals are treated as (or probably better than) one of the family.

The other thing which instantly struck me was that anyone who didn't hoick up debris from the bottom of their lungs, noisily clear their nasal passages, and spit the combined contents voluminously at their feet (or anyone else's) was regarded as distinctly odd by the locals.

This is an accepted mannerism throughout the Third World, and is more to do with the amount they smoke than out of any devotion to Punk Rock music.

I was lucky enough to get the front seat on the bus, if lucky is the right word. It was a good position for photography, and a good position to die, I quickly realised, having observed the totally random and reckless movement of the traffic.

There is one rule in Third World driving, and that is that there are no rules. The main road from the airport to the city is like a race track. It is a wide expanse of tarmac, with no lanes and no markings. At one point we were overtaking a bus with at least twenty people either on the roof or hanging from the sides. The bus was overtaking a *tuk-tuk*, which is a motorised rickshaw and the main means of hired transportation. The *tuk-tuk* was overtaking a rickshaw, which was overtaking an old man on a bicycle. Coming towards us was a taxi, which was overtaking a lorry, which was overtaking a bus with a similar number of people hanging from it.

I was convinced that my trip, and my life, were about to end. But somehow, interweaving like the marching brass band at Wembley before the cup final, we all got through. It was at least half an hour before I worked out which side of the road they were supposed to be driving on.

At a roundabout two boys on bicycles, clad only in turbans and loincloths, threaded their way through the traffic carrying between them twenty or so bamboo poles of over thirty feet in length. Beside them trotted their goat. At home they would been required to have a Long Vehicle sign at their rear!

Ahead of us an ancient London double-decker bus, with no windows and various panels welded on the back and sides, spluttered oily black smoke in our faces. We came to a major crossroads where a traffic policeman on a podium whistled and gesticulated in a totally arbitrary and futile fashion.

Crippled beggars sat pathetic and motionless by the side of the road. Begging women with small emaciated babies thrust bony arms through the windows of our bus.

Through the chaos, an irate-looking moustached young man wearing a monocle and wearing something resembling a nightshirt jostled and shoved the rickshaws and bicycles, clearing a path for himself like Jesus in the temple with the money lenders. At home he would have stopped the traffic, but here he was the norm. This was not home, it was time travel away.

Apart from the occasional Land Rover or Toyota, which probably belonged to Embassy staff, the vast majority of cars were battered relics with starship mileage, imported from parts of the world where they were considered too mechanically and ecologically unsound to warrant further upkeep.

To be fair, our guide did his best to show us the less squalid parts of the city, and there were several buildings – the houses of government ministers, hotels and embassies which were set in fine grounds, and rivalled any in most Western cities. The trouble was, the filth and poverty was not confined to the back streets, and was so evident that it merely highlighted the human suffering and the vast chasm between the rich and poor.

We stopped down a side street, and got out to take a look at the Dhakeshwari Temple, which with its lush gardens was something of an oasis. It is a Hindu temple, is of little architectural interest, and was closed in any case. Built in the eleventh century, it is one of the oldest buildings in Dhaka.

It was here, with shades of Mallory, that I turned the video camera on instead of off, and shot a fifteen minute film of people's feet.

Other than the gardens there was not much of interest. Rather than stand around sheepishly with the others, too polite to voice what everyone was thinking, I went for a wander through the back streets. Despite the stench and the squalor, it was vibrant, and I wanted to feel the pulse of the city.

It was a threatening and oppressive atmosphere, and I felt the envy and hostility of the eyes that burned my back. It was hardly surprising. I was the epitome of an affluent Westerner. Panasonic video camera, high-tech Olympus SLR, small instamatic camera in a case around my waist, Oakley sunglasses, and baseball cap. The sunglasses alone were worth more than most of them would earn in a year. Beggars continually pestered me, and the people in the shops called and gesticulated.

Ahead of me was a pretty blonde girl from our party with piercing green eyes and a purposeful chin. I joined her, more from a sense of duty, like a good Sir Galahad. I was soon to find out that she was quite capable of looking after herself.

"Filthy, isn't it," I remarked. "How the hell do they live like this?"

I pointed my video at a reasonably friendly-looking half-naked youth, who waved, smiled and asked for money. I realised it was still recording.

"My name's Richard, by the way," I said awkwardly.

"Hi, I'm Annabel," she replied, confidently.

I could see that from her name badge. Dr Annabel Carter.

"You're a doctor?" I asked, stating the obvious.

"That's right."

I was sure I could identify an Antipodean accent.

"What part of Australia are you from?" I enquired.

"I come from New Zealand, actually, Richard."

Nice one.

\*

Our next stop was at the National Assembly, (Parliament House) referred to as 'the architectural wonder of the region'. Built in the 1960s, it proved more than anything that 60s architecture was as crass in the Third World as it was in the West.

The building was a concrete structure consisting of circular towers in each corner guarding the central part which rose above the others. The only windows were either in the oblong slits where the towers joined the walls, or set back in triangular alcoves. It was impossible to tell if these were for defensive or aesthetic qualities. Access to the building was via a drawbridge which crossed a filthy-looking moat on one side and equally dirty artificial lake on the other.

If this was regarded as an 'architectural wonder', I wondered what they would have made of Sellafield.

This should have concluded our trip, but we had one further unscheduled stop to make. Our guide was insistent that we should call in to see his boss. His boss was the Minister for Tourism and, despite time marching smartly on, he would not be deterred from the detour to the Department of Tourism. We were ushered reluctantly from the buses, and marched into a large artificially lit room with a huge circular table surrounded with chairs. We were told to be seated, and those who missed out in the scramble for chairs stood behind.

Time passed, and no one appeared. We grew restless.

Eventually, a little man in a dark suit entered, escorted by two armed guards.

"Please stand for the Minister of Tourism," one of them said.

We looked at each other, and stood.

"Thank you, please sit down," said the Minister.

We sat down.

"Welcome to Bangladesh, honoured guests, runners of the Everest Marathon."

No one volunteered that Everest wasn't *actually* in Bangladesh.

"We hope that you enjoy your stay. Thank you. Now we will go outside for some photographs."

Half an hour later the photographer, as frustrated as we were, abandoned the impossible task of arranging almost fifty people in a tiny courtyard so as to include them all in his photograph, and went for the easier option of photographing the minister with our leaders.

No one complained as we climbed back onto the bus, and headed for the airport.

*

Our itinerary had suggested that we would be given lunch at the airport, but this did not materialise. After a lengthy wait to get back into the building, we were told that we should each purchase a bottle of spirits from the duty free shop and donate it to "grease the wheels of officialdom," should problems be encountered at a later date. Any left over would also give the punch a bit of a lift at the prize-giving ceremony on the last night.

The problem was that we didn't have our passports, as the leaders had them. However, with such a vast group instructed to spend money, the officials decided, in time-honoured fashion, not to let petty bureaucracy stand in the way of good commercial sense, and reluctantly we trooped off to buy the cheapest whisky on offer.

After another lengthy wait we were ushered into the departure lounge, and ultimately aboard a much smaller jet bound for our destination, Kathmandu. There was very little in terms of locker space, and even less in terms of seat space, so most of us had to sit in cramped conditions with our hand luggage on our knees., Most people declined the meal, as they were more likely to end up wearing it, so I managed to acquire several extra meals and assuage my hunger.

On our approach to Dhaka, I had had my first sight of the Himalaya. Far to our left, with the early morning sun beginning its ascent over the distant white peaks, it was a sight I shall never forget. Now, as we flew west, we could see them again, far away on the horizon. As we flew to the south of Bhutan, then Sikkim, we got the first inkling of the vastness of the mightiest mountain chain in the world. Stretching over two thousand miles, a distance similar to Moscow from London, we flew past Kanchenjunga, Makalu, then the Everest group, Cho Oyu, Gosanthian and, in the distance, the Annapurna range, stretching far beyond Kathmandu, our destination.

Still unsure as to which was which, I refrained from joining the undignified scramble to point a camera at a window.

The plane was absolutely full, and had used every last inch of runway at Dhaka. Now, suddenly, we dropped like a stone, beginning our descent at an alarming speed. This, of course, was perfectly normal. Once you clear the foothills, you have to come down very quickly, but my knowledge that Kathmandu has no radar, and is notoriously the most dangerous airport in the world, did nothing to put me at ease.

The tarmac was coming up very quickly, and there were the usual looks of consternation and total complacency which people, who may very well either be about to die or begin a holiday, fluctuate between. We hit the runway very hard, nose first, seemingly with all the wheels touching down at the same time, and slewed from side to side for a few agonising seconds. Overhead lockers, where ice had formed during the early part of the flight, and then proceeded to drip on those seated below, burst open, and showered their contents on the unfortunate occupants of the aisle seats.

After an eternity, the plane came under control. It had been a bumpy landing, but we had survived it. To me, the definition of a good landing is any landing you can walk away from.

I heaved a huge sigh of relief in the realisation that I would not have to fly again until after the marathon.

One thing at a time, sweet Jesus.

# "There's a One-Eyed Yellow Idol to the North of Kathmandu..."

There are, in fact a very great number of one-eyed, two-eyed and three-eyed yellow, bronze and mahogany idols, to the north, and all points south, east and west of Kathmandu.

In much the same way as we litter our towns and cities with vast, steel skyscraping structures, icons to the gods of materialism, the Indian sub-continent is littered with gods of all shapes and sizes, intermingling a curious mixture of religion and culture in a manner that would never be tolerated in the west.

For one thing, they'd never get planning permission.

But my appetite for things cultural, limited as it is, was not awakened yet. Walking across the tarmac of Nepal's International airport, I was conscious of two things: first, that the oppressive heat of Dhaka had been replaced by the pleasant balm and warm breeze of a Kathmandu November evening. And secondly, the massive ring of hills from which we had just descended surrounding the valley.

Once in the pleasantly modern terminal building, the queuing began in earnest. First was passport control. Like virtually everyone, I had regarded the information that a visa could be obtained upon arrival at Kathmandu airport with a certain amount of scepticism, and had sent off for one. However, not only did those without a visa get through much quicker, it was also cheaper by ten dollars.

Once we had cleared passport control, there was a vast amount of equipment, mainly medical supplies to be reclaimed, checked, and removed. My video camera, still cameras and palmtop computer had to be inspected and noted on my passport.

Eventually we were out of the building and being greeted by smiling girls who welcomed us and presented floral necklaces.

It was instantly noticeable that we were in a different country. There was a less oppressive atmosphere, both in terms of the climate

I heaved a huge sigh of relief in the realisation that I would not have to fly again until after the marathon.

One thing at a time, sweet Jesus.

travelled extensively. He had left at home a wife and young baby, which made me feel a little less guilty about leaving my brood.

Behind me was Nat Padhiar who lived in London and was a podiatrist. He would be kept busy on the trek. He had also travelled broadly, and had climbed Mount Kilimanjaro.

The allocation of rooms was made for our two night stay, and we trooped off to find our room, which would have been cosy for two people, and was made even more so with the addition of a third bed. Still, we fared better than some who, presumably due to the hotel being overbooked, were squeezed into the maids' quarters in the bowels of the building.

Dinner was a choice of hot or cold plates served buffet-style, and was very welcome. I enjoyed my sixth curry in thirty-six hours, and afterwards we were summoned to the ballroom for the briefing meeting. Most of the party had now assembled, with the exception of those who had been granted permission to join at Namche Bazaar. In the main, these were the elite runners, which consisted of the Gurkhas, Hari Roka, the Nepali Olympic runner, and Sheldon Larson from Colorado, who had won several prestigious mountain races. Pierre André Gobet, the French-Swiss runner who had won in '91, would be trekking independently with his father, his girlfriend and her parents, and would also join up with the main party at Namche.

Also to join us later were John Thomson, his partner Liz, and Mark Woodbridge, who were on holiday in the region, and for whom it would have been very inconvenient to meet in Kathmandu.

There is no doubt that the additional time spent at altitude, and the training which improved acclimatisation permitted, benefited these runners significantly, as their performance in the race would subsequently prove. All except John, who was carrying a bad ankle injury and was happy to complete the race, and one of the Gurkhas finished in the top twenty.

However, with the exception of Ray Brown, a New Zealander who lived in Perth, and who had somewhat illogically been refused permission to meet up at Namche, no one minded too much. For most of us, the race was just one day, and, however important that might be, Dieter had impressed upon me not to let disappointment spoil the rest of the trip.

Ray and I were later to become close friends, and one of the things we had in common was a great love of moaning. We were also very and the people. The Nepalis may not look totally dissimilar to the Bangladeshis, but they had little else in common. They smiled more, they were helpful, not aggressive and obstructive but, in keeping with everyone on the sub-continent, they were totally unhurried.

On the bus to the hotel I sat next to John Webster, a Church of Scotland Minister from Glasgow. John was running his fiftieth marathon at the age of sixty, and this was his third 'Everest'. He was one of the runners making their own travel arrangements, and had joined us following a visit to India, where he had spent a large part of his working life.

John had a wonderfully wicked sense of humour, was the most unlikely parish priest I had met, and we got on from the word go.

As we drove around the perimeter of the city in the dusk of our first Kathmandu evening, similar smells greeted us, and a similar pattern of frantic human activity unfolded before our eyes.

The Blue Star hotel has four star status, and is one of the best in Kathmandu. Crossing a busy road, which almost resulted in the fatalities of both man and beast, we entered a little courtyard surrounded by affluent-looking Western-style shops, and the mayhem abruptly ceased.

Inside, the hotel did its best to combine the splendour of the Raj with the post colonialist comfort demanded by the affluent European traveller. A lot of thought had gone into the decor, and the ambience was good with soft but adequate lighting from crystal chandeliers and deep comfortable-looking leather armchairs in the spacious lounge.

Our arrival did much to spoil the peaceful atmosphere enjoyed by those having an early evening drink.

Again, our welcome was warm, and this time girls applied a spot of red dye to our foreheads. I had the devil of a job to get it off later, and decided this was one local custom I would do without.

Someone had the bright idea of forming a human chain to remove and stack our huge amount of luggage, and with general agreement, we set to work. General, but for one rather fussy little man, who walked up and down complaining about everything from the way the luggage was being handled to where it was being stacked. I invited him to help, if he wanted to be useful, an offer which he declined.

On either side of me, by coincidence, were the two guys I would share a room with. Ahead of me was Simon Petrides, a young doctor from Milton Keynes, who had his own sports injuries clinic, and had

Westerners to see Nepal for well over one hundred years. However, in many ways, the Nepalis remained loyal to the British, and in 1858 much of the Terai was restored to them (not that it was much use to the British) as a reward for their part in suppressing the Indian Mutiny. Gurkha soldiers, who acquired a reputation as ferocious fighters, have fought in the British army ever since, and will long be remembered by the Argentinean troops during the Falklands War.

Despite being isolated from the outside world, and progress being virtually nil for a century, under the Rana dynasty of "Prime Ministers" Nepal maintained its independence.

Then two things happened. Firstly, in a palace revolution in Nepal in 1951, King Tribhuvan, who had been very much a puppet, replaced the Rana family through an agreement negotiated by India, herself now free of the British Raj.

Secondly, following developments in Tibet, Nepal saw the perils of continued isolation, and the possible advantages of being a buffer state between China and India. Ironically, three years before, in 1947 in Tibet the Dalai Lama had his horoscope cast. As a result of gloomy predictions which foretold that he would be threatened by foreigners, there was a ban on outsiders until 1950. The predictions proved to be correct when the Chinese invaded in October 1950.

The Swayambhunath temple is better known as the Monkey Temple. It is infested with Rhesus monkeys and pedlars. Basically a Buddhist temple dating from AD 460, it is a curious and fascinating melange of Hinduism and Buddhism. Hinduism is the largest religion in Asia and the official religion of Nepal. Despite the Buddha being born in Nepal, Buddhism only arrived in about 250BC. Having spread across from Tibet, it is the main religion in the high Himalaya and is an easy bedfellow with Hinduism in the lower valleys. It was quite a revelation, particularly to an Ulsterman, that two such diverse religions can share the same temples.

The central feature is the Eastern stairway leading to the huge circular stupa with its prayer wheels, topped by the gold-coloured square block with the eyes of the Buddha looking over the valley from all four sides.

Inside the temple itself, for a few rupees we could remove our shoes and wander freely, photographing novice monks at prayer. They seemed to be keener on posing for the cameras than praying.

Back in the bus, we made our way to the outskirts of the city. Kathmandu is the capital of Nepal. However, it is a little confusing as there are three cities, which developed separately as city states, despite virtually running into each other. Kathmandu is the largest, with Patan the second largest, separated from Kathmandu by the river. The third city is Bhaktapur, which is to the east. Being slightly more isolated, the pace of its development was slower, and it retains much of its medieval appeal. To add to the confusion, each city has a square, named Durbar, meaning palace, where most of the temples and buildings of interest are to be found.

We left the bus, and set off through the streets with our guide. It was utterly fascinating.

The city of Kathmandu is like nothing I had ever seen. A vast colourful tapestry, in places it has changed little since medieval times. You can close your eyes, step into a time machine and embrace the sounds, sights, and in particular smells, that overload the senses. It is an intricate web of narrow streets and alleys, with carved wooden balconies spilling over open shops. The squares are like living museums packed with the most incredible monuments and temples, a vast exhibition of antiquity, heritage and history.

There are vibrant markets, hawkers and traders, buying and selling anything. The constant throbbing of humanity. The choking engine fumes and dust, hooting traffic edging to its destination, nudging you along in its path. There are stinking gutters and the poor who sleep in them like the living dead. Animals frequently accompany you along streets lined with windowless shops selling their brethren, and Western billboards advertise opulence beyond the expectations of all but a few. And the maimed beggars. Everywhere, the maimed beggars.

There is a huge gap between the rich and the poor, which good humour, self-respect based on a highly developed work ethic, and integrity transcends. The streets may exude stench, disease and squalor, the likes of which I had never seen, but these are no mean streets. They are safe to walk – at day or at night. There are no vigilantes, there is no nightclub, no McDonald's. This is not a playground for the idle rich, there are no Ferraris, no Porches, and Gucci handbags still belong to their original four hoofed owners.

This is Kathmandu. Mystical, magical, and still just a touch inaccessible.

good at it. However, he had serious aspirations of winning the race, which proved well founded, and resented the fact that Gobet might benefit from that extra little edge.

Our party in Kathmandu numbered eighty-four, which would swell to one hundred and three on reaching Namche Bazaar. In addition to the seventy-two runners, there were ten doctors, six leaders, including Diana, and fifteen 'companions', friends of the runners, who had come along for the trek, and would act as marshals in the race.

We were split into two groups, the Early Birds and the Late Birds. The Early Birds were those who hadn't chosen either the option of white water rafting or a visit to the Chitwan National Park after the race, and the Late Birds were those who had.

I had almost opted for a visit to Chitwan, but had been talked out of it by Dieter on the grounds that three days of freedom in Kathmandu were infinitely more fun. By virtue of this, I was placed in the Early Birds. It was a decision I was not to regret.

I looked around the ballroom at my fellow runners. Runners come in all shapes and sizes, and it was impossible to predict those who would do well. Some were ultra-distance runners, men and women who got their kicks from what I called the 'Gerbil Factor' – running around a track for twenty-four hours. There were road runners, capable of sub two hours thirty, or even twenty, marathons. There were world class fell runners and Ironman Triathletes. There were also people who were best described as 'professional adventurers'.

And then there were people like me who didn't fit into any of these categories, and were beginning to wonder just what they were doing there.

There had been a lot of banter which I had overheard about recent races, as some of them sized each other up. My 'friend', who had commented on my predilection for beer at Heathrow had run every race known to man, and I was thankful that he was a Late Bird. A month of that would have been very hard to bear.

I was grateful to be sharing a room with two non-runners, as this avoided any need to be competitive. Actually, Nat had run more marathons than I, and Simon jogged around the village to keep in shape, but their interests were more medical than performance related.

Diana welcomed us, and gave us our itinerary for the next two days. The Early Birds would have one day in Kathmandu and depart early on Wednesday morning, and the Late Birds would follow a day behind. We were then issued with the clothing which we had ordered, and essentials such as kit bag, down jacket, and survival gear. This included bivvy bag, pencil and pad, whistle, and several chocolate energy bars, most of which I had eaten by the time we left Kathmandu.

The doctors adjourned to a further meeting, and I adjourned to the bar, until I suddenly realised that I hadn't slept for forty-six hours, returned to my room, and sank into a deep sleep, too tired to be aware of my surroundings.

## Tuesday 9th November

We woke early, the smells and noises of this strange and exciting city filtering through our open window. I thought of going for a run, but easily persuaded myself that getting to know my two companions was more important.

Simon and Nat knew each other from medical conferences and the like, and talked with great passion about their specialist fields which was way beyond the depth of my meagre knowledge of physiology. However, we had plenty in common, especially apprehension about the coming month.

After a good breakfast there was a sightseeing trip laid on for the Early Birds, which we decided to take.

First call was the Buddhist temple of Swayambhunath, situated high on the top of a hill to the west of the city.

The outer streets of Kathmandu were much reminiscent of our journey through Dhaka, with bustle, dust, gutters full of indescribable filth and chaos very much the order of the day. But as we climbed the short distance out of the suburbs towards the temple, we got a better impression of the fertile and delightful Kathmandu Valley. It was incredible to think that this haven had been cut off from the rest of the world by the vast Himalayan peaks to the north, and the malarial jungle of the Terai to the south, until comparatively recently.

Not until 1950, when China invaded Tibet and ultimately closed access to the Himalaya, did Nepal welcome foreigners. In 1816, when Britain removed Sikkim from Nepali territory, and eventually added most of the Terai to the Raj, Nepal decided it could manage quite nicely without Western interference, and closed its boundaries to all but British residents living in Kathmandu. These were the only

In awe I wandered away from our party; most of whom were transfixed by the erotic art carved on the wooden struts of the Trailokya Mohan Temple.

Suddenly, I realised I had drifted far away from our group down a side street where an extremely fat, but nonetheless athletic, rat ran across my path. Eventually I found my way back to Durbar square only to discover that they had gone. I wasn't unduly concerned; my only worry was that they may be looking for me.

Three very frustrating hours later I arrived back at the hotel. Although I didn't know it at the time, it is a Nepali custom not to give negative answers for fear of disappointing you. So when I enquired as to the direction and distance to the Blue Star Hotel, the reply was invariably, "Ah yes, sir, Hotel Blue Star, straight down this road, not very far." Whereas the answer should have been, "It's bloody miles, mate, get a taxi!" There was an element of truth in the answers I received. It was possible, by following the perimeter of the city, to get back to the hotel, and this was in fact what I did.

It was an interesting walk, and I wasn't particularly concerned. Our next meeting was not until three o'clock, so I had plenty of time. On the outer reaches of the city, the dirt and pollution were more evident. It even got to the Nepalis, and many of them wore masks to prevent the worst of the smog entering their lungs.

A man lay in a gutter, undeterred by the flies which landed on him and the dog that peed next to his legs. Nobody took any notice of him, and it crossed my mind that he may be dead. On the other hand, it was more likely that he came home extremely late and very drunk and found his wife had locked him out.

It was hard to judge if it was more dangerous to walk on the pavement or in the road. In the road the surface was marginally better, but vehicles would not deviate to avoid you. The pavement was frequently blocked by huge piles of household rubbish, and often the contents of the little shops spilled over to the verge of the road itself. The paving stones were as broken and erratic as the path I was to find beside the Khumbu Glacier.

At one point I was joined by an emaciated-looking quadruped with large horns and rather the same resigned and sardonic expression on its face that I would have after a week of trekking. We walked along for a while until we came to a butcher's shop, with an open window, where sat the most unsavoury and gangrenous collection of meat I had ever seen. Sell-by dates are unheard of in these parts. The shop also played host to an international convention of the world's biggest and nastiest looking flies. None deterred, my bovine companion sniffed, then licked, several pieces of meat. Deciding to defer a purchase, it lifted its tail and deposited breakfast on the pavement. The flies transferred their attention from one food source to the other.

I continued my walk alone.

Soon, to my relief, I recognised the National Stadium, which we had passed several hours earlier, and not far distant was our hotel.

At the entrance to the little courtyard stood the Bluebird supermarket. Inside, smartly dressed deferential assistants sat statuesque and silent, like line judges at Wimbledon, staring at the waxed wooden floor. Warehouse-like shelves were stocked with everything one could possibly want to buy, from bare essentials to Western luxuries, although the choice of brands was rather limited. Prices were sky high compared to the little shops in the city, but still compared favourably to home.

I purchased a few essentials, such as water – after an inspection of the city's water supply, the Vishnumati River, which doubles conveniently for sewerage disposal. It goes without saying that it is asking for trouble to put anything that comes from a tap anywhere near your mouth.

Following an acceptable, if unspectacular, chicken sandwich (I remembered that one shouldn't eat the salad as I consumed the last mouthful) in my room, I set off to join the others in one of the conference rooms.

\*

We formed a large circle, and I sat between Simon and Annabel. Our leaders had been identified the previous evening, and sat opposite us. The overall leader was Dave Blakeney who, as previously mentioned, had been involved with the marathon since the beginning, and had helped to measure the course. To the uninitiated this was quite comforting as, if anyone ought to know what they were talking about, it should be him.

Dave was a short, stocky guy, who always, without fail, wore the same clothes. We never worked out whether it was because he didn't have any others, or because he was sentimentally attached to them.

His wardrobe consisted of a pair of boots, rugby shorts which had seen better days, and a black tunic similar to those traditionally worn by men who deliver coal for a living. He had an adventurous spirit, and had, among other things, been a member of the Spanish Foreign Legion. He had also been a fireman, and at present is based in Spain where he manages an adventure holiday centre.

It was Dave's job to ensure that things ran smoothly. In particular, to liaise with the Nepali trekking crew who would be responsible for making camp and feeding us. He had to ensure that we knew where we were going, and that no one got lost. This was fairly undemanding, as it is virtually impossible to get lost on what is known as the Everest Highway. He had to consider demands made by the film crew and medical restrictions which the doctors might wish to impose. Moreover, he had to ensure that we had some idea of what to expect, and how best to cope with it, in this voyage into the unknown.

It has been said that every expedition needs someone to work out their anger and angst on, to unite against, and so make them a tighter, better bonded unit. In 1953, Hunt's party which set two men on the summit of Everest for the first time, turned their hatred on the Secretary of the Himalayan Committee back in London, for the austerity of the provisions.

Most important of Dave's functions, was to fulfil this role, a fact which Annabel, who had also been on the '91 marathon was quick to point out. Although he discharged his role as leader satisfactorily, his quasi-military approach to the trek was at odds with a lack of patience and intolerance of anything which wasn't supposed to happen, or of which he did not approve.

The irony was that we didn't really need a charismatic leader, if indeed we needed a leader at all. Dave became something of a caricature, and contributed to his own downfall by producing a ludicrous hat which was to be presented to the person who, in the judgement of our doctors, performed the most idiotic feat of the day.

It was little surprise to anyone that he won it for the first three days. In fact, if Annabel had had her way, he would have worn it for the entire trip.

Dave's co-leader, or deputy, was Wish Gdula. Wish had as varied and diverse an ethnic background as it is perhaps possible to have, being Polish-Welsh. A builder from Lampeter, he spoke fluent Welsh, and did so on every opportunity to Alun Hughes, one of the film crew.

To look at Wish, you could be excused for not immediately concluding that here was a world class athlete. But his unkempt Rasputin-like appearance belied the fact that he was a runner of some stature, and amongst other things had already run two 'Everests', and had proved that he was no slouch.

His leadership duties seemed to be fairly non-specific, and he generally strolled along towards the back of the trek. I didn't know it at the time, but he would be running the race as well.

The meeting started with a memory game. The first person introduced himself, then the person on his left did likewise, then recited the names of everyone on his right. It was fairly easy to start off with, but by the time it got to us, seated about half way round, it was impossible. To begin with, I am utterly hopeless at memorising names. At the beginning of each term, I have forgotten the names of most of the kids that I teach. Come to that, I've forgotten the names of most of the staff. Also, as many of those in our group were foreign, I couldn't pronounce most of the names, let alone remember them. Anyway, I hadn't been paying attention. It came to my turn. I decided to apply a little psychology.

"I'm Richard," I began. "As we're not going to spend the rest of the trip sitting around in these exact positions, I don't wish to give offence to those whose names I forget in ten minutes time."

If nothing else, it meant that our leaders remembered my name.

Most people took up the challenge. Some did incredibly well. Richard Uridge, a presenter with Central Television who would be conducting the bulk of the interviews and piecing together the documentary, was the last to go and got everyone's name correct. Now that was impressive as there were over thirty of us.

The preliminaries aside, we began in earnest.

"Right", said Dave, "the main purpose of this meeting is to tell you what you will find on The Hill."

Half an hour later, I wasn't much the wiser. He simply confirmed much of what I had gleaned from Dieter. What I wanted to know, he could not answer. For instance, how would *my* body cope with the ravages of altitude and the intense cold? Would I be healthy and fit enough to start the race?

Many people had questions, ranging from who would provide the toilet paper, to whether it was possible to train on the trek. Dave promised to provide the toilet paper, and confirmed that training on the trek was largely a matter of personal preference. He considered that the trek was arduous enough to maintain fitness, provided that the requisite training had already been done.

This, in fact, was a question that not even top physiologists could answer. There is a lack of accord as to whether training at altitude helps or hinders acclimatisation. Dieter had been quite insistent that, two years ago, those who had trained regularly had found it harder to acclimatise, and consequently had run very disappointing races. Dieter had run very little, but freely admitted that training time had clashed with beer time, and it was important not to muddle one's priorities!

I decided to wait and see.

There was then a lengthy discussion on health matters, in particular, altitude sickness. We were reminded of the symptoms to watch out for in yourself and your companions. Although this had been outlined in Diana's highly detailed booklet, this was probably the most important information, and I was happy to go through it again. Everything else was procedural. This was life or death.

"Right", Dave continued, when there was a lull in the questions, "now to the question of kit. The porters will carry a maximum of twelve kilos of your kit, which must be in the sausage kit bag provided. They will not carry rucksacks. The reason for this is they tie two bags together, and strap them to their heads. Anything extra which you will require during the day, or when you arrive in camp, you carry yourself. You may find some of the porters are fourteen year old girls. They walk all day with twenty-four kilo loads for about one pound fifty pence. As a consequence, sometimes they do not arrive at the campsite until after dark. Personally, I carry all my own kit."

There was a general murmur around the group, more from consternation than hero worship.

"Here we go," said Annabel, yawning noisily. "Right on cue. This is where we get to see what Dave keeps in his rucksack."

"Now", obliged Dave, "I'm going to show you what I keep in my rucksack."

He produced a rucksack that Dick Whittington would have had a job to get a cheese sandwich into for his trip to London, and laid out the contents on the floor.

"Starting from the inside working out", he began, "one clean pair of underpants, one pair of socks, one spare T-shirt, one fleece, one pair over-trousers, one fleece jacket, one sleeping bag..." He continued through his collection of survival equipment and toiletries "One toothbrush, one comb..."

Someone else yawned.

"Condoms next," said Annabel, without a trace of wishful thinking.

They weren't.

He had replaced everything.

"Total weight of pack: under ten kilos."

It was clear that Dave had spurned Diana's kit list, which recommended sewing and boot cleaning kit, camera, accessories and film, writing materials, and included optional items such as binoculars, inflatable pillow, umbrella, paperback books, playing cards, Walkman and tapes, and last but not least... photos of your family, home and friends.

My thoughts turned to my own essentials which in the light of Dave's revelations, I was beginning to think might be a little excessive.

Apart from an armoury of underclothes, T-shirts and thermals which would have seen Dave through several Himalayan millennia, I had my state-of-the-art hi-tech gadgets to consider. First there was my compact instamatic camera for snapshots. Then there was my large SLR. Added to this in the photographic department, was the video camera which I had been lent by Panasonic, through the generosity of Ford's, a local electrical retailer owned and run by a family with children at my school. Although this was a mere midget in comparison with earlier generations, it was still a bulky piece of kit, and with the heavy duty batteries that were essential to preserve power at altitude in extreme temperatures, it added considerably to my luggage.

And then there was my palmtop computer. No, this was more than the ultimate pose. I had learned from my previous experience that diary writing was a pointless exercise unless the resultant squiggles triggered some dull chord of memory. If I was going to keep a diary, I was going to do it properly. As my writing was so illegible, this was the perfect solution.

Of course, if I hadn't time to make detailed notes on the computer, I had my micro-cassette recorder.

That just about satisfied the 'preserving for posterity' demands of the trip. As for entertainment, it is unthinkable that I would go anywhere without music. However, I managed to limit my selection of tapes to be played on my Walkman to a mere ten. Luxury items they may well be, but a little luxury was an important thing. After all, on the Everest expeditions of 1922 and 1924 led by Brigadier General C.G. Bruce, tinned quail and champagne were to be found on the menu.

When it came to keeping warm, I was not prepared to skimp. If I was going to be sure of one thing, it was that I was not going to spend teeth-chattering sleepless nights cursing myself for not being properly prepared. To this end, I had spent some two hundred pounds on a top of the range three piece suit, which was lined with fleece fabric on the inside and Pertex on the outside. Worn together, the salesman assured me, it would keep it's occupant warm in the coldest most hostile environments on earth.

"It better had," I had warned ruefully, as I parted with what I considered to be an excessive amount of hard-earned cash. "At this price I could have a week in a centrally heated four star hotel!"

A good sleeping bag was essential. In fact, I had not one, but two. In addition to a down, four season bag, costing roughly the same as several weeks in Lanzarote, I had brought my lightweight down bag, perfectly adequate for the vagaries of the British climate. Also, I had bought a thermal self-inflating mattress, and had taken along Dieter's bivvy bag, just in case.

Just in case of what, I wasn't quite sure, but I was taking no chances, and in the event this was something I wouldn't regret.

My washbag would probably have rivalled James Bond's, containing, in addition to all the usual essentials, shower gel, body gel rub, Eau de Toilette, deodorant, nail scissors and so on.

Just in case.

And then there was a vast supply of batteries necessary to run my high-tech toys, a dozen rolls of film, a book, which went totally ignored throughout the trip, guidebook, snap shots of home and family, hand-warmer, and all the other bits of paraphernalia recommended by Diana.

We were encouraged to leave any non-essential items of clothes or equipment in a locked suitcase in the hotel. In the light of this, that could be quite a bit. I would have to look carefully at my priorities.

Next, we played an extremely silly game. We split into three smaller groups, and, forming a circle, crossed our arms, and held the hands of the person on either side. The idea was to untangle the group without breaking the chain. It was supposed to be a way of getting to know each other, and, I suppose, to some degree it succeeded.

There were those who, like myself, could see little point in the exercise, and who reluctantly joined in. There were those, like Simon and Nat, who regarded it as a serious test of initiative and set about marshalling the troops. And there were those like Valeri, the amiable and good-natured Bulgarian masseur, who was just happy to be there.

And then there was Richard Uridge, who was also happy, but for a different reason. Here was a heaven sent opportunity to grope several different women at the same time.

However, it was me who was virtually suffocated by the more than ample chest of Jerri Lee from California, while husband Mike, a cardiologist, on my other side, gave the solution his urgent attention.

Eventually, it was Zvoni, a wealthy industrialist from Germany, who clearly wasn't intimately entangled with anyone vaguely interesting, who gave voice to everyone's thoughts :

"This is impossible, let's cheat!" So we did, only to find, that the other groups had come to that conclusion long ago.

On that note, the meeting broke up, and we went our separate ways. Nat, who was involved in studies to analyse the effects of exercise at altitude on the body, went off to collect blood from volunteers.

Although much is known about the effects, treatment and prevention of Acute Mountain Sickness (AMS), there is still very little known about why certain people are more prone to it than others. Some people can romp up to twenty thousand feet without so much as a headache, while others have a ceiling of eight thousand, which seems to be the threshold of ability to tolerate diminishing levels of oxygen.

At the start of the marathon, there would be roughly half the oxygen present in the air that is present at sea level. Fitness or age are no yardsticks as to susceptibility to this crippling and potentially fatal illness. Nor is having been at extreme altitude on previous occasions a guarantee of immunity. It is like playing Russian Roulette. Indeed younger fit people are often thought to be more susceptible, as they are prone to rush up hills too quickly.

Several things are currently known about the effects of altitude, and our trek to the start of the marathon was designed to take these into account.

Firstly, gradual acclimatisation allows the body to adjust to the reduction of oxygen. As the blood develops more viscosity by producing more red oxygen carrying cells, the ability to cope with a decreased flow of oxygen is improved. Hence, we would commence our walk in from Jiri tomorrow, rather than fly to Lukla, which would have reduced the trek by a week.

At altitudes of above eight thousand feet, it is beneficial to sleep lower than the highest point attained during the day. Acclimatisation generally occurs during the night. One distressing but harmless symptom of acclimatisation is what is known as Cheyne Stokes respiration. Or, in effect, lack of respiration. During sleep, the metabolism is adjusting to the reduced oxygen. Respiration is extremely heavy and stertorous. Suddenly, breathing stops, sometimes for as long as a minute, and just as suddenly restarts noisily.

It is generally considered unwise to gain more than three hundred metres, (around one thousand feet), in one day. The symptoms of the onset of AMS are commonplace, and it is easy to attribute them to something else.

Most people suffer from some degree of headache at some time above 11,500 feet, an altitude which appears to represent another landmark. Many lose their appetite, which is easy to attribute to the food or the time spent waiting for it, or sleep badly. As I rarely sleep well, this would not be much of a yardstick.

The onset of puffy eyes and fingers, dizziness and vomiting, and a rapid heart rate after rest are irrefutable danger signs. Unless immediate steps are taken to descend to a lower altitude, deterioration is rapid, and death, from either cerebral or pulmonary oedema can result in as little as thirty minutes. You would, of course, have to be extremely unfortunate to go downhill as rapidly as that, but it was a possibility that could not be dismissed from our minds. In all honesty, along with all the other unknown factors, this danger added spice to the adventure.

The history of the exploration and eventual conquest of Everest is littered with sad testament to the army of men and women who died, suffered from, or whose ambitions were merely frustrated by AMS.

One bizarre tale concerns a forty-five year old Belgian, Jean Bourgeois, a member of the French Winter Attempt of 1982–3 (known as the Couzy Everest Expedition). Attempting to gain access to the West Ridge, Bourgeois began to feel unwell, and, recognising the onset of AMS, attempted to retreat to Camp 1. Strong winds forced the rest of the party also to retreat. However, Bourgeois failed to arrive back at Camp 1, nor did he appear at Base Camp. Futile efforts to trace him over the next few days forced the party to conclude that he had fallen to his death down the steep face of Lho La.

The expedition was thereafter abandoned, and evacuated to Kathmandu, where, to their surprise, Bourgeois appeared in perfect health, a few days after their arrival, with a strange tale to tell,

After a few hundred feet of his descent, he slipped and fell. By sheer good fortune, his glissade took him towards the Tibetan slope. Had he veered towards the southern slope, he would have fallen to certain death.

Eventually, he came to rest on the Rongbuk Glacier, and was left with no alternative but to push on into Tibet, and seek help. Finding the Rongbuk monastery (the oasis of earlier expeditions) deserted and ruined, he continued. Two days later, and close to exhaustion, he arrived on the outskirts of a small village. Here, he was nearly devoured by ferocious Tibetan guard dogs and forced to bivouac out of their reach for a third night in extreme conditions.

Eventually he was detained by the authorities for several days while they tried to establish his identity. At last, satisfied that he posed no threat to national security, he was taken by jeep to the Nepali border, given five hundred rupees, and sent on his way.

Now, just exactly what Nat's specimens before and after the expedition were hoping to establish wasn't quite clear, but it gave him something to do, and perhaps gave some scientific justification to the inclusion of so many doctors on the trip.

\*

I needed some exercise. As I had been warned off going for a run other than before dawn, because of the intense heat, the dust and the smog which hangs permanently over the city, I decided to investigate the swimming pool.

The good news was that I found it quite easily. The bad news was that I found it contained no water.

So, a run it would have to be. Anyway, it couldn't be *that* bad, I thought. After all, I had regularly run alongside the Great West Road in West London, the main artery to Heathrow, whilst a student.

Ten minutes later, changed, stretched and ready to go, I bounded down the steps into the lounge, and out into the searing late afternoon heat of the little courtyard.

A further ten minutes, and I was back. Frustrated and irritated by my total lack of progress, I conceded defeat. Like Canute, I could not turn back the tide, and was enveloped by a stormy sea of little brown men, and women, jabbering and hoicking their way homeward towards the river, away from the heat of the city.

I could neither run on the pavement nor the road. Even beyond the busy main street from the hotel, the less commercial thoroughfare leading towards the airport was similarly awash with one way traffic. The scorching heat, the choking fumes, and the gritty dust which I felt permeating my lungs, soon persuaded me that I was doing myself more harm than good.

Back in the sanctuary of the hotel room, I settled for some exercises, and was just enjoying removing the street grime from my body in the shower, when the lights went out.

Luckily, there was a candle and box of matches beside the basin.

'How very thoughtful of them,' I mused.

I popped my head outside the door of the room to see if anyone else was experiencing a similar problem.

Along the corridor, and in reception beyond, hotel staff were busily lighting candles in a well ordered manner, suggesting this was something of a ritual.

"Any idea what the problem is?" I asked one reasonably intelligent-looking lad.

"It's a power cut," he replied, helpfully.

"Any idea what caused it?" I continued tentatively, expecting the reply that it was as a result of failure of the electrical system.

"Oh yes sir," came the answer, "it will return at seven o'clock!"

Satisfied that he was either a fortune teller or a complete idiot, I returned to my candlelit shower. I was not particularly surprised to find that the water had now gone cold.

\*

Two sad and unfortunate incidents cast something of a shadow over the proceedings that evening.

The first occurred upon the completion of my cold shower, and resulted in a prolonged stay in the bathroom.

Simon returned from helping Nat deliver the blood he had collected, and was clearly a little agitated. "Look, I'm going to make a phone call," he said, decisively.

"Give me a second", I said cheerfully, "I'll slap on the old aftershave and bugger off."

"No, don't hurry – I didn't mean that. It's just that my grandfather had a stroke shortly before we left. His chances didn't look terribly good, and I'm dreading ringing home."

"I'm sorry, Simon", I said, awkwardly, "mind you, you'll be lucky if you get through." I had tried several times the previous evening to no avail.

Simon set about making his call, and I returned to the bathroom to complete my ablutions. He got through straight away. Despite the bathroom door being closed, I could not avoid hearing every word.

The news confirmed his worst fears. His grandfather had died. I decided it was best to stay in the bathroom until he had finished on the phone so as not to intrude. Grief is a private affair, and the fact that it is being shared by people thousands of miles apart makes no difference.

At last he hung up, and I emerged from the bathroom after a discreet pause amid noisy toilet flushing.

Simon told me the news, and how close he had been to his grandfather, who had been in excellent health prior to his stroke. He would continue to do what he had come for, as that would have been what his grandfather would have wanted.

I said how terribly sorry I was, and felt rather awkward. There wasn't much I could do, especially as I hardly knew Simon. And yet, with the trip barely forty-eight hours old, there had been a bond established, and the sharing of this sadness was to strengthen it.

\*

The other sad incident could have been avoided. After dinner that evening, we went to our rooms to organise our kit for the following morning. This was a job which I had been dreading.

After much inward wrestling, and outward wrestling, which included muddling a good deal of my kit with Nat and Simon's, I decided to leave many of the clothes I had brought for safekeeping at the hotel. I placed my down jacket, spare batteries, book, and a few other odds and ends in my running rucksack, and put this in the sausage bag for the porters to carry. Everything else I would carry myself in Dieter's ancient Berghaus.

This was a decision I was to regret when I went to pick it up, but I told myself it would be good for maintaining fitness, and I could always rearrange things after the first night if the going was too hard.

Dave Blakeney was waiting in the main lounge to weigh the bags which would be carried by the porters. Weighing consisted of putting a bag over his shoulder, frowning, narrowing his eyes then directing them at the ceiling as if for inspiration, then emphatically pronouncing its weight.

Despite the presence of a perfectly good set of scales provided by the hotel, Dave would only actually weigh the bags that were in all likelihood over the limit. As a means of reminding us how incredibly clever he was it failed dismally. Annabel passed a comment about knowing who to blame if there was a porters' strike on the first day.

It was at this point that Martin Campbell, one of the Late Bird leaders bounded down the stairs calling for a doctor. Simon, Nat and Annabel responded instantly, leaving me to sort out their bags.

John Oliver, one of the Late Birds billeted in the poorly lit maids' quarters, had for some reason been wandering around the corridors in his bare feet, and had stepped on broken glass.

Not only had he lost a lot of blood from a severe cut in his foot, but was suffering shock and had to be sedated. Ultimately, despite Simon and Nat's expert stitching and patching, his injury had not improved sufficiently by the time the Late Birds departed, and he decided to return home.

It was the sort of misfortune that could have happened to any of us, and rotten luck.

\*

While my roommates were earning their keep with John's foot, I set about changing my money. Once on the trek tomorrow, there would be no banks, so I decided to change virtually all the currency I had brought. There wasn't much point leaving it in a suitcase in Kathmandu.

I had brought four hundred US dollars, and I converted three hundred dollars into Nepali rupees, which gave me around fourteen thousand of the latter.

We had been warned that teahouses on the trek would not change large denomination bills, so it was best to obtain your currency in notes not greater than one hundred rupees.

That was a lot of notes. In any case, the cashier wasn't happy about relinquishing all his bills of that denomination, especially as I wasn't the first person to approach him with such a request. In the end, I settled for accepting half of the money in five hundred rupee bills.

I headed for the bar with a wallet as thick as a pillow, and the buzz of excitement at the prospect of being close to the beginning of the real adventure.

*

I should have known better than to expect a quiet night.

My good intentions were to have a couple of quiet beers followed by a good night's sleep.

But the road to hell, as they say, is paved with good intentions. And so I enjoyed a couple of quiet beers, followed by several more extremely noisy ones.

The bar was fairly quiet as I entered at around 10 p.m. My body clock was on overdrive, coping as manfully with very little sleep over the last seventy-two hours as my brain was coping with the sensory battering it had received.

I joined a couple of Late Birds who were at a table in the corner. Martin Mann Heatley was a fifty year old farmer from Nuneaton. I had had a drink with him and his family, who were seeing him off at Heathrow. Roger Manly, from Norfolk, was a year older. Both these guys could be counted amongst the more normal runners within the party, but had considerable marathon experience. Both would be glad just to finish this one.

Several others joined us, including the doctors who had finished their duties. At eleven the bar closed, and we were ushered out into the lounge, where unfortunately the deferential waiters continued to ply us with beer.

The beer itself was uninspiring, extremely gassy, and not particularly cold. It appeared in litre bottles, brewed locally under the names of San Miguel and Tuborg, which should have guaranteed some quality, but did not. There was a third choice, a local brew called Iceberg, which was no more or less palatable than the other two. There was, of course, no draught beer. To cool it, bottles were placed in large wooden casks containing ice.

The company was convivial. We were joined by Gaye Sarma, a nurse from Hampshire, and Rob Haworth, who was the senior doctor, as he had been on the previous Everest Marathon. A seasoned campaigner with a great capacity for tobacco, whisky and humorous stories, he had just retired from general practice in North Wales. He remembered Dieter well, as did everyone who had been on the previous trip!

It was around two thirty before most of us had sufficient sense to go to bed. Curiously, this was the parting of the ways as far as the two groups were concerned. Apart from the evening after the race, when most people would be too knackered for much partying, this would be the last social contact we would have with the Late Birds until the final evening in Kathmandu in almost a month's time. We didn't know it at the time, but the fact that the expedition was in reality two separate expeditions, one moving a day either ahead or behind the other, would lead to a curious sense of detachment and almost rivalry between the groups.

In three hours time we would be woken, eat a quick breakfast, use a proper toilet for the last time for three weeks, and prepare to embark on our adventure into the unknown.

I fell into a deep exhausted sleep, conscious that the muted night-time noise of the city outside our window was a world away from where I would be tomorrow night.

Wherever that may be.

# The Road to Jiri and a Voice in the Dark: "Namaste! Give Me Pen, Give Me Bonbon!"

## Wednesday 10th November

At 5.30 a.m., I rarely feel at my best, particularly after less than three hours sleep, and considerably too much beer. My stomach was uneasy, and the prospect of a nine hour bus ride over rough mountainous terrain, followed by a three hour trek did nothing to allay my discomfort.

Still, the Blue Star's attempt at providing something that resembled the Great British Breakfast, with grease oozing and sizzling from sausages which tasted curiously of curry, washed down by gallons of tea, perked me up considerably.

I could, after all, sleep on the bus.

We gathered outside in the small courtyard, where there was an animated conversation in progress between Dave, Wish, and two Nepalis who, I assumed correctly, were to be our coach drivers.

I have never been moved to study body language, but it was fairly obvious that Dave wasn't pleased about something. Hands raised heavenwards, then on hips, head lowered with eyes raised, then tilted to the right, as the points of issue were clearly emphasised by the smacking of the left index finger into the splayed digits of the right hand.

These were the gestures that we would grow to know and love over the next three weeks.

Finally, when agreement could not be reached and it was time to send for ACAS, there was the half pirouette on the left heel, with the hands sunk deep into the pockets, and the disappearance of the neck, as the head sank into the shoulders.

Alternatively, if a compromise had been reached and accord restored, this was acknowledged by the raucous schoolboy laugh, shoulder to shoulder hug, and hearty slap on the back, forceful enough to loosen the teeth of the unfortunate native.

It was an apprehensive-looking group who stood around chatting excitedly as the film crew captured these final moments of civilisation.

Apparently it was the insistence of the film crew to record us boarding the buses and our departure that was causing the row. The drivers, conscious of the length of the journey, simply wanted to be on their way. This would be a recurring theme throughout the journey.

There were two buses, similar in most aspects to buses anywhere in the Third World. However, these could probably be accorded the status of luxury coach due to the absence of farm animals, and the fact that there would be fewer than fifty people inside and a further thirty clinging to the roof.

On the front of each bus, a large blue banner had been tied bearing the legend "Reebok – The Everest Marathon". It served as a reminder of what we were here for.

At last, shortly after six thirty, we drove out of the courtyard, picked up the film crew, and set off on our journey.

Behind us we left an oasis, an anchor of familiarity and order in an alien environment which was about to become considerably more alien.

Behind us, the last toilet, wash-hand basin and proper shower we would see for three weeks. No telephone, no television, no taxes or shops that accepted credit cards. No deferential waiters, or matronly women in colourful sarongs sweeping non-existent particles of dust from your path.

So how was a three-showers-a-day, *Times*-crossword-on-the-toilet-man going to cope with such basic deprivation? I wasn't sure. Especially with the noises which my stomach was making.

There was plenty of room on the bus, and most of us had a bench to ourselves. The seats were hard and uncomfortable, surrounded by chrome pillars and rails, designed so that any sudden braking (and there would be plenty of that) would precipitate a violent collision between skull and chrome.

The decor, and in particular the curtains, was hideously gaudy and, in fact, reminded me of my ancient camper van. Perhaps it had been fitted out in Nepal.

Although there were a few faces I had yet to put a name to, I knew most of the people on the bus.

Simon and Nat sat at the back. In front of them was Ray Brown, the Kiwi teacher who lived in Perth. Beyond Ray was John Matesich, a fifty-five year old teacher from San Pedro, California. John was rather loud, and regarded everything new with the same gauche childlike over-excitement as do most Americans. However, like good wine, he matured well on the trip, and was a guy I was to grow very fond of. Like most Americans, he was generous to a fault, and this was to save my bacon on one occasion.

In front of me was the doctor I had been allocated, Stephen Hassan. A somewhat spaghetti western-like figure, with his beard and broad rimmed hat, Stephen had travelled extensively and had been a member of an expedition which had climbed Makalu. Unlike John, Stephen rarely got particularly excited about anything, but went about the trip in a quiet and helpful manner.

Also on the bus were Wish and Dave, Joy Williams, the policewoman from Haverfordwest, Mike and Jerri, Lloyd Scott and Andrew Burgess, and two members of the film crew, Alan Hughes and Ron Isles.

Lloyd Scott was lucky to be alive. A one-time fireman and professional footballer for Watford, where he had played in goal, Lloyd had been struck down by Leukaemia. Fortunately, he found a bone marrow donor in Andrew Burgess, whom he did not know at the time. They were now firm friends, and had run a couple of marathons together, raising large sums for charity. Lloyd was now employed by a charity as an events coordinator. Andrew was an electrical engineer, and a keen cricketer. Also with them, as a companion, whatever that meant, was Sue Sayers, a London policewoman. Sue was a warm and vivacious character, with a huge capacity for laughter, and would contribute hugely to the morale of the group.

Ron Isles, head of the camera crew, was a portly middle-aged man, whose physique did not immediately suggest suitability for the rigours of a three week trek. Ron lived in Arthog, Gwynedd, and was a television producer employed by Studio Coleg Harlech. This was the first time a serious attempt had been made to film the event, and he had already encountered many problems, not least persuading a sponsor to part with the necessary cash to make the film viable.

Eventually, a major sponsor was found in Reebok, who contributed twelve thousand pounds and made the project feasible.

Ron recruited his son Stephen, a writer, and Alun Hughes. Al, also from North Wales, was a professional cameraman who had considerable experience of Nepal, having spent three months filming on the recent Makalu expedition. Martin Stone, by profession a computer analyst, was on the trip in the official capacity of cameraman. However his real motivation for making the trip was an attempt to break the world record from Base Camp to Kathmandu after the race. Martin, who I had eventually sat next to on the flight from Heathrow, had won many prestigious mountain marathons, including the gruelling five day Back of the Dragon race from North to South Wales. This he had won with his girlfriend, Helene Diamantides as his partner. Diamantides and Alison Wright broke the record in 1987 for the fastest journey by foot from Base Camp to Kathmandu with a time of three days and ten hours.

The final member of the film crew was Richard Uridge. Richard was one of the smoothest people I have ever met, and always managed to look immaculate, even at eighteen thousand feet. He had an incredible repertoire of both chat-up lines and jokes, and for sheer entertainment value he earned his place on the trip. We were fortunate to have him in our group.

*

The city was starting to stir as we drove out towards the airport, scene of my futile run of yesterday.

At 6.45 a.m., there was a stillness that hung, like the smog, over the city. Dust lay still, waiting for the inertia imparted by a million pairs of feet rushing headlong to their destinations. Lazy dogs stretched, and cocked legs on mounds of street rubbish. The traffic was thin, but grew in volume as we approached the airport, winding its chaotic and erratic way, ceaselessly tooting horns, aimed at no one and everyone. It was incredible that I hadn't seen a single accident yet.

Leaving the city behind, we took the Kodari road, which ultimately crosses the Friendship Bridge into Tibet, and leads to Lhasa. We would not be going that far. The entire day's journey to Jiri would be just under two hundred kilometres. Long enough, I mused after the first half hour.

It wasn't long before we stopped. We were all asked to leave the bus, so that diesel could be put into it. The reason for this was not immediately obvious but became apparent as the driver and several willing helpers performed a bizarre ritual, which involved vigorously rocking the bus from side to side. This complete, the bus was filled with diesel, we reclaimed our seats and were soon on our way again.

The views were not exactly awe inspiring. For one thing, the mist which hung over the valley was slow to clear. For another, we were still in the Kathmandu Valley where presumably the inhabitants were too busy farming to finish building the houses they lived in. Practically every roadside dwelling was incomplete. In the villages, there were blocks of flats, which had one, or in some cases even two, stories complete, but above them were exposed girders and piles of brick and rubble. At least it looked as if they were trying to build them properly. Not much difference between here and Spanish holiday resorts, I thought.

It wasn't long before we stopped again. There was an extremely unhealthy noise coming from the rear of the bus. It sounded as if the rear axle were about to break.

Closer inspection revealed a huge stone firmly wedged between the rear nearside tyres. The driver was trying to free it using a large stick as a lever. Now, I have come across this problem before. Out on a morning run a couple of years ago, I came across two frightfully nice ladies with a horse lorry experiencing the same problem.

No amount of pushing, prodding, kicking or cursing will move the thing, and prolonged shoving will only make the situation worse. The only solution is to remove the outer wheel to free it.

This, I duly pointed out to the driver, who was at first suspicious, then, reassured by Dave, took my advice. Eventually, we were on our way. We soon caught the lead bus, which had stopped for some filming, and another delay ensued.

"At this rate, we're going to be starting the trek in the dark," I observed grimly to Simon. That wouldn't be far from the truth.

As we started to climb into the hills, the fog cleared, and our sense of anticipation grew. Farmers now had to eke out an existence on the small terraced fields cut into the sides of the hills.

We crossed the Sun Kosi, one of the major rivers, for the first time, and stopped again for more photography, and the production of various permits at the police checkpost. Some steps led to a dwelling above us. Two small children sat observing the curious group of foreigners emerging from the buses. I pointed my video camera at them, one nudged the other, and they both giggled and waved. They had seen it all before.

The second bridge over the Sun Kosi was a much more substantial affair. Here the river was much wider, and the Swiss had constructed a sturdy steel-girdered suspension bridge several years ago. We stopped again before crossing it. It was now warm, and with the prospect of approaching the gateway to the world's mightiest mountain range, I wanted to put Dieter's advice to the test.

"The only way to travel is on the roof of the bus," he had told me. Having obtained Dave's tacit approval, I climbed up the ladder, and found a comfortable lair amongst the baggage at the front of the bus. I was joined by several others, including Nat, Simon, Joy and John.

The crossing of the bridge was again filmed, and I was rewarded for my efforts, as this was to be one of my two cameo appearances on the final documentary.

Beyond the bridge the road narrowed significantly, and at home would have borne a 'not suitable for large or heavy vehicles' sign. It also started to climb significantly. As we wound our way up the narrow mountain road, I questioned the wisdom of where I was sitting, as the front of the bus would appear to go over the edge of one hairpin bend, then miraculously accelerate out, and hurtle up the grass-verged straight, to fling itself into the next one.

"Do you think these things have MOT certificates?" I asked Nat.

"No. And I don't think the drivers have any certificates either," he replied.

"We're the ones who should be certified for sitting here!" said someone else, at the back.

It didn't appear quite so daunting through the lens of the video camera, and the results probably would have been spectacular had I not inadvertently pressed a button which caused the bottom half of the picture to appear blank, and the top half to be blacked out. Why is it necessary to put buttons like that on cameras? Still, at least there was nothing wrong with the sound!

Eventually, we stopped at a village where several other buses were also stopped. We all naturally assumed that this would be our lunch-stop, as it was now after 1 p.m., and a very long time since breakfast. However, this was not the case, and we were instructed to return to the bus in ten minutes.

The village was made up of one long street. On either side was a large trench which appeared to double as a refuse tip and the village's sewerage system. The smell was horrendous. Beyond this moat were little shops and unappetising teahouses (*bhatti*) to which access could be gained by crossing shaky small wooden bridges.

I bought a Coke, and watched one of the public buses preparing to depart. The driver blasted his horn relentlessly for around a minute, which brought the response of hoards of little men and women scurrying and jostling for a perch. He slammed the bus into gear, and lurched off up the hill. If you missed it, or were not quite ready for departure, too bad. To be a bus driver in these parts must be to be all powerful.

Our departure was more sedate. To everyone's surprise, once around the first bend we stopped again. On the right hand side of the road was a large grassy verge, a natural car park, which would be our lunch stop.

Lunch was distributed. It consisted of one foul tasting sandwich of indeterminate contents, a piece of fruit which no one could identify, a boiled egg, and an orange.

I picked at mine and, having found my toilet paper, set off to find a suitable site to open my account of crapping in the wild. I couldn't find one. Despite my stomach's protestations, I resolved to try to hang on until we got to camp. Although Dieter had forewarned me about the total lack of sanitation facilities, I assumed that this was simply Dieter being Dieter. It was unthinkable that an expedition of highly tuned athletes would be expected to go for three weeks without some kind of reasonably civilised latrine arrangements. Boy, was I ever wrong?

Back at the buses, there was a riot in progress. A game of catch with an egg had predictably got completely out of hand. Eggs, and then oranges, were being thrown from one bus to the other. As I climbed back to my perch at the front of the bus, I got pelted on the head with an orange, and hit from behind by friendly fire with an egg. My response was swift and decisive, in the context of the battle.

Correctly attributing the instigation of hostilities to be the work of one Rev. John G. Webster, I responded with a direct hit on the latter, squarely between the eyes, with the remnants of the orange which had hit me. The UN peacekeeping force then moved in, in the form of Wish, who told us, "Not to be so bloody childish".

This incident, needless to say, was not recorded by the film crew.

Back on the road, we were joined on the roof by Ron Isles and his camera. He was rewarded for his efforts with distant glimpses of our first snow capped peak. Far off to the north, it was probably Ama Bamare at 5,325 metres, which is close to the Tibetan border.

The villages flashed by in a blur, just names on the map: Perku, Muldi, Nigale. Children ran behind the bus, with dirty smiling faces, hands waving frantically. In one village was a school. I knew this because it had a board above the door claiming that *"Education is the chief defence of the nation."* How very true, I thought, and wished that our politicians would aspire to such a worthy sentiment.

On our guided tour of Kathmandu I had asked our guide about education. He informed me that less than forty per cent of children receive any education, and only seven per cent were girls. As the trip progressed, I was to realise the value which is placed on education even in the remotest of parts, which is in stark contrast to how it is undervalued in some circles at home.

Charikot was a fairly large town, and another stop for the public buses. We, of course stopped as well. It was an opportunity to use the public toilets, and here you had a choice. Either the tree-lined brick wall on the right of the fountain, or the more exposed, but offering a better view, barbed wire fence to the left of the fountain. The latter was presumably the source of the town's drinking water.

Charikot also had a police checkpoint, and bored and fussy uniformed officers checked our passes, in the self-important manner of petty officials worldwide. We had been issued with trekking permits, which were necessary to move in the Solu Khumbu. These had been stamped in Kathmandu, and bore details of passport, length of trek, starting and finishing point and contained a photograph of the owner.

I remembered having mine taken in the booth in the Post Office in Exeter as my four year old daughter, Rosanna, had pestered me until I had one taken with her in it. That was only last week, but seemed like a million years ago. It would seem a lot longer as the trip progressed.

The police were not at all happy about our riding on the roof. Despite being against the law, it is apparently quite acceptable for Nepalis to swing from every handhold. If they fell off it was their own fault, and there would be no suing the bus company. However, the ramifications of Westerners being involved in an accident as a result of breaking the law were politically unacceptable, and so we reluctantly took our places in the bus.

A quarter of a mile down the road, we stopped and got back onto the roof.

It was at this point that a faint and highly unpleasant smell that we had been vaguely conscious of for some time, became less faint and considerably more unpleasant. It was the unmistakable odour of human faeces.

"Okay, who's stood in something?" I asked.

We all looked at our boots. The culprit was soon exposed. Behind me sat Simon and Joy. The sole of Joy's right boot was liberally caked in excrement, which she had applied unwittingly to a random selection of the blue kit bags on which we sat. As the smell had been present for some time, it was likely that it was also on our clothes, what with all the musical chairs before and after Charikot.

There was a general chorus of "Eeeeuuch"!

"My God, this is appalling," said a voice from behind, who had just discovered what he was sitting on.

"This is Nepalling," I offered, still able to wallow in the delights of British toilet humour, having first satisfied myself that I had avoided contamination. Joy did her best to clean up the mess using tissues and some of the baby wipes which Simon had thoughtfully brought with him.

Her boot was then removed and confiscated by Nat who hung it over the back of the bus, where it kicked against the back window, irritating those sitting inside. The smell at last dissipated.

"Ah well", said Joy, "what's a little bit of shit between friends?"

"Yes, but whose little bit of shit?" I replied.

\*

The hills were getting bigger. These still may not yet be the foothills, but they were the foothills of the foothills.

It was mid-afternoon, and it was rumoured that we were within a couple of hours of reaching our destination. The villages flew by, and beyond Kirantichap we crossed the last river, the Tamba Kosi. Mist and low cloud now obscured the sun. At first, the drop in temperature was welcome, but as we climbed, the air became decidedly chilly, and soon we were huddled together for warmth.

Our stops had become fewer, as the drivers pressed their claims for urgency, which was also reflected in the driving. Having followed the other bus quite happily all afternoon, our driver suddenly decided it was going too slowly for him. Finding a straight piece of road with a widish grass verge, he pulled out without warning to overtake.

"I don't bloody believe this," I said, horrified, and clung with white-knuckled fingers to the rail.

We drew level with the other bus.

"Hi, Richard", called Annabel, "what's the matter? You look ill!"

The end of the verge was rapidly approaching, and ahead was certain death in the form of a sudden drop, as the road hairpinned round to the left.

Our driver was not going to concede defeat. I got ready to jump.

Miraculously, at the last minute, amid irate tooting and gesticulation, our rival took his foot off the throttle, and we rejoined the road in the lead, to watch, horrified, the earth fall away to our right. It had been close.

But we recovered quickly and were soon gesticulating our triumph to those sitting atop the other bus.

Our final stop was almost within sight of Jiri, and we were asked to get back into the buses. By now it was genuinely cold, and no one objected. Inside the bus, I made final adjustments to my kit, and spent a little time getting to know what functions, if any, the various straps on Dieter's rucksack performed. Not surprisingly, I found the clasps which secured the top and the waist buckle to be totally beyond comprehension. I enlisted Stephen's help, and despite his patient efforts to educate me, I was little the wiser, and sat with the thing strapped to my back, like a paratrooper waiting to jump. It would be several days before I felt entirely confident with it. Of course, it was simplicity itself once I understood which way round the straps were supposed to go, and introduced the plastic buckles to each other facing the correct way.

We drove into Jiri at five thirty in the gathering gloom. It is a prosperous village, with a main street lined on either side with substantial three storey shops and lodges, white walled buildings made from stone and timber, with sloping tiled roofs. It is a flat and fertile area, and wealthy little farms are dotted on the outposts of the village, and nestle in the hills beyond.

Jiri, which is at 1,905 metres (6,287 feet), not only has a STOL (short take-off and landing) airstrip, but also a weekly blue-sky bazaar. Both draw people to the village and considerably contribute to its prosperity. After our marathon bus journey, despite my hatred of flying, I was wishing we had been flown in. Of course, this would have greatly increased the cost, and fog in the Kathmandu Valley, and the unreliability of booking procedures makes flying anywhere a total lottery.

The villagers are said to have been descended from a father who belonged to the Tibetan Kamba tribe, and a mother named Jirel, who was a Sunmar, the Nepali gold and silversmiths.

From Jiri to Everest Base Camp, along what has become known as The Everest Highway, takes around thirteen days. The name Everest Highway, is more than a little misleading. What passes for a road stops abruptly at Jiri in a small square beyond a narrow bridge. This was presumably where the bazaar is held each Saturday. It is not a 'National Trust, enjoy-your-visit-take-your-litter-home' type of square, but more a 'This-is-the-end-of-civilisation-as-you-know-it-get-out-and-walk' sort of square.

Beyond that, a path disappears into the trees, and meanders its rugged and boulder-strewn way, cutting across the valleys, amassing a staggering nine thousand metres of ascent, which is similar to the full height of Everest from sea level, before arriving on the barren glaciers which approach the foot of the giant and its attendant smaller peaks.

It is a well-worn trail, and the journey is done in set stages from which guides and porters steadfastly refuse to deviate without great financial inducement.

In order to give us the best chance to rest, acclimatise, and arrive at the start of the race in some form of relative fitness, our trek was designed to take sixteen days. This included four rest days in Namche Bazaar and beyond.

Getting out of the bus in Jiri was a struggle. Although faced with a two hour trek to camp with nightfall rapidly approaching, I did not feel any urgency. Despite the extreme discomfort of the last ten hours, the bus was my last link with life as I had known it for the last thirty-seven years. It was a kind of umbilical cord which linked me, albeit tenuously, with the mother comforts of my established existence.

Beyond the bridge and the square lay a world outside my experience, and conscious of my hangover and rumbling guts, enthusiasm to boldly go into the great unknown was just a little lacking.

Still, the sooner I got going, the sooner I would get there, and, as I was now looking forward to a welcome session in the latrine tent, I strode off purposefully up the street.

Most people had already made their departure, so I set off at a brisk pace. Dave had told us that two years ago, "A super fit marine (Dieter) had reached the camp in under an hour", and I had resolved not to be much outside that.

After twenty minutes, I was making good progress, but was finding it hard going. I don't actually enjoy walking (which begs the question what the hell was I doing here?) and very rarely go for a walk for the sheer enjoyment of that form of physical activity. My boots, which were brand new and the sturdy leather type, felt heavy and ungainly, and I was much too hot. Before starting, I had put on a sweatshirt, fleece jacket and gloves, as I was cold after the inactivity of the bus journey.

Now I had to stop and strip off. This meant a prolonged and frustrating argument with the clasps of the rucksack. Eventually, I persuaded the thing to close, but the buckle resisted all my efforts, and I had to proceed without the waist belt fastened. As a result of this, all those who I had passed had now passed me, and I was virtually at the back again. This was the first of many lessons learned: no matter how cold you feel at the start of trekking, wear a minimum of clothes, as you very soon warm up.

Before long I was sweating profusely, and feeling better for the physical exertion. My pack was heavy, but not uncomfortable. The trail was virtually all upward, and required a very different type of muscular response than what I had been used to during my training.

It was thirsty work, and I remembered Dave had mentioned something about teahouses at frequent intervals. So far I hadn't passed anything other than the occasional foul smelling shack. I became aware that I hadn't passed any of my companions for some time either, and there was now a thick fog which, added to the descending darkness, left me feeling uncertain as to whether I was going the correct way.

Suddenly ahead I made out the outline of a couple of small buildings, and heard the sound of laughter, the clearing of throats predictably followed by spitting on the ground, and the harsh, guttural tones of the native tongue.

Towards me, out of the ghostly luminescence, ran several small shapes.

"*Namaste, Namaste, Hello!* Give me pen, give me bonbon!"

I had a few pens and other odds and ends, which I intended giving to the children in the highlands, closer to our destination.

I was surrounded by a jostling, shoving crowd of small boys.

"*Chhaina*", I replied, which means no, and was the only word I knew. I walked on towards the buildings, followed by my hopeful entourage, who were as rude and objectionable as crowds of jostling, shoving small boys at home. I know this because I teach them. Smoke billowed from the chimneyless jerry-built wooden shacks. It was a pungent sickly-sweet smell of wood burning in the open stone stoves in the one roomed dwellings, with nowhere to escape other than to filter slowly through the cracks in the roof, and mingle with the foul smelling evening mist.

The path led me close by them, and I peered inside. A kerosene lamp cast a warm glow amongst the shadows, and a woman with leathery skin dressed in simple but colourful skirts, fed the stove with wood, while the flames licked the blackened bottoms of the pots and kettle above.

Around the perimeter of the room above the earthen floor were fragile-looking benches covered by dirty mats, presumably the bedding for the family, or travellers too tired to go further. At the far end, were shelves neatly stacked with cigarettes, small bottles of rum, Coke and water, packets of biscuits, and batteries. So this is a teahouse, I thought. Who in their right mind would buy tea from here?

I resisted the temptation to investigate further, as I was finding the smell hard to bear. It was something I would quickly grow accustomed to, but for now the smoke, the pungent smell of sweat ingrained in the clothes and bodies of the people who passed by, and the spicy food smells emanating from the stove, formed a hideous and almost unbearable olfactory cocktail.

Perhaps they liked it. Certainly they were oblivious to it. We in the West go to great pains to rid ourselves of unpleasant smells, and spend a fortune in enhancing our own. Whose head has not been turned by the lightly scented fragrance of a pretty girl passing by on a summer's day?

> *Gardenia perfume lingering on my pillow*
> *Wild strawberries only seven francs a kilo.*
> *The song that Crosby sings,*
> *These foolish things,*
> *Remind me of you.* [1]

It occurred to me that, in a few days, we would probably smell as bad as the indigenous population. But would we be equally oblivious to it?

I was beginning to wonder what I had let myself in for. I pressed on along the path, still followed by the host of animated small boys.

"Mister, pen! Bonbon! Give me! Give me!"

*"Chhaina, Chhaina!"*

Most of them had dispersed, but one or two persistent ones still followed, touching my backpack, and pulling the straps.

It was at this point that diplomacy was replaced by my growing irritation:

*"*B-u-g-g-e-r o-f-f!*"* I roared. This, although perhaps losing something in the translation, was altogether more effective. They got the message.

It was virtually dark. Luckily I had kept my head-torch handy, and was able to reach it without having to engage my rucksack in a further bout of prolonged wrestling. Others were not so lucky, as our leaders had not anticipated trekking in the dark, and therefore the necessity to keep torches to the fore. Most people's were safely tucked away in the bags which the porters were carrying.

However, when I turned it on, the beam simply bounced back against the dancing particles of mist. Visibility was limited to a few feet, and my progress was like a blind man feeling his way down a busy street. We think we have a monopoly on mist in Britain, and places like North Wales and the Lake District rejoice in being "clagged in". But even there no one in their right mind would set out in pitch dark over totally unfamiliar territory. Mentally I began to

---

[1] As recorded by Bryan Ferry – believed to be written by Maschwitz & Strachey.

calculate how long it would take to retrace my steps back to Jiri, if the worst came to the worst.

I almost bumped into John Dunning. It was only the sight of his little white floppy hat (which he didn't remove throughout the trip, until it was replaced by something completely absurd in Kathmandu) which prevented me from flattening him.

John was in his sixties, from Redcar in Cleveland. He was one of the small group who were actually crazier than the runners – he had come for the walk! John loved walking and had completed a walk from John O'Groats to Lands End. He had come on the trip as a companion, with his friend Mike Harper, also from Redcar. Mike, who was fifty-seven, was an ultra-distance runner, and aside from twenty-four hour races and the like, had won the Annapurna half marathon in 1992.

John was on his own, without a torch.

"Any idea how far?" I asked.

"Ey, can't be long now," he replied. I didn't ask how he knew. We walked together, and I enjoyed his company, the conversation doing much to revive my flagging spirits, and take my mind off my most immediate problem, namely my guts.

Soon, we caught two small children, a girl and a boy aged about eight and ten. They also had a torch, and the boy spoke good English. At home it would be unthinkable for young children to be out on their own in the dark in such conditions. Here they didn't give it a second thought. Together we clambered down a steep and slippery bank, and came to a junction where the path divided.

"Mali?" I asked.

"This way," said the boy, and we followed, grateful to have avoided the possibility of taking a long detour. As it turned out, others were not so lucky. The path improved, and soon we found ourselves in downtown Mali, which consisted of five or six wooden huts exuding the by now familiar ethnic stench which accompanies all habitation in these parts.

Our companions said goodbye and disappeared into the doorway of one of the huts, having pointed the direction to the camp.

The noise and the beams of light reached us as we clambered up the little hill to stumble into a mist-enshrouded sea of blue canvas. We had been allocated a tent, which Dave had numbered. That number corresponded with the number of your blue bag, carried by the porters, so, in theory, when you arrived at camp your tent would be erected, and your kit bag placed outside it. That was the theory, anyway.

My number was fourteen, and my tentmate was Simon, who apparently had not arrived yet. The tents were brand new and, as far as tents go, perfectly adequate, being reasonably spacious ridge tents which could accommodate two people. However, the prospect of spending the next three weeks in these things did little to disperse my mood of gloom. I felt about as cheerful as a song by Morrissey. Having tripped over several guy ropes, causing concern to those inside, eventually I found tent fourteen.

"Home sweet home," I sighed, and started to arrange my kit for the night. It was not long before I unearthed the first problem. There were three zippered doors. The one on the outside drew the outer flaps together, and was impossible to close from within the tent. The second line of zips came together in an inverted T, as did the third or inner door, which was a thin nylon mesh, presumably to repel insects. The trouble with the two inner doors was they could only be adequately closed from the outside. This meant having to put your hand through the flaps in order to open and close them from the inside. This did not bode well for night time peeing.

As the sweat dried, the temperature rapidly fell, and I put on several layers of clothing. Just as important as not starting off wearing too many clothes, was replacing them when you stopped before you got cold.

Having located my toilet paper, I set off to relieve my nagging guts. I found Dave numbering tents close by.

"Which way to the bathroom, my good man?" I asked.

"Nearest bathroom, ah, one hundred and twenty miles that way!" he replied.

"I'll settle for a nice long session on the toilet, then."

"You'll be lucky! You'll find the green latrine tents on the perimeter of the camp. Wash your hands in the bowl outside, and don't leave a mess."

I set off to seek out a suitable tent, and tripped over more guy ropes on my way, eliciting noisy curses from inside.

I didn't have much difficulty finding the latrine tents. Standing sentinel around the edge of the camp like green AA phone boxes, they afforded little in the way of privacy. The hideous noises coming from the first easily persuaded me to pass on.

When forced to use public toilets at home, it is normal human behaviour to treat them with suspicion. Wait and see who emerges, if they are all occupied. No, don't like the look of him. He didn't wash his hands. So pretend to comb your hair, and wait for the next free cubicle. Aha! Trap four is vacant. God, He's peed all over the seat! Still, what would you expect from a kid. And look at those cling-ons! There's enough for three episodes of *Star Trek* down there!

I arrived at the most remote tent and unzipped the door.

Nothing, no amount of words, nor vivid description, could have prepared me for what lay before me. Secretly, I had suspected it might be bad. But not this bad. The beam from my torch fell on a hole in the ground, roughly a foot in depth, and eighteen inches square. Earth was piled up behind it.

What was piled up inside it was evidence that I was not the first person to use it. What foul being had done that? Not content with almost filling the hole, some previous occupant had acrobatically left half a turd some way up the back wall of the tent. Either that, or it was *The Thing from the Pit* trying to escape. I was about to bare my bottom, when it suddenly occurred to me that it might be a leech, but closer examination proved that this was not the case. In any case, leeches were only supposed to be a hazard during the rainy season.

The next problem was which direction to face. This was a subject on which there would be great debate, and no uniformity was agreed by the end of the trip. Some preferred to go with the slope, and there was some logic in this, as it was certainly easier on the quads.

Some preferred an *al fresco* approach, and presented their posteriors to the semi-open tent flap. This was all well and good, although not particularly pleasant for those waiting. However, you then ran the risk of reuniting yourself with what you had got rid of if your trajectory was slightly out, and you stepped in it on your way out.

I preferred, if prefer is the right word, from such a limited choice, to perform the nightmarish operation facing the entrance.

I was in and out in record time. It is commonly accepted that expeditions attempting to climb Everest have the best chance of success when they "get in, get up and get out", as quickly as possible. The same might be applied to bishops and chorus girls, and can certainly be applied to latrine tents. It goes without saying that the pong was unbearable.

I tried to restrict my use of toilet paper to three sheets, (one up, one down, and one to shine), which was difficult, as I use half a rain forest at home. I covered my deposit with a layer of earth from the pile at the back, which was risky, as I couldn't guarantee that earth was all that it contained.

I emerged, relieved from unleashing my load, but full of trepidation at the final confirmation that this was it for the next three weeks. I noticed the bowl of blood-red fluid outside the tent, placed there for sterilising hands at the same time as my left foot made contact with it, spilling its contents.

Back at the camp, deferential little men wrapped in hooded blankets, with floral-printed vinyl mats on sturdy wicker trays, hovered in the mist offering tea and biscuits. It was now well past seven o'clock, and lunch, such as it was, but a distant memory. I wolfed down several oatmeal biscuits, and as the warmth of my second mug of sweet black tea began to filter to the remoter parts of my body, I began to perk up.

I attached myself to a group containing one or two familiar faces, and we stood around drinking tea and speculating about the prospect of food, and the prospects of those without torches finding the camp before morning.

There was now some genuine concern regarding the latter. About a third of the group were still unaccounted for, but Dave was largely unperturbed.

"They can't get lost. Some people just walk bloody slowly." In this he was right. It was admirable how slowly some people could trek, measuring each step with the precision of slow motion automatons so as to use the bare minimum of energy. They hardly disturbed the air as they passed. Almost walking without waking.

But there was a general air of concern that our missing companions could have met with misfortune.

Suddenly, the muted conversation was hushed by a blood-curdling shriek from the far side of the camp, accompanied by the violent striking of what sounded like cooking utensils against pots:

"Ssssooouuuuuupppprrrreeeaaddyyyyy!"

"What the hell was that?"

It was Wish who answered: "That, ladies and gentlemen, means that dinner is served."

As one, we forgot about our missing companions and trooped off after Dave and Wish to discover the dining room. This consisted of two long mess tents containing tables placed end to end with a row of small collapsible stools on either side. There was a warm glow from the three kerosene lamps which lit the tent. The tables were covered in sheets of the same floral-printed vinyl fabric as was on the trays, and there were several little vases of flowers and candles on the tables.

Someone had gone to a lot of effort and we were, to a man, impressed. There was, however, more than an air of apprehension as to the contents of the huge steaming caldrons which appeared the instant everyone was seated. Small aluminium soup bowls were circulated, which gave us a clue as to the contents of the caldrons. Ladles appeared, and those nearest began to serve the soup. The ladles were too small for any rapid distribution of soup, and with growing discontent at the ends of the table, a soup bowl was substituted, which proved to be much more efficient.

To accompany the soup, several large bowls containing popcorn appeared. Although popcorn may not immediately spring to mind as what the chic restaurants in Knightsbridge might choose to serve alongside soup, once the latter had been tasted, one reason at least became apparent.

The soup had body to about the same degree as a tug-of-war team with Twiggy as the anchor man. It was warm, it was wet, it was lightly spiced, but even your Campbell's consommé kicked sand in its face by comparison.

By augmenting it with popcorn by the fistful, the soup acquired a degree of both body and taste, although it was still of highly questionable nutritional value.

Smiling with obvious satisfaction that we had passed the first test, the cooks removed the empty dishes. There was, of course, nothing left.

The next course was what my mother-in-law would refer to as lobby. It is made thus: take a pot, lob into it anything you can find in your fridge and larder: vegetables, (particularly onions), old scraps of meat, Vapona fly tape, next door's cat, broken crankshaft; bring to the boil and simmer for two hours, then serve.

Alongside this we had bowl upon bowl of spaghetti-like noodles, which was an obvious clue that the carbohydrate loading was beginning early and, of all things, green beans. The latter looked as out of place as a condom in the Vatican.

The *coup de grâce* of the meal was the pudding. It could only be described as sludge. Yellow sludge. Those brave or greedy enough to eat it lost the power of speech for minutes afterwards, and then referred to it as a sort of "Fairy-Liquidy, lemon-curdy sort of thing". Spilt on the table, it had much the same effect as sulphuric acid or the gunge that came out of the Alien. Needless to say, most of the bowls were removed untouched by the still smiling cooks, delighted to find that, true of any group of eating humans, no matter how repulsive the food, there is always a pig who will have a second helping.

Valeri, the Bulgarian masseur, it was who was tucking into his third helping, when the highlight of the meal appeared. This came in the form of large steaming pots of tea, water and milk. Add large quantities of Cadbury's drinking chocolate, a smattering of coffee, and heaps of sugar to the sterile tasting powdered milk, and you were in seventh heaven.

Throughout the meal, conversation had been fairly muted, and invariably reverted to the latrine tents. Spaces were filled, as our tardy torchless comrades filtered in, casting black, ominous glances at our leaders. They consumed their food ravenously and silently. By the time the drinks had appeared, Dave had accounted for all but one member of the party. Several roll calls later, it transpired that the only absence was a degree of arithmetical competence and, much to our relief, everyone had now in fact arrived.

During the course of dinner, two things happened that would stay with me throughout the trip. The first was that I acquired a nickname. I moan a lot. I know that. I like moaning. Not in a particularly whingy and miserable moany sort of way, but when I first address a new and unfamiliar set of circumstances, I naturally look for the black humour in the situation. Take the toilet situation, for instance. I suppose my account of my introduction to defecating in the wild helped to earn me the nickname Marvin the Moaner.

This was Annabel's brainchild. Marvin was apparently a maladjusted robot in a TV science fiction spoof which I'd never heard of.

"Do you ever stop moaning Marvin?" enquired Annabel. "I mean, are you ever really cheerful?"

"No, never," I replied. "Can you pass the milk please?"

"There's none left."

"Bloody brilliant."

"There you go again, Marvin."

And so it went on.

The other thing was something that I apparently said. Although I have no recollection of so doing, I was later quoted as having said: "I can't be done with all this bloody culture crap," with reference to the joys of the ethnic differences experienced so far. It was addressed to Wish, and was no doubt said in an attempt to wind him up, as he was the self-appointed guru of all things cultural. Anyway, it was to come back to haunt me later.

Embarrassingly so.

\*

As the last of the night's supply of drinking chocolate was consumed, and the last horrific detail of the latrine situation and lack of anything resembling sanitation discussed for the hundredth time, there was a general realisation that it was bedtime.

The party broke up slowly, as people put off the evil moment of the first night under canvas after the luxuries of the Blue Star and Kathmandu.

Outside the mess tent were two large, white plastic water containers. One bore the legend washing, and the other drinking. It was important not to confuse the two. The latter contained water that had been boiled, and was fit for consumption. To drink the former was to invite disaster. I filled my water bottle and cup with drinking water, and set off to wash my teeth. Gradually I was mastering the art of performing this act without using the amount of water consumed by a small brewery in a day. By using less than my customary inch and a half of toothpaste, I discovered I could rinse my mouth with the contents of one mug.

Simon was already asleep as I settled myself into my sleeping bag, only to remember that I had forgotten to have a pee.

Outside again, I made my way to the rear of the tent, only tripping over two guy ropes this time, and relieved myself. I turned off my head-torch. The blackness was total. It was oppressive and uplifting at the same time. There was no clue as to our surroundings. What was out there, I wondered?

And, more importantly, what would tomorrow bring? These ponderings were interrupted by an unexplained warm, wet feeling.

To my horror, I realised I was peeing on my foot.

However, a good meal and good companionship had done much to banish my negative mood following the later stages of the bus journey and the trek.

Tomorrow would be the real beginning. Days of strolling carefree over hill and valley amid some of the world's most spectacular scenery, basking in warm sunshine, as the roof of the world came ever closer. I was not simply in the theatre. I was on the stage.

Back in tent Fourteen, with the three zip security procedures complete, I crawled into my bag, exhausted. Before turning out my torch, I glanced at my watch. It felt like midnight.

It was 8.30 p.m.

# Mali to Bhandar, Farewell to the First Latrine

### Thursday 11th November

Way, way back in the roaring 20s, in those early pioneering days of Everest exploration, the main problem which faced intrepid mountaineers was one which, as usual, legend accorded to none other than George Leigh Mallory. Namely, "First find the mountain." Not that there's that much chance of missing the mountain. One would have to be pretty stupid or unfortunate to get lost on the Everest Highway, particularly on the lower approaches. But the lengthy approach to Everest, particularly from Jiri, is as arduous a switchback as it's possible to find anywhere in the world. The path is bumpy, treacherously steep and slippery, and dusty with the erosion caused by the comings and goings of a million pairs of feet.

Also, it's a very, very long way. The foothills of Everest will not yield their beauty and mystery without a considerable outlay of physical effort on behalf of those wishing to enjoy them. Perhaps rightly so.

However, as in the best horror movies, the bright and welcome sunshine that heralded the dawn gave no clues as to just how horrendous the next week would be. We were not to know it but, at best, it could be described as a tedious slog. At worst, as the body fought to overcome the uneven battle between what it had become accustomed to in terms of food and hygiene, and the almost total lack of sanitation with which it was now presented, which culminated in the frequent eruption of fluid from every orifice, it could be described as a nightmare.

Barely had my head hit what I had contrived as a pillow, than I plummeted into what for me were new depths of unconsciousness.

Some eight hours later, I gradually awoke to the unfamiliar sounds and smells of the camp coming back to life.

The clanging of cooking utensils and the harsh, guttural tones of the men laughing and calling to each other, no doubt jibing and joking over what lay ahead for another naive and unsuspecting group of Westerners. The mystery of their unintelligible language and, of course, the ever present clearing of throats and the spitting.

It was five thirty, and as daylight began to filter through the blue canvas, I was once again gripped by the thrill of waking in another world.

I attempted an intricate manoeuvre with the object of opening the tent without leaving my sleeping bag. In my haste to see what wonders morning would reveal, I knocked over my cup of water, and spilled the contents over my sleeping bag, Simon's sleeping bag, and a large portion of the floor of the tent.

"Are you awake, Simon?" I asked the motionless shape next to me.

"I am now", he replied, "and showered."

"Sorry."

I opened the two inner zips, and was relieved to find my boots still outside, even if they were drenched with dew. After a struggle in which it gave clear notice that it was not going to last the trip, particularly when ice came into the equation, the outer zip obliged and I stuck my head out of the tent.

The sight which greeted me just had to be the highlight of the trip so far. It easily surpassed anything else.

We were camped on a plateau which rose sharply behind us to a wooded hill. Ahead of us, looking into the rising sun, the view was simply spectacular. The plateau fell away to the left down into a deep valley from which, on the other side, tree covered hills so close you could smell the pine, were dwarfed by distant snow-capped peaks. High above the trees an eagle soared with almost divine indifference to the majesty of its environment.

Although the sun had barely cleared the ridge of the plateau, the sky was the deep blue of a perfect English summer's evening. It was totally cloudless, and the clarity of the light quite remarkable.

This was a big country, and a country of big contrasts. Just as my spirits had sunk to the laces of my boots on the previous evening, now they soared with the eagle. The early morning sun bathed my face, and the gentle warmth of its rays helped consign the memories of our arrival in this spectacular wilderness to the back of my mind.

The stillness and serenity of the moment was lost forever as someone in a nearby tent noisily broke wind.

"You dirty bastard!"

It sounded like Nat.

"Plenty more where that came from," replied the breaker of wind. "A woman's only a woman, but a good fart's a relief!" I guessed it was the unmistakable northern tones of Bryan English, the young doctor from Sheffield. It later transpired that Bryan was in the same year at Sheffield University as my brother-in-law, Rob. Right now, he was making himself very unpopular with his companion and fellow medic.

Back in the tent, Simon had completed the mopping up operation and was beginning to pack his kit. Mine could wait. I wanted to savour one of the moments I had been looking forward to for months. I stretched out on my mattress, and looked at my watch. It was five fifty-five. Not long now.

In all the official literature, in all the accounts both spoken and written, the day began at six o'clock, with "A steaming hot mug of Bed Tea thrust through the tent flap." This was meant to precipitate purposeful action in much the same way as Superman would nip into the nearest phone box and reappear with his underpants outside his tights.

Sure enough, the clattering of the metal mugs heralded the approach of the posse of obsequious little men. One carried the by now familiar floral print covered wicker tray bearing upturned mugs, another carried two huge pots of tea. Presumably inferior in rank, two further youths followed carrying milk and sugar.

"*Namaste*, Good morning, you like tea?"

"Does the Pope wear a big hat?" I replied, confusing the issue.

Two mugs of tea appeared, although they were not, in all honesty, either thrust through the tent flap or steaming.

Still, with three heaped spoonfuls of sugar it was an acceptable beverage, and I was soon on my second mug. This was a part of the day, as the trip wore on, which I was to savour. The lull before the storm, before the frantic packing, the treatment of blisters, and the ever increasing haste to find a seat at the breakfast table, before anything worth eating disappeared. It was a quiet moment, during which Simon and I frequently enjoyed bizarre conversations such as can only be shared by strangers in a strange land, on a strange journey.

Today, however, we silently contemplated the tea, and waited patiently for its mystical properties to take effect.

None did, but that didn't detract from the thrill of anticipation on that first morning of the trek.

Simon was packed and ready for action in an instant. Despite having an hour to assemble my belongings and vacate the tent with my blue bag for the porter to carry placed outside, I was still struggling to get things in place by five past seven. My porter had arrived and, despite his ready smile, this little brown leathery leprechaun of a man, with trousers which ceased abruptly well above his ankles and wearing trainers that at home no self-respecting tramp would have worn, was clearly chafing to get on with it.

His colleague arrived and they exchanged grunts, presumably to the effect of, "Is this arsehole going to be here all day?" and he began to dismantle the tent, which was a clear indication that my departure was required.

One of the problems with carrying virtually all my own kit was that everything that came out had to go back in, and things had to be arranged in such a way that they could be found during the day if required.

Also, whilst my self-inflating thermal mattress was the cleverest bit of kit since the invention of the plastic tomato sauce bottle, getting the thing to deflate was quite another matter.

Eventually, I expelled most of the air from it and had my belongings packed into my Berghaus in something resembling order.

I put on my wet boots, and set off to find the mess tent.

There was none. It had been removed and packed away, the tables and little stools left where they had been last evening more for their convenience than in consideration of our appreciation of the spectacular scenery.

Still, spectacular it was, which was more than could be said for the food. The little shell-shaped tin bowls which had been used for the soup and pudding, needed a thorough examination lest there should be the remnants of last night's dessert lurking in some shadowy corner.

There was a choice between something which vaguely resembled muesli, and something which vaguely resembled porridge. I chose the muesli, and whilst it was as exciting as dried dog food, except perhaps to a dog, with a little milk and copious amounts of sugar it became palatable.

The kitchen staff then arrived with huge, steaming silver trays of scrambled egg and chapattis, which were delicious, especially when rolled up with the egg as filling and enhanced by liberal applications of both honey and peanut butter.

Several helpings later, I was replete and ready for anything, even another visit to the latrine tent. There was limitless tea, and boiling water for those who preferred coffee.

When most people had completed their meal Dave stood up, still resplendent in his hat. First of all, he introduced us to the host of little men who were to look after us for the next three weeks.

Not only would they cook, wash up, erect, dismantle and carry our tents and equipment, they also had to buy the produce which we would eat along the way, from the people who produced it. There was no question of popping out to the local Tesco's for another bag of spuds. They were the purchasing, the quality control, the preparation and presentation all rolled into one. Chambermaid, cooks and chief bottle washers. In short, they would attend to our every need. And they would do it all with a smile. Come hell or high water.

We were given implicit instructions not to interfere with arrangements that had been made by dealing directly with the cooks or porters. It is a fair point that good workers best serve but one master, and that master was Dave. Any complaints, requests, problems or bribes should be referred to either Dave or Wish.

The chain of command and authority was as well-established as the route we would take and, like the mountains themselves, commanded respect at the top and was a touch unpredictable at the bottom.

The word Sherpa literally translated means people from the east in the Tibetan language. The Sherpa peoples are Buddhist hill folk famed for their hard work, tenacity and bravery, particularly with mountaineering expeditions. Suddenly, in the early 1950s, a fairly insignificant and little-known ethnic group was shot into the international spotlight through the achievements of one highly resourceful and charismatic man – Tenzing Norgay.

The word 'sherpa' has come to mean 'trek leader'. The point here, pedantic as it may seem, is that not all sherpas are Sherpas. Although the best known and the most prolific, the Sherpas are only one of eight tribal groups which are to be found along the Everest Highway. The Sherpas live in two areas, the Solu, which is the lower and begins at Shivalaya, and the Khumbu, which is the higher, and begins at Khari La, near Lukla.

Ethnic diversity is as much a feature of up-country Nepal, as it is of downtown New York. The tribes can basically be divided into two main families, the Indo-Aryan and the Mongoloid. Although the traditional caste system was in fact banned by the king of Nepal some years ago, it still continues to dominate tribal society.

Nowhere is it better defined than in the guys to whom we were being introduced.

The Sirdar is the leader and organiser of the trekking party. He hires and fires, leads from the front, and is the management and union rolled into one. In short, he is a very, very important person. A leader of an expedition who fails to recognise this, and act accordingly, does so at his peril.

Despite a social conscience commendable in a man of his background, even Captain John Hunt succumbed to an inevitable bout of class division and failed to recognise that the arrangements for billeting the Sherpas in Kathmandu before the departure of the successful 1953 expedition were to lead to severely strained relations before the trip even got underway.

While the climbers slept comfortably in the British Embassy, the Sherpas were billeted in a garage in the Embassy grounds. Furthermore, the garage lacked any toilet facilities. The following morning, they were not unreasonably found urinating over the road in front of the garage, which caused outrage amongst the Embassy staff.

The outrage spread to Hunt when he discovered that the papers had got hold of the story. The Sherpas were given a severe dressing down, which did little to improve relations.

The Sirdar on that occasion was one Tenzing Norgay.

Beneath the Sirdar there may, on large expeditions, be a deputy Sirdar, who is a sort of Chief Assistant to the Assistant Chief.

Neither the Sirdars nor the guides will carry anything other than their own belongings, and are not to be seen performing menial tasks, such as erecting tents, cooking or serving tea and biscuits. This is not because they are snooty or demeaning to those who perform these tasks. It is simply a practical application of the division of labour. Horses for courses.

While the Sirdar moves quickly on to the next lunch or overnight stop to negotiate camp sites or buy food, the deputy Sirdar and guides will walk more slowly with the trekkers, ensuring that they arrive at the designated place. Our party would, in practice, be very, very spread out. At the front, some of the group, of which I was to become one, would move at supersonic speed, reaching their destination almost before they had set out, while at the back, the tail end of our expedition would arrive up to five hours later. This would be very frustrating not only for the poor doctor whose turn it was to bring up the rear, but also for the unfortunate guide and porters who had to accompany them and carry the medical equipment.

To lose a trekker would be unfortunate, but to lose a doctor with medical supplies would be negligent.

Moving down the hierarchy, each group had two cooks and cook boys responsible for all matters relating to the preparation and distribution of food. Having seen their attempts at washing up after breakfast, I concluded that this was more a ritual they were expected to perform as a sop to Westerners than an exercise that had any real hygienic value. The slick of filth on the surface of the water was so vile that even the bacteria were bailing out.

The cooks, without a doubt, have the hardest job. Their day starts at five when they light the fire, and begin to prepare tea and the breakfast chapattis. One cook will prepare the breakfast, while the other will dash off to the lunch stop to ensure that the kettle is boiling long before the first trekkers arrive. He will then set up the kitchen and prepare the lunch, clean up, and make his way to the night stop to help his colleague with the main meal of the day.

Their day does not finish until the last cup has been 'washed'.

At the bottom of the pyramid is the humble porter. Porters fall into two categories, low altitude and high altitude. It is a generalisation to say that the high altitude porter is the more reliable; there are fewer distractions at high altitude where it grows cold and the population thins out. On the lower reaches, in the semi-tropical pastures, the frequent festivals sometimes cause mass desertions for days on end, and, although there is a steady stream of willing workers, it is not unknown for fourteen year old girls to become beasts of burden as other family members enjoy the festivities.

Above 3,500 metres (11,500 feet), most of the porters are paid off and are replaced by yaks, whose lungs can only function properly at high altitudes.

The load a porter will carry is frequently in excess of thirty kilos. As already mentioned he will carry two kit bags, theoretically limited to twelve kilos. These will be strapped together, with a tent at the top, and attached to a *Namlo*, a wide head band which he places on his forehead to support his load. He carries a strong stick with a cross piece at the top, like a crude shooting stick, which he will park his bottom on during his well-earned but frequent smoke breaks.

Travelling at their own speed, porters will stop some time during late morning when they reach one of the well-established sites along the trail which has a nearby supply of water and firewood. Like a self-catering Little Chef, they will break their journey to light a fire and cook lunch before proceeding to the night stop.

Curiously, the porter is often paid as much as senior trekking staff. However, they have to look after themselves while on the trek, buying and cooking their own food, and seeking out whatever accommodation they can find. They will seldom sleep in lodges, as this would represent considerable financial outlay on their part. In much the same way as lorry drivers usually sleep in their cabs, porters are usually to be found huddled together in the mess tent.

At lower altitudes, where the temperature is usually balmy, a heavily laden porter dressed for the next Ice Age and resembling a Michelin Man is a curious sight. The explanation is simple. As it gets cold higher up, they need more clothes, particularly at night. So they take all their clothes with them, and the only practical means of transporting them is to wear them. This contributes considerably to the stench along the trail.

We were also told that to make a porter really happy at the end of the trek, we could consider passing in his direction any clothing, particularly boots or thermal wear, for which we were unlikely to have a future use.

In principle this was correct, for it did bring a smile to the face of the recipient. In practice he would shuffle off to the nearest bazaar or shop which sold used mountain equipment, get the best price he could for the stuff, and spent the next three days in a chang-induced haze.

Still, happiness is relative.

Having been made the wiser by Dave's lecture on Sherpas and porters, our attention was now drawn to how the day was likely to proceed.

There was a general air of expectancy.

Each morning after breakfast, he told us, there would be a short briefing which we should all attend. We would receive information regarding the terrain we would encounter, where the lunch stop would be, our ultimate destination, and any other relevant information.

"The Nepalis," he began, "believe in the principle that the shortest distance between point A and point B is a straight line. The trek cuts across the valleys, instead of following them. Therefore, there are four types of terrain which you will encounter: up, steep up, down and steep down. Today, the trek will be down, steep down, steep up, up and down. The lunch break will be at Sangbadanda, between twelve and one o'clock, and the night stop will be Bhandar. At a steady pace you should arrive at Bhandar by 5 p.m. Annabel will be the duty doctor, during the day, and Simon will bring up the rear. See you later. Have a nice day!"

It was just after 8 a.m., and more than pleasantly warm. I paid a last visit to the latrine, which by now defied description, and, mindful of the previous evening, stripped down to T-shirt and shorts. Having loaded various cameras and Walkman onto the belt of my rucksack, and threaded my headphones carefully inside my T-shirt so as not to trip over the wire, I was ready to set off. I looked around for a suitable companion. I could find none. Most people had already set off, so I set off on my own and eventually joined Stephen, my doctor, Joy and Andy.

Almost immediately, as predicted, we started to descend. At first, it was gradual and the path was fairly good. But after half an hour or so, the trail had deteriorated into a steeply zigzagging boulder-strewn gully, cut into the hillside, and only distinguishable from the rest of the boulder-strewn terrain by the occasional flat bit.

Twice, I clumsily kicked a rock, and only just managed to regain my balance before nose diving into oblivion. My boots felt cumbersome, and I already began to regret having bought the heavier leather Goretex type which I had been advised would be ideal in snow. Most people seemed to be wearing the lighter canvas type of boot, which were more like a heavy duty trainer, than the traditional boot I had purchased.

There'd better be a hell of a lot of snow, I thought.

For some time, we had been conscious of the ever increasing roar of water to our left. At last we appeared to have reached the bottom of the valley, and emerged into a pleasant clearing on the bank of a small but fast flowing river, where a group of porters were resting on their sticks.

Strange noises were coming from the river. Further investigation revealed the unsavoury sight of a naked Lloyd Scott, waist deep in the water doing his best to drag a reluctant, screaming, but fully clothed Sue Sayers into the water. It was a good place for a wash, and within minutes we were all in the river, all naked except for Sue, whose modesty precluded the removal of anything other than boots and socks.

Simon and Valeri, who had been bringing up the rear, also joined us. It was all good clean fun, until I stood in something of highly questionable origin as I scrambled over the rocks to the river bank. As I felt the soft and slippery texture squidge between my toes, my heart sank.

I stood there for a moment, not daring to look. The expression on my face, like the boy whose finger had gone through the toilet paper, said it all.

"What's the matter, Richard?" asked Joy.

"I think I've caught your disease, stepping in shit!" I replied.

I looked down, and it was everywhere.

"Don't these people know that shitting in their water supply is bloody antisocial! These rivers should have a bloody health warning 'Beware – you are now washing in raw sewage!'" I was furious, particularly as everyone seemed to find it hilarious.

My anger didn't last long. With underwear washed and pinned to the back of rucksacks to dry, we set off, the trail following the bank of the river, which was now, mercifully, for a while level.

We strolled along the floor of the valley, the huge hills climbing ever upwards on either side, enjoying the sunshine and the relaxed conversation that a good uninhibited bathe in the river had helped to create.

Soon we caught Nat, and not long after, arrived at the bank of a considerably larger river, the Khimti Khola, where we were greeted by the sight of our first suspension bridge.

I was surprised by how substantial it was. The planking was solid, and well-constructed, and gave the overall impression that it was built by people who knew what they were doing.

However, in the centre, I just couldn't resist grabbing hold of the wire rails on both sides, and giving it a good shake. Just to see what would happen.

What happened was that it swung considerably more than I had expected, causing panic to ensue amongst those behind me, and much amused Simon, who was ahead of me.

I took a photo of Simon standing on this, our first proper suspension bridge. Simon was wearing the obligatory red Everest Marathon sweatshirt, which the doctors had been issued with. This set them apart from the standard issue blue garments, which were already being worn by some of the group. Red, they joked, would disguise the blood.

Being slightly superstitious, my sweatshirt and T-shirts bearing the legend Everest Marathon were safely, or so I hoped, stored away in the Blue Star Hotel. I didn't want to tempt fate by wearing them before I had completed the race. In any case, the trek wasn't the place for something you would want to treasure for the rest of your life.

Across the river on the east bank was the village of Shivalaya, which is generally accepted as being the gateway to the Solu region.

Here too we encountered the first police post, and trekking permits had to be presented to a somnolent officer, who magnanimously waved them aside, barely stirring from his pre-lunch doze, in the manner of bored officialdom throughout the world.

He beckoned to a large hardbacked book, which was divided roughly into columns which required us to enter name, address, destination, trekking agency, duration of trek and passport and trekking permit number.

"How are you supposed to remember your passport number?" I asked Simon, dumbly. Our passports were back in Kathmandu, with the trekking agency.

"It's on your trekking permit if you really want to be precise. But I would do what everybody else does and write down the first thing that comes into your head."

"Is that what you do when you write out a prescription?" I joked.

"I hate unnecessary bureaucracy. Anyway, being a doctor no one can read my writing!"

Shivalaya is a small but prosperous and clean-looking village which, with its picturesque setting, is a natural magnet for trekkers looking for a watering hole to break the journey to or from Jiri.

There are several lodges teahouses and well-stocked shops selling a wide range of goods for the discerning trekker. This bode well for the future, I thought. Memories of last night's horrific smoke filled shacks oozing dirt and stench on the road to Mali had filled me with trepidation.

On the right was the Mysterius Lodge and Restaurant, a solid brick built three storey building, with a proper pitched tile roof and a balcony attractively decked out in white and blue wooden panels.

Opposite this was the Trekkers Lodge, Hotel and Lodge, which was a building similar in stature. A large contingent of our party had stopped here, and were gathered around the flimsy wooden tables randomly placed outside, enjoying tea and biscuits.

It was a long time since breakfast, and tea and biscuits seemed a good idea. It is part of the mystique of these places that you never know who is in charge. I tried two enthusiastic youths:

*"Namaste!"* I began, stressing the middle syllable.

*"Namaste,"* came the reply, stressing the third syllable. The different pronunciation made it sound a different word. Like the difference between nasty and have a nice day. I preferred the latter. It was altogether more sunny, more of a greeting and less of a grunt.

These musings didn't bring me closer to getting tea. Before I could experiment with my first meaningful utterances in Nepali, the youths had disappeared.

Eventually I found an old woman at the back of the shop.

I decided to skip the formalities.

*"Chiyaa, dudh kosi,"* I requested, loud enough for the others to hear, "please," I added, more quietly, proud to be up with the pace linguistically on day one.

The old woman looked at me blankly.

I was obviously dealing with a halfwit, and was about to resort to sign language, when Simon asked me why I had asked for tea from the large river north of Namche Bazaar.

*"Chiyaa, chhaina dudh"*, he corrected me.

"Ah," said the old woman, a toothless smile lighting her face, *"black tea!"*

"Yes. Black tea", I confirmed a trifle irritably, "and a packet of coconut biscuits, please."

She poured from a heavy blackened pot on the stove into a glass tumbler and I parted with eight rupees for the tea and biscuits.

\*

Beyond Shivalaya, the path started to climb. We climbed and we climbed. And we climbed. I enjoyed the physical exertion, so much so that I failed to notice that I had increased my pace, and was now on my own.

I stopped three times to admire the view and photograph where we had come from. At first, the river was the focal point of the valley. Then it faded into the background, a thin line of blue, reflecting the sun, and all but eclipsed, when set against the vastness of the towering terraced hills on my left. Soon, it was no longer visible, as I rose above the other side of the valley. My map told me that we had dropped over six hundred metres from Mali to Shivalaya.

It also told me that there were over nine hundred metres to climb between Shivalaya and Deorali Pass. Nine hundred metres! I thought of our Munros at home. They had to be over three thousand feet to qualify. And that was what we had to climb just to progress less than three miles! Why couldn't they build a tunnel?

That old chestnut – was I still on the right path? – began to raise its ugly head, again. There had been several tributaries to the left and right, which I assumed would arrive at the same point. As I was still climbing, I assumed I would catch up with the others soon. It was after midday, and I couldn't be that far from the lunch-stop now.

The path levelled off, and ahead of me was a hat I recognised. It belonged to Thomas Sharkey, or 'Thomas the Tank' as he would in time be known. Thomas was an Irishman from Roscommon, a self-employed welder who now lived in Birmingham. He was also, I had established earlier, the most miserable son of a bitch on the entire sub-continent.

I had trekked behind Tom for a while earlier that morning. His was a face I recognised, but he appeared to be very much a loner, and had hardly said a word on the journey to Jiri. But here was a good opportunity to get to know a fellow countryman, as Ireland is also my country of origin.

My cheery, "Hi, how's it going?" was greeted by a monosyllabic grunt, and my "Ever done anything like this before?" achieved a short, "Yes, in the Alps, but they're not as high." Even my, "I'm from Belfast, what part of Ireland are you from?" elicited the information requested without any embellishment.

"Some country, eh?" I remarked.

"Sure is." It wasn't apparent whether either the question or the answer were about Ireland or Nepal, but it didn't really matter. Here was a man who wanted to keep himself to himself. I turned on my Walkman, and passed him on the climb out of Shivilaya.

Nepal would have a different effect on us all. Few people would go home without some little part of their psyche altered, albeit temporarily. Maybe it was just the purchase of a bracelet or a pair of trousers that you wouldn't give the dog to lie on at home.

But in Tom's case it was more than a mere physical metamorphosis manifested by buying extremely silly clothes back in Kathmandu. The metaphysical or philosophical changes which his mind underwent towards the end of the trip were as at odds with this serious, ultra-cautious, uncommunicative Irishman, as the Pope would be trying to reach the Buddhist state of Nirvana. I dread to think what would have happened to the Irish community in Birmingham if Tom's luggage had ever got home!

Tom was a steady walker, and he passed me with a grunt as I paused for photographs. Maybe he'd got on the wrong plane at Heathrow. He certainly didn't look as if he was enjoying himself. But there again, I probably hadn't looked much different last night, and he certainly hadn't moaned as much as I had. Neither did he look like a marathon runner. Probably in his early forties, I guessed, about five foot nine and stocky to heavy build. But, as I well knew from past experience, you don't judge a book by its cover.

I had caught up with Tom.

"Is this the road to Everest?" I asked, again hopeful of initiating something more than a simple yes or no.

"It'll take you there, eventually," he replied, with just the hint of a smile.

Okay, that was a little progress. That'll do for now. But there was something about Tom that suggested that he had the capacity, deep within him, to know a good time. I mean, he couldn't be this serious all the time, could he?

We walked in silence, until we reached a semi-tropical fertile-looking clearing on the side of a hill, which swept round in a horseshoe with buildings dotted about on various levels of the terraced steps, where the villagers lived and farmed.

On entering the village, we came across our first *mani wall*, which indicated that we were entering a Buddhist region.

It occurred to me, as we strolled along, that maybe Ireland and Nepal were not entirely dissimilar. Entering the Bogside in Londonderry, a huge gable mural announces that "You are now entering Free Derry", with all the cultural, religious and political implications that that announcement conveys to the passer-by. The Catholics are the Jews of Ireland and, whilst they have never been persecuted to the extent of Hitler's Final Solution, they were the subject of considerable political, social and religious discrimination which drove them into their particular ghettos.

Buddhism spilled over the high passes from Tibetan Lamaism over the centuries, and was carried by the wings of trade to the Solu Khumbu. The Chinese occupation of Tibet, with all the religious intolerance of the Cultural Revolution did its best to destroy the physical fabric of Buddhism in Tibet, and resulted in the destruction of, among others, the Rongbuk monastery, home of the Rongbuk Lama, and one of the most sacred places in Tibetan Buddhism.

Mani stones, wheels and walls are carved with the Tibetan Buddhist chant, *Om mani padme hum,* meaning, 'O lotus-seated god of the celestial jewel'. It is in accordance with their beliefs to pass these on the left.

Upon entering the village, we were surrounded by a tribe of smiling ragamuffin children, pointing to a clearing below us about a hundred yards away. There, we could make out the familiar blue banner and, spread out on large sheets of blue polythene, lunch was being consumed by those who had got up the hill quicker than us.

"So, this is Sangbadanda," I said to Tom. "Sounds like the sort of place that Butch Cassidy and the Sundance Kid might have had a shoot-out with the Mexican army."

In the clearing, kitchen boys were distributing food and drink. Hot lemon, which tasted suspiciously like Lemsip, was available from a large teapot, and lunch consisted of coleslaw, salad, tinned meat, something that resembled nan bread, and tinned fruit salad for pudding. It was quite palatable, but there wasn't very much of it.

I took off my T-shirt, which was soaked with perspiration, and hung it on a bush. It was still a beautiful day, and I did what everybody else seemed to be doing, dozing in the sun.

At last, one by one, people began to stir and gather belongings into rucksacks in preparation for the remainder of the day's journey. It was rumoured that we had cracked the hardest part, and once we reached the pass at Deorali, it would all be downhill. Not that I had found that significantly easier.

There was the temptation to try to go downhill too fast, and I had come close to turning an ankle on several occasions. My boots, although no doubt designed for this sort of thing, gave the impression that they didn't really know what they were supposed to be doing, and I had about as much confidence in them as if I had been wearing a pair of clogs.

However, on the positive side, so far my right knee, which has had more surgery than the gas mains outside my house, had shown no signs of protestation. It had behaved well all through my preparation, but it would only need one violent twist to put into question my prospects of completing the race.

I walked over to collect my T-shirt, only to find that it wasn't where I had put it. In fact, it wasn't anywhere. Annabel, hadn't set off yet, so it was pretty likely that she had something to do with its disappearance.

"Okay, Annabel, where's my shirt?" I asked, plaintively.

"I haven't got your shirt." She was having difficulty controlling her laughter. "What would I want with your shirt, Marvin?"

There were others preparing to leave, who were finding something very, very funny, and I couldn't help but think that their humour and the disappearance of my shirt were in some way connected.

Just then, a tired-looking quadruped with crumpled horns and a bored expression, appeared from behind the bush where I had placed my shirt. As it stared at me with the same vacant expression that I normally associate with pupils in my history lessons, I became aware that it was chewing something that looked like a white cotton rag. Closer investigation revealed that the cotton rag bore the legend Panasonic Business Systems, which was curiously similar to the slogan that was on the T-shirt, donated by Fords with the loan of the video camera.

"Okay, Annabel, how much did you bribe that bloody cow?"

It had to have something to do with her. Why else was she hanging around? Not to be found out is not to be noticed.

"To eat one of your T-shirts, Marvin? I couldn't afford that," she replied. "It could only happen to you, Marvin – you're a real loser."

That was it. I was going to have to find some way at getting back at her. For me, that became almost as big an obsession as the race itself.

I took a clean shirt from my rucksack, and set off.

*

Leaving Sangbadanda behind, the path continued to climb steeply, and required a greater level of concentration, as it became more precarious. It was, after all, only a path because it was where people walked, and not through careful planning and construction.

If it zigzagged, it did so to avoid the worst excesses of the particular hill you were climbing, and if it went straight up, you had to choose your own course over the boulders. It was worse than I had expected. If it was this bad here, what would it be like higher up, I wondered?

At last some solid-looking buildings came into sight, and the ground levelled out. This must be Deorali Pass which, at 2,713 metres, was the highest point we would reach today. It was also, at almost nine thousand feet, probably the highest point I had ever reached in my life.

Deorali was a neat little village, with well made stone walls and wide welcoming steps leading to a sort of village square where there were several tea shops and a couple of two storey brick built lodges.

Outside the bigger of these, the Namaste Hotel and Lodge, on the stone courtyard, a festival was in progress. It could have been anything, but as Richard and the film crew were showing a considerable amount of interest, I assumed it must be an official bash.

The Nepalis live for their festivals. They occur mainly towards the end of the monsoon season, in August and September. Sometimes they can last for several days and there is no telling when they will take place, due to the complicated system they have for numbering the days in accordance with the lunar calendar.

Although it is generally accepted that the sun rises every twenty-four hours, moonrises can vary from between twenty-two to twenty-seven hours. This makes things rather complicated but, as I witnessed, it didn't seem to detract from their ability to enjoy a good festival, once they had decided when to have it.

To a cynic such as I, they are an excuse for the men to get roaring drunk and scrounge as many rupees from unsuspecting passing trekkers as they can. But the music, dancing and colourful costumes are as deeply ingrained in their culture as the dust from the path is in the pores of their skin.

I had a cup of tea, and watched for a while, until I could take no more pestering from the smiling little brown men demanding money from me. Still, if I gave them something, they might go and plague someone else with their somewhat untuneful instruments.

I handed over twenty rupees, which was a mistake. Their spokesman feigned insult and demanded one hundred.

"On your bike, pal!" The message seemed to get through. He put his hands together, bowed his head, and got on his bike.

They were collecting for the local school. Which was fine, and a cause worthy to support, except that there seemed to be at least ten local schools, none of which appeared to have a pencil between them.

We had been told that there was a cheese factory at Thodung, a short detour from Deorali. As I have no great fondness for either cheese or detours, I set off to get down the hill to Bhandar, and our overnight stop, to put my feet up.

Sure enough, I hadn't gone fifty yards from the lodge when the path began to drop as dramatically as it had climbed before Deorati. Even the zigzags had zigzags.

I was concentrating so hard on not breaking my neck, that I didn't notice I had company.

Three teenage girls were following in my footsteps, nudging each other and giggling, in much the same way as teenage girls anywhere in the world nudge each other and giggle. They had open smiling faces, and gleaming black hair in braid or simply fastened back. On their backs they wore what looked like leather school satchels.

Their English was good, and we fell into conversation. I learned that they were returning from school in Deorali, and lived in Gholunda, a small village beyond Bhandar, or Changma, as it was better known. In fact, when I later looked at my map, I realised Gholunda was a very long way beyond Bhandar, almost at tomorrow's lunch-stop.

"I go to Everest; *Sagarmatha*," I said. That would impress them.

"*Sagarmatha*, yes." They nodded. "Most Westerners on this trail would finish up somewhere near Everest. You weren't here for the fishin'."

"To run a marathon to Namche Bazaar, from near Base camp," I continued. I pumped my elbows a bit to give it credibility.

"No!" Heads shook in disbelief, "A marathon?"

"Yes, The Everest Marathon."

They clearly thought I was pulling their legs. And it was such a stupid idea, particularly if the path on day one was anything to go by, that it begged the question, was someone pulling my leg?

We parted company shortly after, as the girls took what was presumably a short cut to their village.

What a curious world. Here are three pretty, well brought up, intelligent girls. They walk, in thongs, for at least four hours a day over some of the world's most rugged terrain, simply to get to school. They learn about a world they will never see, and which will have no bearing whatsoever upon their lives, save brief encounters with strangers passing through their land. They will understand what a motor car is, and that the sea covers three quarters of the world's surface. Yet, throughout their lives, they will see neither.

Nor will they ever use toilet paper or a tampon or a hairdryer. They will be married to the man to whom they have been promised, and be pregnant by sixteen. By twenty they will have a tribe of bare-assed kids who use no nappies.

And yet... I remembered the phrase that had impressed me on the bus journey to Jiri: 'Education is the chief defence of the nation'.

In a land where life is a constant drain on the human mind and body simply to survive, education could well be considered a frill, a waste of manpower. But they don't look at it that way. It is seen as an opportunity, and one worth making a considerable sacrifice for. The defence of the nation is defence through combating ignorance. This is more important than bombs and bullets. The acquisition of knowledge is a privilege, and whilst it is maybe only available to a minority of the population, some day the trickle might become a flood.

On the outskirts of Bhandar or Changma was a gompa, which is a Tibetan Buddhist monastery. This one was particularly distinctive, as the walls had just been whitewashed, and was bedecked with brightly coloured flags, perhaps in a more sober recognition of the same festival that was in progress at Deorali.

There didn't seem to be anybody about. Maybe they were all at Deorali celebrating. I was joined by Sue Sayers and Dave English, and we checked it out, absentmindedly taking a couple of photographs.

Round the corner was a courtyard, which appeared to be the hub of downtown Changma. Several members of our group were gathered around a table outside a teahouse. Most were drinking tea or Coke, but Mike Harper and John Dunning were on the beer. They had come to enjoy themselves.

"What's it like?" I asked. I was curious.

"Not bad", replied John, "bit gassy."

I can't explain why, but beer had lost its appeal for now. I bought a tea, and a bar of soap. On a sudden impulse, I bought a small bottle of local rum for sixty rupees. Simon had recommended a very moderate alcoholic intake to nullify any impurities that may be present in the food. It sounded like a good excuse. Besides, I didn't want to live like a monk.

The village, or villages as they seemed to be, were spread out on a fertile plateau, and it was a good walk from the bhatti to the campsite. I followed Annabel's footsteps into the camp, hoping to detect some form of weakness which could be embarrassingly exposed later, but was only impressed at the pace she set.

The porters were still erecting tents, and I was pleased to find Number Fourteen already in situ. I was surprised to find that I was one of the first to arrive. Ray was there, of course. I hadn't seen him since breakfast. It was still warm, although the sun had long since disappeared behind cloud, then behind the hills on which stood Deorali.

"Been here long?" I asked.

"'Bout four hours," he replied. That would have meant that he reached the night-stop at about the time I reached the lunch-stop.

"Did you run?"

"Naw, just didn't bloody hang about."

That was impressive. This morning's wash, and one or two tea stops apart, I thought I hadn't hung about either.

Ray Brown had a strangely magnetic quality about him. As we chatted, it became clear that he had not come here for the trek or the scenery. He had come here for the race, and although he never said it, he had come to win. Perhaps he knew that that may be beyond him, but he would not accept that until someone crossed the finish line ahead of him.

He had left his native New Zealand for Perth, where he was a housemaster at Aquinas College, a large boarding school which valued its staff enough to give them sabbatical breaks at regular intervals. His wife and two sons planned to fly into Lukla, and they would meet up in Namche after the race. Ray had the advantage of acclimatisation he had gained from a 'teashop' trek to Langtang, and had training runs at over four thousand metres under his belt.

Like Tom, Ray's mood in the early stages was grim, but in Ray's case the cause was clear. Diana, apparently, had insisted that Ray join the trek at Kathmandu, rather than make his own arrangements, as others were doing, and fly into Lukla to meet up at Namche.

Ray's answer to this was to get to the night-stop as fast as possible, get cleaned up, and bellyache until it was time to set off the next morning.

On that first full day of the trek, I couldn't understand how Ray could be such a Philistine. But to him it must have been like skiing down the red run, then being sent back to the nursery slopes.

To me, the nursery slopes were exhilarating, and, I was surprised to find, exhausting. In training, I had pushed myself to the limit with frequent runs of over four hours, and the occasional run of over six hours. I had been physically drained afterwards, but this was a different sort of tiredness. I was not used to a day's walk where ascent and descent combined came close to seven thousand feet, with a load in excess of twenty kilos.

Bhandar was a prosperous farming settlement, and beyond the campsite were several well-cultivated small fields, separated from each other with roughly made low stone walls. A stream ran along one side of our field, and disappeared over a bank from which it cascaded down six feet or so in a natural waterfall to a shallow pool below.

It was the ideal place for a shower, and I stripped off and stood beneath the water, armed with my tube of Mountain Suds, which claimed to wash anything from pots and pans to hair in any temperature of water. And, of course, was environmentally friendly.

The water was pleasantly warm, and I was so engrossed in my ablutions that I failed to notice the crowd of staring small children that had gathered to spectate.

"*Namaste,*" I said.

"*Namaste!*" came the enthusiastic reply.

I grovelled around for my towel and made myself decent. Andrew Burgess had also discovered the 'shower', and was waiting for me to finish.

"Plenty of hot water left," I said. "Make sure you turn the taps off when you're finished, and watch out for shit on the floor!"

Later, we were scolded by our leaders for our 'exhibitionism', and breach of Nepali custom.

The tea and biscuits appeared, and, armed with a mug of steaming black tea, and my micro-cassette, I set off to make some notes for my diary.

I walked to the rear of the field away from everyone else and, sitting with my back to the camp, perched on one of the little walls, I began to talk into my recorder.

"Nepal diary, day one," I began, conscious of the prat I was going to sound when I played it back.

"Left Kathmandu on the road to Jiri..."

A strange noise came from somewhere behind me. It sounded like an animal in great pain. I glanced round, but could see nothing. I continued.

"The early morning mist dissipated as we climbed higher into the foothills, revealing..."

"...Aaarrrrrghhhh. Eeeuuuhhh. Oooooooohh!"

What the hell was that?

"Ppphhhhhaaarnppphh. Ooooohh sssshit."

I swung around with increased urgency. One of the green latrine tents had been erected behind me. The noise was coming from inside.

I wrestled with my conscience as to whether to intervene or leave whoever it was to their own personal battle, against whatever demons they were fighting.

Before I could come to a decision, the door was unzipped and out came Mike Harper. He looked like death.

"Are you all right?" I asked. He clearly wasn't. He walked, bent almost double, and I gave him a hand to get to his tent.

"Some beer, eh?" I said.

He tried to smile.

"If that's the beer, then I'm giving up drinking!" he said. "Must be a touch of sun. I'll be all right when I've had a lie down."

I wasn't so sure, and went off to find a doctor.

\*

At dinner that evening, the atmosphere was subdued. There were a few, like myself, in various degrees of fatigue, who had found the day's exertions a bit of a shock to the system. There were others, like Mike though not as serious, who had been affected by the sun, and whose ailments ranged from headache to slight nausea.

And then there were others, like Tom, Ray and the little Latin contingent from Spain and Italy, who were either just plain quiet or just plain miserable.

There was an absence of flowers on the table, and the sole lighting was from the temperamental kerosene lamps rather than the subtle light of the candles that had been placed on the tables the previous night. Many people, including myself, wore head-torches, and the ambience was more of supper down a Yorkshire mine shaft than a bijou, clandestine marquee supper party.

The food was much the same as it had been last night, except that poppadoms appeared with the spicy dishwater that passed for soup, instead of popcorn, there was a different form of pasta with the stew, and the sludge was a pink colour. It was adequate, but not, in all honesty, very appetising. Still, sludge apart, there wasn't much left over.

Sue won The Hat for steadfastly refusing to remove her clothes in the river. Bryan English and Richard kept us amused over coffee and chocolate with a joke telling duel, but most people had slipped off to their tents by eight thirty. It wasn't long after that when I began my night-time ritual.

Tent Fourteen was crammed fuller with bodies than Fred West's patio. Only these were very much alive, and demanding pills, potions and all kinds of medical reassurance from Simon who, I had just discovered, was the night duty doctor.

Several people had headaches and were concerned that they were suffering from altitude sickness. Simon confirmed that the chances of falling prey to AMS at this early stage were remote, and I had the feeling that the chances of either of us having a good night's sleep were equally remote.

"I hope that bloody phone isn't going to ring all night!" I told him. "And if you get called out, don't rev the car too much."

We settled down to read, or write diaries, head-torches piercing the darkness. The waterfall in which I had earlier showered roared like a torrent, and a dog barked in the hills; the same vacuous, persistent litany that dogs in hills bark at home.

Soon my aching limbs cried out for sleep, and I drifted off into the oblivion of my second night in the wilderness.

# Bhandar to Sete: "Got to Keep the Loonies on the Path"

## Friday 12th November

I was right.

All hell broke loose shortly after midnight. I awoke from a deep sleep which felt as if it had lasted for several weeks, to the sound of violent vomiting. I could tell it was approaching our tent by the increasing noise of the spew splattering on the ground.

I struggled to open the tent flaps, and was greeted with something that resembled a scene from *The Invasion of the Body Snatchers*. Two men, talking in an animated fashion, were dragging a third man of similar stature. The unfortunate character in the middle appeared to have lost control of his lower body, and was moaning and vomiting alternately.

It was Mike, and he was in bad shape.

I nudged Simon, who reluctantly stirred from a deep sleep.

"You've got a customer," I told him. "It's Mike, he's being sick."

"Thank you, your initial prognosis appears to be spot on," he replied. "Let's get him back to his tent. Can you give me a hand?"

Mike had been discovered wandering around the camp, presumably looking for our tent, by a couple of the porters, returning from having a skinful at the local lodge. God knows how long they had been dragging the poor fellow around the field. They didn't look capable of finding the mess tent, let alone the duty doctor in the pitch dark.

To make matters worse, one of them had strayed into Mike's line of fire, and his trousers were covered in sick.

We got him back to his tent, where John, his companion, snored loudly. Mike was shivering violently, and we got him into his sleeping bag. I left Simon to do the technical bit, and climbed back into my sleeping bag.

Eventually, I got back to sleep, only to be awoken by the sound of what could have easily been the Notting Hill Carnival outside our tent. I looked at my watch. It was approaching five o'clock. I went outside to investigate. The noise was coming from the mess tent, where the cooks and kitchen boys were commencing preparations for another day. If they had to be awake, then it seemed reasonable that everyone else should be too. One kitchen boy was telling the others his latest batch of Khumbu Girl jokes, which evidently proved highly amusing.

I gave up trying to sleep, and set about writing my diary on my computer, as my attempts to get down a few notes on the microcassette had been none too successful last night.

The day began, following very much the pattern of yesterday. There were boiled eggs and pancakes for breakfast, and Dave informed us that the trek would basically be downhill in the morning and uphill in the afternoon. Lunch would be at Kenja, and we would break for the night at somewhere called Sete.

Mike was considerably better, having had a relatively peaceful few hours. His fever had gone and, although he was still wobbly, he felt fit enough to continue. In reality, there wasn't much choice, although we did have the Late Birds following a day behind, so anyone who fell ill could have a day's respite.

Once again the weather was beautiful, with not a cloud in the sky. It was cold enough to require a fleece at breakfast, but once the sun had cleared the hills to the east, the temperature rose swiftly.

It still took me the best part of an hour to pack my kit, and a further half hour to arrange all my intricate electronic gadgets so that I could get to them when required. By that time most people had left, and the camp was once again an empty field waiting for the next group of trekkers to arrive.

I set off on my own, and switched on my Walkman.

> *...And then one day you find ten years have got behind you*
> *No one told you when to run, you missed the starting gun...*

So Pink Floyd informed me. It was highly probable, I mused, highly probable. Still, I wasn't in a hurry.

Leaving Changma/Bhandar, the trail dropped steeply down to Gholunda, where there was a small teahouse with an inviting-looking balcony overlooking a river. It was packed with trekkers mainly, but not all from our group. Curiously, this was the first time I had seen Westerners other than from our party since leaving Kathmandu. I decided to keep going.

From Gholunda the path levelled out and improved significantly, following the western bank of the Likhu Khola. This was a huge river and, reaching a substantial-looking bridge which spanned it, I had to make a decision whether or not to follow the path which went straight on. The bridge looked tempting, as I knew we had to cross the river at some point, but a little voice in my head told me to stay on the path.

I stopped, and turned my Walkman off, to consider my dilemma.

"Stay on the path!" I turned round. "How loud have you got that bloody thing? We've been yelling for ages!" It was Andrew and Lloyd. I thanked them, a little sheepishly, and carried on, turning my Walkman on again.

> *...The lunatic is on the grass,*
> *The lunatic is on the grass,*
> *Remembering games and daisy chains and laughs,*
> *Got to keep the loonies on the path...*

I passed a house close to the bank of the river. Opposite it was a structure which I had seen several times yesterday, and had intrigued me. Made from long bamboo posts rising from four corners and curved to meet at the top and support a sturdy cross piece, it looked like the skeleton of a long-deceased, giant spider. This one looked particularly haphazard, as two of the legs originated some way up the hillside, well above the level of the other two, in the manner of a dog taking a pee. From the cross piece hung two pieces of rope and above the bamboo stanchions, prayer flags fluttered in the gentle morning breeze.

I had assumed the structure was connected with their religious beliefs, perhaps this was how they built a gompa – first erect some scaffolding, get the prayer flags in place, then when the gods are with you, build the rest of the thing. However, it was too much of a coincidence that half a dozen would be in an identical state of non-development.

No, there had to be a simpler explanation. As I watched, it presented itself to me. Two children appeared and fixed a flat piece of plank to the ropes. One sat on the wood and the other pushed her. It was a swing.

Shortly afterwards, I arrived at the second bridge. I had no doubts that we had to cross here as there was no alternative path, and Richard and Alun stood poised with camera and microphone to pounce on their prey.

"Do you mind road-testing the radio mike?" Richard asked.

"No," I replied, "as long as you don't want me to do it underwater or anything."

"No, nothing like that. Just attach it to your shirt and walk across the bridge. Ron's on the other side, he'll take it from you, and you can carry on."

For a cordless mike, it had a hell of a lot of cord. And for some reason, presumably aesthetic, it had to be threaded up the inside of my T-shirt. Eventually, I was wired up to Alun's satisfaction, and was ready to set off.

"What do you want me to talk about?" I asked.

"Doesn't matter. Anything you like," said Richard. "Tell us your life story, but speak clearly. And turn your Walkman off."

I set off. I couldn't think of anything to say. For once I was lost for words. I turned round and went back.

"I can't think of anything to say," I told Richard, pathetically.

"Well... tell a joke or recite a poem," he suggested.

I tried again.

"A poem about my life..." (nothing). "This, is a poem about my life." (Still nothing). Then I had an idea.

*I was born and brought up in Belfast*
*That's a bloody long way from Nepal,*
*I don't really know what I'm doing here...*
*No, I don't really know that at all.*
*I've come here to run in a marathon,*
*From a mountain they call Everest,*
*It's a bloody long way to the start line,*
*This trek's going to be the main test...*

Two porters passed me, walking in the opposite direction. Their expressions conveyed much doubt as to whether I had previously visited anywhere on a small blue planet called Earth.

> *Each night we sleep under canvas,*
> *At my age I should have more sense,*
> *But the worst part is having to crap in*
> *Those hideous green latrine tents.*

I had reached the end of the bridge. I am not much of a poet, and was quite pleased with my spur of the moment effort. You never know, they might even use it in the documentary. Ron was waiting for me.

"Get it all'?" I asked, expectantly.

"Not a dicky bird," he answered. "These damned things are bloody temperamental. It's a good job it was nothing important."

"All the same, you media types," I said, as I handed him back the mike. "All hype and no soul."

He looked at me blankly.

\*

Once across the river, the going was pleasantly flat, and without consciously meaning to, I broke into a jog. Despite the weight it carried, Dieter's Berghaus clung tightly to my back and shoulders, and I was pleased to find its load was well enough distributed so as not to cause discomfort.

Along the path, little groups of porters were crouched over fires preparing lunch. They looked at me suspiciously as I passed. I glanced at my watch. It was only ten thirty.

I rounded a corner, and what I saw stopped me dead in my tracks. To be honest, the views had been lacking just a little in the slam-you-between-the-eyes department, which was why subconsciously I had increased my pace throughout the morning. You couldn't quite accuse the scenery of being dull, but after thirty hours of the same sort of stuff, it was beginning to lack a little of its initial mystique.

But this was different. This was what I had come to see. Ahead of me at the end of a long valley, distant snow-capped peaks rose majestically to reign in splendid isolation over the more mundane green terraces of the Likhu Khola Valley. My map told me that the highest of these was Borjung, which at 3,720 metres was a midget in the context of where we were going. In fact, we would trek to almost that altitude tomorrow. But the sight of distant white summits set in a clear blue sky, reflecting the brightness of the late morning sun, aroused the dormant little men in the anticipation department of my brain.

So did the sight of the small bridge over the Kenja Khola, beyond which lay the village of Kenja, our lunch-stop. I exchanged pleasantries with a less somnolent police officer and signed the book. I was a little surprised to find that, apart from Ray of course, I was the first to arrive. I pointed to the hills that lay beyond the river, and proudly said "Everest!"

He smiled and, with universal sign language, raised his thumb, being much too polite to inform me that I had pointed, perhaps with shades of Mallory's "First find the mountain", to the south-west, when in fact Everest lay diametrically in the opposite direction.

Kenja is a pretty little village made prettier by its quite spectacular backdrop. Its name means 'Entrance to the Ascent' and, as I was to find out, boy, did ever a place have an appropriate name! The path snakes its way through the ten or so residences, lodge and bhatti, which make up the village. This in itself is unusual, as most villages we had passed through had a long, straight 'street' with buildings on either side, but this gave the impression of a much larger settlement. The buildings were well-constructed, most with whitewashed stone walls and wooden balconies, but the fact that the roofing material was anchored by large, randomly placed stones suggested that that we were getting deeper into remoteness. There was not a tile in sight.

A little girl on a swing smiled warmly at me. The two thin strands of rope were tied to fragile-looking struts on a balcony above. There would certainly be no equivalent British Safety Standard stamped on the bottom of that. But there would be equally few recriminations and litigation when the thing broke.

To my surprise, flimsy-looking power cables hung from several of the houses, indicating a supply of electricity. We had been told that there was no electricity between Jiri and Namche. The bhatti looked welcoming, but in my naivety I was more interested in familiar faces than sampling unique cultural experiences. A small terrier-like dog wagged its stump at me, and I made his day by taking a photograph of him.

On the other side of town there was a clearing by the river bank where the familiar and comforting blue plastic blanket was set out to indicate our lunch-stop. I dropped off my rucksack and went to investigate the impromptu kitchen, which was bustling with activity. The lunch that was being prepared looked considerably more appetising than yesterday's. A huge pot of rice was simmering, and a sort of lentil soup with curried vegetables called Dhal Bhat Tarkari, which is their staple diet and the Nepali equivalent of a vegetarian Irish Stew, was being prepared. I smiled and made appreciative noises to the cooks, who smiled and made appreciative noises back. I didn't know it then, but their appreciation of the meal would be intrinsic, whereas mine would be aesthetic, as it was being cooked purely for their consumption and we would be served the same Western-orientated rubbish as yesterday.

After an extremely cautious approach to the river, I had a thorough, if slightly more discreet, wash and was joined by several other arrivers. I discovered that a good way to wash a pair of underpants and preserve decency at the same time was to remain inside them.

It was beautifully warm, and an hour or so later when even the slowest members of our party had arrived, lunch was served. This, food apart, was the highlight of the day. It was wonderful to lie in the midday sun and think of a bleak November day at home.

I was sorry to leave Kenja. Although stopping short of planning to return for a holiday, it deserved further exploration than a mere lunch-stop. I wandered around the village with my video camera, much to the amusement of the locals who sensed, quite incorrectly, possible financial gain from posing cheerfully for the camera.

The path that led out of Kenja rose steeply from the river valley and continued to rise all through the long afternoon. In fact, it would be Saturday afternoon before we would arrive at our next downhill bit. I had intended to belt up the hill, and push myself on to the night-stop, but before I hit warp drive I was set upon by Adrienne.

Adrienne was a very chatty, very bubbly doctor in her mid-forties, who didn't look her age. She had an unintentional been-there-done-it air, which was a little unfortunate, as she had been there and done it. Why she wanted to team up for the afternoon with a morose bastard like me was quite beyond my comprehension.

It wasn't long before I realised that my involvement in the conversation was required more in an auditory capacity than as an active participant. Still, it was a welcome diversion, since my Walkman was beginning to be as tedious as the trek was rapidly becoming, as my first set of batteries gave notice of fatigue. I learnt that she lived in the Bahamas but had a home near Berkhamsted, where her three sons went to school, and where I had once turned down employment, preferring my present post. Doctors living in the Bahamas obviously command a nice, steady income.

This was Adrienne's second Everest and, as her preferred pastime was sub-aqua off the temperate shores of the Bahamas, I found it puzzling, particularly as the weather deteriorated and the temperatures plummeted, as to why she would want to inflict this on herself.

Some way up the hill we came to Chinbu, which was little more than a smoky teahouse. I bought our tea and, as the sweat cooled on my back, noticed that the temperature had dropped significantly. Removing my Oakleys, I also noticed that the sun had disappeared behind thick cloud and it had become a rather dismal afternoon. We set off again, and ten minutes later I realised to my horror that I had left my glasses behind. I sprinted down the path and, to my vast relief, they were where I had left them. Nepalis were, we had been told, honest to a fault, with the exception of a tiny minority who had learned from the corrupt exploits of Western visitors. However, we were also told, that if you left behind something of value, there might be a small time lag before they run after you to reunite you with your precious possession. Indeed, sometimes they may thank the relevant god in the providence department for the unstinting generosity of Western visitors.

It was an uninspiring afternoon's trek, and the certainty that the only way was up did nothing to alleviate the monotony. I was glad to have Adrienne's company. She was a gentle and well-meaning soul, who would have made an admirable social worker had she not chosen a career in medicine.

I was also deliriously glad when the hill yielded just enough flattish ground to permit the existence of the tiny settlement of Sete. My guide book had claimed that around four and a half hours should be allowed from Kenja, but Adrienne and I had managed it in just over two at a steady conversational pace. It was difficult to see how it could take that time, but there were some who managed to take even longer.

Of course, some had their reasons. Like John Dunning, who had stepped off the path into a bush to relieve himself only to find, alas too late, that several generations of porters used this as the major defecation point between Kenja and Sete. Somehow, he managed not only to attach the stuff to his boots but also to smear it all over his trousers, which he had presumably dropped in the process of performing his toilet. It was an offence for which he was later to be unanimously voted the third winner of The Hat.

Sete, at 2,575 metres (8,500 feet), contained three lodges and was no more than a place to break the uphill journey. The peoples who farmed the terraces of the surrounding hills lived on the land, and so there was no real hub or community to this settlement.

Our camp was perched precariously on two narrow terraces, each about fifty metres in length, on which there was just about enough room to erect a tent. As we arrived, the first tents were being erected under the dubious gaze of those who had arrived ahead of us. I didn't like the look of it. It was a cast-iron certainty that I would have to leave my tent for a pee at least once during the night. It was as unlikely that, with my propensity for accidents, I would complete the necessary without falling over the edge of one of the terraces as a flock of lemmings learning to abseil would arrive safely at the bottom of a cliff. That would either result in, if our tent were placed on the upper terrace, the likelihood of landing on a tent below or, if on the lower terrace, falling off the hill and disappearing into the darkness in the direction of Chinbu.

The alternative was to spend the night in one of the lodges. The terraces on which the camp was being erected belonged to the first of the three lodges, grandly named the Solu Khumbu New Green View Blue Sky. I decided to investigate.

The entrance was at the back up a small erratic flight of stone steps and led directly into a warm, dark smoky kitchen where I could make out familiar faces huddled around a small table drinking tea. We exchanged greetings.

On the other side of the entrance was a dark corridor leading to a small dormitory which contained four rickety but tempting-looking beds.

Simon was amongst the group in the kitchen.

"Are you looking at what I think you're looking at?" he asked.

"Looks tempting, doesn't it?" I replied. It was beautifully warm in the lodge and getting colder by the minute outside.

I greeted the senior woman, or *didi* as they are known, who was slaving over the smoky stove. I asked for tea and enquired the price of a bed.

"Seven rupee," she replied without looking up.

"Seven rupees," I replied. She nodded. "En suite bathroom?" She uttered a curious nasal noise which I took to mean no.

I located my palmtop computer and did a quick calculation.

"That, by Wednesday's exchange rate, is 5.11 pence. I don't know. Seems a bit pricey to me. Shall we try to knock her down a bit?" I asked Simon. "What do you think?" I wasn't ready yet to spend the night in self-imposed exile from the rest of the party, in total isolation.

"Can we see the room?" Simon asked. The *didi* shrugged her shoulders, indicating that financial ruin did not hinge on our acceptance of her hospitality. We walked along the little dark corridor into the dormitory. The corridor was L-shaped, and beyond the first dormitory was another smaller room containing two beds. It had wooden bars which rose to the ceiling from a waist high wooden wall thus giving the impression of a Wild West jail. A curtain hung in the doorway. Rucksacks had been deposited on the beds, indicating that they had been claimed. Pity. Beyond this was a third dormitory in which were five unclaimed beds.

"This'll do," I decided. "It'll be more noisy closer to the kitchen late at night." Also, the gable window overlooked the terraces where the blue tents were almost all erected. I didn't want to miss anything.

"Further to go for a pee," Simon pointed out.

"Pee out the window," I suggested. There was no glass in the windows, just wooden shutters. The window ledge was broad and quite high, requiring a degree of balance that I wasn't totally sure I could guarantee, to perform such an operation.

"Great view," I said, looking out of the gable window.

Below the window, porters were struggling to erect the blue mess tent on the widest part of the lower terrace adjacent to the lodge. It was never going to work.

"Bet you the price of a bed for the night that doesn't stay up," I said to Simon.

"You're on."

We watched as they struggled to position the canvas without falling from the terrace into oblivion. They beavered away, erecting the poles and pegging the side that backed onto the upper terrace, displaying as much optimistic enterprise as I had scepticism. For a moment I feared they might actually succeed, and may well have done had they not begun to set out the tables and stools inside the tent before it had been satisfactorily anchored.

In his haste, one unfortunate porter tripped and grabbed the nearest thing to hand which sadly, for all concerned and Simon's wallet, happened to be the centre pole. A sea of blue canvas wafted majestically over the edge of the terrace, the extremities of the tent dancing on the breath of the cool evening air before fluttering down to earth, engulfing those beneath who, like drowning men, clutched at anything to escape the blackness in which they had become ensconced.

When we had recovered sufficiently from the hysteria this had caused, Simon went off to pay for the beds and I continued to enjoy the scene from the window. The other curious sight from where I stood was the shack beneath the window where the cooks were busily engaged in the preparation of dinner. There was nothing particularly abnormal in this, but on the fragile-looking roof of the shack lay a dead goat with straw up its bottom. Whether this animal was so regaled and situated for culinary or religious beliefs, I was never to find out.

Simon returned with two pieces of information. The first was of more concern than the second. Apparently, if one slept in a lodge one was expected to eat there, and the second was that our leaders were taking a very dim view of our voluntary segregation from the others. Simon had told a porter erecting our tent not to bother and had been severely ticked off by Dave for interfering in arrangements of which he was in sole charge. I suppose I could see his point. But Wish's accusation that we were adversely affecting the morale of the group by destroying the bonding I consigned to the bottom drawer of my mind labelled "complete and utter bollocks". We were planning to get a good night's sleep, not form a splinter group and make a takeover bid. Wish's insistence on group solidarity was beginning to annoy me and accelerated my frustration at the slowness of our progress.

I asked the *didi* for some hot water which, when it eventually arrived, was cold and went out the back for a good wash. As I undid my belt the lid of my small Camera Care System case flipped open and I watched in horror as my Olympus Instamatic fell ten feet to the rocky ground below, tumbling down the slope to come to rest outside the shack where the cooks were slaving. One of the cook boys picked it up and he and his mate brought it over to me. To my surprise it didn't seem to be damaged, but I didn't hold out much hope that it would still work.

I thanked the boys and, without thinking, pointed the camera at them. To my greater surprise, not only was there a reassuring click as I pressed the shutter, but the flash also worked, and it wound on to the next exposure. It was then I remembered that it is bad form to take photographs of Nepalis without first obtaining their permission. Some believe that being photographed will shorten your life, whilst others believe that, as we use toilet paper and they do not, it follows that we will use their photographs to wipe our bottoms. I could not allay their fears on the first, but as to the second I went to pains to try to point out that I personally did not consider photographic paper to be a suitable material with which to satisfactorily clean my bottom. I'm not sure that I was entirely understood and probably succeeded only in causing greater offence than had the taking of the photograph.

Dinner that night, due to the collapse of the mess tent, was served in the ground floor room of the lodge, which was a welcome departure from routine. The room was entered by large outward opening double doors giving it the appearance of being a cross between a garage and a stable, although neither would have had the slightest relevance given our surroundings. The atmosphere was good, and there was nothing to suggest that anyone else shared Wish's concerns over our decision to sleep in the lodge.

There had been no attempts, despite Dave's insistence that there would be, by either the *didi* or her very drunken, very noisy husband to coerce Simon or me to eat in the lodge. In fact, we almost did so voluntarily as the trek food, with a slavish adherence to carbohydrate loading, was rapidly losing its appeal. That night over coffee, as the jokes were told, I passed round my tiny bottle of rum which was returned to me empty.

Simon and I were amongst the last to leave. Before we had dispersed I called across to Dave: "Make sure the cook boys know where to bring our tea in the morning, will you!"

This was well received by everyone except Dave, who simply glowered at me.

Simon had agreed to examine Kathy Crilley who was having problems with her back. Kathy, from London, was something of an anomaly in that she had taken part in the '91 Everest, been ill, had come last and freely admitted to having hated every minute of the entire trip. No one could fathom out why on earth she had wanted to come back, particularly after day one when her body went into a rapid state of disintegration, details of which we had inflicted upon us at regular intervals. Maybe the fact that she was one of the lunatics who couldn't think of anything better to do than run around a track for twenty-four hours might go some of the way to explain her obvious masochistic tendencies.

As Simon was treating Kathy, the lodge owner burst in muttering something in Nepali, and although the precise translation was beyond us, the meaning was quite clear. He was not going to have women sneaked into his dormitory in his lodge, thank you very much. Not, at least, without them paying their seven rupees. Simon attempted to convey what he was doing, and made it clear that he was not going to part with any more money. Our host, who would have comfortably beaten the proprietor of Fawlty Towers in an Alienate the Guests competition, left the room slamming the door and, tripping over a rucksack left in the corridor, cursed loudly and slung it against the wall.

Kathy left, and we set about preparing for the night. The beds were wooden framed with folding legs, and each mattress was cardboard thin and covered with cloth which was ripped and ingrained with grime from the backs of generations of trekkers. I also suspected that there was a longer waiting list for nits, fleas and lice to obtain accommodation in each mattress than there was for a council flat in Knightsbridge. I put Dieter's bivvy bag over the mattress; that should at least keep all but the most resourceful from infiltrating, I placed my inflatable mattress over this, then climbed into my sleeping bag. The bed was considerably harder than the ground beneath the tent had been.

Simon had the solution. There were five beds in all. We were using two of them. That left three free. He had two of the spare mattresses, and I had the other one.

I was just drifting off to sleep, when we were disturbed by a crashing and cursing outside in the corridor. The door flew open and the landlord staggered in shining his torch first at Simon then at me.

In a state of great agitation, he pointed first to the bare beds, than at the pile of mattresses on top of which we were attempting to eke out some form of relative comfort.

He left the room and returned a minute later followed by a rather apologetic-looking little man who deposited his rucksack on the floor, laid out a sleeping bag on the bed opposite me, and curled up, fully dressed, inside it. The landlord continued to rant and gesture with his flashlight.

"Do you think he wants a mattress?" Simon asked.

"Naw, I'd doubt it. He looks quite comfortable to me. They're used to sleeping on the floor, anyway."

"You mean, let sleeping Sherpas lie."

"Something like that."

However, our host did not agree, and it was obvious that he would not leave us in peace until all the mattresses had been replaced to his satisfaction. The latecomer, who was by now sound asleep, was woken up and thrust reluctantly onto a mattress. As soon as he had gone, Simon and I reclaimed the two spare mattresses while our friend, doubtless unaccustomed to the comfort provided by the mattress, resumed his repose, snoring loudly.

I didn't sleep a wink that night. At the best of times, I have difficulty sleeping in the company of a snorer. To make matters worse, when I decided I had had enough and gave the little man's bed a shake so violent that I thought for an instant it was going to collapse, he altered his tactics and talked in his sleep for the following hour before he resumed snoring.

All night, or what was left of it, I tossed and turned, convinced that he had been planted on us by the landlord. Moreover, I was waiting for the door to burst open again and see that look of triumph when he saw the bare boards of the two empty beds.

# Sete to Junbesi: "These Shoes Aren't Made for Walking!"

## Saturday 13th November

Dawn's first light brought an end to my suffering. I opened the shutters to be greeted by another beautiful, bright cloudless morning.

"Another day in paradise," I said to myself as I stretched, more to convince myself than as a statement of belief.

"Sleep well?" I asked Simon, stiffing in his bag.

"Not a wink."

"Me neither," I said. "Don't tell anyone, though!"

"No way!" he said.

The door was flung open and I expected it to be followed by the frenetic entry of Sete's very own Basil Fawlty, with a further heated invective on the subject of the illicit procurement of mattresses.

It wasn't. To our surprise, two smiling cook boys entered with the teapot and mugs, clearly pleased with themselves for having found us.

"Aha! Room service!" said Simon. "How very civilised!"

"Good men!" I said as I shovelled three heaped spoonfuls of brown sugar into the welcome but anaemic-looking tea. "We'd better drink this quickly before Basil does his rounds. He'll probably try to charge us corkage on it!"

On the way to the latrine tents I chanced upon the Hotel Toilet. It was a rotting wooden shack of about four feet by three feet, with several panels missing from the side and a rusting corrugated iron roof. But it was obviously something of which Basil and his wife were quite proud. You could tell this by the fact there was a padlock on the door. That the padlock and the door were both open could either have been the result of a quick getaway by the previous occupant, or a statement of disgust by the same at the measures to which Basil went to ensure standards of hygiene.

I poked my head inside. As expected, the smell was foul. There was a rough hole in the centre of the floor which was surrounded by heaps of excrement and toilet paper, around which buzzed hosts of extremely happy, extremely large flies. The floor itself showed signs of decay, and it was only a question of time before some unfortunate trekker would disappear into the abyss below. 'No, you certainly wouldn't want to have your car keys in your back pocket when using this,' I thought, wryly.

I decided that our green tents were preferable, just, and continued along the terrace.

Breakfast was outside the lodge on the stony terrace beside the room where we had dined the previous evening. Presumably the porters had slept inside as there was no mess tent to shelter them.

Dave informed us that today would be steep up until we reached our lunch-stop, which was a small village just before Lamjura Pass, after which it would be steep down until we reached our night-stop at Junbesi.

\*

I arrived, at what I assumed was the lunch-stop, at about nine forty-five. Frustrated by the lack of opportunity to train, I was conscious that it was now actually over a week since my last decent run. This, I considered, was inappropriate preparation for a marathon which was still a fortnight away, no matter where or over what it was being run.

So, once warmed up, I had slipped into a jog and, despite the uphill nature of the trail, maintained a good steady pace, except in those places where the path was too unpredictable for speed.

Because of the problems with my knee, I generally find that uphill running, although it requires a greater degree of physical effort, is more relaxing, as it can be done with a lesser degree of concentration.

Beyond the tiny village of Dhakuchu, which was little more than a teashop, the trail became flatter and passed along a ridge entering a deeply forested area. The surface of the path was better now, with sand and even mud in places replacing the boulders over which I had clambered earlier. The warm morning sun, and the pleasing response of my body to the physical demands of the climb, helped me slip into a relaxed rhythm, and erase the nightmare memories of my sleepless night.

The land began to open out and I came to a pass where the path forked. As the path to the right sloped steeply downwards, I guessed that one had to traverse the mountain to the left. I had not seen anyone from our party since Dhakuchu, where several of them had stopped for tea, and I assumed that apart from Ray, of course, I was at the front. I was slightly unsure of my whereabouts, but as the path I had chosen was still more up than down I was confident I was still on the main drag. According to my map the descent did not commence until beyond Lamjura Pass, and I felt sure I would have known if I had reached that. Why, I didn't know, if Dartmoor had been anything to go by.

Soon I came to a large clearing with a substantial lodge, a teahouse, and a couple of private residences.

This must be Goyem, and the lunch-stop. I dumped my rucksack on one of the benches and squeezed myself through the tiny entrance of the lodge. I found myself in familiar surroundings: earthen floor, an open stove from which protruded the unconsumed end of an immature sapling while at the other end, beneath a blackened pot, embers crackled welcomingly, illuminating a dark and smoky little kitchen which the sun never reached and where an olive-skinned old woman cackled and cooked, children laughed and teenage girls giggled and peeled vegetables.

I ordered a lemon tea, and then another, and received the news that the price had tripled since Sete with mixed emotions. On the one hand I detest extortion. On the other, it was made with proper lemon, not the concentrated stuff from a bottle, and there was a sugar bowl from which I was permitted to imbue the beverage liberally with some body. And I was over three thousand feet higher than at Sete. Some porter would have had to carry the ingredients up the hill. Let's see, that's inflation at the rate of – I got out my computer one rupee every 787.88 feet Plus the fact, illustrated by this simple example of the law of supply and demand, that we were now passing into remoteness, getting nearer the inner door of this inaccessible wilderness.

Opposite the table where I sat, I noticed for the first time two very blond, very tanned, not totally unattractive females. I correctly assumed that they were Northern European, probably Swedish. Throwing pecuniary good sense to the wind, I asked if they would care to join me in a tea and, as expected, discovered that they spoke excellent English.

They were able to confirm that I was where I thought I was, and told me that they had trekked up to Gokyo Peak and were now headed for Jiri. Not as popular a trek as the Everest Highway, Gokyo provides a superb viewpoint not only for the mountains on the Nepal-Tibet border such as Cho Oyo, Lhotse and of course Everest, but also the mountains to the far east, which Makalu dominates, and the closer Khumbu range including Ama Dablam, Thamserku and Cholatse. Names, distant but familiar names, that I had been reading about for months.

It was mouth-watering stuff, and their enthusiasm fired mine. But if that had been mouth-watering their next piece of information, casually tossed into the conversation, was chilling. There had been reports of six fatalities in the Everest region in the last month. Four climbers had been killed in separate incidents, and two trekkers had died from AMS. Sure, they hadn't seen any bodies, and these things are prone to exaggeration, but this blunt reminder of the fragility of life and the perils of the harsh land that lay ahead sent a chill down my spine, a shiver that owed rather more to apprehension than to the cold perspiration drying on my back.

The girls set off towards Sete, and I put on some warm clothes and settled down to get my diary up to date. Although it was still not quite eleven o'clock, cloud was beginning to build up, the wind was picking up, and a cool wispy mist hovered around the mountainside like a shroud. In the distance I heard the drone of a light aircraft approaching. This was the first time in almost four days I had heard a petrol driven engine, save the generator belonging to the camera crew which droned on remorselessly long into the night.

I walked over to the stony terrace behind the lodge to see if I could see anything. I could – from here the view was breathtaking. The intermittent mist in which we were engulfed was in fact cloud, and below the terrace the land fell away, sloping gently at first then dramatically, down into a deep sunny valley from whence vast mountains rose on either side, as far as the eye could see. The path continued to traverse the mountain beyond the lodge and far in the distance I could make out a dip, and beyond it, a rocky outcrop rising steeply on the other side. That must be the approach to Lamjura Pass which, at 3,530 metres (11,650 feet), was the highest pass in the Solu region and another altitude landmark for me.

The little plane came into sight, plodding steadily up the valley. I recognised it as a Twin Otter, and it was easily close enough to read that it belonged to Royal Nepal Airlines. This, a thirty-five minute flight from Kathmandu to Lukla, was the alternative to what we were doing right now.

It passed at a point that seemed to be level with where I was standing, and it hardly seemed possible that it would clear the pass. It must be right at its ceiling, I thought, as it threaded through the pass with barely fifty feet between the ground and its unretractable undercarriage.

"Now you can see why they don't fly when it's cloudy," came a voice from behind me. It was Tom.

"We've got to fly in one of those baths with wings on the way back," I told him.

"I know." He knew. "It's not so bad on the way back from Lukla. The landing is worse than the take-off."

"How do you know?" I asked, sceptically. "I thought you hadn't been here before."

"No," he replied, and with just the suspicion of a smile he added, in his broad west of Ireland accent, "but I know a man who has."

Another plane passed over the pass, and then another. We were joined by John Matesich, the Californian. He had been finding things hard going of late. While most of us Brits had accepted the culture shock with traditional toilet humour and stiff upper lip, John's system had seemed to have gone into a state of shock, which was only overridden by extremely loud and naive vocal invectives, normally commencing with the words "Christ!" or "Shit!".

"Christ, there's one with its wheels still down!" he yelled.

"They've all got their wheels down," Tom casually informed him. "You see, the wheels don't go up, or down. That way there's less for the pilots to think about when they're takin' off and landin'."

The assistant Sirdar had arrived with an assortment of his staff who were involved in the preparation of lunch. One of the kitchen boys was setting out the blue plastic blanket on the terrace beside us. As another plane flew over he stopped, looked up, put his hands together, shook his head and he drew his index finger slowly across his throat.

"It's that bad, huh?" John asked.

He didn't answer. Looking at us and smiling, his right hand went into a nose dive towards the ground.

"Sssssheeeeet!" said John.

"All done for the tourists," I said. But in my heart of hearts, I was on John's side. On a nought to ten scale of things to worry about, our return flight from Lukla scored at least twelve. But there were one or two other things to worry about in the meantime.

One thing at a time, sweet Jesus.

\*

By the time lunch was served, it was cold, bloody cold. My doctor, Stephen Hassan, had one of those terribly clever watches that calculated the altitude and informed you of the temperature as well as time in every capital of the world. He announced that it was minus five degrees. No one argued.

The little planes which we had watched fly in towards Lukla had again scraped over the pass, having deposited their load and taken on another one for the return trip down the Kathmandu Valley and back to relative civilisation.

I watched each plane until it disappeared from view. This trek was beginning to, feel interminable, and ahead of us still lay five days before we reached the promised land of Namche Bazaar, where we could put our feet up for a day or two. On the wings of my imagination, I could hitch a ride back to Kathmandu, chill out for a couple of days, and meet up again in Lukla... but that would mean two additional flights in one of those things.

As any prospects of another slice of tinned meat, spoonful of coleslaw or piece of bread receded, I grabbed another mug of Lemsip and continued to write my diary. It was going well and I was almost up to date.

I was lost to my toil and so hadn't noticed the small crowd of people looking over my shoulder, watching in fascination as words appeared on the little screen of my palmtop computer. The Nepalis amongst the group had never seen anything like it before, and were simply curious as to what it was. You could have told them it was a child's toy or a thermo-nuclear missile launcher and they wouldn't have known the difference. The Westerners knew what it was, but were curious as to what it could do and its capabilities. Such was the gulf between our expectations of life.

"What exactly is that?" asked Alun, the Welsh cameraman voicing the question on everyone's lips. The crowd edged closer, the Nepalis especially. This wasn't your average Western toy: Walkmans, fancy SLRs and even video cameras were now two a penny. No, this was something different and they didn't want to miss it.

"What this is..." I began, relishing the situation, "...is a state-of-the-art palmtop computer. A 16 bit CPU multi-tasking operating system with a 256k RAM, downloadable into a compatible desktop workstation," the first part of which I read from the small print on the top corner of the machine. I paused, conscious of the rather fetid odours breathing down my neck, "Programmed to kill anyone with bad breath at three paces," I added, "but why stop at breath?"

"What does it do?" someone asked.

"It's a database. Address book, Christmas card list; list of girlfriends that do, list of girlfriends that don't. Whatever you like."

"Who are you tryin' to kid, Marvin?" asked Annabel.

I flicked through a few addresses. "It's a spreadsheet. Keep your household accounts on it." I showed them mine. "Change any one element and it will recalculate your nett surplus or deficit at the end of the month." I increased my salary by fifty pounds, and the figure in the end box jumped from nought to fifty pounds. "Quite useful for calculating how much spending money we'll have left by Namche, if the present rate of inflation continues! It also has a spellcheck, thesaurus, scientific calculator, alarm clock..."

"Does it make the tea?" came the inevitable question from behind.

"...yes, and feed the cat. But it's the word processor which I find most useful." I opened my diary's current file, and found a bit that wasn't too critical of anyone or anything, which was difficult. "Like any word processor, you can edit, which means insert, copy, bring text," I flicked through the menu options, "...and of course delete."

I'll never know exactly what combination of buttons I pressed, whether it was the altitude, or the gods of the mountains, but as I basked proudly in the ownership of this icon of late twentieth century technical achievement, the words on the page faded then disappeared, and the title Week One vanished from the screen. It was lost and gone forever, much to everyone's amusement, especially Annabel's.

"Marvin, you're a real loser!"

I was beginning to hate that expression.

*

I set off in the cloud, feeling thoroughly miserable, towards Lamjura Pass. After the morning's exertions, I had decided to take it easy this afternoon, but the path to the pass was as desolate a wilderness as I had seen. Crudely severed stumps littered the landscape where trees had once grown, giving the surroundings the appearance of a World War I battlefield. Deforestation, along with water hygiene, is one of the main problems of the Solu Khumbu. Although programmes have been implemented to develop systematic foresting, the fact still remains that wood is the only source of fuel in the region. There is no nuclear fuel, no oil, no coal, and although the population is encouraged to use kerosene stoves and lamps, that costs money and needs must when the devil drives. So, the fairly arbitrary hacking down of sections of forest was not only a scar on the landscape but, with the knock-on effects caused by a sizeable and capricious onslaught on the balance of nature, stacked up the odds against the chances of survival for future generations.

The meteoric growth of the tourist industry has accelerated the problem beyond all proportions. As we journeyed deeper into the interior most of the people who populated these mountains owed their livelihood to the trekkers, particularly higher up. But you can't bake cakes without breakin' eggs. Trekkers want hot showers and warm, well-lit lodges, and if your lodge won't provide them, then its as sure a fact as that bears actually enjoy crapping in the woods, someone else's will.

Presently I came to the pass, which was recognisable mainly by the fact that it was clearly all downhill as far as the eye could see. From the pass, a wide steep-sided valley opened out welcomingly before me. Although it was still a grey overcast afternoon, in all honesty not much better than a November's day at home, on this side of the mountain we were out of the cloud and mist. That, at least, was a blessing.

Lamjura Bhanjyang is the highest point between Jiri and Namche Bazaar. Here there is a *chorten*, or hemispherical Bhuddist religious structure, around which one should always walk clockwise. I had no great desire to walk around it either clockwise or anticlockwise, but it was fairly impressive because of the many prayer flags which fluttered to the ground from its apex, causing it to resemble a giant maypole. There was no mystery why it was so placed or why there was such an abundance of prayer flags. Flying is as unnatural form of transport to the Nepalis as it is to me, therefore the more positive divine intervention the better. It was also a damned good landmark for the pilots.

Commencing my descent from the pass the path fell away steeply, zigzagging violently over rough boulder-strewn ground. Throwing caution to the wind, I raced down the upper slopes, passing most of our group. Soon, the path became more level and led through a virgin forest, whose tall pines rose high into the sky, the vast girth of their trunks, intensifying my feeling of wonder and insignificance in this country of big highs and big lows, both emotional and physical. How long would this forest remain virgin, I wondered? If the raping and pillaging on the high ground of the pass was anything to go by, not too long, I guessed.

The undergrowth was dense and green, nourished by the monsoon rains of the summer months not long passed. Between May and September, in keeping with the typical English summer, it rains heavily every day. Beyond the thickest part of the forest, giant rhododendron bushes grew apartment block high on either side of the path. I could imagine how stunning their sea of colour must be in the spring. This was a magical place, as yet not mutilated by either human need, greed or travel agent's brochure; a glade straight out of *Lord of the Rings*.

The forest eventually spat me out into the tiny village of Lamjura La, which is little more than a teahouse and a couple of private residences. But, travelling on from here, the more level ground meant a marked improvement in the path and, contouring the mountainside, I came to the community of Taktor. Taktor, with two solid-looking lodges, is as fertile a settlement as any in the Sulu district, and a prosperous farming community. Here there is abundance and, as in all societies where production exceeds demand, people are well-off. Here, the affluence is relative, but the export of surplus produce allows the villagers a comfortable existence.

As if to emphasise this, I rounded a corner at speed and almost shunted into the rear of a mule train carrying something in bulging sacks towards Junbesi. The width of the mules and the narrowness of the path presented me with little prospect of getting past. I resigned myself to a more sedate pace, and tried to engage the driver in conversation. Too absorbed was he in his task of controlling the reluctant and recalcitrant animals with the arbitrary administration of abuse, both verbal and physical, to have time for small talk. A scant *"Namaste,"* spat with the dust kicked from the feet of mules over several miles of path, was all I got. I was just another bloody tourist.

Then with all the misplaced black humour of a continental lorry driver, he invited me to overtake his mules on a twisty stretch of path. This would prove to be a mistake. I slid past the first two mules, scraping myself against the side of the mountain, and might well have passed the remaining two animals without incident had not the third mule inexplicably decided to turn round. As it did so, my toe caught a stone and hurled me forward in an uncontrolled dive which resulted in a direct hit with my head and shoulder, squarely in the midriff of the unfortunate animal.

I picked myself up, shaken and scratched, but thankful for the soft landing that had spared me more serious injury. The mule, however, did not wholly share my gratitude. With a noise that only a mule in shock could make to another mule, presumably to warn him of imminent physical assault or sexual advances (the look on his face conveyed some confusion as to which was intended), he set off at a goodly lick in the direction of Junbesi. The two mules which I had just overtaken rounded the bend ahead of the muleman, saw what had happened, and drew their own conclusions. Having no great desire to tangle with a mule-butting, two legged, backpacking maniac, they decided to put some distance between themselves and their potential assailant. Unfortunately for their owner, it was in the direction of Lamjura. And even more unfortunate for their owner, he stood between them and the hills for which they were headed.

The muleman got to his feet, following near disembowelment from the mini stampede which I could hardly bear to watch. Lugubriously, he set off after the southbound half of his train, uttering curses which would have made the other eye of one-eyed-yellow-idol pop out.

Some fifteen minutes later, I caught up with the two mules heading for Junbesi. They had paused for refreshment and a reassessment of the situation amidst what appeared to be someone's vegetable patch. The stone wall which separated the path from the vegetable field had provided little in the way of resistance to two supercharged fully laden mules on the rampage. A collection of stones by a gaping hole revealed their point of entry. There was little point in trying to usher them from the field. They didn't look as if they were in the mood to be ushered anywhere, and I guessed that the muleman must be close to rounding up his other two charges and setting off once again towards Junbesi.

The mules eyed me suspiciously as I passed, without interrupting their mechanical consumption of what appeared to be carrots, and I bade them farewell.

The path was now a wide sandy highway which was generally more down than up. On my left the mountain rose steeply but, where terraces could be carved out of the hill these resourceful people had done so. There was little wasted land. To my right the fertile floor of the valley was the agricultural hub of the region. As I approached the basin of the Junbesi Khola, itself a tributary of the Solu Khola, well-cultivated little dry stone walled fields reminded me of parts of Donegal. The cloud that had crept up as the afternoon wore on lowered the ceiling and cut the mountains off at shoulder height, accentuating the comparison. Even the path was not much worse than most of the roads in Donegal.

Agriculture, not surprisingly, is as divinely influenced as anything else in these parts. As at home, there is ritual which must be strictly adhered to, and the roles of men and women are quite specific. Back home, the general scenario is that man goes to work, woman shops, cooks and washes up, and man sits in front of the telly. In Nepal, the men must plough the fields, and even boys of eight or nine are capable of doing this. They must also use male cattle to pull the plough. Buffalo are thought of as messengers of the devil and must on no account be used. Women do the sowing and weeding and harvesting. But in the home, the picture is pretty much the same as it is back home, without the telly.

I rounded a steep left hand bend and paused to admire the view. Another valley wandered off up to the north, and my map told me that a path existed which led to Pangkarma or the Buddhist monastery at Thubten Choeling, should I want to go there. I did not. Also, on a clear day, I should be able to see the snowy peaks of Konyaklemo and the more distant Kala, both of which, at over 4,500 metres, would be big enough to dominate the landscape.

The low cloud denied this, however, but what was of more immediate interest was that not far distant was what must be Junbesi, and the end of another day's trek.

I was about to bound down the hill when something caused me to look down at my feet. I started in disbelief at what I saw. I had a closer look. My heart sank, my legs felt like lead and I felt the months of training float out of the window, like an unwanted smell in the bathroom. All for nothing – my race was over before it had begun.

I had earlier had problems with a blister on the top of my right big toe. It had burst and despite Nat's careful patching up at Kenja, had continued to be irritated by my boot. By Sete it had become a mushy painful mess. I had decided to consign my boots, which in any case were about as comfortable as a pair of concrete clogs, to the bag carried by the porter. I stopped short of giving or slinging them away, due to the fact that they had cost over eighty pounds, and to return home without a plausible explanation to the wife for their absence would be unwise. Also, I had half a mind to see what I could get for them in Namche.

Since Sete I had worn my only alternative footwear, a brand new pair of multi-terrain running shoes which had kindly been donated to me by their manufacturer, a well-known American sports shoe company. These, I had brought purely for the race. But they were extremely comfortable, did not irritate my toe, and were largely responsible for my excellent progress today. But in these parts, comfort and durability do not make good bedfellows.

Now, like my dream of doing well in the race, they were in tatters. Or the toes, to be precise. Where the rubber sole curved upwards to join the fabric at the front of the shoe, there was now no fabric. While the left shoe merely suffered from the erosion of one layer of fabric, and so the sole was still in contact with the upper part of the shoe, on the right shoe there was a gaping absence of fabric of any sort. To be precise, there was a vast hole through which the bloodied end of my sock was clearly visible.

Whilst this had the advantage of stopping my toe from rubbing against the instep of the shoe, and was good for ventilation, it would only be a question of time before a carelessly placed footstep would invite a stone to catch the unattached sole, causing it to further detach from the shoe and throw me off balance, so that I became detached from the mountain. I was quite capable of doing that on my own.

It did not look good. As I was unlikely to find anything resembling a sports shop between here and Gorak Shep, my only hope was to try and get it repaired, and of that I was not very optimistic. In the meantime, the boots would have to come out again, blisters or not.

With a heavy heart, I plodded the remaining half mile down the hill to Junbesi. It had been a curious day and, like the trek itself, one never knew what lay around the next bend or over the next horizon. The highs were big, but the lows were even bigger, and minor problems seemed to exceed all expectations. But without realising it I was already learning to adapt to the deprivation of virtually everything I had come to accept as standard in everyday life. Here, nothing was standard, nor was it sub-standard. It just didn't exist. End of story. It is surprising what you can do without when you don't know you need it. Rather like flicking through an Innovations catalogue full of devices to stop rugs slipping or to remove nasal hair.

And, as expected, it was going to get worse.

*

The Junbesi Chamber of Commerce were nothing if not thorough, and knew a good thing when they saw it. The billboard at the head of the village announced that, amongst other attractions, Junbesi was home to one of the Sherpa Guide Lodges of the Solu Khumbu. Sherpa Guide, I was informed, was to luxury accommodation what Mr Royce was to the motor car. Whether or not they were part of the Forte chain was conjectural. The Sherpa Guide promise included "Serve delicious foods, heated dining room, running hot shower, comfortable rooms at reasonable prices".

This sounded like my kind of town. Junbesi is the Sherpa capital of the Solu district. There are three main centres in the Solu Khumbu. In addition to Junbesi, Lukla, which has grown and prospered due to its airstrip which links the high Himalaya with Kathmandu, and the point of entry for those who had the good sense to miss out the first bit, and then of course Namche Bazaar, the highland Sherpa capital.

Junbesi has about a hundred or so private dwellings, two Gompa, and about six lodges. It also has a fairly sizeable school, and with the flat finger of fertile land stretching gently up the valley that rises to the north, white-walled dwellings are dotted as far as the eye can see.

It was a pleasant scene, but as I walked into the village I realised I hadn't a clue as to where our night-stop was situated. The rough hewn cobbled streets meandered through the town down to the river. I passed the Sherpa Guide lodge, and observed that it didn't look any different from any of the other lodges. As it wasn't central, I resisted the temptation to investigate it further.

I reached the river without seeing a familiar face. Then, as I considered what to do next, a little man approached me.

"*Namaste!*"

"*Namaste!*" I replied.

"Everest Marathon?" he enquired.

I nodded my head. He was probably trying to sell me life insurance.

"Come with me!"

He led me to a lodge inappropriately called the Himalaya White Peaks View Lodge which I had just walked past.

"Everest Marathon in here. Very good apple pie!"

Before I could say that the Everest Marathon most certainly wasn't in there, and that I wasn't crazy about apple pie, I saw Ray sitting on the terrace of a lodge across the path, deep in conversation with a dark-haired bloke I didn't recognise.

"G'day Ray," I called, aping his accent.

"Ah g'day Rich," he replied "Come and join us, you'll get a good graze over here." I was about to reply that I'd suffered enough physical punishment for one day, when I realised that he was referring to food.

I humped my rucksack to the floor and sat down opposite Ray, much to the annoyance of my guide from the Himalaya White Peaks View Lodge who, once he had one bum on a bench, knew that others would follow as would a nice night's takings.

Ray introduced me to his companion Pete, who was from Edinburgh, and was trekking back from Everest Base Camp. He was a runner, and would dearly have liked to have a crack at the race. Ray had already told him that Diana would not permit anyone to tag along even if they made their own logistical arrangements, and I added my weight to this. Quite apart from whether Diana would or would not, I didn't see why any other Tom, Pete or Harry should be able to do it on the cheap, having the same benefits of the back-up which would support us. Especially as they'd already been up in the high mountains and had the benefits of acclimatisation. Pete departed towards Lamjura, leaving the two of us alone.

"Been here long?" I asked Ray, changing the subject.

"Since about eleven thirty," he replied. It was now two forty-five. Ray looked immaculate in the jogging bottoms, pristine running shoes and down jacket he always wore when he stopped. He was a neat little man of about five foot six inches, lightly built, with the lean, wiry physique which stopped well short of the gaunt emaciated took of many marathon and ultra-distance runners.

Ray Brown was forty-two and had only started competitive running about five years ago when he stopped playing rugby.

It was as easy to imagine this quietly spoken little guy snapping at the heels of a maul, orchestrating a bunch of highly charged six foot six inch forwards, intent on tearing each other's heads off, as it was to picture him bouncing his way down the mountain like an Indian rubber ball. There are certain people you meet in life who you can instantly recognise as being driven inexorably towards the achievement of a goal, however bizarre that goal may appear. Ray was one of those people. He had that edge that set him apart from others.

Now, he was one of the finest 'veteran' runners in the world, and I believe would have made a name for himself in athletics had he turned to running earlier.

It was his paradoxical attitude to running which I found impossible to understand, and equate to my philosophy, but it went some way to explaining why it was he hadn't turned to it earlier.

Ray hated running. His anathema was only slightly below his drive to succeed, and diametrically opposed to the reasons why I ran. I ran for enjoyment, my fulfilment came from the sensual as well as physical experience of a three hour run with Floss along the coast path on a balmy summer's evening, or wallowing in frozen muddy puddles across the moors on a frosty winter's morning. For me it had little to do with winning. For Ray, it had everything. He would later write of his reason for entering the Everest Marathon: *It gave me a goal and that brings commitment: I wanted to go and I wanted to do well!*

His goals were realistic, measured out in part his from his previous racing experience, in part from detailed studies from the accounts of participants in the previous races, and in part from a magical coefficient with which he multiplied his road racing times to produce a target time of four hours thirty minutes. By a similar, if not as thorough, process I had a notional target of around six hours. At least I hoped to finish closer to six than seven. Dieter had completed the course in six hours forty-five minutes and, good friend or not, it was impossible to deny that I aimed to finish the race quicker.

I also realised that Ray would probably finish very close to his goal. Unless, of course, the intervention of illness, injury, or the wrath of the gods of the mountains, conspired to move the goalposts. But here we were all soldiers of fortune, moving slowly and uncontrollably towards whatever fate lay in store for us. There was nothing any of us could do about that. But in addition to walking to the left of mani walls, I found myself dragging my fingers along the engraved stones as I passed, and even uttering the odd *"Om mani padme hum."* After all, it couldn't do any harm to enlist a little extra help, could it?

As we chatted that Saturday afternoon in Junbesi over the most delicious vegetable noodle soup I had ever tasted, fried potatoes and gallons of lemon tea, I realised that Ray and I had a lot in common, our attitude to running apart. "I only run cause I'm half way bloody good at it," he told me, and I believed him. In fact, it had been largely chance that he had entered the Everest Marathon at all. Initially, his first choice for his extended holiday had been to take part in the Golden Oldies Rugby Tournament in Dublin. But over the months, the mystique of the mountains had held greater promise than the lure of the Guinness. At this point on the trip, however, the trek was getting to him as much as it was to me. In fact, had a friendly time taxi arrived that Saturday afternoon in Jumbesi, and asked us whether we would like a lift anywhere at any time, we would have happily shared the fare to the Old Wesley Rugby Club, right then.

We didn't talk much about the race. It was still so far away as to be unconnected with what we were doing right now.

I suddenly realised that what I was doing right now was sitting and getting very cold as the clouds became ever lower, and the temperature dropped.

"Why don't you take a shower?" suggested Ray, the devil incarnate. "I had one earlier," he confessed. "It was bloody nice."

I was tempted.

"I don't think I'd be too popular if I was found out. I'd win the hat, for sure," I said, weakening. "I think Dave and Wish take a pretty dim view of showering, don't they?"

"Well, if you like, you can make a bloody one man protest, but that won't stop them cuttin' the bloody trees down. And we didn't come all this bloody way just to please Dave and bloody Wish."

He was bloody right. Ray seldom completed a sentence without at least three "bloodies". And it wasn't that his sentences were that long, he just said "bloody" a hell of a bloody lot.

I booked my shower and, when called by the owner of the lodge, watched him climb up the ladder to pour the caldron of steaming water into the casket above the shower. In the little wooden hut, there was a tap, but that was more to make the tourist feel at home than for governing the flow of water. When you turned it on, the water dripped slowly down from above, and continued to do so until the contents of the casket were gone. There was, of course, no pressure, and by the time the water reached me, what had not long ago steamed, now practically formed icicles.

It was easy to see how the environmentally minded managed to avoid the temptation to shower. By the time I had finished, although I was somewhat cleaner I was not entirely convinced that it had been worth the hassle of removing my clothes, finding soap, cleanish underwear and replacing everything in my rucksack. Still, my five minute shower killed the best part of an hour.

By the time I had finished my ablutions, several others from our party had arrived and the lodge was doing a brisk trade. Ray was deep in conversation with the owner of the lodge, who was also the mayor of Junbesi. He had given Ray a guided tour of the village and the school, and Ray had handed over some pens for the kids. The lodge owner knew about us and the race and in fact, it was from about this point onwards that, wherever we stopped, we were treated, if not quite as celebrities, with more deference than the average tourists. With the probable exception of the late Tenzing Norgay, there is no such thing as a celebrity in these parts.

It was warm in the lodge, and we stayed there for a long time. There was little to be gained from standing in the middle of a field where there may or may not be tents. When we left to find the field which would be home for the night, it was dark. The village was beginning to bustle with activity, and music and the smell of cooking filtered from the lodges and houses we passed.

I've heard it said that you can judge a place by its Saturday night feeling, or lack of it, and Junbesi scored considerably higher than quite a few other places I had visited. I've also heard it said, that the good people of Holyhead find the amenities of their hometown so horrendous, that they evacuate the town on Saturday night and drink and dance the night away aboard the Dublin bound ferry on the Irish Sea, sleeping it off the following morning on the return trip!

Of course, we had arrived during a festival and there would be celebrations that night. The lodge owner tempted us to return with the promise of singing, dancing and the colourful pageant which was part of the festival of *Tihar*, or Festival of Lights.

Eventually, after stumbling around the fields surrounding the village, we found our campsite and I found tent Fourteen, which was placed on a slope of about thirty degrees.

The meal was considerably better that evening, and most people seemed to be in good spirits. Although the meat was tough and of indeterminate origin, the boiled potatoes and fresh green beans were welcome. As always, there was sludge for pudding. Dave English, however, had gone down with a nasty stomach bug and had a high fever. He had been persuaded by his brother to stay in the relative comfort of a lodge where he would hopefully sleep it off and feel better in the morning.

After the meal a small group which included Richard, Simon, Annabel and Nat, decided to go into the village on the pretext of checking on Dave. It was tempting to enjoy the relative normality of a night out, however culturally different it may be, and I considered joining them. I decided not to. I was not feeling well. I was shivery and had a headache, which was part real, part imagined. The more I thought about it, the worse it got. And the more I associated it with my run up to Goyam from Sete, and the rapid gain in altitude, the more I associated it with AMS.

I settled down for an early night, but before I could get my foot jammed against the ridge pole to stop me from spending the night slipping down and crawling back up the tent, the peace was shattered by the arrival of Junbesi's version of the Spice Girls.

Saturday night had come to us and there was no avoiding it. I climbed out of my sleeping bag and joined the throng encircling three well-scrubbed and colourfully dressed young ladies, who sang and danced around their small corgi-like dog. The latter's only participation in the festivities was to yelp loudly when he received a sharp kick from one of his mistresses on his leathery and tailless posterior. On the basis that any attention is better than none, he stayed put at the centre of the dance, whereas a dog of greater intellect or less vanity might have been tempted to move to the perimeter.

I made something of a cross for my own back by fetching the video camera whose light illuminated the scene magnificently, and met with the enthusiastic approval of performers and audience. The girls were obviously highly rated locally as they had a goodly entourage with them who, along with the trekking crew and most of us, sat cross-legged or stood around the impromptu stage.

They weren't bad, and although they occasionally forgot the words of one song, which were pretty much the same as those of the previous song, they were confident and above all were clearly enjoying themselves. Their appeal may not have been universal, but for me they had two big things going for them. Firstly, they were providing live music, and live music of almost any sort draws me like a magnet. Secondly, the one exception to my former statement is country and western. And this had as much in common with country and western as Elvis had with health foods.

Although the dancing, in all truth, lacked much more animation or imagination than three girls called Doris, Sharon and Tracey dancing around their handbags at the Social Club disco, it achieved the simple goal of all good entertainment – namely to get the audience behind them and make them forget their problems momentarily.

After half an hour, I made the excuse that my batteries had run flat, which was actually not far from the truth, and got back into my sleeping bag. Before settling down, I recorded a couple of their songs on my micro-cassette. Why, I didn't know. Probably for posterity.

*

I awoke some hours later with a thumping headache and a dry mouth, and a noise like a pneumatic drill close to my ear. I had slipped down the tent, and found myself crumpled by the constraints of what was more of a straightjacket than a sleeping bag. The noise, I realised, was coming from Simon. He was snoring loudly. I gave him a shove. He stirred, but continued to snore.

It occurred to me that although the unfortunate Sherpa who was forced to sleep on a mattress in Sete had been clearly guilty of snoring, he might have had an accomplice. Simon of course, according to him, never snored. I switched on my micro-cassette. Try denying that, old boy.

Some minutes later, satisfied that I had compiled enough evidence, I wound back the tape and hit the play button to check that it had recorded. Unfortunately, I had forgotten to turn down the volume and the little machine belted out, at considerable decibels, one of the girls' songs which I had recorded earlier.

Simon awoke with a start.

"What the hell was that?"

"What was what?" I asked.

"Christ, I thought we were being attacked by Apaches!"

"You probably just had a bad dream, see you in the morning."

We both settled down.

What a useful little machine. As a 'Snorebuster', it had proved itself to be highly effective. Similar to a gadget I had once seen advertised in *Innovations*, which promised to stop noisy dogs barking, called a Barkbuster. Moreover, it occurred to me, I could have some fun with this.

With just the sniff of a plan to get one over on Annabel, I drifted down the tent and off to fitful sleep.

Outside, however, someone else was very much awake.

# Junbesi to Tragsindho La: "Everest? I Must Have Mist It!"

## Sunday 14th November

One of the dubious advantages of being parked next door to the mess tent was that we were amongst the first to be served bed tea. Not that this really compensated for the racket that had been going on since four thirty, when the cooks and cook boys had started to prepare it. Didn't they know it was Sunday?

I had now had very little sleep in the course of the last three nights but was relieved to discover, as I began to get my world together, that I didn't feel too bad. It was another very cold, frosty morning and I suspected that the mornings would only get colder and frostier from now on. But, once again, the sky was a brilliant clear sapphire blue and I felt considerable optimism that it might stay like this for a little longer today. On what this optimism was based, other than optimism, I didn't know. Little more than the illogical British philosophy that clear blue skies will someday, somehow accede grey ones.

At breakfast, Dave English rejoined us and was feeling much better. However, there were quite a few others who were suffering from diarrhoea and stomach upsets and the doctors had been kept busy throughout the night.

Someone else who had been busy through the night, unlike the diarrhoea, could not be tracked down and eliminated. This was the thief who had entered Rob Howard's tent while he slept and had made off with all his photographic equipment.

As Rob was a professional photojournalist whose living depended on covering events such as this, this was a bigger blow to him than holes in my shoe had been to me.

Of course, there was no hope of catching the thief. Even had there been a policeman in Junbesi, there would have been very little he could have done to bring the perpetrator to justice. There are no sniffer dogs or Interpol helicopters out here. One of the drawbacks of a country where there is very little crime is that there is very little law enforcement. The forces of law and order, such as they are, are not geared up for either the detection or apprehension of villains.

To add insult to injury, the theft had to be reported and a certificate obtained from the police for insurance purposes. And the nearest policeman was way, way back in Kenja – a day and a half's trek retracing footsteps up over the hills.

Rob set off at once, travelling light, accompanied by a porter who had been suitably bribed to do three day trek in one, with the hope that he would meet up with us again that night.

Rob was no stranger to the Himalaya. He was an experienced traveller who had taken a year out to travel the entire length of the mountain chain, some two thousand miles, with a companion in the early eighties. But there was more than a little of the innocent abroad about him and, perhaps as a result of falling prey to several minor ailments, he fell some way short in the life and soul of the party department. For someone who spent most of his life covering mountain marathons, he didn't seem to be particularly at home in the mountains. In fact, by comparison, Ray and I were a comedy double act. At least we saw the funny side of things. Not that there was anything remotely funny about having your cameras stolen.

We weren't the only ones suffering trek fatigue. At breakfast, Joy sighed deeply and proclaimed "Do you know, the day after the day after the day after tomorrow, we'll arrive at Namche!"

There was a further air of expectation following Dave's morning briefing "Today, if you're lucky, you'll get your first sight of Everest. Over the Junbesi Khola, it's steep up to Sallung which should take you around two hours. Provided you get there before eleven you should have a good chance of seeing Everest. Any later, and it's likely to be covered by cloud."

A small group, accompanied by Wish, Alun and video camera, set off to visit the Buddhist monastery at Thubten Choeling. It was a lengthy detour, and even the promise of an audience with the Lama only enticed the most culturally motivated amongst our ranks.

Being slightly misanthropic, the thought had crossed my mind that where Alun and his camera went, Wish and other members of the Welsh speaking union tended to follow. Of course, there was to be a subsidiary documentary in the Welsh language for S4C to collect footage for, so there was little point in interviewing either Ray or me. But it seemed, to my cynical mind at any rate, that the cultural cart was being put before the cultural horse. Which, of course, was being taken to water from which it was liberally assuaging its thirst. In other words, a butter tea with the Lama in a temple deep in the heart of the Solu Khumbu was as good a backdrop for a programme in the Welsh language as a remote and primitive cottage in Scotland was for a coffee advert. It must have been confusing for the poor Lama, though, some of them speaking English and Wish and Alun yacking on in Welsh.

I left Junbesi just ahead of Adrienne who, being the doctor bringing up the rear, had to wait for me. On the way out, we paused to inspect one of the two gompas, which appeared to be deserted. Contrary to the lack of security elsewhere, particularly around our camp, the windows and doors were protected by expanding metal gates similar to those found in primitive lifts. After a quick look around, we left. Adrienne had to go at the pace of the porter carrying medical supplies, so I bounded across the river and set off at a brisk pace up the hill towards Sallung.

It was a climb of about one thousand feet, but felt like more, as the uphill was punctuated by several gentle downhill sections. The scenery was pleasant, if not spectacular, as the path snaked through rhododendron, blue pine and prickly leafed oak forests. Again, I felt like a stretch and got to the top ahead of all but Ray after a steady fifty minute trot.

Sallung was little more than a teahouse, the Everest View Nak Cheese Production Center, a terrace to admire the view from, and a damned good toilet. However, my first priority was to get a look at Everest.

The owner of the teahouse was serving tea to a bloke seated on one of the wooden benches, who looked as if he had been whisked in a time machine from the King's Road in the late 60s. The flat peakless leather cap which he wore was straight out of a poster of Che Guevara, and the round glasses were vintage Lennon.

I asked him where was the best place to get a view of Everest, not wishing to reveal that I wasn't quite sure exactly what I was looking for.

"Over there, man", he said, and pointed his roll-up towards the mountains which I had failed to notice on the horizon beyond the path. "On the left, between the hill on the left of the path and the cloud."

I hadn't noticed the cloud either. As he spoke, the mountain I had just shortlisted as a possible Everest disappeared from view behind thick cloud.

"That's it, man. You won't see that babe again today. Life's a pisser, huh?"

"Life's a pisser," I echoed, which reminded me that there was a very presentable-looking toilet to be inspected.

It was a good toilet, with porcelain foot plates, and a porcelain neck which hastened one's effluent away to the earth beneath, out of body, out of sight and out of mind. There was even a jug of something which resembled Jeyes fluid to banish any lingering remains.

Much heartened by this experience, I enjoyed a lemon tea and admired the view. Although Everest was obscured, the bhatti owner pointed out Makalu to the east, which, at over 8,400 metres was certainly deserving of a long range photograph. The proprietor was equally fascinated by my micro-cassette into which I was surreptitiously dictating a few notes for the diary. I tried to explain what it was and invited him to talk into it. He was very reluctant and lurched backwards as if stung when I played back some of Simon's snoring.

But, encouraged by the recording of the girls' singing, the curiosity as to what his own voice sounded like got the better of him and before long I could hardly wrench the thing away from him.

"How much?" he asked. I wasn't sure whether he wanted to know how much I had paid for it, or how much I would sell it for. I decided the former might conclude the conversation quicker. I took out my palmtop computer to calculate the cost of the machine in rupees and his eyes bulged in their sockets.

"What is that?" he asked.

"Oh, just a computer," I replied and did a quick calculation. "Three thousand rupees," I told him, rounding it up.

"Three thousand rupee?" he repeated open mouthed. "And how much that thing cost?" he enquired, pointing to the computer. Again I calculated. "Twenty-one thousand, three hundred rupees," I announced. He looked confused and I drew the figures in the dirt with my finger.

"How much is the tea?" I asked, wanting to be on my way.

"Five rupee." For the combined cost of my computer and microcassette, I could live here in the most luxurious settings money could buy for several months. I could understand how strange we must appear to these people. How we must seem at once both affluent and yet curiously impoverished, slaves to a technology which here had no value in any currency other than the coinage of curiosity. Only our advanced technology would not come to the aid of our delicate Western stomachs or the ravages of altitude.

I remember once returning from Florida with one of those baseball caps which was designed to hold two cans of beer, one above each ear, from which one drank simultaneously through a clear flexible plastic tube. At a party where I sported my cap with pride, a friend asked how much it had cost. I told him I had paid ten dollars for it. The look of incredulity he gave me was not dissimilar to the one with which the bhatti owner now regarded me. To someone who perceives an object as having no use, it has no value, and the cost has little relevance save only to confirm the insanity of the purchaser.

*

I was about to set off when Richard asked if I would do a short interview in front of the camera, being as I was the first one not to see Everest.

I didn't give him the answers he was looking for and, not surprisingly, it was consigned to the editing room floor. I steadfastly refused to go down the line of Everest representing for me a holy grail and didn't like the sound of personal pilgrimage at all. Pilgrimages, I told him, had by all accounts been bloody unpleasant affairs, undertaken by those whose conscience or public image were beyond the redemption of other less arduous forms of rehabilitation, and should currently be considered by several prominent Tory politicians. But since he asked, yes, I could see certain similarities between the trek so far and a medieval pilgrimage. I had come, I told him, to enjoy myself and to do well in the race, neither of which I felt I was making terribly good progress with at the present time.

The interview which appeared in the final documentary was with Zvonimir Grobenski, the German captain of industry, whose genuine enthusiasm included four "fantastics" and three "beautifuls", and was a whole heap more positive than mine had been, if not, perhaps, as entertaining.

*

Despite my negative sentiments, I was actually in good form as I set off downhill towards the Ringmo Khola and the lunch-stop.

There were several things which cheered me. Firstly, the sun was still shining. Secondly, I felt good. Although my trekking boots which I had been forced to resume wearing had not got any more comfortable or easy to steer, they had not appeared to accelerate the disintegration of my toe.

And thirdly, David Bowie was putting some very classy, if somewhat curiously juxtaposed notes into my headphones in the form of his version of the old Jack Bruce number *I Feel Free*.

I bounded down the hill in a little world of my own. My only concern was that there wasn't quite room on my head for headphones, Oakley glasses and baseball cap, and to satisfy the demands of each meant a little positional compromise from the other. At the speed at which I was going it was difficult to keep my head still and eventually I came up with the solution, which was to wear my cap back to front. At home, this would quite rightly have invited considerable verbal abuse along the lines of, "complete and utter dickhead."

But here no one cared.

I felt free.

*

I almost missed the lunch-stop at the Ringmo Khola. I had descended through Sallung on a good path which gradually contoured down to the river, and was about to cross the bridge and start the climb to Ringmo, when I glanced back and saw the Everest Marathon banner and the blue Polythene blanket on a flat terrace above the river.

In spite of yesterday I had decided to stop. This was for two reasons. Firstly, it was Remembrance Sunday and John Webster, the Scottish minister, had offered to hold a short service. I liked John and wanted to support him. If he could be bothered to work on his holiday, then I would make the effort to attend.

I felt strangely moved by the notion of paying tribute to those who had died in two world wars, here in a country which had barely been effected by the passage of two millennia, let alone the turmoil into which the world had been plunged twice this century. Perhaps it had something to do with their ultimate sacrifice to buy our freedom, the freedom which I was celebrating now. And the price of my freedom to travel and be myself was the solemn recognition of what that freedom had cost. Perhaps.

Secondly, I wanted to wash some socks, and this was the last river before the Dudh Kosi, where the water was apparently much too cold to wash anything in.

I washed my socks and idled the time away chatting with young Ang Nima, the assistant Sirdar, whose English was good. I lent him my Walkman and, to my surprise, David Bowie's *Black Tie White Noise* got the thumbs down. I would have thought that the wild dissonance of the wind instruments, rising and crashing discordantly over the subtle melody lines, bound together by a powerful rhythm section, would have had a shared ancestry with Nepali music and, as such, would have been right up his street. He preferred Dire Straits.

Zvonimir, or Zvoni as he came to be known, was the first to arrive. Zvoni was a Slovenian by birth, and perhaps that explained why he tended to trek with Valeri, the masseur. He was very sociable, had a great sense of humour and a profound sense of propriety, as would befit someone who had scaled to great heights in the business world. Above all he was genuine. At this stage I only knew two things about him, both of which I approved of.

Firstly, each night after supper he lit his pipe, and smoked a tobacco of the most delicious aroma, which transported me far away from the reality of the world I was in to one which only now existed in my dreams. When Zvoni lit up, I was almost there again. He had, in fact, brought seven pipes, one for each day of the week. He wasn't going to bring any of them but his wife had insisted. Well done, Mrs Grobenski! If ever I wanted to take up smoking, it was at around seven each evening. In fact Nat, a complete non-smoker, was so impressed, that he begged Zvoni to lend him a pipe and give him lessons!

The second thing about Zvoni which impressed me, was his insistence on detailed information. After the third morning, Dave had learned to conclude his briefings with: "Has anyone, apart from

Zvoni, got any questions?" Zvoni always had questions. Dave didn't like questions. They were generally the sort of things that the rest of us would like to know, but couldn't be bothered to ask. If Dave found his questions irksome, we found Dave's reaction predictable and highly amusing. If we had been the class and Dave the teacher, Zvoni would have spent a long time standing in the corner. Which, to Ray and I, was not a bad thing as it deflected some of the 'bad boy' heat away from us. Not that we cared that much.

Zvoni told me that he ran one marathon a year. When he had been accepted for The Everest, he had been elated as it was the ideal opportunity to combine his yearly marathon with a trip to somewhere he had yearned to visit all his life.

In addition to getting to know Zvoni a little better, that lunchtime we got to know our itinerary a little better.

\*

Over lunch, as we basked in the sun which still shone brightly, the subject of Namche was again raised. This was the oasis which lay a few days ahead, the promised land which Dieter had raved about, and those in our party who had been there before had misty eyes for.

For Dieter, apart from the race which had been a necessary evil to justify the trip, his time in Namche had been unsurpassable. Like a Greek tragedy, the real action revolved around Namche. There, we would meet some of the key players who had not yet stepped onto the stage and the plot would begin to unfold. From thence, rested, we would depart for the highlands leaving those behind who would greet us in our final hour when, flushed by success or ravaged by misfortune or foe, we would return to claim the prize and drink from the cup of fellowship awhile. We hoped. Or fall upon our swords. Offstage.

But now, like the horizon, the closer you got to it the further it seemed away.

"When exactly do we get to Namche?" asked Andrew, dragging Dave back reluctantly from his sepia daydream on the balcony of the Tawa lodge.

"Thursday we get to Namche."

"Excuse me, Dave, it says in the itinerary..." said Zvoni, with measured Teutonic precision...

"Wait for it," muttered Dave.

"...that we arrive in Namche on Wednesday evening."

"We get to Namche on Thursday. Always have done. Always will do."

Silence.

"Well can you explain why it says Wednesday in the itinerary?" asked Zvoni.

Dave couldn't, and instead counted out the days on his fingers, like a referee counting out a boxer on the canvas.

"Sunday, Tragsindho; Monday, Karikholi; Tuesday, Lukla; Wednesday, Monjo; and Thursday," he said triumphantly, raising his eyebrows, "Namche!"

The boxer was down, but not quite out.

"But there's no mention of Lukla in the itinerary," protested Zvoni, impervious to Dave's grotesquely narrow eyes and wide smile, "at least not until we trek back after the race to fly out."

"Let me see your itinerary." Now the referee was himself backing into the corner. Zvoni handed it to him, and he studied it in silence for a moment.

"Sunday, Tragsindho, yes; Monday, Karikholi, uh-huh; Tuesday, Phakding? Phakding? We've never done that before! What the hell's she playing at? No, it's Lukla on Tuesday, Monjo on Wednesday, and up the hill to Namche on Thursday. That's the way we've always done it, and that's what we're doing." The contest was over. The referee had abandoned it.

Annabel had been thumbing through her diary from her previous visit.

"Yep, that's what we did two years ago." Dave looked vaguely surprised to have received support from such an unlikely source.

"Anything meaty in there Annabel?" I asked.

"If there was, do you think I'd tell you, Marvin?" came the predictably acrid reply.

"It's all been prearranged with the trek crew, in any case," added Dave, as if to rubber stamp it.

"We could go from Lukla to Namche in a day though, couldn't we Dave?" suggested Annabel, voicing the general sentiments of the group.

"Well, if that's what you want to do," replied Dave with an air of conciliation which Captain Bligh might have been prudent to adopt.

"I'll see what I can do. But I can't guarantee that the tents and your kit will get to Namche on Wednesday. That's a two day trek, and we're not paying the porters double."

"Who gives a damn about tents and kit!" I said, with a false bravado brought on by three virtually sleepless nights. "We might as well trek through the night and get there quicker."

\*

The Rev. John G. Webster held a service which was both short and moving.

There was no sign of the monastery contingent, and by two o'clock, with people anxious to move on, around ten of us gathered by the river. It was, of course, optional, and only Lloyd and Andrew had been requested to attend by the film crew. This was so that John could do the bit about the gift of life, with reference to Andrew's noble donation of bone marrow to Lloyd.

This, he also had been requested to do by the film crew.

I hoped that the service had a somewhat better effect on our souls than it had on the weather, for by the time we set off, thick cloud had descended. As we climbed towards Ringmo, the mist was so thick that it could be classed as drizzle. Visibility was poor, and even the most ardent trekkers now only wanted to arrive at our evening's destination.

Beyond Ringmo, which is nothing more than a dozen or so white-walled houses scattered on the narrowly terraced mountainside, we entered a forested area. From here, a new trail to Namche Bazaar had been built in the 80s, which avoided many of the steep climbs which the old route had featured. Not long after, to my relief, I came to the Tragsindho cheese factory. This was not because I had any remote desire either to inspect or buy the cheese it produced, but because journey's end was not far off. Climbing onwards, I came to Tragsindho La which, at around 10,500 feet, is the second biggest pass in the district after Lamjura. On a clear day, the view ahead to Lukla, or back to Lamjura, would have been spectacular. But it wasn't a clear day, and there was no view. Instead, the cold and the damp of a dismal Sunday afternoon made me yearn for a hot bath and an armchair by a roaring fire.

Dropping down from the ridge in the mist, I almost stumbled into the Tragsindho gompa and, on the wings of a light wind, the eerie sound of a priest reciting a sutra flew across the mist to me.

There is little at Tragsindho, save the monastery and two lodges, and it wasn't hard to find our field. It was below the gompa on yet another slope, where Ray stood, Michelin man-like in his down jacket, passively surveying the dismal scene.

"This is it?" I asked him, hopeful that it wasn't.

"This is it," he confirmed.

"Been here long?" I asked again, knowing what the answer would be.

"I've only been in this bloody field long enough to know what a bloody cow must feel like."

There was no sign of tents, kit or fellow companions, but there was a hosepipe which carried water to the field from a stream above the monastery. I stripped off and had a shower. The water was ice cold and gave me a severe headache, as I stupidly decided to wash my hair and had it in a lather before I had realised just how cold the water actually was.

In the middle of my shower, Annabel arrived and took a picture of me hopping around the field in my underpants, with the hose, trying to get the suds out of my hair without inducing hypothermia. I wished that the water pressure was more than a trickle. Had it been, I would have been unable to resist the temptation to turn the hose on her. When I had finished I was numb, but relatively clean.

After a quick inspection of the *gompa*, the three of us ventured into the nearest of the two lodges. The *gompa* was a large colourful building attached to other smaller, functional buildings where the monks slept and ate. The entrance was the most interesting feature, with huge mossy stone steps and ornamented gateposts, behind which a curtain hung from an ornate pelmet so that the entrance resembled a stage.

The lodge in which we found ourselves resembled in part a private residence and in part a farm building. Both purposes it no doubt served, and there was considerable evidence to suggest that the *didi* had made a very, very, recent entry into the trade. Had it not been for the existence of a menu and tariff of prices, one might have concluded as recently as when she saw us walk in.

At least the stove made it warm and, very gradually, I began to regain some sensation in my limbs. Ray told us that he had trekked through Tragsindho earlier, mistaking it for Ringmo, and had got to the next settlement, Manidingma, which was a substantial village with a stone-paved street, three storey buildings, and comfortable-looking lodges. In fact, the logical place for a night-stop. To his horror, the realisation gradually dawned on him that this was not it, and reluctantly he made the return trek back to Tragsindho with its chanting monks and sloping field.

We were joined by Mike and Jerri Lee, the couple from California, and Zvoni. Nothing could induce me to join them in an order of chips, and I winced at the sight of the old lady slowly and deliberately slicing the potatoes into the rancid blackened fat which melted and spat in the pan. Being a man who likes to stick to something he knows, I ordered the vegetable noodle soup. It took over an hour to materialise, and when it did was a pale comparison to yesterday's. It took me almost as long to pay, and the others had long gone by the time I had completed my meal and paid.

I got into conversation with a young Danish couple in their early twenties, who spoke excellent English. The girl was blond and incredibly pretty, and was having a good time. The boy moaned about everything, and was not having a good time. She wanted to get to Base Camp, and if he ever saw any sort of camp again, it would be a day too soon. However, at this point they were still talking to each other.

\*

Halfway through supper, Rob Howard arrived. He had had an utterly harrowing day and was absolutely shagged. With his seventeen year old companion, he had yomped flat out back to Kenja, which had proved to be a totally wasted journey. Officialdom being what it is anywhere in the world, the police officer had steadfastly refused to issue him with evidence of the theft unless Rob could first produce evidence of ownership of what he had claimed to have had stolen. I doubted if anyone had brought receipts for their valuables with them. It simply wouldn't occur to you.

Yet ironically, at Kathmandu airport, the customs man had written above the visa in my passport that I possessed a video camera and a computer. Ironic, because if they got stolen this would do me absolutely no good, as my passport, with everyone else's, was back in Kathmandu in the offices of Highland Sherpa.

There was, according to Rob, a fairly frank and acrimonious exchange of views on the matter of evidence and ownership, before he set off up the long hill to Sete and Lamjura empty-handed.

This, and the miserable weather we were experiencing, led to a subdued atmosphere at supper. There was a temporary uplifting of spirits when I carried out my threat to play the recording of Simon's snoring which duly and deservedly won him The Hat.

The only people who appeared to have had a good day were the monastery party. The small group, including Tom, Simon, Wish, Alun and the Latins, who had made the detour to the Thupten Choeling monastery, had enjoyed an audience with the Lama, which included being blessed and sharing the mixed blessing of a brew of Tibetan butter tea. This potion, which was made from rancid butter, was apparently as revolting as it sounds.

Not only had they acquired spiritual cleansing, they had also acquired one of the Lama's dogs. Buddhist monks apparently rate the dog quite highly, and in fact regard them as reincarnations of their former colleagues. So, if one has to come back to this life as a dog, it is preferable to do so where the prevailing religious influence is Buddhist rather than Hindu. The latter, as I saw last night, have a more European approach to the treatment of man's best friend.

This particular beast, for some inexplicable reason, rated Wish quite highly, and had followed the group all the way to Tragsindho, despite their best efforts to shake him off.

He spent the night lying outside Wish's tent and was still snouting around the camp the next morning when we set off. Presumably, he eventually made his own way back to his master and spiritual mentor.

My stomach was making protesting noises and I had to make several unscheduled visits to the latrine tent during supper. One of these coincided with the minute's silence with which it had been agreed to mark Remembrance Day. Unfortunately, the involuntary noises which issued from my backside were clearly audible in the mess tent, making the minute's silence anything but a minute's silence.

I decided to turn in and have an early night, but we had an invasion in our tent in the form of Nat and Annabel who wanted to play cards, and it was after ten thirty when I eventually settled down to sleep.

For once, I went out like a light. I was awakened at two thirty by the sound of heavy rain pelting down on the tent. It was a pleasant sensation, lying snug and cosy in a warm, dry sleeping bag, until I remembered that I had left my towel, clean underwear and, more importantly, boots outside. I unzipped the tent flaps, and retrieved my sodden boots, emptying the reservoir of water from them. I was past caring about the rest.

"Dear Lord", I prayed, "give me a brain. And please put a user's manual in with it!"

# Tragsindho La to Lukla: "Stairway to Heaven or the Road to Hell?"

## Monday 15th November
## Tragsindho La to Karikholi: Speed Trekking with Ray

I set off in mist after breakfast. Today, for the first time, there was no morning sunshine. It was a foul day with visibility down to around twenty feet, but the damp misty conditions spared us from one fate worse than death – playing Dave's game of International Giants, Wizards and Dwarfs.

I caught up with Ray after half an hour and we moved together, alone, each barely recognising the presence of the other. We were intent on the path, our concentration totally focused on the rough and rocky trail that led relentlessly on towards something better.

We moved at a pace faster, I thought, than my previous jogging and yet we were only walking. Ray looked so sure footed, so agile and confident, I thought, that I would never maintain this pace; but also I knew that I would. There would be no falling behind. Although I'm sure that Ray didn't see it as such, it was a challenge, and the first challenge I had had in over a week, other than simple survival.

The first thing that told me that Ray had fallen was the sickening sound of skull against stone. I was wondering what his feet were doing up in the air when it happened. At first he didn't move, and I approached him terrified of what I would find. But, to my surprise, there was no immediate evidence of blood, his eyes were open, and he was conscious. He lay there, shocked, assessing the damage, then, miraculously, he got to his feet, stunned but apparently uninjured.

"You okay?" I asked.

"I've had worse," he replied, shaking his head. He was a tough little guy, and I imagined he had regularly and voluntarily run into obstacles just as hard as the boulder he had head-butted on each Saturday of his Rugby career.

"If I ever do this again, I'm going to bring my cricket helmet," I told him.

"If I ever bloody do this again, I'm going to have myself committed!" he said.

He had a long, thin cut on his forehead, which in itself was no problem. It was the concussion that may be lurking behind the injury which was the worry. He hadn't lost consciousness, his head was clearing rapidly, and he appeared to be in control of his faculties.

We trekked on through Manidingma, which for Ray had the element of déjà vu about it. Neither of us could understand why this solid and prosperous-looking village had not been used for last night's stop. It had everything, *gompa* apart, which Tragsindho hadn't, especially flat ground where we could have camped. It had taken us less than an hour to reach it from Tragsindho, and that included Ray's fall.

Leaving Manidingma, we rounded a corner and were confronted with the curious sight of a dead mule lying across the path. It looked to have recently departed this life, but its bloated belly showed signs of a build up of gases from the decomposition of its last meal.

We leapt over it with a strange detachment.

"Another victim of this bloody path," commented Ray.

"At least we're ahead of the kitchen boys. If they'd got here first, he would have ended up in tonight's stew."

"You never know, he'd probably taste a bloody sight better than what they usually put in it!"

We were moving together now, still fast, but no more as strangers alone in a strange land. I would talk, and he would listen and rest, and then it would be his turn.

The miles went by, as we descended alongside the hillside farming fields. We passed through Phuleli, a small Rai community where the women hang a strange collection of rings from as many parts of their head as they can find space for. If Ray was being more cautious than before his fall, the difference was negligible as we hurtled down the hill towards the Dudh Kosi. On several occasions, I felt my ankle turn, placed crudely on a hazardous stone by a cumbersome boot. This is crazy, I thought; one bad twist, one bad fall, and all this toil, all this deprivation, all this misery will have been for nothing. I would be out of the race. Assuming, of course, I had shoes in which to run it.

We paused on the western bank of the Dudh Kosi. There was a *bhatti*, and we drank tea and ate chocolate before crossing the relatively new suspension bridge which replaced the one which was swept away in the summer of 1985 when a glacial lake high up in the Thame region overflowed. Most of the bridges over both the Bhote Kosi and the Dudh Kosi had been destroyed, causing considerable distress throughout the region.

The Dudh Kosi was a significant landmark on our journey. Henceforth, instead of travelling west, we would be heading north, towards the big mountains and our ultimate journey's end. Although the trail continued to snake eastwards away from the river, from Lukla we would follow the waterway, crossing and recrossing it, with the worst of the climbs behind us.

The Dudh Kosi is the biggest river in the Solu Khumbu. Its source is in the Imja and Lhotse Nup Glaciers, the former giving its name to the river until, at Phunki Teng, way above Namche Bazaar, it merges with the Dudh Pokhari, whose source is beyond Gokyo.

It was a measure of the growing understanding between Ray and me that the lunch stop was never mentioned. In fact, I didn't even know where it was and I don't suppose Ray did either. Over the bridge, the climb was gradual at first, until we reached Jubing.

Jubing, with its grass-roofed houses built in a mezzanine style, looked bizarrely out of place, resembling a low-altitude temperate area. From here the climb became less gradual. Oddly, I found the uphill less demanding than the pounding my knees had taken scurrying down towards the river. Concentration was easier too. With frequent stone stairways, foot placement became less demanding. Downhill, it had been more complex than landing a 747 without radar in thick fog.

We paused only once when the path divided. Ray wanted to take the lower trail, which ran off to the right, but I persuaded him that we should stay high. To me, logic dictated that, as we had to gain nearly fifteen hundred feet between the river and Karikholi, we didn't want to start losing altitude after Jubing. I was right, but I felt only concern for the future with the realisation that Ray's route finding appeared to be as bad as mine.

The path levelled and improved as we reached a long ridge which led us on a flat road and into Karikholi. I glanced at my watch. It had just passed eleven o'clock. We had reached the night-stop.

"What do we do now?" I asked Ray.

"We find a half-decent bloody lodge, get cleaned up and have a graze."

"Sounds good to me!"

We didn't bother to explore the village. Towards the centre, there was a festival in progress, which came as no great surprise. We therefore opted for the first lodge we came to, on the basis that here it would be quieter and the further we were from the festival, the less we would get hassled. It was a clean and welcoming lodge and the family who owned it were friendly and helpful. They knew we were here for the day and that others would come, so they were keen to please.

We booked hot showers and I bought a razor and some clean socks. I had left my razor in Kathmandu, welcoming the rare opportunity afforded by the distance from my wife to grow a beard. Now, the stubble of almost a week irritated me, and I yearned to be clean and smooth again.

I bought the socks because I had been impressed by the logic in John Matesich's system. He would wear a pair of socks for three days, until they were almost walking by themselves, then give them away to the porters. I wasn't sure if I could bring myself to do the second part.

"Here you go boy, here's a present for you. Now, close your eyes. Oh, so you've guessed it already. My, that was clever! How did you know it was a pair of dirty socks?"

"But", he said, "they were very grateful all the same."

I realised by now that it was pointless trying to wash clothes. In this climate, without sun, they did not dry. So I would buy socks when I found them.

And so we washed, ate, talked, wrote our diaries, and drank, drank, and drank. Flask after flask of lemon tea came and went. We couldn't get enough of the stuff. The lodge owner informed us that the most important Hindu festival, the Tihar, better known as the Festival of Lights or Deepavali, was in progress. The festival lasts for five days and honours different animals on each successive day. On day two, dogs are honoured and although Hindus normally only honour dogs with a smart kick on the behind, this is the annual occasion when they suddenly remember that, in the afterworld, the dog is supposed to guide departed souls across the river of the dead.

One day of immunity each year seems like a raw deal in exchange for performing such an important task. Settle down to sleep at the hearth in your garland of flowers and tikas, only to be woken with a kick next morning to the realisation that the gloves are off for the next three hundred and sixty-four days.

We received the anticipated 'fleece the tourists' visitation from a rather intoxicated splinter group from the festival. They were all men. Some young, but most elderly, who had decided they needed a break from the celebrations and had staggered to the outskirts of the village. There, they chanced upon two tourists who would only be too happy to pay for the next round in exchange for a bit of stomping, shuffling, staggering and discordant chanting.

But in their condition, they were about as entertaining and as much value for money as a group of England football supporters erratically singing in a bar in Amsterdam, but of course without the accompanying menace. Both Ray and I turned on our Walkmans, and buried ourselves in our diaries. When I looked up again, they were still there, beaming at us benevolently with innocence in their eyes and hope in their hearts.

"What d'you think they'd take to bloody shut up?" Ray asked.

"Let's try twenty rupees," I suggested, reluctantly willing to agree to extortion for a bit of peace. Their spokesman didn't seem to have been insulted by the gift of the two bills. He put his hands together and bowed his head.

"You like?" he asked, perhaps out of surprise. "You like flowers? We have flowers." He produced two garlands of bright yellow petals, similar to those with which we had been welcomed at the airport. Before Ray or I could object, we had been wreathed by the garlands, and parted with a further thirty rupees each for the privilege.

"Still," I said, when they had departed financially more secure than before they had met us, "at least you know your money's not going to finance terrorism or line the pockets of the drug barons. At least, I can't see any 'support the IRA' stickers on these flowers, and I doubt if these damned things are hallucinatory!"

The others arrived around three o'clock, and eventually the tents were put up on a narrow crescent of a terrace at the far end of the village. At least it was flat.

I was surprised to observe how large Karikholi was. In all, there are probably eighty buildings, including the rice farms in the surrounding hills, and at the centre of the village there was a thriving community of at least twenty dwellings, several lodges, teahouses and a store.

That night, there was no room for the mess tent on the narrow crescent and the porters had learned from their unhappy experience at Sete. The food was cooked outside and we ate inside the nearest lodge. This resembled an alpine cabin and was decorated with white-peaked climbing posters to give it a real ambience of the adventure which, we hoped, lay not far ahead. The surroundings were convivial, and there was an excellent atmosphere with another rich bout of joke telling from Richard, Lloyd and, in particular, Bryan English. Even Wish told a joke, although I can't remember what it was about, which had most of us howling.

I slept well, conscious that we were lower at two thousand and four metres. This was good for acclimatisation.

## Tuesday 16th November
## Karikholi to Lukla: More Mist and Bad Guts

The mist had not shifted, in fact, if anything, it had worsened. It was another miserable morning.

Breakfast was in the lodge and hardly worth waiting for. The weather had done much to destroy the feeling of optimism of the previous evening. People jostled businesslike and uncaring to get at what they wanted. The realities of another damp dawn filtered its cold grey light on people who had no time for each other, scurrying to fill their stomachs and be on their way. The same people who had joked and laughed in the warm intimacy of a good hot lamp-lit meal and the prospect of what tomorrow may bring. People who now felt let down and cheated by the miserable conditions.

I didn't know it at the time but, leaving the room, I had my last good fart for several days, which crackled like thunder around the little lodge, much to Wish's annoyance. I set off in my wet Lycra bottoms and thin vest, which was now my staple kit for trekking. I would put on my thermals for breakfast then summon the courage to change into what I had worn the previous day, still wet with the sweat and mist that clung to clothes like dew to the grass on a cold autumn's morning. A touch of Vaseline on the more sensitive places prevented painful chaffing, as another day of profuse sweating began.

Ray had gone on already. He didn't bother much with breakfast, so I said I'd catch him later. He was not at ease in camp and I didn't want my lassitude in getting ready to add to his frustration at the slow progress we were making.

I went up the first four hundred metre climb very quickly, to warm up, and soon saw Ray ahead. My stomach was very dicey and protested constantly, making noises similar to an out of control coffee percolator. I had to make frequent stops by the side of the path, but only passed fluid and wind. I trekked on with Ray in the mist, with knotted guts contorted by concern at my rapid deterioration.

It was indescribably depressing, the only pleasure coming from the perverse pleasure of pushing our bodies to go faster still. Again I worried about the consequences of a fall and came close to disaster on several occasions. It was an acceptable risk. Our plan was to get to Lukla as fast as we could and rest up. Lukla bore the promise of comfortable warm lodges and the hope of something resembling a toilet.

We crossed the Khari La, the pass between the Solu and the Khumbu districts. This should have been another landmark on our journey, but we were unaware of it. Head down, hell-bent over the loose stone highway, all I was aware of were my calculations as to where to place my feet and whether the ball of wind in my stomach would pass or required a stop.

We broke at Phuiyan, which was the lunch stop, for tea and biscuits. From here it is possible to see Lukla airstrip – on a clear day. We were joined by Alun and his camera and, while we waited for tea, Ray and I gave short and not very positive interviews. Neither of us felt like singing the praises of either the cooks or our leaders and this was my second interview to end up on the editing floor.

I made the mistake of using the lodge 'toilet', which was precariously balanced on the hillside below the lodge. As I shifted my weight to the left to complete the paperwork, I froze as I felt the pathetic little structure shift to the left with me. I got out quickly, but not before I had pictured myself cartwheeling down the mountain amid debris, and a suitable epitaph on my grave brought a wry smile to my face:

> Here lies a man who was once so fit,
> Killed by the need to have a shit.

*Down the hill went the loo when he moved his feet,*
*And all for the want of a toilet seat.*

\*

Between Phuiyan and Surkhe is the most uninhabited stretch of the entire Everest Highway. It doesn't merit much being said of it, so I won't. But from June to September each year, when the monsoon arrives, it becomes leech city, populated with millions of the little sticky things you least want to find in your sleeping bag. It is a waste of land, a waste land, conjuring jumbled thoughts of Eliot's *The Waste Land*:

> *...breeding...*
> [leeches] *out of the dead land, mixing*
> *Memory and desire, stirring*
> *Dull roots with spring rain.*

We belted down the hill to Surkhe and came to a tributary of the Dudh Kosi, the Surkhe Khola. This was crossed by a substantial wooden bridge, beautifully constructed with lattice-framed sides and thick wooden panels. The sort of bridge that my local town council would be only too happy to spend thousands on to enhance the image of dog-shit alley, and local yobbos would be only to happy to deface in minutes.

On the other side of the bridge was a large lodge, which we didn't take much notice of, but beyond it there was something of which we took a great deal of notice.

This was the divide in the path. Take the old road, the path that goes straight on, and you will travel through Chaumrikharka, on to Phakding, and ultimately to Namche. Take the high road, and you will go to Lukla. Ray and I looked wistfully at the lower path. There was no mistaking it, Phakding was marked on a rock with an arrow pointing to the lower path.

"Seems a bloody shame," said Ray, voicing what we both felt. "We could be in Namche in three bloody hours from here."

We would have been going some, and then some more, but we could have done it. Instead we took the stone stairway, and began the long haul up to Lukla, almost one thousand feet above us.

"Stairway to Heaven, eh?" I jibed, hauling myself over the uneven steps and cursing as my toe kicked a boulder.

"More like the road to bloody Hell!"

There were no more jibes as we left each other to the mental and physical battle of getting up that hill. High above, in the mist, I heard a helicopter and my mind registered surprise that anything would fly in these conditions. 'It must be a bad stretcher case,' I thought.

My stomach was hell, and I felt the first telltale signs of dehydration set in. The fluid lost, and unreplaced, and the effort required to keep up had taken its toll. I strained every ounce of energy to stay with Ray. It was just up the hill, it won't be far. It can't be that far!

Oh Jesus, it can't be that far! The pace was relentless, the path remorseless.

'Now let me see if I've got this right,' said a voice in my head. 'First of all you voluntarily agree to run a marathon from the foot of Mount Everest. You then set out to walk for over a week with minimal comforts and even more minimal sanitation arrangements, in foul weather conditions. Then, to cap it all, of your own volition mind you, you team up with a fanatical mad Kiwi bastard who doesn't know the meaning of the word stroll!'

Enter those familiar little puffy white clouds that float on the periphery of my vision to tell me that I'm running on empty; the needle has dropped off the gauge. It's time to stop; too late for water. Soon they will grow matchstick legs, and become the woolly sheep of children's drawings; they walk, staring, and bleating across the threshold of my consciousness so that I begin to lose touch with reality. And then the sheets, the white-starched sterile sheets of hospital beds; bright, white light, and blood-drained doctor's face looking dispassionately down towards the chasm of my indifferent surrender.

At last we stopped.

"Are we there?" I asked. I hadn't got as far as the sheets. Beyond the sheets, beckons a vortex; my white-out, my goodnight, my all systems shut down. And, thank God, I've never got that far – yet. But I've come close.

We stood in a level clearing, amongst man-high boulders of contrasting irregularity, yet with some sort of acquiescence to methodical order that was curiously familiar. It could have been a

Celtic burial barrow on a Cornish moor, or a cairn on a Scottish island. It added to my feeling of disorientation.

"We're near," said Ray. "I think the end of the runway's just above here." The clearing was a maze of intricate trails, each trail leading to a clamber over boulders with the promise of a path which ended abruptly in nothing. We had lost the path. In my confused state of mind it felt as if someone, or something, didn't want us to find it.

"We must have come off the path lower down, before we got to that clearing," Ray said. "Shit, man, you look bloody rough!"

"I feel bloody rough!" I replied, and dived behind a rock to pass more fluid, as if confirmation was required. I rummaged through a pocket of my rucksack, and found a Power bar, half of which I crammed into my mouth and eventually swallowed. I drank the last of my water, and began to feel a little better.

"If the runway's above us", I said, thinking aloud, "then why don't we go that way?" I pointed to the boulders. There was no foliage – experience had taught me never, ever to follow a barely perceptible path into undergrowth. And, there was something about this stony hill that suggested it had been cleared for a purpose. It wasn't much to go on.

"Why not?" Ray shrugged his shoulders, and we started to clamber over the mossy rocks. Neither of us wanted to admit to the possibility that we might be lost, and neither of us wanted to go back down to look for the path lower down. We had been concentrating so hard on covering the ground quickly that we had missed a vital clue and had come off the main drag.

We climbed for about ten minutes. There was no discernible path, but enough evidence to suggest that we weren't the first to take this route. Wherever it may lead. We ploughed up two hundred feet of scree-like rubble and, through the mist, could see the crest of the hill ahead of us. Whatever lay beyond that would tell us if my hunch had been right. It could just be a spur, with the mountain running on beyond it, shrouded in trees, through which there would be no passage. I tried not to think about that. Or, it could be the runway. And, of course, if it were the runway it was just possible that there might be a plane trundling down it.

Cautiously, we stuck our heads over the top. This was it. There was no spur beyond it. Ahead of us, disappearing into the mist was a flattish expanse of hardened stone-strewn earth, forty metres in width and sloping gently upwards in the direction we had come. On either side of it was a deep ditch, and beyond that stone walls, more for demarcation than to restrict access. Beyond that was scrubland, little fields with low stone walls.

"Welcome to Lukla Airport," I said, caustically. "Home of 'Gut Rot' Airlines. Enjoy your stay in the Khumbu. And don't forget to visit our well-stocked duty free shops and select your gifts from our enticing range of luxury goods for the discerning traveller."

"Is this the bloody runway?"

"This must be it," I said, praying that I would be wrong.

"I wouldn't ride a bloody mountain bike on that surface, let alone land a bloody plane on it!"

We decided to walk up the right side. It was ironic that we had entered town along the runway – there was a strong possibility I would die on that runway, I thought.

It was doubtful whether this was the accepted way to enter town, but at least if we followed the runway, it must take us somewhere. Out of the mist ahead of us we saw a large stupa which, in its own way, was comforting, as it confirmed that we were still in Nepal.

In front of it, straddling the wall, half in the ditch, as if in the act of reciting its final mantra, lay the carcass of a crashed Twin Otter. Its shell had been picked clean, presumably by the Airline company, of anything that could be used again: doors, windows, seats, all things mechanical in the cockpit, wiring, everything. There was nothing left. Like the sheep on my nightmare Dartmoor run, white boned, totally gutted by the carrions of the night, left as a macabre warning – as if anything else was required to further suspend my disbelief at this tasteless joke of a landing strip.

What we couldn't know then was that, hidden by the mist on the far side of the runway, a further two aircraft lay stricken. Only, their fuselages were twisted and contorted, testimony to human as well as mechanical injury beyond repair. Propellers, wheels and broken wings scattered to the four winds, beyond even the ingenuity of the resourceful and penurious airline. Left as a savage reminder that, if the mountains don't get you, something else just might.

I had already witnessed how the Nepalis took a perverse delight in the Westerner's stock reaction to air travel in and out of the region.

Ray was actually looking forward to his flight. I had seen nothing to convince me that any accounts I had heard had actually understated the experience.

The end of the airstrip come into sight, and with it much of the town. On our left was the control tower. There, the wire fence was crossed by a stile which served no purpose other than to slow down the flow of people crossing the runway at any one time to and from the bulk of the town.

To the right was the apron, where fresh-faced, clean-socked trekkers and climbers would disembark, the scent of their morning bath oil still on their skin. This also doubled as the town football pitch, though this was probably more for the Westerners to work off the frustrations of days spent waiting for the mist to clear.

The airport building was behind the apron, and this side of town looked to have the pick of the lodges. Logic would dictate that if you were in the lodge trade, where better to be than where your clientele could roll out and then roll back in, having learned that their flight would again not be going today?

It was to the left that we turned first. We had no idea where the camp was to be pitched, but that was the least of our concerns. I remembered Dave saying something about a Sherpa Coffee Shop, which was where we were to meet.

Ray wanted to find the Highland Sherpa rep to arrange flights for his wife and kids back to Kathmandu. His initial plan had been to trek back to Jiri with them after the race, but wild horses would not have dragged him down that path again.

Lukla is a dreary, wet collection of lodges, stores and weary, irritable travellers wandering through the muddy streets killing time until the weather clears and planes can land.

Over thirty years ago, four hundred metres of the southern slope was "levelled" to create the runway which we had walked up. This shot Lukla's status from 'Mutzville, Arizona', to 'Sin City, Nevada' almost overnight. There are joints that call themselves 'Bar', a discotheque; there is a Holiday Inn, and even a lodge which is reputed to have satellite TV. I was dubious. It had, in fact, an appendage which could have been a satellite dish. But it could equally well have been something that had been cannibalised from one of the crashed planes and made to look like a satellite dish.

All this makes the place sound rather grand. Not so. Both the runway and a generation of cheap travel have made this wilderness accessible to those on a modest budget. The physical infrastructure is inadequate, and the cultural tapestry of the town confused, finding its dual role of gateway to the world's finest mountain scenery and home to the indigenous Sherpa, Rai, Tamang and Magar tribes hard to equate.

With an open honesty and the same ready smile that is seen throughout Nepal, they watched their town adapt to meet the needs and desires of those who passed through it, not those who lived there. There's gold in them there hills, but mining it brought a virus of deceit and dishonesty that spread like the dental decay ushered in with the arrival of the first plane. Trust is a dream, fading fast. Here, everything, not just the toilets, are locked.

There is even a jail.

Higher prices, and fewer scruples, are to be found in Lukla than anywhere else in the Solu Khumbu, perhaps throughout Nepal.

The smiling faces of the lodge owners are poker-player expressionless now. They are selling, you are buying; you want to get out of their town but can't. Town is like a huge stagnant airport lounge, on a permanent delay. It reminded me of the scene in *Star Wars* where the traders, aliens and criminals from all corners of the universe are banged up in a bar in a small far flung trading post. Tempers frequently erupt, petty squabbles break out. Boredom and frustration make scoundrels of us all.

You watch your back in Lukla. We had been warned that most theft is perpetrated by Western travellers and not the Nepalis. That probably didn't make Rob Howard any happier.

We wandered through the town looking for the Highland Sherpa rep's office, which we established was in the offices of the Royal Nepal Airlines. He wasn't in. Ray decided to come back later, and we headed for the east side of town and a decent lodge to shower and rest up in. The street was muddy and crowded. A goat scattered a gathering of hens pecking amongst the stones at the entrance to a store. I startled as they flapped and squawked in front of us. A smiling boy, with a long stick between his legs and another across his shoulders beneath his jacket, veered across the street pretending to be a plane. He was the only thing that would fly today.

A chance meeting with an old codger, who probably worked for the place and did a sideline in selling timeshare apartments, took us to the Buddha lodge, which was close to the Sherpa Coffee House. We could leave our kit in a dormitory, have a hot shower and a good meal.

There was a lounge with a lovely warm stove, and although my shower was cold, I soon warmed up, hunched over the stove. Ray decided not to bother with a shower.

We ordered soup and yak steaks with chips. The steak was chewy but quite tasty and filling. I felt better for eating, despite having to make three dashes to the toilet during the main course. We were joined by John from Lancashire, who had been climbing in the Gokyo region, and had already been stranded in Lukla for two days. He had just been informed by the airline office that five days hence would be his earliest departure.

The system works like this: you trek in from Namche in bad weather, planes cannot land; there is of course no radar in either Lukla or Kathmandu. You wait, the weather clears the next day, but those who are booked to fly out do so, and you go to the back of the queue. There are no valid flight rosters – often those prepared to donate the most whisky, goats, or T-shirts will get to the head of the queue.

We persuaded John that, if he was prepared to bribe his porter enough, and prepared to put up with hell for a few days, he could trek back to Jiri in four days. Ray reckoned it could be done in two, but you wouldn't get a porter to stay with you. A further day on the bus sharing the journey with sheep, goats and the motley collection of fowl that people attached to their persons on public transport, would get him back to Kathmandu in time for his flight home.

In the Buddha lodge, there was something that resembled sanitation. Upstairs, a toilet with a porcelain footplate, though of course no seat, vaguely reminded me of civilisation. My stomach was showing signs of further rapid deterioration. I passed liquid which squirted everywhere, and had to pay, on average, four visits per hour.

I made the mistake of rinsing my hands in a bucket of fluid which I suddenly realised was intended to be sluiced down the toilet. Still, it was disinfectant.

The other mistake I made still haunts me. In front of the toilet was a large tin bin which contained bits of torn up toilet paper.

'How very considerate of them', I thought, 'to provide toilet paper.' I was, however, at a loss to know why they had taken the trouble to tear it into wipe-sized strips. It was not until my third visit, with the supply rapidly diminishing, that I caught sight of something curiously suspicious. Something brown. I took a closer look. What I saw made me yelp in horror like a wounded animal.

It had been used before. My God! It had been used before! I looked away and grimaced, dropping the paper as if it had suddenly become alive. It can't have been. Something must have been dropped into the tin by mistake. I looked again. It had been used. By someone else. It was liberally smeared with excrement. Shite almighty! I had been wiping my bum with paper that someone else had used! But what idiot had put it in the tin containing clean, unused, virgin, what one would normally wipe one's bum with, toilet paper?

And then it dawned on me. The tin never had contained clean toilet paper. It was not even intended for clean toilet paper. On the contrary, it was intended as a recipient for dirty toilet paper. And now that I came to think of it, it almost screamed out "Oi! I'll have that, thank you! Not down the loo, stupid. Who d'you think's going to pick it up!"

I got out my toilet paper, which luckily I always carried on my person, soaked it in the disinfectant provided in the bucket, doused myself with the stuff, then gave my nether regions a lengthy scrub. Then I bathed my hands. Right up to the elbows.

I considered the list of diseases I was likely to have contracted. The list was doubtless a long one, and the prognosis not good. I considered yet another appropriate epitaph for my tombstone :

> *Here lies a man whose health did taper,*
> *Struck down by the use of toilet paper.*
> *For he didn't know, nor was it planned,*
> *To use a piece that was second-hand.*

This lodge was entirely geared for young Westerners facing long delays and is directly opposite the departure hut. Loud rock music blared from the ghetto blaster on the bar. The choice of music was deferentially left to the discretion of the customers. One could either select from the assortment of tapes collected over the years from forgetful travellers, or play one of your own.

Ray and I cheered up when someone put on some vintage Hendrix – presumably by mistake. It was not universally popular, particularly with the Rev. Webster, playing bridge with Nat, Adrienne and Mike Silpa next to me.

"Can someone put that ruddy cat out of its misery!"

"Philistine!" I said, and returned to my diary.

Later, we moved out into the night to our tents, placed in a muddy field at the back of an impressive-looking building which we gathered was a lodge. The windows had glass panes – some lodge! Had I known earlier that we were to camp so close to such a magnificent-looking building, I would have gone in search of a room hours ago.

We were told to use the hotel toilet which, although it had no seat, actually had a flush. Next to the toilet cubicle, was a room with an electric light and a sink with a tap which, to my disbelief, issued hot water! Luxury!

After soup and the inevitable pop corn, we retired to our tents. No one wanted, or could be bothered to wait for, the stew, pasta and sludge.

Lukla, of course, now has electricity, as do most reasonably large villages. At least, for some of the day.

But by now we would all have swapped electricity for a little sunshine.

# Lukla to Namche Bazaar: "Heaven Knows I'm Miserable Now!"

## Wednesday 17th November

I slept well, until four thirty. This was my best night's sleep yet. I slipped on my running shoes and went for a pee, a suitable distance from the other tents. Good toilet or not, an awkward and slippery stile lay between the camp and the lodge, so a visit there would only be for more serious and urgent calls of nature.

I crawled back into the tent and removed my shoes. Simon was still asleep; there was over an hour until "bed tea". I was wide awake and feeling good, with that darkest-hour-before-dawn certainty that today would somehow be better.

I had got through the night without interruptions from my stomach and was optimistic that whatever had ailed me might have departed. I lay back, and switched on my Walkman, also optimistic that today was another milestone. We would arrive at Namche, the threshold of our ambitions and the gateway to the world's mightiest mountains. Perhaps, more importantly, we would get off this wretched path for three days and have a chance to lick our wounds.

I became aware that there was a strange and unpleasant smell emanating from somewhere near the door of the tent. It was the unmistakable smell of human excrement. Cautiously, I crawled out of my bag, and snaked towards the bottom of the tent. The smell grew stronger until it was almost unbearable. I turned on my torch, and examined my right shoe. Nothing there. I checked my left shoe. What I saw confirmed my worst fear. It was caked in shit, absolutely covered in the stuff. And not just the sole. Some of it had got into the holes on the side which house those little reflective bits – the bits that reflect the headlights of the car that is about to run you down.

I was about to put on my Buffalo jacket and venture out to clean the offending shoe, when I realised that the inside of my jacket must have come into contact with my shoe and it too was contaminated. The fleecy interior lining had acquired an unwanted dressing that glistened like peanut butter on burnt toast.

I was just wondering if things had got as bad as they could get, when they got worse. To my horror, I noticed that it was smeared on my sleeping bag and on the corner of Simon's sleeping bag.

An hour later, I had removed most of it from most of my shoe. I had done what I could with the sleeping bags and my jacket, but as the only solution for the latter was washing, I decided that smelling of shit was better than being cold and wet.

Simon, of course, was not overjoyed to wake in a sleeping bag that smelt somewhat different from the one in which he had gone to sleep. Graciously, he accepted that the blame lay not with me but with the person who had deposited their load so close to the tents. And we would never know who was the perpetrator of that crime.

Or so we thought. But when dawn's first grey light drew me to the scene of the crime, like a victim trying to lay the ghost of a particularly nasty assault, all the evidence pointed to one tent. For right outside the tent occupied by John Dunning and Mike Harper, right on the main thoroughfare from the field to the lodge, was the offending pile, now squashed flat and bearing the unmistakable tread from the sole of my shoe.

"Are you awake?" I roared.

No reply. If they weren't, they soon would be. I shook the tent. Someone stirred inside.

"Two sugars in each, please, and no milk."

"Bollocks milk. Which one of you buggers did this!" I called to the inert occupants, shaking the tent more from frustration than anger.

"Eh, what's that? Morning Rich, did what?" replied John, unzipping the flaps.

"Did that," I said, pointing to the offending excrement.

"Eh, hold on, let me get me glasses, I can't see nothing without me specs on." He rummaged for a moment, and returned with a pair of spectacles. "Oh shit!" he observed astutely, "That were me. Me bloody torch battery packed up and I were dying for a shit. I 'adn't a clue where I were, but I thought I were closer t'ut fence than that. Looks like someone stood in it!"

"I stood in it," I replied impassively. "Do you own a dog?"
"No."
"Just as bloody well!" I said, and walked away. "Talk about shit in your own backyard!" I added, to no one in particular.

\*

Breakfast that morning was in the mess tent. It was now actually raining and, mercifully, the kitchen crew had persuaded the porters to delay the packing up of the tent until we had eaten. Had it been a 'normal' day on the trek, we would have breakfasted in the rain. But this was no normal day. Today we would reach Namche, and the mess tent would be stowed away for a while. Despite the weather, there was a high octane, end of term frivolity around the breakfast table. It was impossible not to be affected by it.

I even managed to raise a little enthusiasm for The Hat ceremony, held over from the previous evening, and related the sorry and cautionary tale of my close encounter with John Dunning's faeces. I could, at least, repay him with the inconvenience of carrying the stupid thing in his pack for a day.

However, Andrew Burgess kindly related a tale that I had been trying to keep very much under my hat. Namely, that in the Sherpa Lodge last night my computer had once again inexplicably taken leave of its senses and, with them, had taken the first week of my diary into oblivion, which I had just about replaced following its previous unexplained aberration.

This, combined with the fact that having stepped in the shit was considered a greater folly than having put it there (something which I hotly disputed), resulted in having The Hat added to my luggage.

Still, they say that every cloud has a silver lining. From then on, John Dunning was known as John 'Dunging'.

\*

At the morning briefing, Dave told us that the lunch-stop would be at Benkar, on a field by the bank of the Dudh Kosi, by which time we would be well on the way towards Namche Bazaar.

"And I'd be grateful if those buggers who fly past the lunch-stop five minutes after leaving here", he looked at Ray and me, "would be kind enough to wait at the lunch-stop. Unless of course, you want to pay your own entry fee into the National Park."

We didn't.

I've heard it said that lightning strikes somewhere in the world twenty-five times every second. It must have been rampant in Lukla that morning, for Dave's next statement was like a bolt from the blue. He casually informed us that this was as far as our video cameras went, unless we paid the one hundred dollar fee which permitted us to film within the National Park. I was utterly staggered. I had heard rumours about a fee for use of a video camera, but one hundred dollars was a hell of a lot of money. I didn't have that kind of money to spare.

"What happens if you don't, or can't pay?" I asked.

"Then you either leave your camera at the entry post to collect on the way out, or you use it illegally and risk the consequences."

"Which are?" I asked. I had a sneaking feeling that Dave was enjoying this. Ray and I didn't fit in; we didn't laugh at his jokes and, by voting with our feet, we didn't exude confidence in his leadership. We didn't salute. And that niggled him. That really pissed him off. And now my independence was vulnerable.

"A five hundred dollar fine, and confiscation of the camera."

"Shit!" Sue had a video camera, and faced the same predicament. "What are the chances of getting caught?" she asked.

"Oh, the chances are pretty good," was the predictable reply.

We asked Ron Isles if he would list our cameras with those of the film crew and get them through under the corporate fee. I was even prepared to bung him twenty or thirty dollars for his trouble, but he wouldn't hear of it. They'd had enough trouble with officialdom at the airport without further complicating things and putting the film in jeopardy. Which was fair enough, I supposed. But something in the pompous way he said it raised my hackles.

The problem was that we looked at the trip from two very different standpoints. To the film crew it was a job. They had an obligation to produce something good enough to tempt the moguls of nationwide prime time television. Their day extended long into the night, reviewing the day's footage, and planning for tomorrow. They worked hard. To us it was a holiday, a once in a lifetime opportunity.

I felt like saying that if that was the thanks we got for our cooperation in giving interviews, testing microphones and hanging around until they got the shots they required, then he could go piss into the wind the next time they wanted to put me in front of the camera.

I felt like saying it, but I didn't. Because, like it or not, as much as they needed us, I needed them. If I was going to part with one hundred dollars for the privilege of using my camera higher up, I needed the use of their petrol-powered generator to charge my batteries. Without this, when the altitude rose and the temperature dropped, even my heavy duty battery packs would pack as effective a punch as I would against Mike Tyson, and would last about as long as I would last in the ring against him.

If I alienated the film crew, I might as well set fire to my one hundred dollars with the first flash of the battery low indicator.

Anyhow, Sue said it for me. The frustrations of the last few days of sunless discomfort and relentless head-down foot-slogging were all focused into a short, angry outburst at this latest unsolicited blow to morale.

I obtained a promise from Ron that my batteries would be charged, at his convenience. Satisfied with that, I decided to pay. It was only money, after all. The insignificance of one hundred dollars when compared with a lifetime's regret at having a camera and not using it was immeasurable.

I could not risk the fine and, more importantly, as I had borrowed the camera, were it to be confiscated I would have to buy a new one. To leave it at the entrance to the Park was out of the question.

Moreover, I knew I could not use it illicitly. I may have a curious sense of propriety over certain things, but I believe in paying my way. Also, I didn't want to spent the rest of the holiday looking over my shoulder for little brown men waiting to pounce on unlicensed users of video cameras.

Having decided to pay, the next question was how. To pay in cash would leave me considerably short of funds for the latter part of the trip. They sure as hell would not accept a cheque or credit cards. The only alternative was to borrow the money, and thrash my Visa card on our return to Kathmandu, but who would have one hundred dollars to spare?

"I don't suppose anyone's got one hundred dollars to spare until we get back to Kathmandu?" I asked, pessimistically, expecting the question to clear the tent as effectively as one of my farts had done two mornings ago.

To my surprise, John Matesich peeled off five twenty dollar notes from a huge wad he produced from an equally gargantuan wallet.

"Thanks. I owe you." I meant it. I kissed the money, and almost kissed him.

"You'll get it as soon as we hit civilisation."

"No problem, buddy. You give it back when you're ready."

John was already bankrolling Nat, whose wallet had been pinched way back in Kathmandu. I wondered what they paid teachers in California. A damned sight more than they did in Devon.

A huge surge of relief washed over me. It was like losing something irreplaceable, then suddenly finding it right there, just where you expected to see it.

It was also important to me that Dave knew I had paid the fee. I wanted him to see that I was squeaky clean in the moral integrity department. I didn't want any little innuendoes later in the trip when the tensions, like the altitude, were bound to increase.

*

My stomach had once again deteriorated, and I reluctantly said goodbye to the lodge toilet, truly an icon of civilisation in this wilderness, and set off slowly across the airstrip and out of town in the drab mist and rain.

The path to me no longer represented a stairway. It had become a conveyer belt, a Ferris wheel, an escalator. What went up, must come down. It would take me on and up to the top, to within sight of the summit of the very world, and then it would take me back down again, to Lukla.

This is where the real adventure would begin, and this is where it would end. I put the past week to the back of my mind.

Leaving town, I caught Adrienne. She wanted to trek with me, and also wanted to talk. I was feeling worse by the minute and was poor company. Beyond Chaumrikharka, we rejoined the main drag, which Ray and I had reluctantly abandoned yesterday, and on past the small villages of Chopling, Kyomma, and Chumlo. I raised the pace and when Adrienne stopped for tea in Ghat, I continued on my own.

Leaving Ghat, I passed a huge rock inscribed with the Buddhist mantra: *Om mani padme hum*, evidence that we were deep in the Tibetan Buddhist heartland.

The path was fairly level and good except for several sudden and abrupt dead ends, presenting one with much the same problem as a rodent faces in a maze. You either climbed over the boulders where the path ended, or looked for an alternative route, which generally meant scrambling over other boulders.

After the isolation of the stretch across the Khari La from Karikholi to Poiyan, the relatively heavy traffic from Lukla was at once both welcome and irritating. On the one hand, passing sardonic-looking trekkers and climbers headed through the mist for the frustrations of long delays at Lukla at least confirmed that I was going in the right direction. On the other, a steady stream of porters, some of whom wore only flip-flops on their leathery feet and carried more wood than the average builders' merchant's lorry, and fully laden cattle Namche bound, plodding lugubriously where I wanted to walk, only served to frustrate. Still, there was no point in hurrying, as we were duty bound to wait at Benkar.

Cattle and not horses are the pack animals of the lower parts of the Khumbu. Although they move slowly, they are less temperamental and move at a steady pace so that they generally arrive before the people do.

From Namche, where the altitude exceeds 11,500 feet, yaks, or more correctly naks, take over. The nak is the female yak and as applies to both animal and human life in most parts of the globe, the female makes the more reliable and effective beast of burden. Witness, if you will, the weekly scene in the Sainsbury's car park on Saturday afternoon. The female comes back with the goods. The predatory male, with mind on the terraces, cannot be trusted to bring home anything more useful than a six-pack of lager. Perhaps, as with all species, there is an element of 'get it wrong and you won't be asked again'.

Yaks, and naks, have developed a pulmonary capacity which can only function at high altitude.

Around one bend, I was almost flattened by four porters moving at speed, carrying an unconscious man on a stretcher. Behind the stretcher jogged his companion. I nodded to him, but he was oblivious to anything other than his own world of problems. No helicopters would fly in the upper valleys in these conditions, so this was the only way down. No matter how ill you were.

From Ghat, the path slopped gently downwards to the east bank of the Dudh Kosi, and suddenly the mist miraculously lifted and the valley was bathed in warm sunshine. The wondrous scenery revealed by the unexpected change in the weather was all the more stupendous for our world having been entirely cloaked in mist for the past two days. On either side of the valley, magnificent pine and cedar tree clad hills rose sharply from the banks of river. Sunshine danced on the water as it babbled unreservedly down from the mighty mountains and the silent glaciers for which we were headed.

And dead ahead was the end of the valley, where the escalator would rise sharply to Namche. To the right was the west peak of Kangura, towering high above at over 21,000 feet.

Just as the mist had lifted with an unexpected abruptness, so too had my morale. Namche was just beyond the next hill. It was almost in sight! The fact that it lay a good three miles north, and a mile above the Dudh Kosi, along which I was walking, was neither here nor there.

My guts were still grumbling plaintively and as volatile as an extremely volatile but schizophrenic volcano. However, listening to my Walkman and keeping on the move kept my mind off how I felt, most of the time.

*...Hold on... hold on...*

Seal screamed into my headphones. "I'm holding, Seally, I'm holding."

But when my mind tried to analyse how bad I actually did feel, I felt worse.

'Would you be doing this if you felt like this at home?'

'No. But then, I wouldn't be doing this at home. No bloody way.'

'Well, would you go for a run if you felt like this at home?' I broke into a jog.

'No.' I walked again. 'I definitely wouldn't go for a run. With or without a backpack weighing around forty pounds.'

'Well then, would you go to work feeling like this at home?'

'Ah. Questions. All these questions. Who knows? I don't know!'

I gave up. It was folly to compare the comfortable, predictable and sane conventions of home to this unpredictable, uncomfortable, beautiful but crazy, crazy world.

> ...*But we're never going to SUR-VIVE*
> *Unless, we get a little C-R-A-Z-Y.*
> *No, no, never going to SUR-VIVE,*
> *Unless – we get a little bit...*

"You've hit the nail right on the head Seally. Right on the head."

A huge suspension bridge took me over around one hundred metres of sacred river at Phakding. The mountain-dwelling Sherpa has a deep distrust of fast flowing water, sacred or not, and crossing bridges they move slowly with measured steps, praying to the water gods as they go. It occurred to me that I had no real foundations on which to base my blind trust in the permanence of these things.

Phakding is a prosperous village on the flat plain of the east and west banks of the river.

The path was lined with rock walls to prevent cattle intruding and supplementing their diet. This was the last of the flat. From now on, the only way was up.

Leaving Phakding, I was faced with a dilemma as the path left the river, and at a fork there was a choice of similarly unprepossessing paths. I took the right hand fork, assuming that it would lead back to the river, and was grateful to see that it did.

Just before Benkar, I caught Ray and the others.

Lunch took forever, and I got very cold. I couldn't wear my Buffalo top thanks to the coating it had acquired that morning. Unable to bear the smell of shit any longer, I washed it in warm water provided by the Sherpas, an exercise which was punctuated by three emergency dashes into the undergrowth to pass fluid and appease my extremely irritable guts. My jacket would require several days of sunshine to dry, so was of little immediate value.

For now, though, the weather was fine, and we managed to catch a few precious moments lying in the sun. I felt a little better and managed a few press ups and sit ups, mainly to impress Dave English who said I should do them properly. It wasn't long, however, before the weather again deteriorated, with a cold clammy mist whipping up the valley on the back of a strong breeze. Once again our environment became obliterated, and soon it became cold.

The others arrived and we played a game of cricket, which was enjoyable until I got carried away demonstrating my wicket-keeping skills and ostentatiously dived to stop the ball. I landed on a sharp rock, badly bruising my right hip. At last lunch came, which was swiftly consumed, and eventually we were off.

Once again I began to feel dreadful, the cold adding to my discomfort, and just wanted to reach Namche and the relative comfort of a lodge as soon as possible. I drifted along from group to group, as disinterested in the company as I was in the surroundings.

Beyond Monjo we came to the field office at the entrance to the National Park, where our permits had to be scrutinised and where I had to pay for the video. Inside a large two storey stone building, two self-important little men in flashy brown uniforms proved that officialdom is the same worldwide. I was kept waiting for an age before I was told that they wouldn't accept US dollars. I was getting cold again and my head was pounding. I felt sure that my temperature was going through the roof. I could feel the anger bubbling not far beneath the surface.

Eventually I was unable to take any more polite waiting, being ignored while every other trekker who came in had their permit stamped. Dave had gone ahead and had left Wish outside in his official capacity of group leader just in case there were any problems over the permits.

My frustration spilled over into a minor eruption when Wish tried to make light of the situation. "All right, all right. Keep your hair on, man. These things take time, you know. It's Karma."

"Bollocks Karma!" I said, "It's bloody inefficient bureaucracy gone crazy. You make the one with the most to pay wait the longest! Even British bloody Rail haven't thought of that one yet!"

With that I pushed to the front of the queue and got the attention of the more self-important of the two officials by slamming each of my five twenty dollar bills on the counter beneath my fingers.

"One hundred dollars. Take it or leave it."

He spoke to his partner and then addressed me.

"There is a bank in Namche Bazaar. You go and change the money, then I give you permit."

I struggled to contain the ball of anger rising inside. I noticed that a small multinational crowd had gathered around.

"If you think", I said, slowly and deliberately, "for one moment, that I am going to walk up that hill, two miles that way and one mile up, to some shack calling itself a bank which Billy the Kid wouldn't have pissed in, to be told that that they don't exchange dollars, then you must be crazier than a Sanilav salesman in Surkhe. One hundred dollars, take it or leave it!"

He took it. Reluctantly, shaking his head with a look of dogged resignation.

A couple of people clapped, and some idiot yelled "Yo!"

A third uninformed official entered, clearly superior to the other two and the designated writer of receipts for video camera permits. Ten minutes later I was given a receipt the length of *War and Peace*, and got going again, feeling really rough. On the way out I used the office toilet, an unfinished wooden structure with no roof and a jagged hole in the floor.

"Take it or leave it," it seemed to say.

\*

I scarcely noticed either Jorsale or the bridges that crossed and recrossed the Dudh Kosi. The path became a pick-your-own-way procession over large white rocks on the east bank of the river before suddenly and dramatically climbing up through a wooded hillside to a huge suspension bridge high above the river.

Once across the bridge, all that remained to do was gain approximately one mile in altitude by following the well trod path that zigzagged ever upwards through the mist and drizzle.

With faltering steps, my tired and aching body felt every step, every foot gained took its toll as my bruised hip and troublesome guts protested. On a precarious bend, high above the roar of the river, I caught Andrew Burgess perched motionless on a rock. He didn't normally trek on his own and I was concerned that he might be in a similar state to me.

"You all right?" I asked.

"Think so," he replied with a smile.

"We are still alive, aren't we?" I asked.

"'Fraid so." This was no limbo, no dream, no Dante's nightmare world between a life now relinquished and the fiery underworld. We were stuck with it.

"Better get on up this hill then." And with renewed purpose, we trudged onwards, towards Namche.

> *...Unreal City*
> *Under the brown fog of a winter noon...* [1]

My first impressions of Namche Bazaar fell a little short of my expectations. The streets were not paved with gold. They were, of course, not paved at all. But the fact that two men were engaged in digging a vast hole in the path on the outskirts of town, suggested that below ground level there might be something remotely connected with comfort and hygiene.

My first encounter suggested that, for a promised land, it was just a little short in the milk and honey department.

Without meaning to, I must have left Andrew behind on the upper reaches of the hill, and I arrived among the outskirts of Namche alone. My decision to look for accommodation in the first lodge I came to was, for someone fast losing the capacity for making rational decisions, a fairly rational one. It was almost four o'clock. Most of our party would have arrived and Namche would be like Bethlehem on Christmas Eve. I would take what I could get and maybe move tomorrow.

The warmth of the welcome I received in the first lodge I entered was the only warm thing about it. The proprietor was thrilled to be of service to someone running the Everest Marathon. He had himself run in the Namche Bazaar half marathon, which started the whole thing off, some years ago.

Blinded by the friendliness of the reception, I took a room for fifty rupees and to my surprise was given a key. I shuffled down some loft stairs and along a dark passage to find a cold, depressing little room with twin wooden cots and broken window panes. Tentatively, I parked my rucksack on a bed.

Upstairs, the lounge was freezing. A metal stove dominated the centre of the room, but there seemed little prospect of it being lit. I ordered tea and asked if I could have a hot shower.

---

[1] T.S. Eliot: 'The Fire Sermon', *The Waste Land*

The proprietor was sorry, there would be no hot water that day. When the tea arrived it was lukewarm. This was the last straw. I paid the fifty rupees for the room and left. I told him the tea was cold and I was sorry, I would not pay for it. He apologised and we parted on good terms.

My next stop was the Khumbu lodge, which seemed to be close to the heart of the village. It was getting dark now and it was hard to get any perspective of my surroundings. The Khumbu was a large three storey lodge run by a smartly dressed businesslike lady with glasses and a head scarf, who looked as if somewhere, in some parallel universe, she should drive a Range Rover. There were no single rooms left to rent, but I could have a bed in the dormitory for ten rupees. I found a free bed in a room resembling a Rwandan refugee camp, crammed full with haphazardly arranged timber cots and scruffy and untrustworthy-looking trekkers. It was cold, and I had no intention of staying there, but it could serve as a base for the time being.

The room was illuminated by a single naked bulb which hung by some fairly dubious wiring from the ceiling in the centre of the room. I had thought that class of electrical jiggery-pokery was reserved for cheap French hotels. All manner of clothes were hung from improvised lines and draped from windows and anything else that would support them.

The electrical sorcery required to coax the feeble but welcome light from the enigmatic bulb dangling from the ceiling, and the hundreds like it throughout every home and lodge in Namche, comes from a hydroelectric power station. Built in 1985 at the instigation of the self-governing council of elders, the lights that come on each night at five o'clock and go off at ten o'clock are like a gift from the gods of the mountains themselves.

Namche was the first village in the Solu Khumbu to have electricity and is the highest point where electricity is available for the benefit of the general public.

The trickle of electrical power provides light and permits the use of certain electrical appliances, such as radios, tape players and battery chargers for the video cameras of Westerners. But it is not sufficient to make inroads into reducing the vast consumption of wood used for cooking, heating and providing hot showers for trekkers. If Pink Floyd held a concert in Namche, they'd have to bring their own generators. In fact, if Des O'Connor gave a concert in Namche, he'd have to bring his own generator. But Namche isn't ready for either the Floyd or Des yet. And that's no bad thing.

I slung my rucksack on the only free bed which was adjacent to a window. If there were a fire, however unlikely it was that anything would burn in the dampness of this atmosphere, I wanted to be sure that I could get out. I was conscious of several pairs of eyes surreptitiously raised from books and maps following my every move as I rummaged through my kit in the hope of finding something vaguely clean. I looked up suddenly and caught a young man with grubby fair hair and a scraggy beard sprawling on a cot opposite mine staring at me, unable to avert his eyes before mine caught his. He nodded, and I returned the gesture, careful not to encourage any further entente and conveying just the hint of a warning as I returned my attention to my rucksack.

I asked the *didi* if I could have a shower and gratefully received the news that there was plenty of hot water. I followed her directions down to a dark basement where I followed the sound of falling water that eventually led me to the shower.

Strange but familiar sounds emanated from the small wooden cubicle, which I recognised as Simon's singing.

He told me that a large number of our party had obtained either beds or rooms in this lodge. He had, in fact, managed to get the last double room, which was known as the Jimmy Carter suite. Though whether that referred to the Jimmy Carter who farmed peanuts and had presided over the most powerful country in the world wasn't quite clear. It was also rumoured, he said, that the Khumbu was owned by relatives of Tenzing Norgay.

"Nice business to do people with," I said, mindful of the lack of warmth and crowded conditions in the dormitory.

"Mind you, the lounge is warm and the food's good, reasonably priced and you don't have to wait for ever," countered Simon, who had already eaten.

I began my shower in the dark, which is something I had never tried before. It is not, either, something which I would recommend. Totally disorientated, I fell over a block of wood which served no obvious purpose other than to trip me, and landed heavily on my bruised hip, falling through the door of the shower onto the floor outside. I completed my shower wearing my head-torch.

Simon had been right about the lounge. It shared the top storey of the building with the kitchen, which doubled as the family's residential area. The open wood-burning stove in the kitchen and the closed enamelled stove in the lounge combined to radiate a snug, cosy ambience which was further helped by the unintentionally subtle lighting. Most of the tables were occupied. Young climbers quietly poured over maps, discussing their plans in hushed but occasionally animated voices. Young couples talked in muted tones or played cards, older couples sat hunched in the dim lighting, heads buried in books. There was an air of peaceful restfulness that had been absent from my life for too long. The bright ethnic clothing worn by many fellow travellers evidenced that they had gone some way down the road towards living, rather than merely absorbing, the culture. Hitherto, we had been unable to more than dip tentative toes in the cultural water. That, I sensed, was all about to change.

Along the length of one wall was a glass-fronted wooden cabinet containing an impressive collection of books, mostly about mountains and mostly, but not all, written in English. People ate, savouring the food with the quiet reverence normally reserved for moments of secret indulgence during lengthy periods of self-deprivation in retreats such as health farms.

And then I noticed some familiar faces. It was actually Brian's laugh which I noticed first, followed by his impersonation of Valeri's laugh, which he performed to perfection. I joined Brian, Dave, Sue, Lloyd, Andy and Annabel, and enjoyed some excellent soup and Tibetan bread, washed down by lemon tea. Sue was drinking rum, and some of the boys were drinking beer. It was strange how, despite now feeling considerably better, I had never felt less like alcohol. In fact, I remember feeling a little concerned as to whether I would ever feel like alcohol again. I need not have worried.

I could almost have stayed there in the comfort of the Khumbu lounge all night and crashed out with the others in the squatter camp in my sleeping bag, but Annabel mentioned that there was some pretty reasonable accommodation in the Thamserku View Lodge. The Thamserku was our base, the administrative centre where meetings would take place and where the trekking crew would serve the food which they had cooked in the street outside.

I collected my rucksack, thankful to find it's contents still intact, and set off into the night to find the Thamserku. Despite being less than fifty metres from the Khumbu, I went up several blind alleys before finding it. It was dark outside, except for the faint lights which glowed in the buildings which I passed. The light from my head-torch cut no further than six feet through the near impenetrable mist. Tripping through stony, narrow streets echoing bewildering, but familiar, noises of guttural laughter and throat clearing from the shadowy recesses, I could have been in Victorian London: Fanny, without the gaslight.

I stumbled upon the Thamserku View Lodge along a street with only one side. The street was in fact a rampart, some six feet wide, leading past the lodge. I realised this when I almost wandered off the edge and down a ten foot drop into the field where the beam of my torch picked out something familiar and blue. It was, of course, our collection of tents.

The Thamserku was, on first impression, somewhat more Spartan than the Khumbu. Through the entrance there were two large downstairs rooms. To the left was a sparsely furnished room, one corner piled high with our blue kit bags, stretchers, oxygen equipment and unfurled banners bearing our sponsor's name, which brutally reminded me that we had at last arrived at the very gateway to the big mountains. Dave Blakeney was in conversation with the Sirdar and some of the trekking crew. This room was where we would eat during our stay, and also doubled for an annex to the lounge and was used as a storeroom at other times.

The room to the right of the front door was smoky, hot and heaving. As with all lodges, foam-filled threadbare cushions covered stable benches around the outside of the room. Flimsy trestle-type tables, similar to those one can purchase in DIY outlets to paste wallpaper should one be that way inclined, faced the benches. Small round pedestal stools with leather seats grooved by the bums of a generation of trekkers filled the void on the other side of the tables. Most of the benches and the stools were taken by our group. If the lounge in the Khumbu had given the impression of a spiritual sanctum, than the lounge in the Thamserku gave the impression of a spiritual vacuum. It was bedlam.

This room was the hub of the lodge. Here the family who owned it prepared the food, cooked and ate themselves, and conducted all business transactions. The lodge was staffed by three girls, ranging in age from around sixteen to twenty-five, who peeled vegetables, cooked, served and washed up. The *didi*, who appeared to be their mother, looked much older. It was hard to tell her age, people age rapidly in these parts. She presided over proceedings and took orders for food in an unhurried and dignified manner. With a curious indifference to the sudden intrusion which the mist and the path had swept through her door, she passed the order to a pretty smiling girl, who broke eggs into a pan on the stove. I imagined that she would probably show the same indifference towards the pecuniary uplift which the Everest Marathon had brought to her door. But not so the smartly dressed woman in her early thirties sitting at a desk who spoke good English and handled all the money matters.

But if the *didi* in the Khumbu might, in her parallel universe have driven a Range Rover, then in that same world the *didi* of the Thamserku would certainly have driven an ancient and rusting Datsun Violet.

I asked her if there was a free room. She nodded impassively and took a key bearing the number five from a board on the wall. I had no idea what I was getting or how much it would cost, but I accepted the key gratefully and went in search of room five.

It was on the first floor, on a corridor just beyond the top of the first flight of bare wooden stairs. I found the light switch, and an eerie but adequate luminescence flooded the room.

The only furniture in the room was a large double bed covered by a thin grubby mattress over which was draped a worn bedspread. I had no use for anything else. The wooden-framed windows were intact and there were even two pieces of cloth dangling from a string above the windows, which reminded me of curtains in a remote and distant world.

There was sufficient room and the window sill made a more than adequate bedside table. There was even a nail on the wall opposite the bed, where first of all I hung my jacket, until I decided that my wet and filthy towel had the greater need and slung my jacket on the floor.

I felt a huge relief at having established a comfortable, secure and private base. Downstairs I found Stephen, my doctor, and discussed the condition of my stomach with him. As it had gone on for three days and I had eaten little other than soup and bread since my yak steak and chips in Lukla, he was inclined to recommend medication.

"It may bung you up a bit," he warned.

"Well, bung up and be damned, then," I replied. "I don't care if it gives me terminal constipation. I've had enough of this."

The Thamserku toilets, after the luxury of the lodge toilet in Lukla, left a lot to be desired. Despite being kept under lock and key, the two cubicles at the end of the rampart offered no more than a small hole in the wooden floor. Beneath this was a drop of around ten feet to where the effluent simply sat and putrefied until it was absorbed by the earth and the cold of winter froze it into oblivion. Aiming through the hole into the abyss required great skill, but at the back of each cubicle the patron had thoughtfully provided a pile of straw so that accidents could be cleaned up should the perpetrator be moved to do so. It reminded me of the byre on the farm where I spent my youth. Except that it smelled considerably worse. I remembered our old doctor once telling my mother that Tetanus could live on indefinitely in cow dung and described a case in which a man developed Lockjaw through an infection from a compost heap on a farm which had not seen a cow for over thirty years. I wondered just what infectious horrors lived on in the pit below the toilet floor. It was just too hideous to contemplate.

It occurred to me that the size of the hole in the floor was as much of a quandary for the builders of toilets in these parts as the question as to how high to place a urinal was at home. Make the hole too small, and the thing can quickly become very nasty indeed. Make it too big, and you risk the young, the old or the infirm disappearing either partially or completely into the internal void below.

"Take one now, and one first thing tomorrow. That should do the trick."

"Thank you, doctor," I said and, having bought a bottle of water and paid a final visit to the byre, retired to find that room five still existed and had not been a mirage of fantasy in my mind.

As the marching clouds of sleep rolled up the valley to numb my consciousness, I was aware of one last thought: "It's over eleven thousand feet up here. This is the highest I've ever slept! I'm above the clouds and tomorrow I'm going to see Everest! The hardship of the last few days will be worth it tomorrow. Yes, it'll all be worthwhile."

*'Well now that's done: and I'm glad it's over.'* [1]

---

[1] T.S. Eliot: 'The Fire Sermon', *The Waste Land*

# Namche Bazaar:
# "Introducing the Band"

## Thursday 18th November

Richard Millhouse Nixon who, in August 1974 was not having a particularly good time of it, was quoted as having said: "Only when you've been at the depths of the deepest valley, can you know what it's like to stand at the top of the highest mountain."

At about 8.45 a.m. on the morning of 18th November I got some insight into what he may have had in mind when he uttered those words. Leaving aside the notion that mountains and valleys were purely figurative symbols for the fortunes of politics in general, and in particular the reversals of fortune that a little clandestine bugging can cause or effect, the sentiment was strikingly appropriate to how I felt.

For ahead of me, far up the valley, the thick bank of cloud had suddenly vanished to reveal my first view of Mount Everest. Of course, I wasn't instantly certain that it was Everest, lurking furtively as it does behind the Lhotse-Nuptse ridge. But when my map confirmed that I was definitely looking in the right direction, there was little doubt that I was gazing at the highest point on God's earth.

And behind me, beneath the stony hillside up which Ray and I had puffed and panted half an hour before, lay Chhorkung, a satellite of Namche and little more than a military camp and a collection of houses and small fields. Below Chhorkung lay Namche itself, and then nothing – nothing at all – as the mountain plummeted down into the valley of the Dudh Kosi, a mile below where I stood. Beyond that was the path that led to Lukla and snaked its infernal way back to Jiri. With the early morning sun glinting on the river so far below, the importance of that path suddenly became crystal clear to me. Far from dismissing the last week from my mind, that turgid grind through the mist-shrouded valleys had been an essential penance for an appreciation of the wonders that were now almost within tangible reach.

I had been at the depths of the deepest valley, and now I was standing in the doorway to the roof of the world. Less than twenty miles from where I stood was our journey's end, it seemed so close. It would take over six days to reach it, and I was already plotting to return to Namche in around four and a half hours. Curiously, at that moment, that didn't seem at all important. What was important was that I was looking at Mount Everest.

And in that moment of truth, I learned that had not this privilege been hard earned, it would have trivialised the thrill at the majesty of what lay before my eyes.

*

I had awakened at six o'clock, equally confused by my unfamiliar surroundings and a strange but familiar noise which emanated from the nether regions of my bed. As I shook off the bleariness of some ten hours of uninterrupted sleep which my body is unaccustomed to, I realised that my guts had improved significantly and that I could now fart. It's hard to explain what a simple joy this is. I spent most of the next fifteen minutes doing it to celebrate.

Outside, on the landing, through the open window which ushered in the freezing morning air, I got my first glimpse of the snow encrusted mountains which dwarf Namche Bazaar. Far above the field where our blue tents stood lonely and abandoned, towered the giant Kwangde.

At a touch under twenty thousand feet, this vast wall of rock and ice dominates the south-east skyline, a mighty ridge flanked by two great buttresses, the more prominent of which got the name. In these parts there are too many peaks and not enough names. One would assume that cataloguing anything around twenty thousand feet should be a matter of course, but around here, it's as much a matter of course as knowing your flock of sheep by name is to a Welsh sheep farmer.

The deep blue of the sky was profoundly beautiful against the whiteness of the mountains, caressed by the morning sun and throwing long, dark shadows into the valleys far below.

In the kitchen, the *didi* was brushing her long black hair while the young girl swept the floor and stoked the stove. The morning light brought a softness to her features which the half-light of the previous evening had obscured. There was a quiet kindness in her eyes which I had mistaken for indifference and which I would later come to know and appreciate. Particles of dust danced above the elder girl's brush in the cold morning air as the first rays of the sun crept through the open windows.

Ray sat at a table in the company of three sharp and fit-looking men with crew cuts, who I did not recognise. They were dressed in immaculate blue tracksuits and expensive-looking running shoes bearing the name of Reebok, our sponsors.

I guessed, correctly, that they must be the British part of the elite and highly vaunted Brigade of Gurkhas team. Ray invited me to join them and introduced me to Kevin Davies, Fergus Anderson and Charles Moores. Along with four Nepali Gurkha runners, Gyan Bahadur Limbu, Dharmabikram Sunwar, Birbahadur Balal and Guman Thapa they had arrived in Namche the previous evening and finished off a remarkable feat of training and acclimatisation with the equally remarkable feat of finishing off twenty-seven bottles of rum.

Small though the bottles may have been, that was still probably the equivalent of drinking around two-thirds of a standard sized bottle each. I shuddered to think how they must feel but, being true soldiers, they took their hangovers like men. Their demeanour revealed no telltale signs of internal turmoil.

As they heartily tucked into fried eggs, toast, chapattis and tea, I learned that they had run down from Gorak Shep the day before. This was the culmination of six weeks of trekking and training in Nepal, which had mainly been conducted in the Annapurna region, more specifically at the Thorung La Pass which, at around 17,500 feet, was similar in altitude to the start of the Everest Marathon.

And what better way of making a dramatic entry to the party than to trek up to the start of the race and breeze down in between three and four hours. It was enough to put me off my morning tea. But Ray, being Ray, was more sceptical. When pressed for exact split times in the run, the lads became somewhat evasive, and the conversation drifted away from the race and onto the subject of food.

The fried eggs, I had to admit, looked heavenly, and as I was feeling considerably better than I had done for some days, I decided to order eggs and toast. They came almost immediately and, as I ate, conversation switched to our backgrounds. Fergie, originally from

Scotland, was the only one based in Kathmandu. Kev was in the British Army and expected a new posting shortly after the race. Both of these two were NCOs. Captain Charlie Moores was the officer in charge and was based in Hong Kong. Charlie and I had a mutual friend and, in fact, had a good deal in common. They were a sociable and friendly group and it was clear than their inclusion in the party was going to liven things up considerably.

Friendly and rum drinking they may have been, but there were no illusions as to why they were there. No Gurkha had ever won the Everest Marathon, and Gurkha trophy cabinets in Hong Kong and Kathmandu were as devoid of winners' medals as was the Namche Bazaar general stores of toilet brushes. They had not been given eight weeks to go swanning about the Annapurnas and the Solu Khumbu to come home empty-handed. Good as the crack may be, these guys were deadly serious and although they were officially part of our group, they were on their own, with a self-sufficient independence and solidarity which emphasised that they clearly believed 'elite' was a badge worth wearing.

Aside from the leg-pulling, there was a good deal of humorous, but nonetheless deliberate, psychological subversion aimed at those most likely to thwart their ambitions. Pierre André, the 1991 winner, was, of course, the main recipient of this, but he was completely unruffled by it. After all, not only had he been here and done it, he had been here and won it. That, and the knowledge of what to expect between now and race day, gave him a considerable advantage and one which, with his exuberant personality, he was not slow to recognise.

The psychological warfare had more of an effect on Ray who, like myself and most of the others, had absolutely no idea of what to expect. Of course, unlike myself and most of the others who simply wanted to survive and run as good a race as the gods would allow, Ray was a "not so young pretender" who would mount a serious and legitimate claim to Gobet's crown. He knew, of course, that to do this, he would have to see off the Gurkha challenge, and that challenge was thrown down that first morning in Namche over eggs and toast, unintentional as it almost certainly was at the time.

"You get a fantastic view of Everest from the National Park Museum above the town. You lads should go and take a look," said

Charlie. "But you want to go early while the weather's like this. If you leave it till later, it may get clouded over."

"Sounds like a good idea," said Ray. "How d'you find it?"

"Oh, just follow the steps beyond the toilets that lead up and that joins a path that takes you right past it. You can't miss it."

"How far is it?" I asked. If someone tells you that you can't miss something, experience tells me that you generally can. Quite easily. Although feeling rejuvenated, I was looking forward to a day relatively free from physical exertion. Especially on top of my fried eggs, at the speed that Ray was likely to trek.

"It'll only take you fit young men ten to fifteen minutes, at a steady pace," said Charlie.

Ray looked at him suspiciously.

"Honest", Charlie said with a smile, "Scout's honour!"

I collected my cameras and Ray and I set off, following Charlie's directions. Ten minutes later, I was puffing and sweating in the thin air as we reached the top of the village with nothing resembling a museum anywhere in sight. We paused briefly to savour our first view down on Namche Bazaar with its houses and three storey lodges built on steps in the hillside. The village forms a horseshoe, and looking down, Namche resembles a natural amphitheatre, surrounded on three sides by huge mountains and then dropping off into oblivion to the south.

"Come on", said Ray, impatient to get there, "it must be further on up the hill. While I was impatient to get to the top for aesthetic reasons, Ray's urgency was spurred on by the ticking clock as we went further and further beyond the fifteen minutes that it should have taken us.

Without realising it, we had gone beyond Chhorkung, turning left instead of right which would have led us to the museum. Somewhat more bizarrely, we had come off the main path leading to Tengboche, then off the path to Khumjung, and had begun to climb a barren stony hillside following a barely recognisable path cutting across the grain of the hill. Soon, there was no path at all, except for the tracks made by animals foraging for food on this barren hillside. With my heart pounding and my lungs screaming, I struggled for breath in the cold, thin mountain air. The frost sparkled in the bright sunshine. Sweating profusely as the sun warmed my back, the exertion of the chase up the hill and the promise of what lay ahead were exhilarating.

I called to Ray, some way ahead of me, to stop and I stripped to the waist and looked down on where we had come from. Namche was obscured from sight beneath the brow of the hill and Chhorkung with its little fields and the path leading to Tengboche were visible far beneath us.

"I don't see any bloody museum," said Ray. "D'you reckon those bloody Poms were winding us up?"

"Naw", I replied, "there is a museum." I'd noticed it on my map. "It's down there, somewhere," I pointed towards Chhorkung." We've come much too far up this hill. But if we carry on we should come to the Everest View Hotel, which the name would suggest should have a view of Everest."

For the next fifteen minutes we pounded up the hill, walking hard and scrambling over loose scree in places, until we came to a spur beyond which, to our disappointment, the climb continued. We paused again. My chest was heaving, I was beginning to notice the altitude and find the going tough. Beneath us, to our left, was a long flat clearing, lined on either side with white boulders.

"We're close," I panted. "That's the Shyangboche airstrip down there. We're well above it, so it can't be far to the top!" The airstrip was built in 1959 to airlift emergency food to the hoards of Tibetan refugees who descended upon Khumjung. It is now used for emergency flights and to ferry wealthy, if foolhardy, clients to the Everest View Hotel.

Invigorated by this, we bashed on up towards the skyline and this time we were rewarded for our efforts by reaching a plateau which sloped gently down to the north towards an impressive building in the distance surrounded by the only trees that could be seen for miles.

Far beneath us was the thin finger of path that linked Namche and Tengboche, along which we would later trek and run. That we could make it out from where we were was a good sign.

Perhaps it was the altitude or perhaps it was just us, but at first we both optimistically mistook the building in the foreground for the Tengboche monastery and made the far distant settlement, to be Pangboche.

The zoom lens on my SLR brought the building in the foreground closer.

"Do you reckon the monastery has a helicopter landing pad?" I asked dubiously. We consulted the map, and both felt somewhat sheepish when we realised that we were looking at the Everest View Hotel and that the buildings far distant were in fact Tengboche, which we knew to be around six miles from Namche and would be our first night-stop as we followed the valley of the Dudh Kosi towards our destination. Beyond Tengboche, a bank of cloud obscured the view that we had come to see.

But there were compensations. To our right towered the dramatic and jagged ice flutings of Thamserku, which rose to its 6,623 metres' splendour to the east of Namche Bazaar. Further up the valley of the Dudh Kosi, the magnificent Ama Dablam stood sentinel to the higher mountains, dominating the scenery. At 6,685 metres it reclines, lugubriously, almost posing for the camera. With its Matterhorn-like pyramid of a peak, it is unquestionably one of the world's most beautiful mountains. If a beauty contest were held for mountains, the others would need braces or surgery to straighten out their imperfections and still not hold a candle to this awe-inspiring peak. It is simply drop-dead gorgeous. Its name literally means 'Mother of the star-shaped pendant', and it is instantly recognisable from any angle.

We stayed there for some time, savouring the sunshine, the scenery and the feeling of vastness which contrasted with the introspective world of the last few days. It came as no surprise that Ray had forgotten his camera, so he took some shots of me with mine, with Ama Dablam in the background. It was silent, save for the breeze whistling over the lip of the hill and Ray's mutterings about the vagaries of the path far below, until we heard the drone of an aeroplane engine coming towards us. The little plane came into view and I followed it through the lens of the video camera, as it twice slowly circled high above the mountains surrounding us and then headed back down the valley. It was probably a sightseeing trip from Kathmandu, filled with Japanese tourists frustrated by the cloud that obscured the world's highest mountains further up the valley.

Whilst I was absorbed with the mountains, Ray was absorbed with the race course. Where we stood was an excellent vantage point to get a fair appreciation of what lay between Tengboche and Namche. We could see the path below us, and it appeared to be fairly wide and flat, although we had been warned that this section was extremely exposed, and therefore highly dangerous to tired legs and numbed minds. An error of judgement could result in a fatal tumble down to the river, a mile below.

Tengboche was virtually the same in altitude as where we stood, at around 3,800 metres. But between Sarnassa and Tengboche was a vast chasm which dropped to the Dudh Kosi at Phunki (3,247 metres) and climbed sharply out of the tree-lined valley on the other side. Although on race day reaching Tengboche would mean that more than half of the course had been completed and Chhorkung would be in sight, the nightmarish ascent of over two thousand feet in the thin air on the legendary Sarnassa Hill that would follow struck fear into all our hearts.

I looked at my watch. It was eight thirty.

"I think I'm going to head back. Dave wants us at a meeting at nine o'clock. You coming?" Ray asked me. "To tell the truth, I'm feeling pretty crook. Guess I'll lie down for a bit."

I wasn't ready to go back yet. I shook my head.

"I'll see you later," I said. "Give Dave my apologies. I doubt if it'll be anything important anyway." I welcomed the chance to sit and savour a private audience with the mountains. I also had a strong feeling that it was worth waiting on that windy plateau, that the gods of the mountains were almost ready to reveal the real stars. One by one, they were introducing the band.

I felt a strong impulse to close my eyes. It was like when you were a child and your mother told you to close your eyes before giving you a present.

Go on. Do it. Okay, there's no one around anyway.

I closed my eyes, and sat very still, feeling the chill of the wind combat the warmth of the sun on my back. Time passed. I sat, thinking of the days behind, the days to come, and home and family light years away. And through the turmoil of my jumbled thoughts came uninvited but familiar words; the words of Yeats which I had learned in my youth; words which, as I recalled them, seemed to take on a new significance:

> *Nor law, nor duty bade me fight,*
> *Nor public man nor angry crowds,*
> *A lonely impulse of delight*
> *Drove to this tumult in the clouds;*
> *I balanced all, brought all to mind,*
> *The years to come seemed waste of breath,*
> *A waste of breath the years behind*

*In balance with this life, this death.* [1]

And when at last I opened my eyes, the cloud had gone, and the Everest cluster stood out majestically before me.

\*

Through the viewfinder of my video camera, I could clearly make out the huge south-west face, first climbed by Scott and Haston on 24th September 1975 on the expedition led by Chris Bonington. To the right, rising from the South Col obscured by the Lhotse-Nuptse ridge, which the Swiss had in 1952 described as "...having the smell of death," rose the south-east ridge, by which Tenzing and Hillary had ascended to the summit on that memorable day in 1953, just before the Coronation. On a day when Empire, Commonwealth and all men everywhere who believe that the doing of great deeds is a hopeful sign for our future, set aside divisions and came together, united in the celebration of the climbing of the world's ultimate mountain.

And just before the summit itself, the South summit. Here Evans and Bourdillon had been forced to turn back, and here frostbitten and sleepless, Scott and Haston had been forced to bivouac, before reaching the summit, tantalisingly close, but unreachably distant.

To the right of Everest was Lhotse. No less a giant to the naked eye, the summit of Lhotse, at 8,343 metres, is a mere five hundred metres below the highest point on earth. Rising to a perfect triangular apex from the Nuptse-Lhotse ridge, Lhotse is the greatest of Chomolongma's attendant peaks.

If the 'mother goddess of the earth' is a retiring, almost self-effacing bride, veiled in splendid isolation behind the ridge, then Lhotse is a more voluptuous yet enigmatic bridesmaid. For it was Lhotse that held the key to the summit of Everest. The Lhotse face, where Lowe and Ang Nyima slaved selflessly cutting steps in the ice for five long breathless days, unlocked the door to the South Col and the South East Ridge. Beyond this lay relatively easy access to mountaineering's ultimate goal – the summit of the world's ultimate mountain.

---

[1] 'An Irish Airman Forsees his Death'

But self-effacing Lhotse is not. From the Lhotse vertex spindrift plumed dramatically, high above the summit, powered by a wind of unimaginable force, driving all before it in one of the most inhospitable places on earth. Flung high into the clear blue sky beyond, the fine, powdery snow flumed like a Roman candle in the swirling currents of air, before spiralling angrily down its south-eastern slopes.

A ridge runs from the Lhotse summit, dipping from its eastern flank and then climbing to form the 8,383 metre Lhotse Shar from whose peak the ridge ends abruptly in a huge, sheer, triangular, multi-banded rock face far above the icy walls beneath.

The enormity of the mountains took a long time to sink in. I had not been prepared to be so utterly mesmerised by their size and splendour. What I was looking at was utterly timeless, totally incomparable, more savagely beautiful yet at the same time more terrifyingly dangerous, than anything I had ever set eyes on before.

I could have sat there all day, but just as suddenly as the cloud had dissipated to reveal the jewels of the Solu Khumbu, a curtain of murky cloud was once again drawn across the roof of the world. My preview had come to an end.

The chill of the wind had cooled me and it was time to get moving. I decided to walk towards the Everest View Hotel and, after a steady ten minute walk, I realised that it was not as far distant as I had thought. But the altitude was taking its toll and soon I was forced to stop and breathe deeply every fifty metres.

Suddenly I felt light-headed and, for a second, thought that I was going to lose consciousness. I sat down on a rock and quickly felt better. Then I remembered reading somewhere that the most likely people to suffer from altitude sickness are fit healthy people who climb too high too quickly. That made me feel worse. Christ, I thought, if I'm struggling to walk at twelve thousand, five hundred feet, how the hell am I going to run a marathon at almost eighteen thousand feet?

Resigning myself to walk at a snail's pace, I plodded steadily towards the Hotel. I passed a well constructed Western-style stone bungalow with huge picture windows and a Georgian style front door with ornate glass panes. It had a neat garden and a well-manicured lawn, and even a patio with what appeared to be a barbecue. This just had to be the highest luxury residence in the world and only the galvanised corrugated steel panels on the roof, that are a feature of buildings in the Namche region, convinced me that my eyes were not lying.

Looking across the valley at Ama Dablam, it certainly must have one of the best views in the world. But it looked as bizarrely out of place as my school matron in a Wonderbra advert and I could only assume that it was in some way connected with that other great folly to which I was drawn: the Everest View Hotel.

The Everest View Hotel was built by the Japanese and, by their standards, was an unmitigated disaster. By the standards of a nation whose business acumen is legendary, and whose corporate commercial institutions dominate world markets, this idea was nothing short of financial hara-kiri. In fact, if they wanted to train their Kamikaze pilots to cope with the experience of sudden death before going into battle, this would be the ideal place to do so.

Medical opinion may be divided on many things, but there is more than tacit agreement that flying people straight in to an altitude of over four thousand metres has little beneficial effect on their health.

Their brochure boasts that: "The hotel is reached by a dramatic flight in a small aircraft to the hotel's airstrip at Shyangboche... and then a forty minute walk to the Hotel." It fails to point out, however, that the drama of the flight pales in comparison with the drama when guests begin collapsing from Acute Mountain Sickness on the walk to the Hotel. By the time the temporary respite of the newly installed pressure chamber is reached, guests were frequently well into an advanced state of pulmonary or cerebral oedema.

It would, in fact, perhaps be the ideal venue for Exit, the society which campaigns for the right to end one's life, to hold its annual conference.

However, the Japanese owners had not totally lost sight of good financial sense. The brochure also stipulates that fifty per cent of the cost of the stay and flight must be paid fifteen days before arrival.

I was drawn to the Everest View Hotel by three things. The first was simply idle curiosity. The second was a vague notion that if it bore some resemblance to what one would expect from a luxury hotel without costing the earth, I might be tempted to stay here after the race. In retrospect, any notion of trudging up almost two thousand feet of hillside after running a marathon from Gorak Shep was almost as absurd as the idea of running a marathon from Gorak Shep itself.

The third reason was more rational. The only thing that had made me consider withdrawing from the trip and giving up my place in the Everest Marathon, was that I had obtained a ticket for the match between England and the All Blacks at Twickenham on 27th November, the day after the race. I had considered carefully, for around thirty seconds, and then had given my ticket to a friend.

But having learned of the existence of a hostelry which claimed to offer many of the trappings of Western life, it occurred to me that it was just possible that they might have satellite television. I had no idea whether the match was being screened on satellite, but if the answer to both questions was "yes", then it would certainly be worth a further trip up the hill.

Also, the match had taken on an unexpected importance as my friendship with Ray grew. Being a Kiwi by birth, Ray was giving the Poms about as much chance of winning the match as Saddam Hussein had of winning the Nobel Peace Prize. I was very confident that, on this occasion, England would win on their own patch. Were it not for the fact that Liz, Ray's wife, and the boys were trekking up to Namche from Lukla to join him after the race, I am quite sure that Ray would have been equally motivated to find a way to watch it.

I struggled up the huge, sweeping stone staircase, and entered the Everest View Hotel lobby via an equally impressive plate glass door. The first thing which struck me, other than the fact that I appeared to be the only living soul in the building, was the incredible view of Ama Dablam through the picture window in the lounge ahead of me.

I approached the reception desk and rang the small hand bell. Almost at once, through a door marked 'Manager', a deferential little Japanese man appeared, immaculately dressed in the sombre black suit favoured by undertakers and hotel management throughout the world.

"Good morning sir. How may I help you?" he enquired.

"Do you have a room available next Friday, and if so how much do you charge?"

He consulted his register.

"Yes, sir. We would be able to accommodate you." This is promising, I thought, imagining the took on Dave's face when I asked him to tell the kitchen boys to bring my bed tea up to the Everest View Hotel. "Is the room just for you, sir?"

"Yes, I think so." Simon had suggested he might be interested when mention of the hotel had been made some days ago. It would certainly be an improvement on our previous stay in the lodge in Sete.

"The rate for one person is one hundred and thirty-five dollars for the room per night, plus forty dollars single room supplement. Meals are, of course, extra, and the rates are subject to a ten per cent government tax."

"I see," I said, when I had recovered sufficiently for him not to quote me the price for emergency use of the pressure chamber. "And I presume each room has a shower with hot water and a toilet with a seat?" Not that it made a jot of difference at that price.

The manager smiled and, with the somewhat patronising "Ah, you British..." sort of look, which the French normally reserve for tourists who ask for bacon at breakfast, he replied:

"Of course, normally. But we are having problems with our water supply at present."

"Oh," I said, grateful for an excuse not to lose face. "That's too bad. I will particularly need a shower, as I'll just have run a marathon. From close to Everest Base Camp."

That impressed him.

"Ah, you are running in the Everest Marathon?"

I was, I told him. As he was clearly not rushed off his feet, we chatted for some time. No, there was no television, satellite or otherwise, but they did accept Visa and, should I require a room at short notice, he very much doubted if there would be a problem. In response to my request, he gave me a brochure, which was a sheet of mustard coloured paper with information about the hotel on one side and the tariff on the other. A liberal use of Tippex had helped to amend the prices, presumably downwards in an effort to entice someone to stay at the place.

I thanked him for his time, and said that I might be back but it would depend on how I felt after the race. In reality, though, a lot more Tippex would have to be used on that tariff before a stay would be worth any serious consideration. Had a room come with full en suite facilities, a satellite television on hand and a night's stay costing around fifty dollars, it might have been hard to resist.

A rough mental calculation on my walk back towards Shyangboche told me that I could enjoy a sojourn of approximately three and a half years in the Solu-Khumbu-New-Green-View-Blue-Sky lodge in Sete for the cost of one night in the Everest View Hotel. Even if I splashed out and took a second mattress, I would still have eighteen months for the cost of one night. Neither, at that time, had a shower or private toilet facilities although, to be fair, I hadn't had an opportunity to inspect what the Everest View had to offer in the toilet department. Mind you, I doubted if I would be insulted by the proprietor of the Everest View, or have a torch shone in my face in the middle of the night as by Sete's answer to Basil Fawlty.

It had transpired in our conversation that the manager lived in the civilised-looking bungalow which I had passed on my way up. It went with the job. To add to the incongruous sight of such a fine building in such an unlikely setting, on my way down I noticed a youth lying, presumably asleep, in a bush by the path which adjoined the bungalow's garden. It reminded me one of those irritating lateral thinking games: "By the side of the garden of the world's highest modern bungalow which overlooks the world's highest mountains, a youth is found lying in a bush. What was he doing there?" But there again, there were times when the senses were so bamboozled that the entire country resembled a bizarre mind game.

And little wonder, I thought as I passed, that the bungalow and garden were so well kept and manicured. Judging by the absence of bustle in the hotel, the manager should have many vacant but happy hours to enjoy his home comforts.

\*

I paused below Shyangboche and sat on a rock where a strange-looking animal with thick brown fur and fiercesome antler-like horns stood in silhouette on the hillside and observed me from a distance. By the time my SLR had obtained an answer to all the questions posed by the light, the perspective, and the colours of the hillside and the animal itself, the creature had got tired of waiting, and had elegantly bounded off down the hill.

A couple of hundred feet below my perch was a *chorten*, which is a sort of supa-stupa, beside which a man sat deep in contemplation. Prayer flags fluttered in the breeze and this time it was my video camera which found the scene all too mind-bogglingly confusing and refused to focus.

Looking down on Namche, built into the horseshoe basin of the mountain, it was hard to believe that this was the largest village in the Solu Khumbu and the centre of the entire region. It wasn't discernibly bigger than Lukla or even Junbesi. Yet Namche is the administrative heart of the region and is generally regarded as the home of the Sherpa.

Prayer flags and banners fluttered in the wind from every roof, like bunting on a luxury ocean liner. Even the hillside leading out of town towards Thamo was bedecked with the stuff. The domestic buildings are substantial two storey affairs and the lodges have an extra tier and roofs made from galvanised corrugated iron. It was a tranquil and colourful scene, described in the guide books as bearing a greater resemblance to an alpine village than the Himalayan highland capital. I wouldn't know. I have never visited an alpine village.

Namche Bazaar, as the name would suggest, owes its existence to trade. At some point in the sixteenth century, the first settlers arrived. Driven out from their Tibetan homeland by some long forgotten skirmish, they came over the high mountain passes and followed the valleys of the Dudh Kosi and the Imja Khola until they found this Garden of Eden with an abundant supply of fresh water. Although many of the surrounding villages such as Khumjung, Khunde and Thame are almost entirely self-supporting with fertile plains and summer pastures, Namche's barren hillsides make farming nigh impossible. If you live on the steps of a terraced hillside, you either farm or build, and in Namche, they build. Houses, shops, restaurants and lodges sit side by side like cinema-goers in the upper circle. So close together are they as almost to suggest that, unlike elsewhere in the region, an element of aforethought and, perhaps planning had gone into their aspect.

Namche exists now, as it did then, as a trading centre. At the major crossroads where the path to Thami, and ultimately Tibet, bisects the paths to Gokyo, Lukla and Tengboche, it is the logical place for those who wish to sell to meet those who wish to buy. Every Saturday, around a hundred sellers, mainly Rai and Tamang peoples from the lower parts of the Dudh Kosi, climb up the hill to offer their goods to up to five hundred Sherpas who have made the journey down the hills from the villages of Tengboche, Phortse, Pangboche, Khumjung, Khunde and Thami. The weekly market, or 'blue-sky' bazaar, takes place on the crest of Namche's eastern slopes.

In its infancy, Namche Bazaar had quickly become an important trading post between Tibet to the north, and India to the south. The Tibetans exchanged salt for grain from India. Then in 1950 the Chinese occupied Tibet and one by one the border crossings were closed. Trade was stifled, and the noisy bustle of a busy market town which once echoed with laughter and bargaining, now echoed the silence that spelt starvation for the people of Namche, leaving them the stark choice of either moving or facing extinction.

And then began an economic miracle that, in relative terms, would have surpassed even Margaret Thatcher's wildest dreams. Moreover, one which was achieved without the sale of a single piece of the 'family silver'. In the early 1950s, starved of trade from the north and prey to frequent embittered disputes with India, the government of Nepal realised that she could no longer survive as a buffer between two Asian super-powers in isolation from the rest of the world. Every country has its assets – Britain had North Sea oil for about five minutes, Nepal had had its mountains for about five hundred millennia. It was just a question of recognising their value and realising that in the mid-twentieth century it was no longer practicable or even desirable to be an island in the ocean of world affairs.

And so Nepal opened its doors to the world and access to the world's most sought after prize in mountaineering was granted.

This had an almost immediate effect on the fortunes of the people of Namche. For although the trekking boom was still some considerable way off, the race to be the first to the top of Everest was very definitely on.

From the Anglo-American Nepal Reconnaissance Expedition of 1950, which was the first party to be allowed access to the Solu Khumbu, the mountain was "booked" by those wishing to climb it. Even today, there is still a considerable waiting list for a crack at the giant.

Those early Everest expeditions were massive affairs frequently requiring several hundred porters to transport enough food and equipment to sustain them for months. There was, of course, neither airstrip nor road in the early fifties, therefore the 'walk in', as it was referred to, commenced from Kathmandu. At least we had been spared that.

Not only was Namche the logical place to break the journey, but the threshold to the high mountains where the porters from the lower reaches would not and could not go. The physical and psychological aptitude of the high altitude Sherpa for carrying the white man's burden quickly became legendary. Here was an intelligent, honest and reliable people who could walk for days, carrying large loads uncomplainingly in the thin air.

Captain John Hunt, leader of the successful 1953 Everest expedition, calculated in London prior to departure, that his thirty-five Sherpas would be capable of carrying at the high altitude above Camp One, a load of thirty pounds without oxygen. But such was the determination of these people that the expedition should succeed, that at twenty-five thousand feet they were happily shouldering fifty pounds a man. Try selling those industrial practices to shop stewards on the assembly lines at Longbridge or Cowley.

Not only that, but they could climb mountains too. And smile while they did it. It was little wonder that the Sherpa people acquired such a formidable reputation so quickly. Species who survive when faced with extinction are those who can adapt, and few can have done so as successfully or dramatically as the Sherpa.

The Western mountaineering world was thankfully not slow to recognise and reward their worth. Although there are bound to have been countless cases of exploitation, John Hunt had vision ahead of his time to send one on the top of Everest along with Hillary in 1953. But it was more than a diplomatic gesture. Tenzing Norgay was not only a charismatic figure and a fine leader of men. He was also a damned good mountaineer. When questioned on his motives to include his sirdar, Tenzing, in the second summit assault, Hunt replied: "It was probably true that diplomacy did come into play to the extent that I was very keen that a Sherpa, if possible, if suitable, should be one of those to reach the summit." And so, on 2nd June, when the young Elizabeth was crowned, on a day full of romance and hope which some foretold as the dawn of 'a new Elizabethan Age', the success of Hillary and Tenzing put Nepal on the map. The Sherpa legend was born.

However, like everyone else, the Sherpa has an Achilles Heel. Perhaps it is the monotony of the food itself, perhaps it is lack of imagination, or perhaps it is a desire to feed the Westerner what he thinks the Westerner wants to eat. Perhaps it is a combination of all three. But the Sherpa, from those early days of Everest exploration acquired the reputation of being the world's best porters but the world's lousiest cooks! They say that the proof of the pudding is in the eating. And the sludge of assorted colours which we had been served for pudding each night during our trek from Jiri had done nothing to convince us that this was a reputation without justification.

In 1953, two years before I was born, when Captain John Hunt's expedition walked into Namche, the two New Zealanders in the party, Edmund Hillary and George Lowe were appalled by what they saw. Both had visited Namche before, and both had been impressed by the selflessness and integrity of these people. But in 1953, the people of Namche were amongst the poorest in the world, and this gave fresh impetus to their intent to do something about it. It was not enough, they realised, to come into the region and enjoy themselves without putting something back. And so the big-hearted moment they shared as they lay exhausted and relieved after crossing from Tibet by one of the dangerous high passes while their Sherpas brought them tea and cooked, led to the foundation of the Himalayan Trust. This has helped to improve the living standards of thousands of Sherpa people over the last forty years, and Sir Edmund Hillary is remembered more in these parts as a saviour than the man who first climbed Chomolongma.

Indeed, Hillary's status is almost as vaulted as the gods of the mountains themselves. Her Majesty may have conferred a mere knighthood upon him, but in these parts, he is practically worshipped.

The Khumjung school is a fine example of how the philosophy behind the Trust works. The 'can you help us?' theme was Hillary's brainchild. The principle of helping the people of the Himalayan highlands to help themselves, without compromising their religious or cultural ethos or radically altering their environment, is in keeping with how the Sherpa have helped others achieve their goals on the mountains over the past forty years.

I had hoped to visit the Khumjung school and the Khunde hospital after the race so that I could report first hand to those who were sponsoring me. But fate had other plans for how I was to spend my return to Namche.

*

If there had been moments thus far on the adventure which hadn't quite lived up to the dizzy heights of my expectations, Namche helped to push these firmly to the dark recesses of the mind. The little placards bearing the inevitable question: "What the bloody hell am I doing here?" were beginning to pop up in my mind like no sale signs on an ancient cash register, as they had done on that awful day on Dartmoor. But this was the oasis which I had long awaited.

Namche was everything it had been hyped up to be. And more besides. In addition to the lodges which I had already sampled, and the National Park Office and Museum which I hadn't, Namche had a police checkpost, a bakery, a post office and, of course, a bank, in addition to numerous shops and what the guide books magnanimously described as restaurants.

If Namche Bazaar is at the heart of the Khumbu region, little knowledge, either anatomic or local, was needed to find where pulsed the heart of Namche. My ears led me to the centre and the legendary Tawa lodge, upon whose famous balcony the world's greatest mountaineers have gathered, and where Pierre André Gobet, the Crown Prince of the Everest Marathon, was holding court.

Perhaps Clown Prince is more appropriate, for wherever the Gobet entourage went, laughter, practical jokes and frivolity were never far behind. I had first seen Pierre, or Peg, (a name by which Annabel referred to him, so distorted by her Antipodean dialect, that it took me until the last day of the trip to fathom it stood for his initials), on the flight to Kathmandu. Later, we had exchanged pleasantries in the hotel before he departed to do his own thing in the mountains. At the time I hadn't known who he was, and felt no remorse for not immediately recognising him as one of the world's finest mountain runners. A man who has run across his native Switzerland in a weekend. Simply for something to do.

For in truth, although Gobet's appearance is unmistakably Swiss, it is not unquestionably the appearance of a man who possesses a capacity for endurance beyond the dreams of most of the world's top athletes. Even those ten years younger than he. In truth, Gobet, with his stocky frame, thinning hair and little round spectacles resembling those once prescribed to children by the National Health, is not a man who looks one day less than his thirty-nine years. In truth, Gobet's appearance is instantly more reminiscent of a Swiss watchmaker than an incredible, close-to-perfect human running machine. Now, Ray looked like a runner, the Gurkhas looked like runners, even most of our party looked like runners. But Pierre André... well... er? For sure, appearances can be deceptive.

As I squeezed into the only remaining space on the balcony, which unfortunately happened to be between Wish and someone whom I did not recognise but looked like a shaven-headed football hooligan, I wondered could Gobet really be that good? Was his winning time in '91 of four hours, four minutes, and Maitland's record two years previous, set at three hours, fifty-nine minutes really that outstanding? Would someone not blast down the mountain in around three and a half hours this year? He looked so relaxed, so at ease, almost too casual for someone here to defend a title that some very plausible challengers had come so far to strip away from him.

Next to Pierre sat his girlfriend, Jeanne, whose simple understated beauty reminded me how a pretty face can draw a crowd. Seated on Pierre's other side, with his arm around the runner, was his father, Jean Gobet. Jean, like Pierre, was unmistakably Swiss. Dressed in clothes that suggested he may have come along for the world yodelling championships, he was a generously proportioned man built, one might deduce, neither for speed nor comfort in the mountains. I was to be proved wrong. He was neither an outstanding yodeller nor a slouch when the going got tough on the hills. Jean was a gentle, kind and friendly man, and although he was unable to communicate in our language, that was not a barrier, and he was well liked by everyone he met.

Opposite Pierre sat Jeanne's parents, Marc and Marguerite Bongard. Slim and sophisticated in their early fifties, they were relaxed and smartly dressed, annoyingly devoid of any visible ravages of the trek which had scarred those of us who had endured the foot-slog from Jiri.

Next to the football hooligan with the grade two head shave, was a not totally unattractive girl in her early thirties with a laughing face and curly blond hair. She smiled at me and it occurred to me as odd that she appeared to be attached to the hooligan. Dotted around the balcony packed with fashionably dressed trekkers were Valeri, Zvoni and other familiar faces with whom I exchanged greetings.

"How're the guts, old boy?" Wish asked, in an unusually friendly manner. "Good to see you up and about." He was obviously well into the process referred to as chilling out.

"Oh, much better, thanks, Wish." I replied, slightly taken back by Wish claiming that it was good to see me at all. The last time we had met, I had been pretty vile to him.

"Nice of you to make the meeting this morning." The voice belonged to Dave Blakeney, who was obscured on Wish's other flank. The frostiness in his voice was unmistakable. Despite the beer in front of him, he was clearly not quite so far into the chilling out process as Wish.

"Sorry," I said, feebly. I momentarily considered telling him that if it were a toss up between attending his fairly pointless meeting and savouring the first sight of the world's finest mountain scenery, the coin wouldn't even have got out of my pocket. But why should I be the one to spoil the convivial atmosphere? He could, if he wanted to. I was relieved that he didn't.

"Well, you haven't missed anything *that* earth-shattering." I feigned surprise. "But you will have missed lunch, as you haven't signed up for it. So you'll have to make your own arrangements, but that's what you normally do anyway." He grimaced, a shade triumphantly. "Oh, and by the way, you've still got the hat, as you weren't in supper to wear it last night, or in breakfast this morning!" I received the news with the stony stare and slow, contemplative nod of someone who had just been told that they had cancer, waiting for the information to filter through to the deepest recesses of my mind.

The Hat! I had forgotten about the wretched thing! I couldn't remember having seen it amongst my kit last night. Perhaps I'd left it in Lukla, or it had fallen out of my rucksack somewhere along the path. Maybe I'd left it at the National Park Office during all that fuss over my video camera. If I'd lost the damned thing, I would be an even blacker sheep in the eyes of our leaders, once again adversely affecting the morale of the group by destroying the bonding.

I picked up a menu from the table in front of me, and studied it. The fried eggs were a distant memory and I was now ferociously hungry after the morning's exertions. I managed to catch someone, whom I presumed to be a waiter and asked for coffee. I was left to ponder whether or not he was in fact a waiter, or whether or not he had understood.

The Tawa lodge is an institution. Like Piccadilly's Hard Rock Cafe in the late seventies, it is the place in which to be seen. You could meet your future partner, have a relationship if you were American, rear children and get divorced, in the time it takes to be seated and served. It is the one place in the Solu Khumbu which could almost be described as chic, and precisely what I had come to get away from. But after a week of total deprivation I was drawn to it like a fly to shit.

Fleeces and expensive sunglasses may have replaced the Afghan coats, and the half-pounders may have been traded for various brands of vegetarianism, but the people are essentially the same. Some have acquired social consciences and those who can, when on holiday, grow beards. Many are now in their forties and freed from the shackles of financial acquisition, they worship at the shrine of a different god. They have completed the metamorphosis from ancient Beetle through GTi to BMW estate, catalytic converter, of course. They recycle everything, particularly bullshit, and some have even saved the whale.

Others, however, are still on a journey of self-discovery, through the university of life. But with or without the smell of pot that lingers on, the atmosphere is as high as the mountains themselves.

We were different, of course. My advanced state of cynicism I attributed to my advanced state of dishevelment. We were there because it was a seat in the sunshine and after the previous nine days who could deny that we deserved one. And because they served the best apple pie in town.

Eventually I managed to order food. The skinhead on my left turned and spoke to me.

"Are you a runner?" he asked in a broad Scottish accent.

"I was before I came here. I'm not so sure now," I replied, without a trace of humour.

"So was I," he said with a broad grin, holding up a heavily strapped ankle. "What happened?" I asked.

He introduced himself as John Thomson who, with his partner Liz, had been travelling independently and had just arrived in Namche to join our group. Two weeks ago in training he had severely twisted an ankle and had torn ligaments. He was not optimistic about being able to start, never mind complete, the marathon, but seemed to accept this with a quiet complacency which I found difficult to understand. The reason for this, I soon learned, was that both John and Liz were devout Buddhists, although Liz hadn't had the haircut yet. She was also one of the four directors of the Glasgow School of Shiatsu.

John, from Inverness, was a PE teacher who found both living and teaching in London as spiritually uplifting as I found one of Dave's early morning meetings. Together they had decided to quit the rat race, and on their return from Nepal, they were headed for the white glistening mountains of the Scottish Highlands and the Moray Firth. John had quit his job and would look for work when they had established themselves in Scotland. They wished to start a family as soon as nature would permit.

I felt slightly envious, until I remembered that I lived in a location which most people would envy. But there is something hopeful and romantic about making a fresh start, particular one as spectacular as theirs.

They were rather unlike the Buddhists I had come across thus far on the trip. For one thing, they were not constantly knee deep in prayer. For another, they both had a huge capacity for humour and certainly knew a good time when they saw one. I liked them instantly. As with the Gurkhas, they were another welcome inclusion in our group.

Several millennia later, my food arrived.

*

After I had eaten I took a stroll around Namche Bazaar. I soon realised how small and compact it was by the fact that it was impossible to go more than fifty yards without bumping into someone from our party.

The bank was an imposing building with a board above the door upon which, under the Nepali hieroglyphics the English translation read: "Rastriya Banija Bank, Branch Office". I entered more from curiosity than a real need to do business. I was greeted by a friendly clerk who sat at a desk behind a wooden counter. Yes, I thought, this would go down well with Butch Cassidy and the Sundance Kid. No guards, no security cameras, not even glass, bullet-proof or otherwise, between the cashier and the customer. Nonetheless I doubted if the bank contained enough loot to keep Ronnie Knight in cigarettes for a fortnight, never mind support a life of luxury on the Costa del Crime.

I exchanged a few ragged and frayed bills, which we had been warned would not be accepted higher up, for some nearly new notes. The cashier beamed a broad smile as I thanked him and crammed them into my already bulging wallet.

"You run the Everest Marathon?" he asked.

"That's right," I replied.

He shook his head in a pitying sort of way and smiled again.

That was comforting. Even the locals thought we were off our trolleys.

Further up the rough, stony street, I found the post office. The authorities had not gone far out of their way to make it instantly recognisable as such. In fact had I actually been looking for it, and not idly ambling around, I would probably have had as much chance of finding it as the Famous Five's den in deepest Devon. For the only clue as to the function of the large whitewashed building with green wooden-framed glass windows, above which fluttered neat little prayer flags beneath a canvas pelmet, was a piece of cardboard wedged between the doors which simply said: "Open 9–1".

Assuming that these must be the hours of opening, rather than a tip for the two thirty at Tengboche and that it must be some sort of office or shop, I opened the heavy green wooden door and entered. Inside a sparsely furnished dark little room sat a young man at a small desk. In front of him were two large piles of letters and cards, the smaller of which he was engaged in shuffling through.

He looked up and smiled, then continued to sort through the letters, placing each in a different pile. He seemed oblivious to my presence. Unlike a sub-post office at home, I hadn't come in to buy a bag of potatoes or hire a video, so he must have assumed I had come in to conduct a transaction which required his participation. Unless, of course, I was simply lost, or wanted to inspect how the post was sorted in Namche.

"Excuse me", I began tentatively, "could I buy a stamp. In fact two, if it wouldn't be too much trouble."

He looked up from his work and with a look of slight irritation, pointed to the letter he held in his hand.

"No, I'd like to buy a stamp, please," I repeated, wishing I'd brought my guidebook, however naff it might look. I pointed to the stamp on the letter he was holding. He shook his head. Obviously I couldn't buy a stamp. I see. I've come to the sorting office by mistake.

I turned to leave, but he called me back. Plucking a card from his other, larger pile, which mostly contained cards bound, I assumed, for civilisation at some future date, he took a stamp from the desk and said:

"Give me card. I stamp." That was it. I smiled and thanked him. Like everything in life, all very simple and logical when you know how the system works. When I later returned with two cards which I had bought and written, I asked when he thought they might get to Britain.

"Soon," came the reply. Soon is relative, I suppose. One arrived the following March and the other in May.

\*

In the kitchen lounge of the Thamserku, the Gurkhas were busy drinking tea in the company of a tall, thin young man with glasses, and an unkempt mop of curly brown hair.

"Hi Rich," greeted Charlie. "Find the museum all right? Told you it'd only take you about fifteen minutes."

"No. We didn't find the museum," I replied, sardonically. "Ray was going too flippin' fast for that. But I did find Everest. Eventually. So we must have been going in the right general direction, thank you."

The new kid in town laughed, and Charlie introduced him as Mark Woodbridge, who had also just arrived in Namche to join our group. Mark was an instantly likeable young man, with an easy going nature and a carefree outlook on life most uncommon in his chosen profession.

Mark was an accountant, a statement which in itself is as unsensational as saying that Noddy drives a taxi. However, every accountant with whom I have had dealings has billed me for everything including the use of his pen, in addition to the time it took to remove it from his pocket. What was almost unheard of in Mark's line of work, was that he had chosen to do it for nothing. Well, peanuts, anyway. Mark was a VSO worker, who was working in Bhutan. On account of lack of funds (also unheard of for an accountant) he had been granted permission by Diana to opt out of the Jiri foot-slog and make his own travel arrangements.

As I got to know Mark over the following days, I realised that he had prepared himself for the race as thoroughly as an accountant would prepare a balance sheet for presentation to the board. And in keeping with the canny accountant who undervalues the assets of the company to represent a capital loss upon sale, Mark never for one moment oversold his prospects in the race.

While at home in England his running experience was fairly limited and his times modest, out here that meant nothing. Living and training at an altitude of over eight thousand feet gave him a huge advantage over us warm-blooded temperate mammals who lived at or close to sea level. I also prised out of him that he had several runs of over six hours under his belt, which, at that altitude, was a solid proving ground and a psychological boost.

But what really impressed both the Gurkhas and me, was that he had trekked up to Gokyo, walked across the Ngozumpa Glacier and crossed the 5,420 metre pass at Chola La. Then he had threaded his way down to Dzonglha and past the Tshola lake to Dughla. From there he had trekked up through Lobuche to Gorak Shep, where the race would start. And then he ran down to join us in Namche. What was particularly impressive about this was that he had been entirely on his own and had carried his own kit.

Some might call that foolhardy. Some might call it downright irresponsible. If there are two of you and one becomes ill, injured or even just plain lost, there is an acceptable safety net. Whether or not it holds you is largely a question of chance. But on your own, the risks become multiplied by whatever mystical coefficient the gods of the mountains choose to throw into the equation.

But I believed that Mark knew exactly what he was doing, knew exactly where he was going, was well aware of his own capabilities and understood the warning signs and how to react to them should the alarm bells start to ring. He knew, like most of us, that this race, this folly, this madness was far beyond anything he had ever attempted before. So all through his preparation he had paced himself, building his fitness with the steadily accumulated growth of a good, solid high-yield investment. His trot down from Gorak Shep proved that the money was in the bank. And pay day was little more than a week away.

Mark's goals were realistic and I, for one, expected him to do well. But that was still a long time away and for now, as we drank tea and chatted, I reflected that here was another good member of our rapidly expanding band.

Having eaten a second lunch in the Thamserku, I set about resolving my most immediate problem, namely effecting the repair of my running shoe. On my tour around Namche I had seen several shops which I thought might be able to help. How, I wasn't sure, but there were several retail outlets selling a vast array of mountaineering equipment, most of which had been acquired from expeditions retreating to civilisation. I felt confident that resourceful traders like these could, for the right price, come up with something suitable to sew or stick onto my shoe to protect it, and therefore me, from further disintegration on the mountain.

I set off filled with optimism, armed with the sorry-looking shoe, but an hour later my optimism had evaporated. Had I wanted to buy or hire, tents, ropes, sleeping bags, salopettes, ice axes, down jackets, any variety of dried foods, cooking or climbing apparatus from the chaotic bulging little emporia which I visited, I could have returned with enough supplies and equipment for a major assault on Everest.

But in each of these dingy but vibrant Aladdin's caves, with kerosene lamps illuminating their inner reaches in a manner that would have had many a good insurance man spluttering into his mobile phone back home, the answer was the same.

"No," followed by much head shaking. "Not possible to fix. We have good boots. Here, let me show you good boots."

I had good boots. But I was damned if I was going to run in them.

And so, demoralised, I headed back to the lodge. Of course some of the shops sold trainers, but they were the thin soled flimsy things that I would refer to as daps. One step up from those hideous elastic fronted affairs; even the youngest kids at my school wouldn't have been seen dead in them. Fashion apart, I saw nothing remotely suitable for running a mountain marathon in.

Out of desperation, I tried the little shop beneath the Tawa lodge. It hardly seemed worth bothering, for it seemed to sell only trinkets and T-shirts. However, the shopkeeper was a helpful young man, who spoke good English, and when I told him why I needed the shoe repaired, he was keen to help.

"Come with me," he said, conspiratorially.

"You can fix it?" I asked excitedly.

"The Tibetan can," he replied.

We walked quickly up the bumpy street which the eastern wing of the Tawa balcony overlooked. Someone called my name and as I looked up to acknowledge the greeting, I tripped on a stone step and was catapulted into the path of a fully laden yak lurching unsteadily beneath its burden down the street towards me. The shopkeeper grabbed my arm and prevented me from falling headlong into the path of the oncoming bovine juggernaut. I thanked him and he smiled. I pressed myself against the wall as the impressive animal lurched impassively past, head low to the ground with mighty horns ready to clear the street of any obstacles they may encounter, human or otherwise. Heavily laden, its girth virtually occupied the entire width of the street.

What this town needs is a traffic-free pedestrian zone, I thought, as we reached a junction, and climbed steps to another smaller street. Eventually, through a labyrinth of narrow alleys, we came to a house with a large wooden gate, beyond which was a little courtyard.

"Wait here," I was told. I waited. The Tibetan was clearly revered by the community.

My friend entered the gate and crossed the courtyard to a door through which he entered the house. He spoke, and I heard a woman's voice reply. An animated conversation between the two followed, occasionally punctuated with what sounded like the gruff groan of an animal in pain coming from inside the window beside which I waited.

At length he crossed the courtyard and joined me forlornly.

"No good?" I asked.

"The Tibetan is drunk," he replied. That explained the noises from the window. "But tomorrow he will not be drinking and he will mend your shoe."

The remainder of the day seemed to drift by in a peaceful haze of food, drink and keeping warm in the lodge, as the mist again descended and the temperature plummeted in late afternoon.

Upstairs, in the dormitory adjacent to my luxury single room I found Ray sprawled on the bed nearest to the door. He greeted me with a wink which momentarily replaced the pained expression on his face, in part due to his stomach upset, and in part due to the little Japanese man sitting on the bed next to him.

Shigemi Chiba, from Tokyo, was in his late fifties and another recently arrived late addition. He had attempted the race in 1991, but had failed to finish. By all accounts, he had not enjoyed it much and neither had anyone else in his vicinity. People do strange things with their lives, but quite why he had felt the urge to return was beyond comprehension. As the days passed and the trek resumed, each of us prayed that our tent would be erected as far from Shigi as possible and then some more. For this little man could snore like there was no tomorrow. His extreme nocturnal nasal noises were enough to frighten any passing Yeti and to cause erstwhile perfectly stable snow to avalanche on mountains miles away.

By 8 p.m., after another indifferent supper provided by the enthusiastic trek cooks followed by a more palatable meal in the Khumbu, I was exhausted, and decided it was time to turn in. There was still no sign of the Late Birds, who were following a day behind. We assumed that they were a less militant lot than us and had followed the itinerary as prescribed by Diana.

Diana herself was in residence at the Thamserku, accompanied by one year old Tashi, who was similar in many ways to one year old Cameron whom I had left at home. Similar, except that Tashi's mother was basically responsible for the health, safety and relative sanity of over seventy basket cases who sought the ultimate in mountain running, but complained when they had to buy their own toilet paper.

## Friday 19th November

Peeing apart, I had quite a good night. On two occasions I prised myself from my pit and staggered my way along the shadowy corridor, groped down torchlit stairs, and along the misty stone parapet outside the lodge, to find the key and do battle with the lock on the 'byre' door. On each of these occasions, I collided squarely with the curiously placed flagpole right in the centre of the path to the left of the door of the Thamserku. Odd, how I hadn't noticed it in daylight. But the bump on my forehead the next morning was evidence of its obduracy.

My third call of nature was an improvised slash over the parapet where our tents had been placed the previous evening, giving the post a wide birth. As no one except for John Dunning and Mike Harper had expressed the slightest inclination to remain under canvas when something approaching comfort could be had for a pittance, they had been packed away that morning. Perhaps John wanted to be closer to the toilet. It occurred to me that if I accidentally peed on his tent, perhaps some sort of justice would have been done.

Passing the dormitory was like passing the epicentre of an earthquake. The wooden floor seemed to vibrate to the rhythmic stertorous violence which Shigi was inflicting on his roommates. Even in the sanctity of my room, the decibels rivalled an Iron Maiden concert. However, I was fortunate enough to have made the last minute purchase of a pair of ear plugs at Heathrow, as Dieter had warned me about this guy.

By the time I had got downstairs to breakfast, resplendent in the errant hat, Ray had run to Thamo and back to investigate 'the loop'. His stomach was still rebellious, but he appeared as content as Ray ever did; despite three shit-stops, he had returned in well under the hour.

After breakfast provided by our cooks, supplemented by another plate of those wonderful fried eggs, toast and fried potatoes, I was ready for anything.

What I wasn't ready for, however, was another shopping trip.

But when a mature and attractive woman takes you under her wing with something approaching maternal concern and offers of help, who was I to resist? Jerri Lee may have been knocking on the door of forty, and the glitz and sterile glamour of suburban Oakland may have been a little tarnished by the grime of the trek, but she was undeniably still an attractive woman. She had also been a long time in the wilderness, and the call of the shopping mall was hard to suppress. A month without shopping to a Californian must be like a month without raping and pillaging to a Viking sentenced to Community Service.

So we set off to scour the shops of Namche for something suitable in which I could run the race, with the same far flung optimism of bargain hunters on the first day of the sales. Just in case the Tibetan had decided that he would, after all, be drinking today, or pronounced my shoe beyond repair.

Whilst waiting for my second breakfast to arrive, I had again visited the Tibetan with my shoe. Anxiously, I had opened the gate into the little courtyard where, on the west side, a double door opened to reveal possibly the world's oldest woman lugubriously turning possibly the world's largest prayer wheel in a melancholy and sombre manner. The colourfully inscribed metal prayer wheel occupied most of the downstairs of the building, and was doubtless of aesthetic as well as inestimable spiritual value. But it was the size of a ship's boiler, and it was hard to see the attraction of possessing such a monstrosity.

I poked my head round the door opposite to see a wizened old man sitting in an armchair amid the squalor and chaos of a room that served as his workshop and living quarters. He looked at me with the far away eyes of the very wise or the very hung over. I pointed to the toe of my shoe.

"Can you fix this?" I asked. He motioned me closer, scrutinised the shoe, and then nodded slowly.

"That's a relief," I said. "How much will it cost?" I didn't care, but it is always better in these parts to agree a price beforehand. He held up four fingers.

"Four hundred rupees!" I exclaimed, a little taken aback. He shook his head and motioned again with the same four fingers.

"Four rupees?" He shook his head, a little more violently this time.

"Ah! Forty rupees!" He nodded. I smiled, and resisted the temptation to try to beat him down to thirty. Haggling had become a way of life. Still, fifty pence should guarantee a good job.

"When will it be ready?" I asked.

Once more, the four fingers were thrust in front of my eyes. It wasn't much wonder he drank on his own. His conversation seemed a little limited.

I bade him good-day and walked through the sunny courtyard where the crone turned the prayer wheel, as oblivious to my presence as to the fact that man had long since landed on the moon.

An hour later Jerri Lee, with the assistance of a convivial shop keeper who knew a sucker when she saw one, had convinced me that I had found exactly what we had been looking for.

What they had found was a pair of green, lightweight, rubber-soled boots with suede and canvas uppers, made in Korea by that well known sports shoe manufacturer Rocky. I had to admit that not only did they look good, but they were also incredibly comfortable. As for running in them, well, I just couldn't tell. The idea of running in any sort of boots seemed unnatural to me. But whereas my costly Brasher boots in full flight handled like a runaway bin-lorry, these Rockys had the comfort and looks suggestive of a Vauxhall Frontera; the sort of things that turn heads in the Tesco car park, but were never seriously intended to be taken over rock and mud.

Cheap, though, they were not. The well-dressed shop keeper who looked, and probably was, closely related to the *didi* of the Khumbu lodge calmly announced that she would like three thousand, two hundred rupees in exchange for them. Three thousand, two hundred rupees! That was around a third of a night in the Everest View Hotel! I shook my head, and stood up.

"No. Too much," I said, and turned to leave.

"Three thousand, one hundred?"

"Oh but Richard, they look ideal!"

"Two thousand, five hundred," I countered, weakening. There is something curiously exciting about shopping with a woman who is not your wife. Perhaps I have led a very dull life in this department, but it is the nearest I have yet come, or wanted to come, to having an affair. There is something unmistakably conspiratorial and exotic about malting even the most mundane purchases. Particularly if you go for a drink or a coffee afterwards and relive the thrill of the chase.

If I had been on my own, I would almost certainly have said that I would think about it and in all likelihood not have come back. But I wasn't on my own, and if I walked away empty-handed I was letting Jerri Lee down. Out of concern, she had persuaded me to embark on a more extensive search and we had been rewarded by the discovery of something which undeniably appeared suitable. After all, why else would this remote trading post stock them? This wasn't exactly Oxford Street. Also undeniable was the fact that, had they cost around fifteen hundred rupees, I would have snapped them up. So why on earth was I being a cheapskate and quibbling over a few hundred rupees when the outcome could make the difference between success and miserable failure? At worst they would be a back up, and a vast improvement on what I was currently wearing, for the rest of the trek.

Before I knew it, we had agreed on two thousand, nine hundred rupees which, at over forty quid, was probably twice what the boots were worth at home. But who cared? Jerri Lee beamed delightedly at me, as if I had just slayed the dragon.

"Do you take Visa?" I asked.

"Visa? What is Visa?"

"Never mind," I replied, and reluctantly peeled six five hundred rupee notes from my wallet. What with video camera licences and boots, it was a good job that you could get a luxury suite for around a quid a night.

\*

"D'you want to take a run out to the loop?" Ray asked me, basking on his bed.

The quiet of the empty dormitory, with bright sunlight flooding through the windows, was a haven of tranquillity in contrast to the nightmare vibrations of Shigi's snoring. I had heard several people threaten to murder him if he repeated that performance again tonight.

"I suppose I'd better find out what it's like to run at this altitude," I replied, unenthusiastically. By the stage of the race when we got down to this altitude, we would be close to the finish. But Dieter had advised me to investigate the six miles to Thamo and back, for this was a gruelling part of the race which had crippled the ambitions of many quality runners.

"Good, I'll come with you," Ray offered.

"But you've already run there this morning," I said.

"I'm fed up of bloody kicking my heels around here," he replied. "Besides, we can take it at a steady pace."

It was now twelve thirty, and some four hours had passed since I had left my shoes with the Tibetan. As four appeared to be the number by which his life revolved, I decided it was worth a visit to see how my shoes were coming along. If they were not ready, or should he again be drinking, then my newly acquired Rockys would be broken in.

To my surprise, my shoes had been repaired. The Tibetan had stitched a crude but remarkably effective green leather patch which bridged the rubber sole and the fabric upper. I examined it carefully before parting with my money. It wasn't pretty, but it was stitched with thread thick enough to anchor the QE2 and I felt optimistic that it would do the job. I handed over the money and went to road-test the repair.

The cloud was gathering in the valley as Ray and I climbed to Chhorkung, and found the path that led to Tengboche. It was important to be clear in our minds which path bypassed Namche and led to Thamo, for to take a detour into Namche after twenty miles would not be a good thing to do. We jogged gently some way along the flattish sandy path. My heart raced, as it struggled to cope with the absurd demands being made on it in the thin air. Ray, in his running kit, looked even skinnier than before. He had fasted for two days, and it showed on his diminutive frame. Whatever weight loss I had experienced due to my own stomach problems was of less concern. At six foot two and twelve and a half stone, the less I had to carry up and down the mountain the better. Ray stopped ahead of me.

"Okay, let's do it."

"Go easy," I pleaded. "Remember this is the highest I've ever been, never mind run."

We turned, and ran lightly back along the track. It seemed slightly downhill and we slipped easily onto the path which traversed the hill above the village and passed above the gompa. The path continued to descend gently. 'This is easy,' I thought to myself, as rested muscles warmed in the cool of the early afternoon mist and heart and lungs began to scream less abusive messages to my brain.

And then we came to the first climb. It was only a gentle slope, rising slowly to where the path contoured around the hill past a *chorten* and on towards Phurte. Suddenly my heart felt as though it were about to burst through my chest and my head and lungs threatened to explode simultaneously. Ray held his stride pattern, running easily and effortlessly ahead while I fell behind, coughing and panting in the thin air. It was pointless trying to keep up with him. I felt like quitting. I felt like crying, I was a failure – Ray had disappeared from view, I couldn't even stay with him on a gentle run. How the hell would I run at almost eighteen thousand feet, if I was struggling to move at a jog at less than twelve thousand?

Gradually, I felt the anger and frustration, as vital a force at driving my will to get over the next hill as all the years of training, begin to kick in. Like the Tuesday morning on the Lizard when I started a thirty-five mile leg of my Cornwall coast path run to finish near Mevagissey. In driving sleet and a force eight gale into which I thought it was impossible to run, I was close to despair. But somehow the anger spat out in obscene invectives at the unseen force behind the wind pulled me through it.

'You haven't come here to bottle out!' screamed a voice in my head. Slowly, the anger helped the pain to ebb away and although it felt as though I were running through glue, at least I was running. The path was seldom level and I could appreciate how the constant undulations would sap both energy and resolve after the rigours of the twenty miles from Gorak Shep. Anyone who simply looked at the 'altitude by mileage' chart which we had been given, and assumed that the last six miles were as flat as they appeared on paper, would be in for a nastier shock than the latrine tent on the first night.

Before Phurte, where the path wound down and zigzagged through a pleasant wooded stretch, I passed two young porters, lads who looked no more than thirteen or fourteen, sitting smoking on their large cargoes of timber.

The familiar heckling I expected, but much to my surprise and annoyance, they first pursued me, then overtook, running just ahead of me laughing and joking, occasionally slowing to draw on their cigarettes.

"Little bastards!" I hissed. "You're taking the bloody piss. Wouldn't be quite so bloody cocky over fifty miles of coast path where you can breathe!" However, I had a suspicion that they probably would be. The natives of the Khumbu were irritatingly fit, despite their predilection for vast amounts of tobacco and rough alcohol.

After half a mile or so, they tired of their game and stopped.

*"Namaste!"* they called, waving me past with mock deference.

"Fuck off!" I hissed to no one in particular when out of earshot, mainly out of the frustration at not being able to move faster than an octogenarian. They were only lads having a bit of fun, innocent joyriders on the trail to Thamo. There was no malice intended: these were no adrenalin junkies puffed up with their own macho stereotype self-image and driven on by the constant need to prove themselves to their peers. People here weren't like that, and besides, they didn't have time for that sort of stuff.

At Phurte I found the only piece of dual carriageway I had seen in Nepal. The path divided where a huge *chorten*, which from a distance resembled a fat policeman wearing a traditional Bobby's helmet, stood guard over the tiny village. The little yellow god's face gazed down in disapproval as I ignored religious custom and passed on the right. To take the left-hand carriageway would have extended my run by a good fifty yards.

Not long after, I met Ray on his way back. To my surprise, he told me that I was near Thamo and the turning point.

"There's a boulder just before you get to the first building. That's where you turn, you can't miss it! See you later." I warned him to be prepared for some unwelcome company on his way back, but felt certain that he would respond to the challenge rather better than I had.

The boys might even put their cigarettes out. He picked up speed again, and I felt a pang of envy. At that pace, he had probably run right through Thamo and half way to Tibet.

As I turned at the boulder in Thamo, I glanced at my watch. I had been running for over thirty minutes, which was a pitifully slow pace for three miles. I suspected that the going would be tougher on the way back and despondently resigned myself to completing the run in around eighty minutes.

To my astonishment, I was wrong. The three miles back to Namche were considerably easier than I had anticipated. For one thing, apart from the long incline down which I had run with my escort, there were fewer uphill stretches than I had remembered. Also, my body had adjusted more rapidly than I had expected and even my headache eased to a dull thud over the last couple of miles. My spirits rose considerably as I realised I was going to be well within my pessimistic estimate of eighty minutes.

As I threaded my way through the boulder-strewn maze of small paths leading to the *chorten* where the path dog-legged down to Namche, my spirits rose still further as my watch informed me that I could finish well inside the hour! It had taken me under twenty-five minutes from Thamo. Far below, I could see our lodge and the familiar blue tents being erected on the muddy terrace above the Thamserku. The Late Birds must have arrived at last.

In my excitement, I somehow missed the path that would have taken me down past the gompa and into Namche, past the post office, the bank, along beneath the balcony of the Tawa, and back to the field beneath the Thamserku, where the race would finish.

A very frustrating three minutes later, I had weaved my way down through the alleys from Chhorkung, flying down steps and stupidly taking far more risks than were justified, to finish on the mud terrace amongst the unfamiliar Late Birds, in just over fifty-nine minutes. I had pushed myself hard and felt utterly knackered. But at least I knew that whatever the path threw at us between Gorak Shep and Chhorkung, it was vital to hold something in reserve for those final six, tortuous, undulating miles.

*

I found Ray in the lounge of the Thamserku talking to Alan Hall from Gisborne, New Zealand, who was one of the Late Birds. From Alan's description of their trek, they had had a much worse time than us. Stomach disorders had been rife, and already several people had succumbed to altitude sickness. Their doctors were prescribing Diamox by the fistful, and already the prospects of several members of the group making the start did not look good.

There were those, of course, like Russell and Viv Prince, New Zealand ultra-distance record holders, who had trained every day, often running on to the next day's destination and back again. We didn't have any such nonsense in our group and, if it hadn't been for the lousy weather condition, Ray and I probably wouldn't have pushed ourselves so hard on the trek.

Listening to Alan confirmed what an odd and diverse group the Late Birds were, and how glad I was that I had cancelled my Chitwan booking and had been placed in the Early Birds. First of all, there was Mr Argumentative, for whom nothing was ever right. He was wearing a bit thin, even with his long-standing chums. Well, I had done my best to fill that role in our group, but had tried to play the part with caustic humour. Then there was little Miss Hypochondriac, who constantly thought she was dying, and Mr Sickbag who usually was, and shouldn't really have come in the first place. Added to them was Mr All-Too-Much who had never travelled further than the nearest market town, let alone leave his native shores. He was finding it a bit, well, all too much. Finally, there was Mr Just-Plain-Odd, who was so alternative that back home he knitted his own yoghurt and grew socks in his kitchen garden.

If any confirmation was required that the Late Birds were, generally speaking, a few mani stones short of a full *chorten*, it was served up by the fact that, almost to a man, they preferred their tents and the food provided by their cooks to the bounty that could be had for next to nothing in the lodges.

Ray apologised for abandoning me and explained that he had felt good, and had pushed himself hard to record the fastest time over the loop, at fifty minutes. He was pleased to have bettered "Gobo's" time of fifty-one minutes, and the fastest Gurkha claimed to have completed the run in fifty-two minutes. Ray had won a major battle in the psychological war. The average Gurkha time was fifty-four minutes and I felt elated at being in touch with runners of that class on my first run at altitude. All the others had trained hard at greater height and, as such, had a considerable advantage.

Dave had organised a guided tour for all runners to ensure that everyone knew the correct path to take out of Chhorkung, where I had gone wrong, when entering Namche, and finding the finish line. I was about to set off with the others, when one of the girls who worked in the lodge informed me that my shower was ready. I was reluctant to give up my last opportunity for cleanliness for over a week, so Ray promised to take a walk up the path later to show me where we would have to come back in. I skulked off and sneaked furtively past Diana, hiding my towel, soap and cleanish underclothes in my small rucksack.

Later on that afternoon, after Ray and I strolled up the hill past the gompa to check where I had gone wrong, we were joined by Charlie, and retired to the Khumbu for a meal. Ray was still on his fluids only purge, but Charlie and I ravenously tucked into an extremely good vegetable noodle soup, followed by yak steak and chips and, to complete the meal, apple pie. We then went back to our lodge for our evening meal.

It was probably at this point that I realised that, just to stay healthy, it would become necessary to eat and drink almost uninterrupted from here to the start of the race. For fat people with a will to release the slim person inside, this is the place to be. Altitude simply sucks the weight from your body.

Over dinner in the Khumbu, there was a fair amount of good-natured verbal horseplay, particularly from Charlie, in an effort to psyche out one another.

"This is going to be our year, you know," he said. "The lads are in top condition and we know exactly what to expect this time. We've at least two who will take Gobet," he predicted. "Just look at him, he's not hungry for it this year." That I doubted very much.

"I wouldn't be too hasty to write off Roka," I said. Another late arrival had slipped into town, almost unnoticed, mixing easily with the people with whom he shared his roots. Hari Roka had run in the marathon for Nepal in the 1992 Barcelona Olympics. Finishing in a creditable position, he had attained the status of a world-class marathon runner. Hari was one of Nepal's few national sporting heroes, and was also a full-time professional athlete.

"Naw, he's basically a road runner," replied Charlie dismissively.

"He's got the credentials," said Ray. "And besides, I'll bet he was bloody running over this bloody crap long before he set eyes on a bloody road."

At seven thirty, in the Thamserku lounge where our food was served, there was a meeting "which everyone *will* attend". Dave and Diana went over the final details regarding the race. Most of the information was received in a stony silence. Much of it I had heard before, but oddly, on this occasion, that served to underline its importance. Until now, the race had seemed distant, far removed from what we were doing. Both groups, leaders, doctors, and sirdars were packed into the steamy little lounge. Although we would now follow in each other's footsteps on the trek to Gorak Shep, we would camp separately and the two groups would not again mingle after tomorrow morning until we stood together on the start line one week hence.

The race was becoming a reality, a day of reckoning which was fast approaching. My thrill of anticipation was shrouded with a thin, cold veil of fear as Dave and Diana informed us that those who displayed symptoms of altitude sickness prior to the race would not be declared fit by the medics and not issued a race number. The good news was that each aid post would be attended by a doctor with a stretcher and oxygen.

We were issued with a sheet which summarised the information we had been given. Dave ran through the week's itinerary and the procedure on race day. We were advised to familiarise ourselves with the course on the upward trek. The course was not marked as markers had in the past disappeared. Moreover, there were several places where it was possible to take a wrong turning. Finally, we were urged to take particular care on bridges and when passing yaks, which were unpredictable and must always be passed on the inside of the path.

An hour later, I settled into the snugness of my double bed to savour a final night of comfort armed with two empty plastic water bottles, cunningly converted to pee-bottles by the surgical removal of their necks.

As I drifted into fitful sleep, my mind reeled with rampaging yaks, spiralled with stony faced, head shaking doctors denying me my race number, and echoed to the silence of the Tibetan wind, its icy tendrils pulling me from the path into hypothermic oblivion, lost for ever on some frostbitten plateau.

Lands End from home on the coastal path: the end of a 208 mile training run.

Pole position on the bus to Jiri. The only way to travel.

John 'Dunging', resplendent in 'the hat'. And who could argue that he didn't deserve it!

Lanjura Pass in the mist: no amount of prayer flags could bring a smile to that face!

The room service was good, but the en-suite left a little to be desired! The sirdar shows disdain for my flagrant disregard for Nepali custom.

Another interview hits the cutting room floor, as Everest disappears in cloud (left). Richard Uridge (right) and Ron Isles probe for Euphoric Vernacular Dementia. None came.

Looking down on Namche Bazaar. The lower camping field is where the ordeal comes to an end on race day. But with relative opulence to be had in the lodges for a pittance, there's no one at home in tent city.

Above the 'road' from Tengboche to Namche. Possibly the best stretch of path on the course, aside from sudden drops to the Dudh Kosi, one mile below.

The 'Early Birds' at Tengboche. The author, fourth from left, back row, is having a 'bad hair' day. Simon, next to Nat (who is in front of Annabel), has 'the hat'.

Loboche, beneath the Khumbu Glacier, close to journey's end.

'Taking it easy' at over 5000 metres with Ray above Loboche on the final rest day.

The night before the race at "Gorak 'get down' Shep". Pierre André, looking relaxed, fourth from right.

'Where chickens dare'. The Lukla runway – the ultimate 'white-knuckle ride'!

Relief at a safe landing shared with Dr Bryan English. Now let's party!

Dressed to kill for the awards ceremony and the end of ordeal party. Left to right: Richard Grainger, Dr Simon Petrides, Dr Bryan English, Pierre André Gobet and Dave English.

# The Road to Tengboche: "And Some Say That There Is No God!"

## Saturday 20th November

I rose late, dozing and listening to music in a hazy reverie of ambiguous thoughts and emotions, reluctant to relinquish the comfort of my bed. My thoughts turned to yesterday's run. I had been gratified with my time, but concerned as to how tired I had been afterwards. Something else struck me as odd: I had experienced a curious sense that something was missing, particularly in the latter part when I had been more relaxed. I suddenly realised what it was – I had no dog. I was unaccustomed to running without a lead entwined around my wrist and a white and black streak darting after this deer or that rabbit, then padding loyally behind, only running ahead when she tired and wanted to make sure I wouldn't forget about her. And always when we set out, the poor bugger never knew whether we were going to run for six or thirty six miles.

Kirsty had said that I should take a dog lead with me. It might make me run better. Well, this time next week, with or without a dog lead, it would be all over one way or another.

It was another glorious morning, and after breakfast we all strolled up the hill to the National Park headquarters where the museum was situated. The Gurkhas were right. It took us about ten minutes to reach it.

The previous evening, we had been requested to assemble at 9 a.m. by the helicopter landing pad beyond the museum for an official group photograph to be taken. It took as long as one would expect for Rob Howard, now operating with cameras borrowed from Charlie and Ron Isles, to create some semblance of order among almost eighty recalcitrant runners who all wanted to be doing something else. At last, when we had been shepherded into three lines, sitting, kneeling and standing, it became apparent that some of our leaders, including Diana, were not present.

And so we waited. And we waited. At first no one was particularly aggrieved by the delay. The sun, after all, was shining, and the view wasn't that bad, either. But gradually as the minutes ticked by, dripping from the hands of the clock like teardrops falling into the vacuum of inactivity in which we sat, kneeled or stood, the grumbling began. At first it was a trickle, then it was a flood, as wave after wave of acrid protests swept over the indignant gathering.

"Can you believe this?" I asked Ray. "Here are we on a perfect morning, standing in warm sunshine looking at exactly what we've come all this way to see. It's not exactly North Wales on a wet, foggy day, is it? We have an uninterrupted view up the valley to the world's highest mountains. You could not have a more spectacular backdrop than what's behind us. And are we happy? Are we bugger! You can't hear yourself think for whinging!"

"What's the matter Marvin?" replied Annabel. "We're not moaning about moaning now are we?"

Eventually Diana sailed up the path like royalty, to a chorus of sardonic applause, with Tashi, Dave and Wish in tow. A few minutes later the gathering of disgruntled runners set off to rinse out their socks or continue with whatever it was that was so important.

Ray and I went for a final stroll around town to take a look at the market and buy a few essential provisions which we had seen earlier. I was in no hurry to get back into trek mode, and was happy to delay my departure until near lunchtime, in the hope that my washing might be dry.

There were in fact now only twenty miles to cover to Gorak Shep. But the distance we would go towards our destination each day would be insignificant compared with the unknown effect of the distance which we would travel upwards. This would be the telling factor. There were two days when we would not trek at all; days set aside for rest, acclimatisation and, for those who wanted to, training.

Today the lunch-stop was at Pungo Tenge, just beyond the bottom of the feared Sarnassa Hill and before the equally fearsome climb to Tengboche began.

The Namche Saturday Blue Sky market was everything it had been cracked up to be. The little streets were awash with the colourful throng of bustling buyers and sellers. There were few stalls. Most who had come to sell simply sat cross-legged over the bamboo panniers called *Rokos* and the sacks or cardboard boxes which yesterday they had arduously lugged up the mountain. Those who had come to buy, mainly dokos (the local people) down from the high pastures to buy supplies, examined the produce and haggled themselves an acceptable price. There was, of course, a smattering of tourists like ourselves interspersed with the traders and punters, but this market had very little to do with tourism. It had been going on long, long before the first plane load of Westerners touched down in Kathmandu.

On offer was rice, wheat, corn and a kind of millet called *kodo*. Many of the everyday essential items such as tea, sugar, petrol and beer had been carried all the way on someone's back from Jiri. Much of it would be for our consumption in the lodges as we progressed further up the valley of the Dudh Kosi. It was incredible to think of the time and effort which had gone into getting the goods this far, and they would go further still. This, of course, would be reflected in the price, but, even if the prices were to treble, most things would still be cheaper than at home. I shuddered to think how high inflation might rise if the off-licence in Sidmouth High Street was stocked by a little man who had walked in from Exeter.

Having done our bit of sightseeing, Ray and I returned to the village centre and found a large shop which specialised in expedition supplies and equipment, and had exactly what we were looking for.

Ray was concerned about his torch. It worked perfectly well, shone brightly where it was required and there was technically nothing the matter with the thing. It was just that it was too damned heavy. But a torch was a part of the minimum equipment which we were obliged to carry during the race, or risk disqualification, and this was causing Ray some concern. On the initial minimum kit list, a torch did not appear. Had it done so, Ray would have obtained an appropriate torch. But last night, the word "TORCH" had appeared in bold capitals on the handout which we had been issued. On this, the organisers were unyielding. No torch – no medal. An appropriate torch to Ray was one which weighed about half as much as a postage stamp, the sort of thing used by surgeons for performing fibre optic, keyhole, cardio-vascular operations. When the shopkeeper produced a small cylindrical black object the length of a matchstick, Ray was manifestly thrilled.

"I don't suppose the battery will last long," I said naively.

"Who said anything about carrying a bloody battery?" he replied. "You heard him, he only said you need a bloody torch. And this is a bloody torch. And a bloody good torch too!" He was like a cat who had found the cream. He almost purred.

Good it may have been, but cheap it wasn't. It cost almost the equivalent of a week's stay in a single room at the Thamserku.

"Besides", he added thoughtfully, "if I'm still on the hill after sundown, I'm going to need more than a bloody torch!"

Earlier we had noted that, amongst the array of climbing and trekking goodies for sale in the store, were packets of dehydrated food. It is amazing what can now be done with food. All sorts of meals were available, from Chicken Supreme, Sweet and Sour Duck, to sausages and beans. Ray was clearly on the mend as his thoughts had once again turned to food, but he was extremely wary of what our cooks would serve up during the coming week. As meat would certainty get scarcer, who knew exactly what they might be tempted to lob into the stew? So this was insurance. All you had to do was ask the lodge *didi* to pop a packet in boiling water for a few minutes and, hey presto, there was a ready made meal.

Ray bought several packets of the more exotic meals and I purchased several packets of beans and sausage. I knew, of course, that the sausages would bear little resemblance to those plump, gristle and fat filled growling digits which sizzle temptingly in the pan, or spit effusively on the barbecue, but they were familiar and safe.

Finally, we bought chocolate. A lot of chocolate. At home my chocolate intake is strictly limited to Sunday nights, but here it was an essential form of instant energy and, with the constant weight loss at altitude, as good an excuse to gorge ourselves on the stuff as ever we would get.

Ray decided to set off and I returned to the Thamserku to collect my belongings and pay. The system for settling one's account throughout the Solu Khumbu is an exercise in both memory and integrity and, as such, one which is unlikely to be adopted by any ambitious Western hotelier wishing to make a profit. Each lodge has a book, usually a school exercise book. As you order food or drink, you record your order and the price. When you come to leave, you add the cost of your bed, any washing you may have had done, plus any other extras, such as toilet paper or water, which you have purchased. You then total them up and present the *didi* with the book and your payment.

The system is as much a temptation to the artful dodger as arms sales to win construction contracts are to the enterprising politician. The unscrupulous trekker can abuse the system with the same impunity as he would at home submit an inflated insurance claim, or forget to declare the rent from his holiday cottage in Wales on his tax return. Honesty aside, it is not a very practical system. Should the lodge be busy, and the book not be available, it is not always easy to remember exactly what one has had.

I arranged my belongings in my Berghaus and found, to my surprise, that I had to think carefully about what had until recently been as automatic a procedure as getting ready for work in the morning.

"Okay," I said to myself, taking a last wistful look at my room. "Let's go camping!"

I paid, thanked the *didi*, who responded with just the hint of a smile, and said farewell. Outside in the bright sunshine I stood and gazed at the muddy terrace below the lodge, where our tents had briefly been placed and, more importantly, where the race would finish in around six days time. I tried to imagine myself running down past the gompa, along the narrow street overlooked by the Tawa, down the steps past the Thamserku shower, through the gap in the wall onto the terrace and through the funnel which I had seen in photographs many times, beneath the blue Everest marathon banner to the finish line. I wondered how it must feel to be the first to take the tape.

Then for a moment, I was lost in a sepia daydream, captured in a slow motioned, cinematic fantasy as I ran down the hill into Namche. Suddenly ahead of me was the leader, Pierre André. To my surprise, I was rapidly closing the gap between us. Before he was aware of my challenge from behind, I was almost level with him. Then, striding, *Chariots of Fire*-like, with sinews tensed and teeth gritted, shoulder to shoulder with him through the narrow streets. Veteran duellists of the dawn encounter now, after twenty-six miles, too proud to give in, each too tired to break free from the other.

Past the post office, past the bank, over the rough cobbles, we asked questions of each other that had not been asked before, and which mere words could not answer, fighting it out to the death like gladiators in this land of smiles above the cloud. With every last ounce of energy, willing to risk everything simply for the right to be the first to cross the line.

And then, it was over.

At the death, he faded, drained and beaten. I surged ahead through the gap, head lolling uncontrollably, a whirl of tired and aching limbs propelling me impossibly slowly towards the tape. I waited for him to come past. Surely he must catch me. The camera angle changed, and I noticed the crowds that jostled for a better view on either side of the funnel. They perched on every inch of the parapet outside the Thamserku and hung from every open window of adjacent lodges. They were all looking at me. And as the tape came closer, I heard them clap and scream hysterical encouragement.

Not far now. I could see the timekeeper study his stopwatch. It could even be a new record.

Then, finally the feeling of almost immortality as I raised my arms aloft and momentarily felt the tightness of the tape across my chest before it fluttered redundant to the ground. I punched the sky in triumph, twice, fists clenched tight in sweet, sweet victory. Diana hugged me, placing the winner's medal around my neck. To the victor go the spoils. Things happened quickly. Cameras clicked, a microphone was thrust into my face.

"Unbelievable. I just kept going, and then I saw him, ahead of me. A new record? Christ! You're kidding!"

Adrenalin kept me on my feet. A cup of water was thrust into my hand. Someone rushed forward and placed a garland of pretty mountain flowers around my neck, and from somewhere else, a white cotton scarf.

Then I turned to look at Pierre, and my heart filled with pity. A sad figure, alone and forlorn amid the crumbling ruins of the castle where once he had been crowned king. Condolences from the new king, a hug and a handshake, before returning to the limelight, leaving him to the mercy of the intrusive microphone. He handled it well:

"I believe that everybody has two legs, yea. One heart, one head. That's all." It was just like Pierre to laugh off his defeat. His cheeky sense of mischievous fun would not desert him, not even in the darkest hour.

And then close by I heard the tinkle of a cowbell, and felt something sharp prod my hip gently, but with enough force as to move me some way sideways and bring me back to the real world in which the fulfilment of my daydream was as likely as Biman Bangladesh winning International Airline of the Year award.

Thus the dream faded, and I was back in the full glorious technicolour of a Namche Saturday morning on the parapet outside the lodge, standing in the path of a train of ostensibly docile, but rather large, fully laden yaks who had a day's work to do. Once they had got past me. I shouldered my rucksack and moved out of their way, recalling the words of Eliot:

> *I have seen the moment of my greatness flicker,*
> *And I have seen the eternal Footman hold my coat,*
>     *and snicker,*
> *And in short, I was afraid.* [1]

Moments of greatness are, for most of us, relative. But there is no law which says that we cannot have them.

\*

If walking out of Namche late that Saturday morning had taken a good deal of resolve, it was almost instantly worth it as I climbed higher on the path out of Chhorkung. Far ahead of me up the valley was the same stupendous view which I had been privileged to witness near the Everest View Hotel, and which had been the backdrop for the world moaning championships earlier this morning. It was an uplifting experience and caused me to re-evaluate my previously grim view of trekking.

For almost three miles the path was virtually level, apart from the occasional scramble up rough rocky steps fashioned by the passing feet of generations of traders. The path was cut into the mountainside, contouring around breathtaking hairpin bends which, even at a steady walk, had me gasping at the sudden appearance of a sheer drop where the land tumbled away down to the Dudh Kosi far below.

I was now on the course over which the first twenty miles of the race would be run. *Falling off the trail could cause severe injury or death; medical assistance may not be timely*, Diana had stated in her

---

[1] 'The Love Song of J. Alfred Prufrock'

notes. I had thought that this was perhaps just a little overstated when I had read it, but now I could see that it was not.

But even the realisation that extreme caution was required was not enough to keep my eyes on the path. The magnetic draw of the mountains was just too powerful, and I found myself coming close to bumbling off the path and into oblivion on too many occasions.

I had resolved to trek slowly. We had been advised that to trek quickly would not be good for acclimatisation. I had ignored that advice on the earlier part of the trek, but the breathless feeling of fatigue, like sudden ageing, on my walk to the Everest View was a warning which I would heed. With only six miles to cover, there was little urgency in any case.

However, I found myself romping along in the comfort of my new Rockys, and before Sarnassa, I caught John Matesich.

"How're you doing, John?" I greeted.

"Fine. I'm doing just fine," he replied enthusiastically. "Why, this really is far out." John was into an advanced state of mountain induced EVD. This, to the layman, is Euphoric Vernacular Dementia. Its early symptoms are the use of phrases such as "Far Out!" and in its more advanced state, words such as "Awesome!" are rife. John's exhilaration at the vast panorama before us rivalled his naive shock at the horrors on the early stages of the trek. And now the word "Awesome!" had replaced the earlier "Shit!" or "Christ!"

"Take a look at the mountain. It's awesome!"

"It certainly is."

At that moment a trader with his three yaks appeared around the bend, plodding uncertainly towards us. There wasn't very much room on the path and, without thinking, I stupidly moved across to the outside to make way for them. Before I realised it, I was perched on a tiny pulpit of rock overlooking a very large drop. Luckily the yaks stopped, and I squeezed myself between them and the hillside.

"Nice yaks," said John. "Want me to take a photo of you?" I handed him my camera and, having confirmed that their owner would be happy to be photographed with his beasts ("try leaving me out of it", I think he said) John snapped away. I then took a photo of him, the yakman took a photo of the both of us, and the yaks probably would have taken a photo of the three of us, but instead decided that this photo call had gone on quite long enough and set off at a goodish lick towards Namche, their owner in hot pursuit.

Sarnassa is the first habitation beyond Chhorkung. It probably owes its existence to the fact that it is the first, or last, relatively flat ground before, or after, the path drops two thousand feet down to the river, depending on which way you are travelling. Either way, it is a good place to break one's journey, and its geographical significance has not been entirely lost on its inhabitants, as it is possible to buy refreshment or find accommodation in virtually every building. Opposite the crescent of lodges and teahouses, traders hawk and harass you into parting with money for the touristy knick-knacks which have curiously doubled in price since leaving Namche.

And then there's the hill.

Dropping to the river, 1,100 feet below Sarnassa, it then rises some 2,046 feet to Tengboche. That is roughly four times greater than the climb from sea level to the cliffs of the East Devon coastline where I had done the bulk of my training. Only here there was roughly half the oxygen present that is in the air at sea level. To say that it would a bit of an obstacle in the race, was a bit like saying that if you were a horse at the Horse of The Year Show facing the very big wall with all the bricks in the Puissance event, you would rather find Harvey Smith than Cyril Smith in your saddle.

Descending the hill was a precarious and arduous slog. For one thing, the surface had deteriorated from the gently undulating but runnable sandy track that had led out of Namche. For another, it was now an extremely hazardous boulder-strewn alley, littered with jagged rocks and scree. As such, it was barely recognisable as a path, hewn between the blue pine and fir trees of the forest on either side, which became more prolific as the river approached.

Oddly, I was much more concerned about the big descents than the big climbs in the race. I was glad that we would not have to run down this, but knew that the descent from Tengboche was likely to be twice as bad.

After an eternity, the path levelled in a clearing where there were signs of habitation. But this was a false dawn. Soon after, it again led deep into juniper forest, taking me down the flank of the mountain, zigzagging frantically as the roar of the river announced its presence, and the end of the ordeal, far below.

My thighs were aching and my knee felt as if it were on fire from the constant twisting and jumping from boulder to boulder, as I crossed the lattice-framed wooden bridge over the Imja Khola.

Beyond the bridge I came to Pungo Tenga, which was the lunch-stop. Pungo Tenga is renowned for its water-driven prayer wheels, which are of as little practical value as the lunch provided by the trek cooks would be of nutritional value, but were duly noted as I hunted for little men carrying trays bearing food. It was about one thirty, and the remnants of both groups were spread out enjoying the bright sunshine on the terraces above the village.

It was tempting to lounge longer in the sun, but the prospect of the long hard crawl up the hill to Tengboche was something I wanted to get over before the afternoon cloud rolled up the valley and crushed the warmth from the day. I had been warned that Tengboche could be bitterly cold and, although we would only gain around fifteen hundred feet from Namche, the relatively temperate and sheltered conditions of the Sherpa capital would seem like a world away.

And so, when I had reminded myself of how indifferent lunch on the trek could be and resorted to consuming two of my chocolate bars, I set off up the hill.

If I had been perturbed by the gradient and condition of the path which we would have to run, walk or crawl up to Sarnassa, I was positively depressed about what lay between the lunch-stop and Tengboche, which we would later have to run down. Dave had mentioned something about looking for shortcuts. Shortcuts? I had enough difficulty just following the path, placing my feet on something relatively flat which would not hurtle me back down the hill like a counter in a game of Snakes and Ladders.

For almost all of the climb, the path snaked erratically through a forest of contrasting trees and bushes, and where dappled sunshine filtered through the blue pine, rhododendron and black juniper, or the trail spat you out on a sunny ledge with views back towards Namche. It was truly spectacular.

It was also truly knackering. I was finding trekking slowly a good deal harder than trekking quickly and so, when Mark Woodbridge caught me, I decided to step up the pace and trek with him. Some way further up the hill, I was struggling to keep up with Mark who was not finding me particularly good company, conversing only in grunts and monosyllabic responses. I had a straight choice between talking or breathing, and after a short and fairly one-sided internal conflict, I decided upon breathing. Particularly with the increased demands in the thin air to carry my expanding wardrobe and the little culinary extras, which had been purchased and crammed into a rucksack now the weight of a small caravan, up the mountainside.

"This is what I like about trekking," enthused Mark. "You get days like this when you've not got far to go, and you can really relax, take it easy and enjoy the sun and the view."

God, what it must be like to be fit, I thought, my heart pounding from the exertion in the thin air. Mark clearly was well-acclimatised and I clearly was not. Just how much the beneficial effects of the next six days would help to level that steeply sloping playing field, I could not tell. I had a feeling, however, that, come race day, Mark and the others with recent high altitude training would have an unassailable advantage similar to playing both halves with the slope.

I was about to tell him that what I best liked about trekking was a hot tub followed by a pint or, better still, not to have to do it at all, when our progress was thankfully halted by a train of four yaks ahead of us, headed for Tengboche. It was some time before we could get past and, when we did, it was not without considerable risk to life and limb. Climbing up the bank of the hillside to overtake the leading animal, I made the realisation that not all yaks possess the same submissive and quiescent temperament. They are not all the large, hairy, docile, picture-postcard, pat-my-nose beasts that they appeared to be. The cowbells which jingled from their sturdy necks, the equivalent of the truck driver's eight-track stereo, carry a warning as well as a unique musical greeting.

Yak, or rather nak, number four was different. She probably prided herself in being different. And it was my misfortune to be squeezing past a yak with an attitude; a yak who clearly didn't want to share the path with man nor beast. Mark had managed to complete the manoeuvre without incident by the time I had reached number four. Unlike the previous three, who had graciously stopped and stood statuesque as I passed, number four closed the gap between me and the rocky side of the mountain, and forced me to pull back. Realising that this was clearly a homicidal yak who would stop at nothing, I wisely refrained from attempting to overtake on the open side of the path.

For the next fifteen minutes, I contrived devious ways to get beyond the obstinate beast in front of me, conscious of the proximity of the imposing cocktail stick-sharp horns of number three not far behind. If she got nasty and joined in the game, I would become the meat in the sandwich, or on the skewer of the kebab to be more precise. At first, it had been a blessed relief to trek at the pace of the convoy, but gradually, as the beast frustrated my every effort to pass, it grew irritating. I did not want to spend my afternoon looking at the back end of a recalcitrant yak.

And then it became personal, like the classic film which launched Spielberg's career, *Duel*. Every ploy I tried was easily countered. Occasionally, the animal would twist its neck one way or the other, sending me black ominous looks, challenging me to try again. "Go on", said the body language, "make my day."

At last I saw my chance. The path contoured around the hill to the left. We had emerged from the forest and the hillside on the right was a bare mass of stubbly undergrowth, with rocks sloping gently downwards for a hundred yards or so before dropping to the valley floor. I could see a faint trail forty feet below me which rejoined the main path. It must have been one of Dave's so called "shortcuts".

Throwing caution to the wind, I hurled myself down the hillside towards the lower path. I had not gone ten feet when my foot came into contact with a rock and my balance went the same way as my patience and judgement, hurtling me head over heels down the bank. To my horror, I realised the gradient was steeper than I had thought and my slide was suddenly out of control and gathering speed. Somehow, I managed to grab hold of a root, and arrest my descent. Greatly relieved that, minor cuts and bruises apart, only my pride had been hurt, I got to my feet and scrambled down the last few feet to the path without further incident. Pumped up with adrenalin through my narrow escape from more serious injury, I practically sprinted up the trail to where it joined the main drag.

If my experience had taught me anything, I thought, as I put some distance between myself and the belligerent yak number four, it was that shortcuts in the race were definitely out of the question.

Rounding the last bend beyond which was the final straight leading to Tengboche, I took one last look back at the yak. Head down, its coal-black staring eyes fixed on me impassively, it almost seemed to have a wry, sardonic smile on its face, as if to say: "I wasn't the prat to tumble down the hillside amid a whirlwind of dust, was I?" The victory had been a hollow one. I half expected the beast to be turbo-charged, and for it to appear behind me at full tilt on the last straight.

\*

Tengboche is not large enough even to be classed as a village. Yet this is a part of the trek which most visitors to the region will remember, after Namche of course, long into their dotage; and, for a variety of reasons, which does not include the quality of accommodation on offer. Whilst it may have the attractions, thankfully it is hardly Blackpool.

At its heart, and one of the principal attractions is a huge gompa, or monastery, which is the chief temple of the Nyingmapa sect of Tibetan Buddhism, founded by someone called Padmasambhava, whoever he may have been. This is the second most significant monastery in Nepal, and in charge is the abbot, Master Nawang Tenzen Jangpo Rinpoche, (which means reincarnate). In his current existence, the abbot was formerly abbot at the famous Rongbuk monastery in Tibet. This was the oasis for the huge expeditions during the early attempts on the north side of Everest and continued to be home to lamas and shrine for pilgrims until raped and destroyed by the cultural revolution. Then, under a more liberal regime which cagily re-opened its doors to climbers and explorers, it was used as a rubbish dump by subsequent expeditions.

The Tengboche monastery also serves as a training school, or *sheta*, for young novices.

At 12,761 feet above sea level, it is situated on the saddle of a hill, where the cold wind, carrying curious smells from the high plains of Tibet, whistles over Mount Everest to meet the more temperate but turbulent currents which blow the cloud up the valley of the Dudh Kosi.

The other principal attraction is that Tengboche has a stunning view of the mountains, described by John Hunt as "A grandstand for the finest mountains I'd ever seen." The explosive scenery which burst over the hill had a huge impact on Hunt, for the beauty and sheer enormity of the scenery caused him to proclaim: "And some people say there is no god!" Whether or not the god of Hunt's cognisance was spelt with a capital 'G' is largely irrelevant.

For it is here, the spiritual home of the gods of the mountains, and home to the October *Mani Rimdu* festival first held in 1930, that there unquestionably pervades an atmosphere as suggestive of a divine presence as in any cathedral, in any city, anywhere in the world.

Something, surely must control the inestimable forces of nature which created this unsurpassable majesty. Just as man is attracted to woman, generally speaking, and we are drawn to the mountains; it must be part of some great plan, and not some improbable random hiccup of nature, which pushed the Eurasian plate beneath the Indian plate and spat out these formidable mountains.

It is easy to understand why Hunt referred to Tengboche as a 'grandstand'. Once through the long roofed pagoda, somewhat suggestive of a car wash without the brushes, and over the crest of the hill, the ground slopes gently away beyond a flattish plateau giving the impression of looking down upon the wide valley towards the world's biggest mountains. The monastery is overlooked by the beautiful, but rakish, pyramid of Ama Dablam and has uninterrupted views up the valley of the Imja Khola to Everest and the other attendant peaks, less than twenty miles away. On the other side the gompa is beneath the shadow of Khumbiyula, a sacred mountain rising to 5,761 metres above Sarnassa, for which no climbing permit is ever granted. The gods who live there are not to be disturbed. North-north-west, there is a clear view up the Gokyo Valley, from where the Dudh Kosi emanates at the Ngozumpa Glacier.

If the sudden visual bombardment after the long haul up the hill had had a huge impact upon John Hunt, it had an equally rousing effect on me. It was like singing *Jerusalem* at Twickenham with the French routed, watching Superman reverse the world's rotation to bring Lois Lane back to life, and listening to Pavarotti's rendition of 'Nessun dorma' all rolled into one.

And then there was the monastery. Gompa are usually built against rock walls or mountains, but not this one. The Tengboche gompa stands proudly just beyond the crest of the hill. A pavilion of splendour surrounded by the lesser buildings, home to the Sherpa priests from the surrounding villages who have dedicated their lives to worshipful self-denial in this wonderful setting.

However, in January 1989, the monks were punished by the mountain gods for their wanton and wilful investment in the frivolous and self-indulgent frippery of the twentieth century. They had a small hydroelectric plant installed. Now, they could have argued with some justification, that the miracle of electric light which banished the long hours of darkness could better equip them to carry out their worshipful pursuits. Perhaps the gods considered that the use of a force which represented the greed of the material world was contrary to their advancement towards a state of rejection of all things material. Who knows? But before they had an opportunity to appreciate its benefits, the wiring developed a fault and caused a fire that destroyed the entire building.

Donations to rebuild the monastery from all over the world poured in, as did practical offers of help. But 1989 was an inauspicious year for building, and so reconstruction did not commence until 1990. Three years later, the work has been virtually completed and the monastery rebuilt on a larger scale, thanks not only to foreign aid, but also the Himalayan Trust, set up by Hillary.

In the annals of the successful Everest expedition of 1953, Tengboche had more than a passing mention. For it was here, not far from the monastery in a grassy tree-encircled field beneath the lengthening evening shadows of Ama Dablam, that Hunt's party occupied the sturdy oblong building not dissimilar to a scout hut, their home for three weeks. From this base, the climbers acclimatised, exploring the valleys and passes, and improved their fitness before moving to the head of the Khumbu Glacier to establish their base camp.

Moreover, on their triumphant return, the expedition called at Tengboche to inform the abbot of their success. The abbot, of course, already knew of their progress, and congratulated the party upon their remarkable achievement of nearly reaching the summit. It was inconceivable that mortal man could attain the same level as the gods.

Our tents were being erected close to the steps leading to the monastery. Number Fourteen had been erected and I gingerly inspected it, mindful of the unwelcome intrusion on the sole of my shoe on the last occasion it had been used. It didn't smell much worse than usual.

Ray had been here since eleven thirty. I had half expected him to have run down the hill and back up, but he was apparently satisfied that there were no navigational uncertainties and was content with his level of fitness. So instead, he had made himself useful helping the porters to erect tents, ignoring Dave's instructions not to: "on any account interfere with the putting up of tents." As a reward, his tent had been sited on the flattest part of what, upon closer inspection, proved to be a steeper slope than at first it had appeared. He had also ensured that the tent which Shigi would occupy was as far removed from his as possible.

An air of quiet tranquillity pervaded the scene, spoiled only by the inharmonious whistling of the porters, and the racket from the cowbells which announced the arrival of the troublesome yak number four and her mates. Number four had slunk to the rear of the procession, and shot me a murderous look as the train passed fifty feet away. The herder, a curious little man with teeth jutting from his mouth at impossible angles and wearing what appeared to be a world war two flying cap, applied his whip to the rump of the beast, and it reluctantly returned to the head of the group. I hoped we would not meet again, particularly not on the road to Namche next Friday morning.

I joined Mark Woodbridge and John Thomson, chatting by the monastery steps.

"What kept you?" Mark asked.

"Oh, I was just testing a few short cuts," I replied, and told them what had happened, pointing at the yak train receding into the distance. "Been round the monastery yet?" I asked them. "Mind you, John, I suppose they'll keep you in, with that haircut!"

They hadn't, so we dumped our kit and went to take a look round. Ray declined to join us. He'd done the cultural bit and stuck his head round the temple door. He said he was suffering from temple fatigue, "...besides, it's bloody noisy in there!"

Up the steps, a gate led to a square courtyard overlooked on three sides by covered palisades. Beyond this, we found the entrance to the temple. Inside, was a beautifully decorated room where monks and novices played instruments, filling the room with a harsh, haphazard and, it has to be said, not very pleasant cacophony of sound which was not instantly recognisable as music. Ray was right, it was bloody noisy. There were two types of instruments. One I imagined to be a type of flute, which resembled a metal candlestick and only appeared to be capable of producing two notes. One sounded like the noise made by a pig in agony, and the other resembled the more urgent sound made by a pig in greater agony. This instrument would make a dirge on the bagpipes sound no worse than something that Linda McCartney might consider worthy of banging a tambourine to. The other instruments were cymbals, which were only capable of sounding, well, like cymbals.

Musical or not, there was unquestionably an atmosphere of sanctity. Perhaps religious music is all the better for lacking the conventions and appeal of other sorts of music. Certainly the music master where I teach appears to hold this view, if the bashing he gives the organ in morning chapel is anything to go by.

The atmosphere had clearly got to some members of our party. Wish sat transfixed, as if undergoing true enlightenment, and Jerri Lee appeared to be in a trance.

The room was dominated with a huge golden statue gazing benignly down, welcoming those, like us, who were simply passing through, and smiling on those who had forsaken worldly desires and existed purely for the search for truth. Tragically, all the painstaking effort which had gone into making the *Mandalas and Thankas*, the Buddhist paintings on cloth which had colourfully decorated the temple, had been obliterated; as all was destroyed by the fire. But with renewed purpose, the monks, temple craftsmen and volunteer workforce had set to work and created surroundings furnished with ornate work of the most intricate detail.

Buddhism, John explained, is a simple religion. About five hundred years BC, a prince named Gautama was born and a fortune teller predicted that he would become a monk upon seeing an old man, a sick man and a corpse. Like the king in Sleeping Beauty, his father decided to confine the boy to a world where such mundanity did not exist. However, despite marrying a beautiful princess, he did not live happily ever after as it was only a matter of time before he came into contact with old age, sickness, and finally, death. He was confused and deeply worried. How could people grow old and die? And how could they escape from their own selfish personality? He decided to find out. Aged thirty, he left his beautiful wife, baby son, and princely palace, and wandered around India as a beggar, seeking the truth. God only knows how he failed to discover sickness and death in one fell swoop himself.

However, despite listening to wise men and starving himself so as to forget the pleasures of life, no answers came. But gradually he discovered that a simple life and three square meals a day helped him to think more clearly. Perhaps that is why many of the most outrageous and successful robberies are planned by those serving prison sentences.

One day, seated under a tree, the solution to life's problems came to him. Exactly what the solution was, no one seems to be quite clear on. The dilemma, as I see it, was reincarnation. To Gautama, or the Buddha (Enlightened One) after he had solved the puzzle, reincarnation was not a good thing. In fact, people were only reincarnated because they still retained worldly desires. Give up these desires, and you will cease to be reborn, and disappear like a 'drop of water in the sea of Brahma', the great spirit. This, he called *Nirvana*, and suggested an eight step plan, known as the Eightfold path, to achieve this blessed state. Chief amongst these were right living, right thinking and right doing.

If Buddhism is a way of life which encourages people to be satisfied with what they have got and to help and love others, I can see little wrong with it. I resolved to find out more about it.

Outside the monastery, just for a moment, I felt a strange sense of calmness at the unexpected and moving insight as to how the lives of the monks dedicated to selflessness were shaped by their belief. If we believe in something enough, we reflect that belief in our behaviour. If the mores of that belief are humanitarian and intrinsically good, then our behaviour benefits others and our existence is all the more important. If we have no belief, perhaps we have no soul; our existence is important only to ourselves. If Windsor Castle catches fire there is national indignation and a detailed forensic search for clues to establish the cause or perhaps apportion guilt. If Tengboche monastery burns down, you get on and rebuild it. It did not matter that the thousands of hours of detailed work in the monastery had gone up in smoke. It was part of life and you accepted it. It was *karma*.

And then the moment passed, and I was myself again, full of worldly desires and uncertain beliefs.

\*

My moment on the road to Damascus was shattered by the incongruous sight of what appeared to be a game of cricket in progress on the open ground beyond the tents. The Rev. Webster (the owner of the tennis ball) was bowling to Lloyd Scott, who was preparing to take strike with a rough wooden club which looked even heavier than the bat used by Graham Gooch.

Behind the wicket (a rucksack in front of a jacket supported by a tent pole), was Andrew Burgess. Dotted about the field were Bryan and Dave English, Al Hughes the cameraman, Charlie, Tom and John Dunning. The fielding side was augmented by several bemused-looking porters, one of whom had unwittingly moved into forward-short-leg. With his hands together, there was some doubt as to whether he was waiting for the bat-pad catch or simply deep in prayer, unaware of the danger his proximity to the bat put him in.

"Right then Richard," ordered the reverend. "Deep square leg please, and don't keep us waiting. We are very, very needful indeed of a breakthrough!"

My turn to bat came as Wish, who had emerged from the temple, came on to bowl. He was irritatingly accurate, but my innings, although short, lacked nothing in the planning. On the first delivery, I went down the track giving Wish the charge and, seeing a sudden dip in the ground behind Brian English at deep mid-wicket, clubbed the ball skyward in his direction, hoping to lure him to tumble backwards into the dip in an effort to take the catch. Unfortunately, I hit the ball too hard, and it cleared him by a considerable distance. It rolled down the slope, gathering pace towards the site of the Hunt's scout hut.

"I think that's a boundary. Drinks break anyone?" I suggested, as Brian set off towards Base Camp to retrieve the ball.

"Once more down the hill, and you're out!" pronounced Webster, who was obviously the umpire as well.

Wish's second delivery, thankfully, was short and just outside off-stump. Noticing Simon walking up the monastery steps, I made room for myself and savagely cut the ball over the head of the close fielders and beyond the tents. It whizzed past Simon's right ear and thudded against the gate to the courtyard, rebounding back to the fielders.

"Into the monastery is out as well!" warned the umpire.

My third and final ball was a good length delivery on middle-and-off and, much to my chagrin, I was clean bowled as I attempted to reverse-sweep Wish into Ray's tent.

The subtleties of cricket were lost on the porters and, as they were getting bored simply standing around in the outfield, we played a game of catch instead, hurling the ball high into the thin air for someone to claim. Charlie had a damned good arm and an absorbing contest developed between him and one of the porters, who had hands like buckets.

It was well after three and it was getting cold. The clouds which always threatened in the afternoon had arrived with a vengeance, and the wind had increased.

We had been warned that the latrine situation might worsen. At Tengboche, there were 'public' latrines for people passing through and expeditions were not supposed to erect their own tents. I wasn't sure if this would be a blessing or a curse. Diana's handout had urged us, in the absence of our familiar green tents, to use the 'grot spot' designated by the leaders. In the event, however, the tents were erected and so it was business as usual.

The Late Birds were camped on the lower part of the plateau, well away from our base. From the moment the tents were erected, we became two separate groups again, each oblivious to the existence of the other.

As darkness fell, it became seriously cold. Simon and I huddled in our tent, reading and writing diaries beneath the pale uneven light from our head-torches, until it became too cold to do anything other than climb into our sleeping bags. As we envisaged a long and probably sleepless night, we decided to check out the one decent lodge in which the Gurkhas had taken up residence. Predictably, everyone else had shared that idea and it was packed. Most of the occupants of the dimly lit first floor lounge were Early Birds, and the others were mainly from a separate trekking expedition, camped higher up the slope some distance from us. In addition to this, there were a few independent trekkers, and I recognised the young Danish couple I had last seen at Tragsindho. The pretty blond girl greeted me warmly. The man barely looked up from his book. As I had expected, the communication between the pair was now barbed and their relationship appeared tense and brittle. Perhaps they were here on a Danish version of *Blind Date*.

The view from the lounge must have been truly magnificent in daylight. Like an airport control tower, three sides consisted entirely of glass above the level of the seating. John Webster made room for me beside him and I squeezed into a gap opposite the little stove which belted welcome warmth into the room. I was tired after the exertion of the cricket and running about after the tennis ball, and found myself drifting in and out of a jerky, unrefreshing doze.

"What's the matter, Marvin?" asked Annabel. "Can't stand the pace?"

"It must have something to do with the company, Annabel," I replied.

The owner of the lodge spoke little English, but eventually we learned that he would not be cooking until six thirty. That was over an hour away, and most of us were starving. It would be even longer before the cook boys fired up the kitchen and got the inevitable soup, stew and gunge on the go.

The reason that the lodge owner was prepared to turn away good business was let slip by Charlie, and did as little for the popularity of the Gurkhas as Rennies does for a dose of dysentery. They had booked the kitchen for their evening meal at six o'clock and the food they had ordered would occupy the entire culinary facilities and manpower at the disposal of the lodge owner.

If Junbesi had something of a 'Saturday Night' feel about it, Tengboche, monastery or not, was severely lacking in this department. Here, it was forever Sunday, waiting for seven o'clock to come around and the pubs to open.

To make matters worse, when the smells which emanated from the kitchen filtered through to our nostrils as the preparation of the Gurkhas' meal got under way, my hunger knew no bounds.

And when at last the mounds of food appeared and the ravenous Gurkhas enthusiastically tucked into their meal, under the envious, near-salivating gaze of everyone in the room, it was too much to bear.

Simon and I forced ourselves out into the cold night to investigate the prospects of food in the mess tent. They were not good. The cooks and cook boys were sitting drinking tea and chatting, and although they greeted us in a friendly manner, our presence and animated search for signs of food was not suggestive enough to trigger some action. Even my desperate appeal in sign language was in vain. Pointing to my mouth, my stomach, and then pointing to my brain and drawing a finger across my throat, I hoped to convey the message that my stomach thought that my throat was cut. They laughed and nodded heads in agreement, probably mistaking it for, "If I have to eat that rubbish again tonight, I'll probably go mad and kill myself!"

In the end, we resorted to returning to our tent and pacifying the worst of the hunger pangs with the chocolate I had bought and some biscuits which Simon produced.

Back in the lodge, the Gurkhas were finishing their meal and reclined with the exaggerated contentment of Roman patricians, smugly savouring the situation.

"Bit of bread going spare, Rich," said Charlie. "That was great, but I couldn't eat another thing."

"I hope it gives you bloody indigestion!" I replied. Then, after a short inward conflict, which I lost, I scoffed the bread.

Meanwhile, the reverend had managed to order some soup and bread and, when that eventually arrived, things began to look up.

Supper, when it was finally served, was fraught with the tensions which were creeping through the party, fuelled by the cold, the prospect of it getting colder and the swelling of numbers in our group resulting in less space and less food.

Stephen Hassan, my doctor, had one of those watches that measures everything, anywhere in the entire universe, and informed us that the temperature was minus twenty degrees. The fact that the tent was now so crowded that the end flaps had to be open, and late arrivals had to sit beyond the canvas, did not help. The tent served as a wind tunnel and the wind whipped down the length of the dinner table, making eating without wearing balaclavas and thermal gloves distinctly unpleasant.

Up until now, even if the food had done little to reflect the position of man relative to the animal kingdom, at least our manners had retained the vestiges of civilised society.

Now, "Sorry to trouble you, would you be so kind as to pass the..." was replaced by "CUP-CUP-CUP!" Henceforth, supper became a battle for the centre seats, where the tent was warmest, and where it was also possible to claim a right to food from either side. Henceforth, it also became a question of getting in, getting your head in the trough, and getting into pole position for the goodies which now had to stretch still further, namely the hot chocolate and milk.

Of course, there was still humour, over the coffee and chocolate, after the tensions of the battle had passed.

We had now been joined by two other runners. They may in fact have joined the party in Namche, but if they had, I hadn't noticed, mainly because they weren't all that notable. Except when they were together at the supper table and in their tent.

Sheldon Larson was thirty-three and from Boulder, Colorado. He had won prestigious races in his own backyard, the Rockies, and was widely tipped to do well. Eckart Lemberg was, at sixty-five, the oldest runner, and he was not widely tipped to do anything, but just hoped to finish. He was also from Boulder, Colorado. That, and the fact that alphabetically they were placed next to each other, was all that they had in common. Yet we all made the erroneous assumption that their relationship went deeper. Initially, the pair were labelled as grandfather and grandson. 'How quaint,' we thought, 'how very touching. What a wonderful relationship they must have, to attempt this together.'

Wrong. On all counts. They were neither related, nor did they have a wonderful relationship, and they certainly did not wish to attempt this or anything else together. They had simply been on the same plane from Colorado and now had the misfortune of having to share a tent.

At the supper table, Eckart droned incessantly on and on, in the same dull, monotonous drawl. I found being trapped near him at supper about as stimulating as being trapped in a fourteen mile traffic tailback on the M25. But, not to be outdone, Sheldon moaned on and on equally tediously about being stuck with the old man. These two were definitely Late Bird material.

Sheldon, away from the old man, was a quietly spoken personable young man, aside from having more than a passing resemblance to John Boy Walton. That, of course, was not his fault and he was pleasant enough company. But, within a fifty foot radius of Eckart, he underwent as severe a transformation of personality as Dr Jekyll. Put together, there was more bitching between them than contestants at a Madonna lookalike contest.

There was little temptation to linger in the mess tent that night. There was little temptation to undress either, as ice had started to form on the inside of our tent. I climbed, fully dressed, into the gradually encircling warmth of both sleeping bags, inside my bivvy bag. The only part of my body which was exposed to the air was my nose and, when I could feel it no longer, I put on my balaclava and my woolly hat, and pulled the top of the bivvy bag over my head.

And then the headache started.

At first, I hoped it was just the intense cold that caused it. Or maybe my Walkman was too loud. But then, it got worse. As each throb of pain pulsed through my head and taut muscles drove my neck into my shoulders, I waited for the next vicious stab to arrive.

And then I remembered that there was a doctor beside me. He may not officially be my doctor or even the duty doctor, but he would have medication to ease my suffering. My head was too sore to go out into the freezing night looking for the duty doctor.

"Simon," I hissed.

"Mmmmph."

"Are you awake?"

"No!"

"Stop pissing about. I've got one hell of a headache."

"So have I," he replied. "Go to sleep."

"I can't. Can you give me something for it. A pill or something."

Slowly he sat up and rummaged through his bag. He passed me a painkiller, taking one himself.

"Is my face puffy?" he asked.

"No. Why, should it be?"

"It's a symptom of AMS, that's all. Your hands, feet and face swell up as fluid accumulates."

"Well, you took normal enough to me. Although it's a bit difficult to tell under that beard."

We settled down again.

"What time is it?" he asked.

I fumbled with my torch.

"Eight fifteen."

"Is that all?"

"Yea. Only eleven hours to go until breakfast," I said.

"Twelve," he corrected. "We get a lie-in tomorrow."

"Just what you want really. A lie-in, after twelve sleepless hours in a frozen tent."

My headache had thankfully begun to recede, and I tried to think of sleep.

"Christ I'm hungry," said Simon, a few minutes later. So was I.

"Well, look on the bright side," I said. "If you haven't lost your appetite, you're unlikely to be suffering too seriously from AMS. You can't have it both ways, you know."

After a prolonged search of my rucksack, I found my remaining chocolate bar, which we polished off, along with what was left of Simon's biscuits, and settled down once more to search for sleep.

But my mind would not switch off.

"I don't think I'd make a very good Buddhist," I said, reflecting upon the events of the day.

"Why's that?"

"Well, I think I'd keep on being reborn. After the fiasco in the mess tent, I'm having a bit of trouble with the bit about being satisfied with what I've got. And the bit about helping and loving others, come to think of it."

"But it's not a doctrine of total self-denial, is it? They eat well, have a simple but sufficient existence, but without the pursuit of worldly pleasures."

This really was something. Talking philosophy at minus twenty degrees, with altitude headaches, in a frozen tent with a long comfortless night stretching ahead.

"And that's another thing," I said, "I could do with some worldly pleasures right now. I could kill for a steak, a pint and a decent bed. Anyway, I wouldn't really suit the haircut. It wouldn't go with the BMW!"

We fell quiet. I felt the first visitations of sleep begin to numb my mind, as wild fancy and grim reality danced away. Then Simon dragged me back.

"Wake me up if I start Cheyne Stokeing."

"Thanks Simon. You mean if you stop breathing for a long period of time?"

"That's right."

"No chance! If you're not breathing, you can't be snoring!"

\*

I awoke at 4 a.m., bursting for a pee, but grateful to find that the bulk of the night had passed.

Outside it was cold, bitterly cold. The wind had dropped and the world was still, save only for the sleeping noises that people make.

The stars lit the sky with a faint, milky luminescence, and the mountains cast dark shadows down the valley, across the roof of the world.

As my eyes grew accustomed to the faint light, the white peaks pierced the darkness of the night sky, white knights standing guard against the demons of the dark, and behind, the monastery stood out in a magnificent and stately silhouette. Gradually, I became aware of a faint orange glow heralding the distant approach of morning. I was not cold any more.

If there was a grain of logic which drove us to put ourselves through the rigours of deprivation and the risks of high altitude, it must surely emanate from a desire to experience a moment like this. I remembered the strange sensation I often experienced as a child, that if I were not here now, at this moment, it would not exist. Just as home, at this moment, did not exist.

But tomorrow, and long after tomorrow, days would dawn exactly like today. Long after I was gone, I knew that this would always exist, and no matter where I went, it would be here, unchanged. "Time would not weary, nor the years condemn" these mountains, and long after I had grown old, others would come and experience this wondrous sense of timeless serenity.

Perhaps, unless the world to which I belonged enveloped this world with the same headlong death wish that threatened to choke the life from its own children, and their children's children.

> *Now you are gone*
> *Far away from me*
> *As is once will always be...*
> *Earth and sky,*
> *Moon and sea.* [1]

---
[1] Crowded House

# "High Plains Drifter": The Mad Axe-Woman of Dingboche

## Sunday 21st November

I had been up for an hour before the ritualistic bed-tea arrived, and had spent most of that time capturing the setting with my video camera. It was excruciatingly cold and everything looked blue through the viewfinder. The view back to Namche was spectacular. A thick layer of cloud covered the village like an unwelcome blanket, but above it the sun danced on the white peaks to the south-west of the settlement.

It was comforting to know that we would be above that cloud, should it arrive early up the valley, like an unwanted guest.

To the north, Everest and the Nuptse-Lhotse ridge basked serenely in the early morning sun, but it would be several hours before the first rays cleared the pyramid of Ama Dablam and warmed the frozen soil of Tengboche.

The familiar early morning sounds, of cooks and cook boys whistling tunelessly, and porters coughing, spitting and groaning as they shouldered their heavy loads and prepared to set off, announced the inevitability of another day's trek and the hope and promise of breakfast.

We ate in the open air, the mess tent having been packed away. Somehow, as I chatted to Ray, I had failed to notice that we were under starter's orders for the race to the table. I was too late to get a seat, so I hovered behind, grabbing pancakes and a boiled egg from the cook boys as they passed with their heavy trays. The tension, which the crowding and shortage of food had caused last night, was back with a vengeance and threatened to erupt on a couple of occasions. The generally congenial and relaxed atmosphere previously present at mealtimes was already a memory.

Those who could get, got; those who had had enough looked for a little more, and those who were out of reach got nothing except by reaching over others. It was a situation reminiscent of life itself.

And all the while, Eckart droned on and on.

The flashpoint finally arrived when Rob Howard, who I was beginning to conclude was totally humourless, asked us to pose at the table for an official photograph. As I had neither a seat or food, and deciding the latter to be of greater importance, I seized the opportunity caused by the diversion to purloin a couple of pancakes and liven them up with a little jam and peanut butter.

"Can you come and sit down, please," he asked.

"On what?" I asked.

"On your arse," suggested Wish.

"Would you like me to sit on your lap, Wish?" I asked.

"Look, either sit down or get out of it!" said Rob. "I've got a lot to do this morning."

I decided to get out of it.

"You won't be in the official photograph," warned Wish, who clearly would, sitting right at the end, in front of the camera. "You'll be sorry when it arrives and you're not in it."

"Well, I'll just have to say I was that unidentifiable bobble hat sitting half way down the table then," I replied. "Besides, I'll be even sorrier if I don't get something decent to eat this morning."

"Can we just get on with it!" demanded the cameraman.

"Sure, you're the boss," I said. I grabbed a couple of pancakes and a tub of peanut butter and sat on the monastery steps to finish my meal.

As I walked away, Wish made a derogatory comment which I missed, but to which Ray replied on my behalf.

I had to risk frostbite and remove my glove to spread the butter with my finger but it was worth it. It was heavenly.

Rob Howard finished capturing the breakfast scene, minus one very disgruntled runner, and set off to record a similar scene at the Late Bird camp, down the slope. Similar, except that they had no view of Everest behind them.

Official photography was, in fact, the order of the morning. Once breakfast had been completed, we were summoned for group photographs beneath the monastery with the mountains as a backdrop. I didn't want to miss this one, particularly as we were paying for it.

And so I stood, with a face like a waxwork without a willy, between Eckart and Sheldon who had carried their latest disagreement from the breakfast table to the gathering in front of the camera.

After that, we were invited to change into our running kit and pose for the camera whilst running up the hill. The film crew were particularly keen that as many of us as possible should do this. If any of us unexpectedly did well in the race, they could slip some footage of us 'training' into the final video.

They had no shortage of volunteers. A steady stream of runners stripped and donned their kit to belt up the slope towards the monastery. I considered it as utterly pointless an exercise as bungee jumping. I wasn't going to be springing light-footedly up the hill after fourteen miles, so why pretend? I suppose I could have jogged up, but my altercation with Rob Howard still rankled and I was childishly reluctant to be further obligated to his photographic services. Anyway, he probably would have taken two shots of the sky as I slogged up the hill and later informed me that they hadn't come out. That's what I would have done to someone who had just proved themselves to be an uncooperative and stroppy bastard. It's a good job most people don't think like me.

Ray, at first, was also unwilling to pose for the cameras but, when pressed by the film crew who considered him a good bet for the Vets' prize, he changed into the most hideously lurid running kit I had ever seen. Dressed in fluorescent yellow tights, a matching long-sleeved shirt and hat, with a pair of shorts outside the tights, he resembled a canary wearing underpants.

Both Rob Howard and the film crew were clearly unimpressed, and this did much to lift my spirits.

"Can't you wear something, well, more normal? Surely to God you're not going to run in that get-up?" demanded Ron Isles.

"Who says I'm not?" replied Ray, "I'm not going to run any bloody slower just because it hasn't got the bloody maker's name splashed all over it!"

Ray was somewhat nettled by the fact that, despite his running pedigree, his requests for kit and equipment from leading manufacturers had all been rejected. All he had managed to scrounge was this quite hideous canary outfit, which no manufacturer in their right mind would admit to designing. On the other hand, his fellow Kiwis, the Princes and Alan Hall, had all been the recipients of vast quantities of booty, varying from hugely expensive running shoes to absurdly expensive designer sunglasses, generously donated and emblazoned with the names of the benefactors. These were now paraded before the cameras, and there was a general air of accord that this was the sort of kit befitting those with serious aspirations of doing well in the race.

But Ray, the birdman of Tengboche, stole the show. I sat on the steps of the monastery enjoying the first heat of the mid-morning sun and the remnants of a packet of biscuits which I had bought from the lodge. From here, I observed the scene below and noted that Tengboche was not only a grandstand for the world's finest mountain scenery, but also an admirable grandstand for watching the world's daftest mountain farce.

Runners were issued with their number for the purpose of running up the hill for the camera. Rob could not guarantee a photograph of everyone on race day, so if you wanted one of the four photos to which you were entitled to act as proof positive that you were there, this was the answer.

The scene was quite chaotic. At the bottom of the hill, runners waited for the signal to start their charge towards the camera. Most set off as if it were a fifteen hundred metre race and were reduced to a crawl by the time they were within range of the camera. Some were asked to do it again. Some treated it as an opportunity to show a clean pair of heels to the runner behind them. And, of course, some just did it to pose.

When it came to Ray's turn, he strode up the slope in his comical kit with little visible effort. Behind him, a little man in his fifties from the Late Birds stalked him, straining to the limit to stay in touch.

"Go for it, Ray," someone called, urging him to respond to the competition.

We are all human. Ray increased his stride length, and a large gap suddenly opened between him and the impostor. It was impressive. Ray was a naturally balanced and relaxed runner, whose pace was deceptive. If I had even lingering doubts of his capacity to be right up there with the leaders, they were now gone.

"Blimey", I said as he joined me on the steps, "I've never seen a canary move that fast!"

\*

Tiring of the pantomime, I prepared to set off. The first leg of today's trek was to Pangboche, where lunch was available. From there, it was on to Dingboche, where the overnight stop would be and where we would spend a further rest day for acclimatisation, training, foraging for food, or wherever your priorities lay.

The most direct route to Gorak Shep was via Pheriche and up the valley of the Khumbu Khola to Dughla. Pheriche was home to a small hospital run by the Himalayan Rescue Association in conjunction with a clinic run by the Tokyo Medical University. Here, their speciality and raison d'être, not surprisingly, was altitude sickness. There were many more patients ferried into casualty suffering from AMS than road traffic accidents or sports injuries. Consequently, they were very good at dealing with it. It would therefore not be a bad place to be should one start to display serious symptoms of mountain illness.

Perhaps, more importantly, Pheriche had several good lodges and 'restaurants'. It was a natural stopping point for those retreating down the valley and acquired the more stimulating cuisine left behind by international climbing expeditions.

But, heck, why talk about Pheriche? We were not going to stay at Pheriche. We were going to Dingboche, which had nothing, and was technically a detour. Anyway, at that point they were both just names on the map. It was clear that Dingboche was some way off both the race course and the trail to our ultimate destination, but it was assumed that there must be a good reason for the detour. If there was, it remained a well-kept secret.

I paid a final visit to the latrine tent before departing. One of the few beneficial effects of the severe overnight drop in temperature was to freeze the contents of the latrine. If defecation was still some way removed from being a pleasure, at least it was less horrific than on the earlier part of the trek.

Walking down the grassy slope towards the stone steps that led north, I felt a pang of sadness to be leaving Tengboche. I imagined that when I retraced my steps in around six days time, my body would already be aching and my mind would be fixed rather more on negotiating the drop to the river and the climb to Sarnassa than on the beauty of my surroundings.

The path led steeply down through a wooded area of juniper and rhododendron, and past a large *Mendan*, a long wall of mani stones, generally built on the side of the road. This one occupied the centre of the path and something about the setting gave me the curious sensation that I was walking through someone's garden. Beyond this was Deboche, which is little more than a commune of nuns. The path led on through Milingo, which is a tiny community consisting of only a couple of shacks and a teahouse.

Here I caught up with Simon, who was traitorously trekking with a couple of Late Birds. I joined them for a tea and confided in Simon that my headache of the previous evening had returned. The warmth of the sun had taken the temperature into the high twenties and as I hadn't switched my Walkman on all morning, I could no longer kid myself that it was due to anything other than the altitude.

Simon gave me some Panadol and urged me to take it very easy. I promised that I would, and set off down the continuing slope to the bridge where the path crosses the Imja Khola. The headache eased almost at once.

I had generally considered, up to this point, that much unnecessary hoo-ha had been made concerning the suspension bridges. Most of them, the odd missing plank apart, were as well constructed as you would wish them to be and considerably better than I had expected. Sure, they swayed a bit when you crossed them, and a bit more besides when you side-stepped heavily across for the benefit of someone with a nervous disposition behind you. But I had not crossed anything where I genuinely felt I was in mortal danger.

Until now.

If suspension bridges were rated for their safety in the way that motor magazines rank the safety of motor cars, the bridge beyond Milingo would fall into the same category as a 2CV with defective steering and faulty brakes; *sans* airbags, *sans* ABS, *sans* SIPs, *sans* everything. You would no more bet your life on safely crossing this structure, than you would on surviving a night in the little pig's house of straw when the big bad wolf was in town.

With great trepidation, I gingerly tiptoed across the bridge, which sagged ominously and creaked plaintively in the middle. I was concerned as to how I would cross it in the race, and prayed that it would be yak-free.

Once across the river, the trail started to climb for the first time. Leaving Tengboche, the path had more or less led downwards and quite steeply on occasions. How to tackle this on race day would be crucial.

According to the map, the climb was only around three hundred feet, but it felt like a lot more. Apart from the two obvious steep climbs that would confront us on our return, one from the bridge and the other through the grove up to Tengboche, the path would climb at a more or less gentle but significant uphill gradient. To arrive at Tengboche exhausted could be disastrous, not only to my race aspirations, but to my health, as I expected the drop to Pungo Tengen and subsequent climb to be one of the most demanding phases of the race. To arrive at Tengboche feeling relatively fresh would allow me to push on for a competitive second half of the race. Dieter had warned me that the real race did not begin until Tengboche. Whether this was relevant or not, only time would tell. But I would certainly enjoy the race a lot more if there was more to the last twelve miles than hobbling home and praying that I could muster enough strength and resolve to limp across the finish line.

And that wasn't what I had in mind.

Having crossed the bridge, I was confronted with another problem, that of direction. Until now there had been little to worry about. Trekking through Sarnassa, it could have been possible to take the path where it forked to the left and find yourself on an unwanted detour to Khumjung. It may also even have been possible to find yourself on a central fork leading towards Gokyo. But travelling from the opposite direction, one would have to be very dim or very confused indeed to choose one of these paths. Moreover, as there would be a check point and aid station at Sarnassa, I felt confident that this would not be a problem.

We had been warned to expect certain navigational difficulties once on the west bank of the Imja Khola, and the first presented itself once I had safely negotiated the bridge.

There were three paths to choose from. I immediately discounted the one on the left. Although on my map it appeared that this path should not be here, but should in fact have crossed the river by a non-existent bridge just beyond Milingo, maps of the area are notoriously inaccurate. This path joined the Imja Khola with the Dudh Kosi before crossing the latter by an equally non-existent bridge and joining the main route to Gokyo.

I chose the middle path, which climbed sharply up treacherous, roughly hewn steps before levelling off into a pleasantly clear trail which followed the river a hundred feet below. The path was good, and I noted that it should be possible to make rapid progress here during the race.

The lower path had been the most tempting of the three. It followed the river, so clearly went in the right direction, and appeared to be the third side of the triangle which the middle path formed. However, as I approached Pangboche, I had found no evidence that it was a shortcut, or even rejoined the main drag, and so discounted it. My only concern was that from the path, the bridge was out of sight and there was no warning whatever that you were approaching it. It would be easy to miss the steps which descended to the bridge and to be oblivious to the mistake until well beyond it. A mistake like that would make my experience on Dartmoor seem like entering the public toilets by the exit door.

\*

Shortly before reaching Pangboche I came to a single *chorten* which I recognised. I had seen it many times in many photographs. In fact, with Ama Dablam towering in the background it is probably one of the classic scenes which visitors to the Khumbu record on film. Which is probably why I didn't take a picture of it. Beyond the *chorten*, the path led beneath a Buddha stupa gate, or Khangni and over rough terrain where a high level of concentration would be required in the race.

Suddenly, I changed my mind. Retracing my steps back to the *chorten*, I took the photograph which everyone has at the front of their album. After all, I thought, the bulk of my sightseeing would have to be done in the comfort of my living room when my films had been processed.

Pangboche, at 3,985 metres, over 13,000 feet, is the highest village on the Everest Highway to have year-round habitation. It is, in effect, two villages. The lower village is the prettier of the two with solid two storey residences built on a terraced hillside overlooking fields leading down to the Imja Khola. There are several lodges, teahouses and shops, but it was clearly harder to eke out an existence in the harsh living conditions than in the relatively temperate pastures of Namche. The available arable land is even less than in Namche and, upon closer inspection, although the houses are well built, they are smaller and shabbier. Some of the one storey dwellings were so primitive that they wouldn't even be used to shelter cattle at home. If there were few frills to life on the path from Jiri, there were even fewer here.

I bought some chocolate and water, and noted the predictable increase in price.

Around the next bend I bumped into Tom, who had a problem. He was hammering at a large rock by the side of the path with a stone. I was intrigued.

"What're you doing?" I asked.

"I'm marking the way," he replied.

I was none the wiser.

"Why?"

"Well, you see, if you look back, you'll see there are two paths."

I did, and there were. I hadn't even noticed the other path.

"Now, which path have you just come along?"

"The lower path, of course. No, hang on..." There was something familiar about the upper path. I couldn't be sure, and I'd only walked on it a few minutes ago. Paths often don't look the same from the opposite direction. "The upper path, I think. I give up, I'm not sure."

"It's the lower path. So I'm marking an arrow pointing down."

"That's very clever. But why don't you mark a rock on the path itself?"

"Well, because you'd have to guess which path you'd marked before you could look for your mark. And that would cost you time."

I was becoming fond of this quiet, watchful Irishman. The solemn earnestness with which he had approached the early part of the trip were still occasionally present, but, as we got to know each other, Tom unveiled a good sense of humour and became a popular member of the group.

"They both probably join up again anyway," I said doubtfully. I couldn't remember seeing a path forking off to the left.

"Well, they might do," replied Tom thoughtfully. "But there again, they might not."

Enough said.

It was probably at about this point that I became aware of a couple of things. The first was a nagging little doubt which I realised had been gnawing away at my mind all morning. Namely, that it had occurred to me that running the Everest Marathon was not actually the best way to enjoy the stupendous scenery of the upper reaches of the Everest Highway and get to know the Khumbu region.

While the pre-Namche trek had been simply a walk to get from Jiri to Namche, the post-Namche trek was a recce, a large part of which would be spent looking backwards. Come the big day, and we would not only be running away from the mountains which had drawn us to the area, but so absorbed would we be in navigation and placing our feet as to render our environment irrelevant. What would overcome this would be an additional week after the race using Namche as a base, but where it would be possible to trek either as a group or individually to revisit places we would like to have another look at. Of course, that would not only extend the trip but would cause it to become fragmented, with the possible logistical and medical problems which could arise as a result.

It was also at about this point that I became aware that if I survived this trip, I would have to come back some day.

But some day was a world away.

\*

Tom and I found the lunch-stop without much difficulty in a stone-walled field dominated by the growing presence of Ama Dablam. As it grew in stature, Everest receded like a shy child hiding from strangers behind the impressive and obliging mother's skirt of the Nuptse-Lhotse ridge.

Lunch was the same as usual and not really worth writing about, so I won't. Dave commented on what an honour it was to have the company of both Ray and myself at a lunch-stop. Ray replied that the honour was Dave's entirely.

Consulting my map and guide book over my fifth mug of lukewarm Lemsip, I deduced that Tom's upper path almost certainly did not join up with the lower path. To take the upper path would result in another considerable detour. As far as I could ascertain, it led to a three hundred year old monastery which offered inspection of some Yeti remains, including a scalp, in exchange for a few rupees. Tracks of the Yeti, or Abominable Snowman, had been reported in Sikkim as early as 1889, and these giant footprints were witnessed by Mallory in 1921. General Bruce's 1922 expedition was casually informed by the Lama of Rongbuk monastery that there were five Yetis living in the upper reaches of the Rongbuk Valley. The Yeti had a fearsome reputation for drinking the blood of yaks, killing the men and carrying off the women from the villages they raided. Their appearance was said to be similar to a very large man, but their bodies were entirely covered with long hair.

Despite searches for the Yeti, such as the well-publicised expedition undertaken by Norman Dyhrenfurth in 1958, there was little solid evidence either to prove or disprove the existence of the beasts. I decided that the trek up to the monastery was not worth the considerable effort that it would demand.

After lunch, Dave told us it would be a good idea to trek to Dingboche via Pheriche, instead of taking the direct path to Dingboche. This would allow us to inspect another crossroads where it was possible to take a wrong turn. I lazed in the warm sun beneath a stone wall in the lee of the freshening wind which would later bring the clouds. It was only twelve thirty, and I reckoned I could make Pheriche in under an hour at a leisurely pace, and it would only take an additional half hour or so to reach Dingboche. There was no need to rush.

So like a mad dog or an Englishman, I sat out in the midday sun.

\*

Beyond Pangboche, the landscape changed quite dramatically.

For one thing, there were no more trees. Ever since we had stepped off the bus in Jiri, several millennia ago, trees had been a feature of the landscape. Great forests of pine, cedar or juniper clothed the sides of the mountains whose valleys we passed through. In more accessible areas, trees were hacked down for fuel, building or simply to clear the land for dwelling or farming. But now, we were above the tree line and nothing grew apart from bracken and scrubby little bushes.

For another, the villages from here on are summer pasture, or *kharka*, only, and this heightens the sense of remoteness. There are fewer dwellings and they are much less substantial. Not only are building materials harder to come by, but also the buildings are only required to shelter the herders during the summer months when weather conditions are considerably less severe.

Another remarkable feature of the scenery is the profusion of dry stone walls which enclose the little fields where animals exist in the summer months. They are, of course, no more remarkable than dry stone walls in north Yorkshire. But the fact that so much time and effort has gone into enclosing such small areas is indicative of just how hard life for these people must be. In fact, from Pangboche, mountains apart, the walls became the most prolific feature of the landscape.

Up here, they build walls like there is no tomorrow. What is surprising is not simply the intricate web of walls which corral each allotment-sized field, but the quality of their construction. Hundreds of years must have gone into the careful arrangement of stones in these magnificent fences. We spend our leisure time at the golf club, or watching satellite TV. Up here, they liven up the boredom of their empty moments by putting a few more stones on their wall. The recreation boom ain't even a whimper yet.

At lunch, it was clear that a number of people were ailing from the effects of the altitude. It was rumoured that some of the Late Birds, despite guzzling Diamox as a prophylactic measure, were already suffering badly. I was relieved that since taking Simon's painkillers, my headache had subsided and I felt strong.

Adrienne was quite poorly, although she maintained that her illness was not connected with the increase in altitude. Being a doctor is no guarantee of good health. With a rest and plenty of fluids, she had felt well enough to continue and had set off in a small group about an hour before I reluctantly dragged myself away from my suntrap in Pangboche.

Just before Shomare, where the path was lined with stone fences announcing that we were approaching the tiny summer community, I caught Adrienne's group. Her condition had deteriorated, and she didn't look as if she ought to be travelling anywhere let alone further into the interior. But she had clinically assessed her own condition and was determined to reach Dingboche where it would be possible to lie low for a day if necessary.

I offered help, but she was already in good hands. Tom, Mike, Jerri Lee and, in particular, John, had the situation well under control. John, demonstrating that there was more to Californians than neurosis, *Baywatch* and body-sculpting, had devised a method for pulling Adrienne along. Tying a rope around his waist, he had attached a stick to the other end and given it to the unfortunate doctor to hold. With Tom and Jerri Lee steadying and helping her along, and Mike fussing and supervising, Adrienne thus became probably the first person to land ski up the Everest Highway.

Wish need not have been so concerned about the group bonding that Simon and I had thrown into question so long ago at Sete. The only time that bonding becomes an issue is when people simply do not like each other and a problem arises. Then all that singing-around-the-campfire crap is instantly forgotten and self-preservation takes over as each individual retreats into the security of their own prejudices. But by allowing each other space in a world without privacy, by not demanding more from one another than was forthcoming, and by respecting individuals for their own differences, we were closer now. Closer than any amount of trekking at a snail's pace, or enforced stopping at the lunch-stops could have achieved.

And that closeness would be essential for coping with the problems that now would confront us. For there would be problems, and we all feared them. From now on, we were stealing apples from the giant's orchard, and no one had bothered to check if he was at home. But together we were stronger, and that feeling of unity and support made us individually stronger. And that strength was greater than the fear.

John had demonstrated that with his compassion and ingenuity. But that didn't excuse a lousy taste in music, and I returned the tape he had lent me on the road to Tengboche and set off on my own towards Orsho.

There may be little in the way of permanent habitation in this remote area, but that does not deter those who people this high wilderness from that other great recreational pursuit: the engraving of the scriptures on huge mani stones by the side of the path. Before Orsho there is a magnificent example of this intricate sculpture, a mixture of religion and art, perhaps a prayer to the gods to beg for protection for a journey deep into the interior.

Beyond Orsho, which is a lone house on a hill where tea can be bought, the path continued to follow the banks of the Imja Khola, carved into the side of a steep hill.

Although narrow, it was relatively flat, and I noted that this would be a good stretch to open the legs. Ironically, I would be right, but not quite in the sense I had intended.

Past Tsura two workmen were toiling over a stone bridge which spanned a narrow but deadly-looking crevasse. They looked up and smiled as they heard me approach.

"*Namaste,*" I greeted.

"*Namaste!*" they replied. Like workmen worldwide, they broke from their labour, thankful for the diversion caused by a stranger.

"Keep at it lads," I said. "Make sure it's finished by Friday!" Quite possibly it lost a little in the translation, but the smiles were a much more pleasant response than I would have received for a similar comment at home.

Somehow, beyond Tsura, I missed the turn to Pheriche. We had been told that it was clearly marked on a rock. How I missed it baffled me later, as not only was it marked, but it was also quite obviously the main highway. Perhaps the sight of the towering and formidable Lhotse at the head of the valley was just a shade more compelling than the tedious business of watching where I was going.

By the time I had realised my mistake, the temptation to return and find the main path was much diminished. The path dropped once more to the river, which I crossed by a solid wooden bridge, and wound upwards for some time. This was a mundane foot-slog, particularly as the hills obscured the view up the valley. It became even more mundane when I caught up with an agonisingly slow yak train. Mindful of my experience of the previous day, I resigned myself to walk at their funereal pace, turned on my Walkman and retreated into my private universe.

The clouds that flocked up the Imja Khola Valley, with the brisk afternoon wind snapping at their heels seemed to mock me. They seemed certain to be in Dingboche long before I would.

\*

The climb came to an end abruptly. Around a long left-handed bend, the hillside finally fell away and the valley opened up to reveal the most remarkable vista. The stony, scrub-covered hills sloped gently down to the river, beside which were situated the flat, green, summer pastures of Dingboche ahead in the distance. A large *chorten* stood proudly below the naked hillside some distance from the *kharka*.

Chorten and mountains apart, this could almost have been spaghetti western country. For this indeed bore a striking similarity to the high

Spanish plains where Eastwood drifted, Wallach leered and Van Cleef squinted. So suggestive was the scenery of the stomping ground of the cinematic heroes of my youth, that I almost heard the sound of approaching horse hooves, the striking of a match against a rock, the sweet aroma from the butt of a cheroot, and the husky drawl of a poncho-clad enigmatic stranger imploring me to "get three coffins ready!"

Dingboche was Stone Wall City. In Pangboche, the walls were a feature of the landscape. In Dingboche, the walls *were* the landscape. Entering this settlement was like entering a stone maze. From the slightly elevated approach, it is a patchwork quilt of tiny fields through which a walled path runs the length of the narrow strip of arable and pasture land. It is not even a community, yet there is enough of the lucrative trekking trade, which deviates from the main Everest thoroughfare, to support three lodges. Beyond Dingboche and on past Bibre, is another *kharka*, Chhukung, which is considered one of the best scenic galleries in the area. Here the view opens up into a vast mountain and ice panorama and rewards those who made the detour with spectacular views of the glacier zone to the east, where the Lhotse Glacier meets the Imja Khola. Further to the east is Makalu, another of the giants at 8,463 metres. From here also there is an outstanding view of the huge rock wall which fluctuates in height by as much as nine thousand feet in places, and connects Nuptse with Lhotse.

Chhukung also has its own peak, but more significantly is the closest habitation to the base camp of Imja Tse, better known as Island Peak. What makes Island Peak so special is not its outstanding beauty, although its big, triangular south-west face is impressive enough from Dingboche, but the fact that, for an affordable price, it is possible to trek to its 6,189 metre summit.

And that is a lot of mountain to get to the top of for relatively little financial outlay, and without the hassle of having to spend years learning about mountaineering, or the encumbrance of being tied to a large expedition. So, for those whose goal it is to get as close to the ceiling of the world as possible with minimum cost and experience and without specialist skills, Island Peak is a huge attraction.

The first attraction which I came across in downtown Dingboche, was a small stone-built lodge with smoke billowing from a metal chimney, which was home to some familiar faces. In the field in front of the lodge, Charlie sat reading and Pierre André sat shaving. We exchanged greetings. I had no idea as to which part of the maze to begin looking in for our base, but after the freezing conditions at Tengboche, a night in the warmth of a lodge was tempting. Particularly when the temperature began to drop as the cloud obliterated the afternoon sun, promising a long, cold night. It was a measure of the increasing cold and altitude-induced apathy which was creeping through me like a disease, that I considered a tour of Dingboche to see what else was on offer an effort not worthwhile.

The Gobet entourage and the Gurkhas were in residence, which was a good enough recommendation. Inside was a dimly lit kitchen where the family who owned the lodge cooked and lived. Through a curtained entrance was a long L-shaped room which served as dining room, dormitory and lounge. At one end of the room, there were three private rooms, although the flimsy wooden divides and curtains that separated each meant that privacy was very much in name only. There is probably more privacy, and more room, in the changing cubicle of a public swimming pool.

A long table in the centre of the room, with a bench on one side beneath the only window and stools on the other, were the only vestiges of furniture. This was the residents' lounge.

It was three thirty, and already outside the day was turning decidedly chilly. The heat from the kitchen filtered into the lounge, and a small stove near the 'private' accommodation did its best, but provided an apologetic amount of additional warmth.

Fergie found me a bed, and I threw my kit onto the thin, narrow mattress which only really served to house parasites and to show you how much of the wooden rack you were entitled to for your twenty rupees. The lodge appeared to be crowded, and there was a curious-looking case that resembled a Gladstone bag on the mattress next to mine. There was no telling who belonged to it. I caught the fleeting glimpse of a knowing exchange between Kev and Fergie and, when Charlie entered with a grin which he found difficult to conceal, I knew that I was about to become the victim of what passed for Gurkha humour.

"Did Fergie find you some accommodation then, Rich?" asked Charlie. There was little doubt that I was the fly to have flown into their spider's web. The mug they had waited for to walk through the door.

"Is someone sleeping here?" I asked, poking the wafer thin mattress next to mine suspiciously.

"Oooph, ah... I don't know, Rich," Charlie replied. "That looks like kit on it, though, so it's probably been taken."

"Kit?" I said, "It looks more like a Gladstone bag. Any idea who owns it?" It was becoming quite obvious that they knew only too well to whom the curious baggage belonged.

"No idea," answered Charlie. "Have you any idea, Kev?"

"None whatever. Sorry can't help you, Rich." Kev returned to his book. "Mind you", he said reflectively, "you don't half get some weirdoes up here. It's the last place on earth you'd think you'd find them. But there's something about the place that draws them."

"Yea, I know. I've met one or two of them," I said, thinking of some of the Late Birds.

"D'you remember that Aussie bloke we ran into at Gorak Shep?" said Fergie. "He'd half his leg missing. Said he'd lost it shark fishing. Well, he lugged his fishing tackle all the way up to Base Camp. He reckoned he never went anywhere without it, just in case."

"Did he catch anything?" I asked cynically. This was all part of the wind up.

"Yea", answered Kev, "he caught bronchial pneumonia. Had to be carried down to Pheriche by porters."

"And there was that yank in Lobuche, remember lads", encouraged Charlie, warming to the game, "who carried an old gramophone player with him and was trying to prove his theory that the Khumbu Glacier was formed by some sort of nuclear fusion from an alien spaceship ten thousand years ago."

"And did he?" I asked. This was the best cabaret I was likely to find anywhere in Dingboche.

"No, he got fed up with that. But he did claim to have proved that old 78s break when dropped from a lower height at sixteen thousand feet than they do at sea level."

"A useful piece of research then," I said.

I ordered tea from the kitchen, settled down at the table, and started to write my diary. At least my bed was at the end of the row, so I would only be in close proximity to one person. And however odd they might be, it would only be for one night. If I were to remain oblivious to any slight peculiarities which my neighbour would obviously display, that would take the wind out of the Gurkha sails.

And then she arrived. I heard her before I saw her.

I was jolted from my notes by the strident voice and unmistakably home counties accent of a middle-aged English woman, who had just entered the kitchen.

"I'll take tea in the lounge, now, if you'll be so kind. Be a good man and bring it through, will you!" It was not a request, it was an order, as savage as it was unexpected.

"Who the...?" but before I could finish the question, the owner of the voice filled the room with a physical presence as striking as the voice. She was a very large woman. Not tall, not stout, but very large in the very sense that one might refer to a concrete wall as a very formidable obstacle. This redoubtable woman was dressed more for an expedition in the high street than an expedition in the Himalayan highlands. The only concession she made to her surroundings was itself a curious one. In one hand she held a black patent leather handbag, but in the other she held a shiny ice axe. As it was unlikely, attired as she was in a knee-length gabardine overcoat, head scarf, and well worn fur-lined ankle-high boots, that the axe was to assist in the crossing of icy passes or to brake an uncontrolled fall down a snowy face, it must therefore be for defence.

Or, of course, attack, I considered, as she slung it beside the Gladstone bag on the mattress next to mine. My heart sank as the Gurkhas could contain their laughter no longer.

"Good afternoon, gentlemen," she said, removing the head scarf to reveal a mop of unkempt blue-tinted hair. "I've had a wonderful walk and feel quite refreshed. I shall take tea now. You will join me, I trust, and tell me more about your great battles."

And then she noticed me. Or, to be more precise, she noticed my rucksack next to her bag. And then her eyes followed to where I sat, defenceless behind my little computer

"And who might you be?"

I told her.

"Well you must sleep somewhere else!"

"It's all right, Mrs P., you've nothing to worry about. Rich is an honourable man. He's almost one of us."

"Well, you'd better not get up to any funny business, young man. I don't usually sleep beside strange men." She eyed me with mild curiosity and then added: "Besides, I carry two rape deterrents, you know!"

Tempted though I was to say that she was a walking rape deterrent, I watched and said nothing as she produced two devices from her handbag and proceeded to display them.

The first was a siren which made a hideous shrieking sound, even worse than the voice of its owner. Taken by surprise, the brave Johnny Gurkha boys dived for cover, and the little man who owned the lodge scuttled in with uncharacteristic haste expecting to find that his lodge had been overrun by aliens.

The second was a small tube which squirted some sort of gas that temporarily blinded the assailant. Its usefulness as a deterrent was proven by the fact that there was no one left in the room to observe its effect at close hand. We had no desire to be blinded, temporarily or not, and an undignified exodus had ensued.

Moments later, we slunk back in to find Mrs P. drinking tea and examining my computer, which I had carelessly abandoned in my haste to avoid being the recipient of the contents of her little aerosol.

"What in heaven's name is this device?" she asked, holding it to her ear and shaking it violently like a child with an unopened Christmas present.

I told her, as she handed it back, grateful that she had not tested its durability with her ice axe. My flask of lemon tea arrived and, switching on my Walkman, I settled down to continue my diary in peace, hopeful that my body language spoke loud and clearly that I wanted nothing other than to be left alone.

But the message was either not understood or not heeded. My eyes were unavoidably drawn to a frenzied waving of arms in front of me. This woman would not be ignored.

"I say!" The piercing voice penetrated even the screaming Stratocaster of a Clapton lead break.

I took off my headphones.

"Excuse me, young man! I was talking to you."

I gave in.

"I say, are you some sort of writer? Do you know, I used to do a lot of writing. A lot of writing." For the next fifteen minutes, I was treated, if that is the right word, to the phenomenal literary works of the mad axe-woman of Dingboche. She had written on all subjects known to man and, if anything she said was to be believed, which by now I very much doubted, her work rate made Barbara Cartland's daily output of seventeen thousand words look as paltry as 8G's history homework. Eventually, I managed to stem her flow by asking the question which every hopeful writer hates to answer.

"Have you ever had anything published?"

"Well, no. Well not exactly. Of course, there's been plenty of interest in my work, its just, that... well, I can't sit here all day talking. I have a great many people to visit."

And with that, she scooped up her handbag and ice axe and swept from the room.

I sat, shell-shocked, in the sudden vacuum of her departure. Like an earthquake, she had ceased and departed as abruptly and unexpectedly as she had arrived.

"Well done, Rich", said Charlie, " you've upset her now!"

"Who the flipping hell was that?" I asked, when I had recovered sufficiently.

"Mrs P." replied Charlie. "She's barking. Absolutely bloody barking. But unfortunately not as totally harmless as she appears."

The Gurkhas had first come across Mrs P. in Kathmandu, where she had stood out from the run-of-the-mill tourists by her somewhat unsuitable, if not unfashionable, clothes, and the fact that she carried a shiny metal ice axe in addition to an ornate antique parasol. Whilst there was every reason to carry the latter in the thirty degrees heat of a Kathmandu autumn afternoon, any practical need for the former was highly questionable.

Tiring of the city in the heat of autumn, she now wandered the high Himalaya, pouncing on unsuspecting trekkers who were either too polite, too gullible or just plain intrigued by her seemingly innocent eccentricity, to treat her with other than deferential respect.

But there was more to Mrs P. than a harmless basket-case who had escaped the grim prospect of spending her twilight years mistaking her false teeth for sugar cubes with Henry and Doris in a Dorking Day Centre. Mrs P. had a most unpleasant pastime: spreading malicious and totally unfounded gossip. She was well known to the small English speaking community in Kathmandu, as most of them had at one time or another suffered from an acrimonious and untrue piece of tittle-tattle perpetrated by this seemingly harmless walking anachronism. Even Diana had been the focus of her absurd pronouncements and, in a country where libel laws are as effective as those banning dog shit at home, there was little way of silencing the woman.

And so, when she had said that she had a great many people to visit, it was far from certain that the pleasure of the visit would be entirety mutual.

But what was certain, by the Gladstone bag next to my rucksack, was her intention to return, and the prospect of spending the night next to an axe-woman of questionable sanity did not fill me with deep joy.

And so, with that in mind, I wandered up the path, which was more of a stony river bed down which icy water was rapidly flowing, until I spotted the field where the familiar blue tents were being erected. Closer inspection revealed that they belonged to the Late Birds, but ours were easily identified on the other side of the path. I was pleased to note that Number Fourteen had been erected, and even more pleased to note that for once it was located on a piece of relatively flat ground. The campsite was entirely dominated by the towering mass of Ama Dablam which rose from the east bank of the river, and was more or less in a bowl. I decided that we would be relatively sheltered from the worst of the wind.

I returned to the lodge, and was relieved to find that the axe-woman was still doing the rounds. I collected my kit, paid for my tea and the bed which I had abandoned, and wished the Gurkhas a pleasant night. I felt a twinge of regret as I left the warmth of the lodge. But then Simon would have to snore some, and then some more, to stand side by side with the mad axe-woman in terms of points scored for nuisance value. Even if we had the misfortune to be close to the epicentre of Shigi's nocturnal onslaught, there would be no competition. Game, set and match, Mrs P.

But that wasn't quite the end of the matter. A few hours later, I dragged myself out of the comfort of a gloomy but warm Island Peak View Lodge, where I had waited an hour and a half for a plate of chips which would have been worth twice the wait, to attend the Sunday service conducted by Rev. John Webster. The service was to be held in the mess tent prior to supper and, in all truth, what motivated me more than absolution was a guaranteed seat near the centre, where there would be an abundance of warmth and food.

Few had made the sacrifice, preferring the relative comfort of the Island View, and the third lodge close to the Late Bird encampment, until summoned by the familiar scream : "Ssssooouuuuuupppprr-reeeaaddyyyyy!" This signal would empty the lodges as effectively as the signal to Scramble would have activated a Battle of Britain fighter squadron on alert.

To my surprise, upon entering the mess tent, amongst John's small and diversely motivated flock, sat a familiar face. For between the Rev. Webster and John Thomson, demurely sat the mad axe-woman of Dingboche, engaged in the hushed conversation of churchgoers everywhere.

"This is Richard, a fellow Celt. Have you two met?" asked the Rev.

"Oh yes," I replied. "We've already met." I wondered whether John had been advised of her two rape deterrents, should the closeness imposed by the shortage of space be construed as taking Christian fellowship too literally.

John and Liz, either unaware or unprejudiced by the woman's reputation, had clearly taken her under their wing, although, by the expression on John the Buddhist's face, the next hour or so was going to be a solemn test of faith.

John, the Vicar, conducted a simple and short but moving service for his small congregation and, following the battle-cry to supper, the tent began to fill up.

However, the axe-woman showed no sign of vacating her seat, despite several members of our party glowering at her and dropping hints about hoping that tonight there would be an adequate amount of food. John Webster did what anyone in his position would have done. He cordially invited her to join us for supper, stating that there would be ample food for everyone. The objections from both ends of the table became as vocal and plaintive as from a resident pack of spotted Hyenas whose freshly killed Wildebeest had just been hijacked by a larger nomadic pack. And, I had to admit, had I been seated at one of the extremities of the tent, I would have been equally concerned about what would be left by the time I got my snout into the carcass.

The axe-woman, sensing more than just a hint of hostility, took her leave, but the atmosphere lingered on throughout the meal and into the night. And for once, Eckart and John Boy had little to do with it.

If her reputation was indeed true, then the woman had a split personality and what she needed was help. When I had earlier put this to the Gurkhas, they had suggested that what she needed was a bullet in the head. Perhaps they deserved each other tonight, I thought, as I paid a final visit to the frozen latrine. Although I was relieved not to

be spending the night in her proximity, I felt some sadness a
had been treated. We humans have an incredible capacity for ᴗᴗ_
compassion and indifference, and man's inhumanity to man never
ceases to amaze me.

My guess that the campsite would be sheltered from the worst of the wind had proved correct, and the cold was nowhere near as intense as at Tengboche. However, it was still bitterly cold, and my headache returned with renewed ferocity as Simon and I prepared for sleep, at around eight thirty. Again I confided in him and he gave me an anti-inflammatory pill, which resembled a miniature rugby ball and was about as hard to swallow.

Over dinner, the tense atmosphere was not improved by leaked news that there had been a heated exchange of views at an earlier meeting between the doctors and leaders of the two groups. Apparently one of the Japanese women from the Late Bird group had been suffering from altitude sickness since Tengboche. Her condition had deteriorated after the lunch-stop at Pangboche and doctors from our group, being the nearest on hand, had taken the decision to evacuate her immediately to lower altitude. The Late Bird doctors, whose ranks included the Chief Medical Officer, felt that they should have been consulted, and so a row ensued. Again, this reinforced the impression that we were on two separate treks.

Many of the Late Bird group, particularly the older members and the Japs, were now in poor health and giving their doctors, who were working the hours of hospital juniors compared to our senior registrar 'Tee off at twelve sharp' types, cause for concern.

Headache apart, I felt fine. But my diary entry that night only registered the relief. *I dread the next four days, and just want to get on with the race. Anything can happen between now and then. Each day that passes and gets me closer to the race in a relatively fit and healthy state is ticked off with a blessed sigh of relief.* Hardly the sentiments I had envisaged in the weeks and months leading up to departure. But then the mistake I had made was to shut from my mind the inevitable conflict between a once in a lifetime experience and an inestimable physical challenge. The trouble was that I neither knew what to expect, nor how I would cope with a subtle but not insignificant change in my priorities which gradually put success in the race above anything else. The apathy, which was discernibly shutting down the sightseeing mode of my priorities, was unexpected, but was a feeling prevalent amongst many of us. Ray, after all, had been like it since Jiri.

My motivation was fear of failure. And the yardstick with which I measured failure was becoming longer.

For now I felt strong, and that was all that mattered. Tomorrow's goal was simply to stay healthy and to maintain my strength.

As I drifted into steep, my last conscious thoughts were of the mad axe-woman of Dingboche listening, long into the small hours of night, to the stories of great battles, dragged from great sleepless warriors, and I recalled the words of Wilfred Owen:

> *My friend, you would not tell with such high zest*
> *To children ardent for some desperate glory,*
> *The old Lie: Dulce et decorum est*
> *Pro patria mori.*

# "Some Things Hurt More, Much More Than Cars and Girls"

## Monday 22nd November

When I was a kid, I dreamed of owning an Aston Martin. No other car would do. I would save up my pocket money, clean out the chicken shed twice a week, and some day I would buy a silver DB5. Just like James Bond's. But without the fancy toys. Because people in the real world did not drive cars with ejector seats, machine guns in the bumpers or deflector shields that rise from the boot. And I lived in the real world.

But by the time I passed by driving test, I had learned that people in the real world did not drive Aston Martins, and so I dreamed of owning an MGB. No other car would do. And so my father, in a fit of generosity I put down to his survival of a major heart attack, helped me to buy a two year old white MGB, with Recaro racing seats, stainless steel spokes, raised rear suspension and, of course, chrome bumpers. It was the most beautiful car in the world, and I was in heaven. At nineteen years of age, it was the knees of the bee, and I was king of the ball park.

One week later, returning home from cricket in a state of total inebriation, I piled it into a concrete bollard outside Antrim police station, lost my licence, and brutally shattered my own childhood dreams.

The following day was the worst of my entire life. My father took me to survey the wreckage that had been towed to a salvage yard. I will never forget how I felt looking at the stoved-in front wing, crumpled bonnet and broken steering rack. It was as if I had taken a kitchen knife and mindlessly slashed my very own Van Gogh. It probably did little for my father's recovery from recent cardiac trauma, either. With third party insurance, the car a virtual write-off and beyond my means to repair I had not only had my dream snatched violently from my grasp, but faced a long period of disqualification and telephone number insurance quotes. We sold it to the scrap dealer for a hundred and fifty quid.

I was utterly devastated. I hadn't even had an opportunity to pose in the thing at college. I simply could not comprehend how I could have wrought such abject misery on myself. In the days when drinking and driving in Ulster was virtually compulsory, with the forces of law and order huddled in armoured cars rather than sitting with smug menace at roundabouts, the only way to get caught was to drive into a police station and give yourself up. And I had done the next best thing. But the experience, which still brings me great pain to recall, taught me two lessons.

Firstly, that nothing worthwhile is achieved or gained without considerable personal sacrifice and effort. That I had thrown away so carelessly the dream cherished for so tong indicated that its realisation had not been sufficiently significant or hard-earned.

Secondly, and this was the important bit which triggered these painful memories flooding back that Monday morning in Dingboche, that life is fragile and the price of recklessness is high. It was a lesson of which, over the years, I constantly needed to remind myself. To undertake a pursuit or goal which is dangerous is perhaps understandable, if questionable. To chase that goal in a reckless manner when all good sense indicated that the odds of success outweighed the risk is foolhardy. But, over the years, I had put bits of my body where they shouldn't really have been, to retrieve an oblong ball from an irretrievable situation, or to hurtle uncontrolled down a slippery hillside, using my head as a brake, with the inevitable consequence that bits of my body now didn't work very well.

And now, living at almost fifteen thousand feet, recklessness was again tempting me to push to the boundaries the fragile good health which at present I enjoyed. But I had to realise that my dreams of achieving something that I would took back upon with pride, rather than the agonising regret of the morning after I wrecked my 'B', were also fragile.

Sure, it would be good to trek to Chhukung and maybe scramble up an easy trekking peak or two. Or, perhaps, march straight through to Gorak Shep, and have a preview of Everest from Kala Pattar, which had been suggested by some of the already acclimatised runners. But, in the circumstances, if the price I had to pay to know that I had given myself the best possible preparation for the race was to skip out the side trips, then that was a sacrifice I would be prepared to make.

After all, this trip itself was full of paradoxes and conflicting aspirations which needed much the same juggling and compromise as balancing my headphones, glasses and cap on my head. It was not possible for me to get the very best from five days spent close to the base of Mount Everest, and then to run a competitive marathon. For now, it was enough to be amongst the mountains.

For now we lived in the real world. A harsh, unforgiving world where dreams and reality were distant cousins. And I would have a better chance of buying an Aston Martin, with or without the twiddly bits, than running a marathon suffering from AMS.

*

Hunger got me up before the dawn. Even before the cook boys had prepared the bed-tea, I had risen and, dressed in my complete Buffalo suit, had braved the bitter cold of a Dingboche Monday morning to scour the lodges for food.

I had no success. There is no great rush to greet dawn's first light in these parts, and neither the Island View nor the Late Bird lodge were able to offer anything more than biscuits.

Fuel is at a premium and so stoves are only lit at certain times each day. As there are no trees, the principal source of fuel is yak shit. It is collected, dried, preserved and stacked against the stone walls like peat in Connemara.

The yak is more vital to survival here than the supermarket shopping trolley at Tesco's is at home. But the problem is that you can't have your yak manure cake and eat it, so to speak. If yak dung is used to fuel the stoves, it cannot be used to fertilise the land. Which is why the potato has done for Dingboche what The Beetles did for Liverpool. Dingboche is the potato capital of the Khumbu.

But neither love nor money would get me a fried plateful of them, and so I returned to our camp and settled for some biscuits scrounged from the cook boys, before they did the rounds with the morning tea. I could, of course, have tried the Gurkha lodge, where the owner almost certainly would have been pressed into action, but I was reluctant to initiate another audience with the mad axe-woman.

The tea tasted different that morning. At altitude, water has a lower boiling point, and so the tea acquires a quite different flavour. I actually thought it was an improvement.

Breakfast was in the mess tent, which had not been dismantled due to the fact that today was a rest day. This was not altogether good news. Although to begin with it was pleasantly warm huddled together beneath the green canvas, as the sun cleared the mountains the ice on the inside of the tent began to melt and large droplets of freezing icemelt rained down upon us.

There was a relaxed and genial atmosphere in camp, and the tensions of the previous evening had evaporated. It was soon warm enough to strip down to T-shirt and shorts, as we busied ourselves washing, shaving or simply sitting on the stone walls planning how we would spend the day.

I amused myself by wandering around the field conducting silly interviews with anyone willing to cooperate. Wish explained to the camera exactly how he had come to be awarded The Hat. He had filled two pee bottles at around 6 a.m., and had placed them outside his tent. In the act of leaving the tent, some time later, he had somehow managed to kick both of them over, much to the annoyance of Dave, his tent-mate.

The camera crew had spent the night in the lodge on the pretext of keeping the batteries and camera equipment warm. Richard was man enough to admit that, in reality, it had been the prospect of spending another night with ice on the inside as well as the outside of the canvas which had prompted the decision.

By midmorning, most people had set off to wherever they had decided to go. The more culturally inclined had gone to visit the Nangkartshang Gompa. Some had set off for Chhukung, and a few, motivated by the prospects of a decent meal, had opted to take the theoretically short trip over the hill to Pheriche, where there was more on the menu than one hundred and one things to do to the humble potato. Dave English had yesterday found a pleasant lodge with an enclosed and sheltered yard which made an excellent sun trap. He had returned to this oasis, and I decided to follow his footsteps. Besides, I needed to investigate the path between Pheriche and Tsura, where I had missed the divide.

Leaving most of the contents of my rucksack in the tent, I set off up the hill behind Dingboche. The path was clearly marked and, at the saddle of the hill above Dingboche, there was a large *chorten* which I passed, and descended to a long, wide valley. The scenery was utterly spectacular, with great walls of rock on all sides rising to white, snowy pinnacles framed by the blueness of the clear, cloudless sky. Invigorated by my magnificent surroundings, I slipped into a jog, enjoying the comparative lightness of my rucksack.

The valley was grassy and, although there was no path as such, it was clear that it led somewhere. But gradually it dawned on me that it did not lead where I wanted to go. To my left, I noted that the terrain had ceased to rise steeply; in fact, it did not rise at all, but tumbled away down a steep bank of mountainside to another valley. From the south side of this lower valley rose great walls of rock and ice. I was on a wide terrace above the valley in which I wanted to be and in which I noticed, far behind in the distance, lay what I correctly assumed to be Pheriche. Somehow, once again, I had missed the path that led directly to Pheriche.

As I intensely dislike retracing my steps, I decided to continue. I felt good, and was enjoying the exercise. Ignoring my pre-dawn warnings to myself about overdoing things, I pushed myself hard over some short but sharp uphill sections. Unlike my previous run at altitude, there were no obvious telltale signs and, despite the greatly increased effort which was needed to run at a reasonable pace, I felt strong.

I caught up with a Sherpa cook who spoke good English. He was between expeditions and headed for Dughla which, to my relief, he confirmed was the next habitation at the end of the valley. I walked with him, and we chatted for a while. He told me that he had just returned from Gorak Shep, where the temperature was nowhere near as cold as was normal for this time of year. In fact, he said it was nowhere as cold as Tengboche or even Lobuche, which was to be our next overnight stop.

I continued alone to Dughla, which was nothing more than two extremely basic lodges. I stopped at the first of these, just across the river, whose roofing was in dire need of repair. Large, slate-like stones arranged in a haphazard fashion sagged ominously over the more dilapidated bits, and it was hard to tell whether people just outside or just inside the building were at greater risk. It was a sign of my enduring naivety that I concluded that one would have to be very desperate indeed to stay here.

I ordered tea from the *didi*, a powerfully built young woman in a sort of full length apron and a red headscarf and, as I bent over to remove my video camera from my rucksack, a bizarre thing happened. Someone smacked me firmly across the buttocks. At first I assumed that it must have been one of our group who had furtively watched me arrive and crept up behind me. But when I turned around, there was only the lady of the lodge, wringing her hands and laughing uncontrollably. Across the path, four porters sat smoking and sharing the joke. Was this a Nepali custom unknown to the author of my guidebook, or was she was making a pass at me? Perhaps she just liked smacking tourists. I was shocked, but diplomatically joined in with the joke when I had recovered my composure sufficiently.

When the hilarity had subsided, I ascertained from the smacking *didi* that the lower of the two paths on the Dingboche side of the river led to Pheriche. This was a junction where it would be very easy to make a mistake in the race. I walked further up the path towards higher Dughla to get an idea of the perspective of the path from the direction I would be approaching it in a few days time. As I thought, the Pheriche path was concealed from view until one was almost at the river. The obvious path was the one I had run along from Dingboche. It appeared temptingly flat and contoured the hillside, so that it deceptively appeared to lead in the direction of Pheriche. It would be inviting trouble to look for the path while running down this stony moraine, and so it was vital to be confident as to which one to take. To take the Dingboche path would be nothing short of disaster.

I crossed the little bridge and set off along the path to Pheriche at a comfortable jog. Once around the bulb of the hillside, the path climbed slightly and then I was faced with a long sharp descent over precarious terrain to the valley of the Khumbu Khola, towards the end of which lay Pheriche. I came close to falling on several occasions, but once on flat ground the going was much easier.

Presently I came to the little *kharka* of Phulung Karpa, which the path actually by-passed. However, an alternative path led directly through the stone walls which enclosed the little fields of the summer pasture community. Either someone was a lousy hurdler, or Billy Whizz had been through town, chased by Desperate Dan. I followed the curious line of gaps in the walls; a line which was considerably quicker than following the intended path. I was pleased at having discovered something else that would help in the race. I had had a productive morning.

Less than twenty-five minutes after leaving Dughla, I found Dave basking in the sunny courtyard of the Himalaya Hotel, which was conveniently situated close to the little hospital.

Thankfully neither of us required the treatment which it was equipped to provide, and instead spent a peaceful afternoon sitting reading, writing diaries and chatting in the sunny and sheltered courtyard.

The food was indeed excellent, and only slightly marred by the illicit entry of two *dzopkyo* during our main course. *Dzopkyo*, (pronounced zzop-key-o), are a hybrid cross between yak and cattle. Unlike yaks, who are larger bodied animals, have long, thick coats, and horns which protrude to the front, *dzopkyo* are easily identified by their smaller frame, thinner hair, and horns which point almost directly upwards like television aerials. They are more reliant on their herders for sustenance than yaks and, when the heavy snows of winter descend, are renowned for expectantly hanging around outside barns. Apparently, they are unaware of the existence of their horns, and have not worked out that they can use them to dig through the snow to reach the grass that continues to grow beneath it. This suggests them to be singularly unintelligent creatures, perhaps one step ahead of the humble amoeba and one behind Pamela Anderson, on the evolutionary scale.

But the two who entered our courtyard dining area and interrupted our meal scored well on a different scale, namely delivering fuel right to the door, thus proving that here it is not only acceptable but sound fiscal practice to shit in your own backyard. The owner appeared almost immediately and went through a bit of a charade rebuking and removing the beasts. This was largely, I believe, for our benefit. He then gratefully collected their issue and took it off to dry for future consumption as fuel.

We shared the courtyard with a few other trekkers, but they were just passing through, and Dave and I had the place to ourselves for most of the afternoon. Stephen Hassan, Dave Blakeney and Annabel appeared shortly after we had eaten. Their arrival was timed to witness me standing on the little ledge on the outer side of the courtyard wall with my video. I was trying to capture the panoramic view up the valley, with the wing of the lodge bearing its name in the foreground and the spectacular pinnacle of the 21,252 foot Cholatse towering far above a heap of inscribed mani stones, in the background. The equation proved to be impossible to balance, and I inevitably lost mine, pirouetting hopelessly on the ledge before falling head over heels some five feet to the ground. Somehow, I managed to protect the camera, but landed heavily on the hip which I had bruised doing something equally stupid a few days before.

To add insult to injury, Annabel had observed my undignified demise in its entirety.

"What a loser, Marvin! And all that just to film people's underwear drying on the clothes line!"

"I only film underwear", I replied weakly, "when there's something inside them worth filming. So don't be disappointed if yours don't feature too highly in my video." It was, as usual, an inadequate reply, and only a token gesture.

But I begged whatever gods of the mountains that may be listening to place a banana skin somewhere very close to Annabel's feet. And then prayed that I would be around when it happened. Just once. Please. Because I was so far behind on points that I was beginning to agree with her.

*

Right on cue, the three o'clock wind whipped up the Imja Khola Valley, and also blew and cracked its cheeks upon the valley of the Khumbu Khola. The sky was still a perfect blue, but the clouds would already be gathering. The best of the day had long passed, and it was time to move.

Dave had trekked the path between Tsuro and Pheriche, which I had missed, yesterday, and now headed back to Dingboche by the most direct route. This was, in fact, a path which climbed out of the valley more or less directly behind our lodge. I set off to find the bridge which crossed the river and led to Tsuro. It was a pleasant walk, and I resisted the temptation to run. I had done enough for one day and felt the suspicion of a headache creeping across my brow.

The path was easy to follow, and I had little difficulty in finding the bridge, although it would have been possible to miss it as a path continued to contour the hill, presumably eventually leading to Dingboche.

Across the bridge, the route was not quite so obvious. After a steep climb from the river, several tributaries of the path appeared, all of which seemed to meander in the same general direction. I assumed that the intricate labyrinth of trails must all lead to Tsuro. It was just a question as to which of the three more prominent paths was the most direct. I followed the highest, and was relieved to see the main path, and beyond it Tsuro, some way beneath me to my left.

Rejoining the main path, I noticed a large stone bearing the names of Dingboche and Pheriche, with a large arrow clearly indicating the direction of each. Only a singularly unintelligent creature could miss such an obvious signpost, I thought. Even a *dzopkyo* could find it.

As the clouds rolled up the valley, I repeated the trek of the previous day and half an hour later arrived back at Dingboche. To my surprise, the cook boys were shelling peas. Fresh peas with fresh potatoes was a considerable improvement from the noodles and other rubbish of questionable nutritional value served up on the earlier part of the trek.

But dinner that night was a long time coming. And the temperature dropped. And dropped. Three frozen hours spent huddled together in the lodge next to the Late Bird camp, but curiously devoid of Late Birds, dulled the enthusiasm for anything other than the warmth of an assortment of sleeping bags. Each time the lodge door opened, the newcomer ushered in an icy blast and the fragile warmth of our environment was shattered. Ordering food, of course, was a total lottery. I ordered soup and bread, which came almost immediately. Adrienne ordered fried potatoes, which took an hour and a half. Someone else ordered apple pie, which did not appear at all. At least, not before the battle cry summoned us to supper. The logic behind this was perhaps simple. The *didi* could only cook one selection at a time. Whether one had minutes or hours to wait was therefore either luck or judgement.

*

Most of us had benefited from the rest day. There were those, like Dave and myself, who had spent the day relaxing. And there were those who had enjoyed more energetic pursuits and had wandered up the Imja Khola Valley to Chhukung and beyond. There was a much improved atmosphere over supper that night, despite the intense cold, which could not solely be attributed to the improvement in the food.

The conversation turned to the making of the film, and there was much speculation as to what its title should be.

"How about 'Perishing in Pheriche'?" suggested John the vicar. "Or 'Shivering in Shivalaya'?"

"I think we should call it 'Not Another Day Like Last Thursday'", said Annabel. This met with more than general approval. This phrase had been the punchline of a joke told by Richard early in the trip. In all honesty, I have heard many funnier jokes, but the punchline had acquired a cult status all of its own, being frequently quoted for no good reason other than people simply liked saying it with the pleasure of imbuing each slowly pronounced syllable with a rich and fervent Indian accent.

It would be impossible to do the story any sort of justice without Richard's embellishments of accent and simulated radio static produced by blowing into his semi-clenched fist. But it's still worth repeating.

A British Airways 747, flight 456, bound for Bombay developed engine trouble and was diverted to Karachi. The pilot of the troubled airliner established radio contact with Karachi tower to alert them to the situation and to request permission to land.

"British Airways, flight 456 calling Karachi tower. We have developed an engine fault, and have been diverted from Bombay. Request permission to land. Please confirm Karachi. Do you read me, Karachi?"

"Hello flight 456. Karachi tower, here. Yes, we read you loud and clear man. No problem, flight 456. No problem at all. Plenty of room for you to be landing here. Been nothing in and out of here since last Thursday."

Flight 456 began its final approach, through low cloud, with no visibility. Suddenly, the plane emerged from the cloud to be greeted by the sight of the rapidly approaching runway, some two hundred feet away. But, to the pilot's horror, on the runway lay the scattered wreckage of a stricken airliner, so dispersed as to make any safe landing impossible.

"Karachi tower! Karachi tower!" screamed the pilot, now committed to landing, "there's wreckage everywhere! What the hell do you mean clear to land?"

"Oh no," came the reply. "Oh golly no. I knew I'd forgotten something... Oh no! Not another day like last Thursday!"

And then there was Bryan's suggestion.

"How about, 'Zvoni, you're killing me!'"

This was the cry which, like the song of the lark, announced the fact that Bryan English was alive and well and had the early morning waking camp in stitches. Although Valeri, who shared a tent with Zvoni, had doubtless once uttered these immortal words when reduced to a state of near collapse by Zvoni's uncompromising humour, it was Bryan's ability to imitate Valeri's Scooby Doo-like howls which set the camp ablaze. In fact, it had almost achieved a similar cult status to "Not another day like last Thursday."

"Or we could call it 'Steep Up, Steep Down'," suggested Simon.

And there were others that were equally poignant or equally witty.

But the best one, as usual came from Richard:

"Shortly before supper, I had to pay a visit to the latrine tent. I don't know whose tent I passed, but the three little words I overheard would make the perfect title. It's just a pity we couldn't use it."

Like all good media men, he paused for effect.

"Come on Rich, spill the beans," urged Annabel.

"Whoever it was simply said: 'F-u-c-k! It's cold!'" He pronounced each word slowly and with feeling. This, without a doubt, was the perfect title. Any of us could have said it. For if we hadn't said it, we had all felt it. And after tonight, we still faced a further three nights when it might even get colder, despite the welcome news I had received on the path to Duglha.

"Well, I hate to disappoint you all." The laughter was interrupted by Ron Isles, who clearly disapproved of the lack of deference accorded to his art and, more specifically, at Richard's apparent defection to the rank and file, "But the title's already been decided long ago. It will be called", he announced proudly, "The Reebok Everest Marathon 1993".

*

Leaving the mess tent where we huddled beside the two kerosene lamps, and where the warmth of our laughter had raised the temperature a degree or two, was like walking into a meat freezer. Protected by the thin blue layer of canvas from the inky black cold of a starless Dingboche night sky, Simon and I prepared for what was to be our worst night thus far.

## Tuesday 23rd November

I had been ready for sleep at eight thirty, when we had turned in. I was pleasantly tired from the day's exertion and, despite the headache which had threatened on my walk back from Tsuro, I managed to convince myself that I had not overdone things.

But at eleven, I awoke with my head threatening to explode. Simon was making noises suggestive of being asleep, so I rummaged in my rucksack and found the small first aid kit containing a squashed and crumpled packet of Anadin. I took two and waited for the headache to subside. It didn't. Instead, my stomach started to cramp, then turn somersaults, and I felt a sea of nausea rising like storm waves in my throat.

I was going to be sick. I have only been sick a handful of times in my life, and it is an experience which I detest. There are few things worse. But now I was going to be sick, and soon, and I would have to do something about it. Painfully I groped with the zips and, with throbbing head crawled outside and managed to reach the back of the tent, where I vomited noisily enough to wake sleeping dogs in Duglha.

It was also loud enough to wake Simon, who wasn't able to ascertain whether it was the pills or the altitude which had caused me to be sick. He administered something stronger and, some hours later, my headache subsided enough to allow me to drift in and out of fitful sleep.

I tossed and turned until first light and the sounds of life, coming from the direction of the mess tent, filtered through to my diffident consciousness signalling the welcome approach of a new day. Although the worst of the headache had been banished, I was still conscious of a dull pain pulsing across my temple.

Simon was awake, and admitted that he too had endured an appalling night. He examined me carefully for signs of puffiness around my face and in my ankles and wrists, which would confirm my fears that my acclimatisation had been badly knocked by pushing too hard on the previous day. I was mightily relieved that he found no such evidence and, as my stomach had stopped orbiting the rest of my body, he was inclined to deduce that my nausea had been either caused by something I had eaten, or perhaps the pills had not agreed with me. It could have been anything, but the pangs of hunger which replaced the previous contortions in my stomach suggested that there was nothing wrong with my appetite. This, at least, was an encouraging sign.

A less encouraging sign was that, to judge from our conversation, there had to be a question mark as to whether either of us were capable of the process of rational thought, exercising good judgement or concentrating for any length of time. The deterioration of mental ability is a warning sign that the body is acclimatising poorly.

"I think I might change my underpants today," announced Simon over bed-tea.

"Steady on, Simon, don't you think that's a bit drastic?"

"Well, I never like to wear one pair for longer than a week if I can help it." I assumed this referred to when he was on an expedition, rather than during the course of normal working life. Otherwise I pitied his patients.

"I can easily go through three pairs in a day," I announced proudly. "In fact I manage it quite regularly," I reflected wistfully. "One for an early morning run, another for the rest of the day, and a third clean pair if we go out in the evening. No problem."

We were agreed that one of the advantages of a boarding school education was an acquired ability to endure dirty underwear for prolonged periods. Even at twelve, we never wiped our bums properly. The scratchy Izal school toilet paper was best used rapidly and sparingly and, once the first layer of 'skid marks' were established in our pants, there was little worse that a week's wear could do to them. The school laundry never really got them clean, in any case.

"D'you know, I was the first boy to have coloured underpants at my Prep. school," Simon announced, equally proudly.

"I didn't know that, Simon. Congratulations."

"My aunt gave my brother and me a pair of blue underpants each one Christmas. The matrons didn't really approve. They thought it was the thin end of the wedge: blue underpants today, flares and platform shoes tomorrow."

"Matrons never approve," I said thinking of my school matrons, to whom I was public enemy number one, particularly in the cross country season. And to whom the idea of a good time was to iron and number socks.

Right now, I would give a lot for a pair of ironed and numbered socks.

\*

After breakfast in the warm sunshine, we had a visitor. The American nurse who ran the Pheriche clinic, a confident and eloquent coloured lady in her late twenties, had been invited to lecture us on her specialist subject: Acute Mountain Sickness. As the last of our tents were dismantled, and the porters began the short journey to Duglha, we were joined in our field by the Late Birds, many of whom were already quite knowledgeable on the subject of AMS. Indeed, sickness in general, and in particular mountain sickness, had received such a high profile in their camp, that some of them had practically earned doctorates on the subject. By comparison, I was still only approaching a good pass at GCSE level.

The lecture was concise, polished and depressing. But to what purpose it was intended, I was at a loss to understand. We needed a lecture on the cause and effect of AMS like a drunk sitting in a pub on his sixth pint of extra strong larger with the declared intention of getting brainless, needed a lecture on alcoholism.

We were already in the danger zone, as those who had already succumbed to AMS had testified. We all intended to reach Gorak Shep which, at 5,288 metres above sea level, was still almost one thousand metres higher than Dingboche, and about as good for one's health as tipping a triple brandy into that seventh pint of Tenants. We knew that our fragile, sea-level pulmonary systems depended upon twice the oxygen that was now available to function properly, let alone compete in a gratuitously severe athletic endurance event. We knew how to minimise the chances of illness, and how to recognise the symptoms in ourselves and each other. We also knew that we could be described as anywhere between mildly eccentric and mind-bogglingly stupid for exposing ourselves to such unnecessary risks.

What else, then, was there to know? By the time she had finished, I was thoroughly depressed and unsure whether my headache, which had considerably worsened, was real or imagined.

But although we had heard it before, there were two particularly salient points which were worth reiterating. Firstly, the importance of drinking at least seven litres of fluid each day, to avoid dehydration. At this altitude, we lost a litre a day simply by exhaling. In addition to checking the body for previously mentioned symptoms of AMS, it was essential to check the colour of our urine. Clear meant that all was well. A yellowish colour was a warning that the fluid intake was insufficient, and a stronger reddish colour spelt severe danger.

Monitoring my body closely is something which I am not used to doing. At home, my body is something which I live in. If I treat it reasonably well, it will mostly do what I want it to do. Provided that I maintain the sort of equilibrium to which it is accustomed and avoid more than the occasional excess in any direction, it does not usually let me down. I do not follow any particular diet, but I consider myself fortunate that I do not like eating rubbish. I would like to drink more alcohol, but age has diminished my ability to tolerate hangovers. This, however, sometimes does not deter me sufficiently.

But now monitoring was all important, for it was stressed how easy it was to fall prey to AMS without realising it. Attributing minor ailments to another cause could result in rapid and life-threatening deterioration, and the disappointment of failing to complete the race would fade into insignificance.

It was the hypochondriac's dream.

The second significant point was something over which we had no control. The nurse stressed that at this altitude, a gain of three hundred metres, around one thousand feet, per day was generally recognised as the safe limit. To exceed this was to increase the risk of illness. What concerned me was that I had just worked out that the difference in altitude between Dingboche and Lobuche, today's destination, was five hundred and sixty metres, almost twice the recommended increase. But, to be fair to the organisers, there was no way around this. Had we camped at Pheriche, as most people including myself would have preferred, the climb to Lobuche would have been nearly seven hundred metres. From Tengboche to Duglha would have caused the porters to desert quicker than rats from a sinking ship, and would in any case have meant an increase of over seven hundred and fifty metres. Having a rest day at Dingboche, allowed time for acclimatisation, and those who had sensibly not pushed themselves too hard should not have problems with the extra gain in altitude required to reach Lobuche, provided they trekked at a steady pace.

I cursed myself for my stupidity and resolved to walk slowly.

The nurse held a further meeting where the doctors received a crash course in the wonders of the Gamow Bag, which could provide instant relief in an emergency to a victim in the advanced stages of AMS.

Resembling a body bag, the invalid is zipped inside and air is pumped into the bag with a foot pump so that the pressure almost instantly drops by around one thousand metres.

It is not a cure, for it does not help its occupant to acclimatise. As soon as the victim steps out of the bag, the sickness will return. The only cure is to descend immediately, and the Gamow Bag is simply to keep the patient alive until a lower altitude is reached.

As I gathered up my belongings and prepared for the walk to Duglha, I sincerely hoped that I would not see another one of these. Particularly from the inside.

\*

Maintaining my resolve to walk slowly to Duglha was not difficult. The ground over which I bounded yesterday curiously appeared to have acquired a few more degrees of incline, and it felt like walking on the moon.

But slowly as I was trekking, it wasn't long before I came upon someone who was trekking slower.

Now, there had been several sights hitherto which had made me question the messages my eyes were sending my brain, and made me look again. But the sight of Donald James MacPhee dressed in a heavy tweed suit and deerstalker hat was as bizarre as anything I had yet seen.

I had, of course, noticed this character thus dressed on the flight from London, and assumed that he was either part of a publicity stunt, or a complete basket-case who had somehow been coerced into a venture about which he had absolutely no idea. As it transpired, there was a little of both in Mr MacPhee.

MacPhee, or D.J., as he was known, was the Head Keeper on the Dunlossit Estate on the island of Islay, in the Hebrides, and not a man normally given to foreign travel. He did not in fact possess a passport. Nor would he, had not Ron Isles hit upon the idea of finding a Gaelic speaking runner in an effort to raise money for the film from a Scottish television fund. The search led to D.J.'s rather barren door and, although he spoke little more Gaelic than Wish spoke Nepali and the television fund refused to cough up, he went anyway, and was allocated to the ranks of the Late Bird party.

But now he was regretting it. It wasn't just that no one had told him that tweed suits, admirable as they may be and the envy of the porters, had been replaced in the High Himalaya by rather more practicable gear about half a century ago. Tweed suit or no, D.J. was suffering badly. He walked slowly like an automaton, with staring eyes, zombie-like, fixed on the ground ahead. I asked if I could help, but he replied that he was fine and just wanted to take it easy. For a while I walked beside him, but I sensed he relished my company little and there was not much I could do for him in any case. With the knowledge that there was a doctor behind us, and no way that he could wander of the path into oblivion, I bade him good morning and carried on alone.

The lunch-stop was at Duglha, in the field belonging to the higher and marginally more substantial of the two lodges. I had slunk past the lower lodge, anxious not to invite another assault from its proprietor, when I heard a blood-curdling cry followed by a deep laugh behind me. I turned round to see the *didi* standing, hands on hips, smiling menacingly at me. With a muttered *"Namaste"*, I quickened my step towards the upper lodge.

It was a measure of how slowly I had been trekking, that most of our group had already arrived and were basking in the sun on the sheltered stone terrace beneath a vast neatly stacked tower of yak shit.

Duglha, dominated by the presence of the 6,440 metre Cholatse, is situated right at the southernmost tip of the Khumbu Glacier, and is the gateway to some very, very barren country indeed. Many people turn back at this point and, for those suffering from the altitude, it is unwise to continue. The path leading to Lobuche is singularly uninviting. There is, in fact, no path. Leaving Duglha, there is a three hundred metre scramble up a rocky moraine to the lip of the glacier, over which it is necessary to clamber to access the more level higher plateau of the Khumbu Khola Valley, which runs parallel to the Khumbu Glacier.

Looking at this interminable rock-strewn hill, I felt defeated. It suddenly struck me, for the first time on the trip, that here was an obstacle which might be insurmountable. I took off my rucksack and slumped down against the wall next to Ray. I was tired, and right now I didn't care if I never took another step towards Everest. I wanted to be at home. I longed to once again listen to the roar of the sea.

"You okay?" he asked.

"No," I replied. "I don't think I can go on. I'm not sure that I can get up that... that thing." I pointed in the direction of the path. In my mind, it had already acquired a forbidding and hostile personality. My head and my heart were pounding, and I felt breathless. They're all coming together, I thought, ticking the symptoms off one by one. All coming to get me. I took my pulse. It was ninety beats per minute. My normal resting pulse rate is between thirty-five and thirty-eight.

"Take it easy, and you'll be all right. Have plenty to eat and drink, and have a good rest. There's no hurry to get to Lobuche, and we've got another day's rest ahead of us". Ray fetched me some of the foul tasting hot lemon, and ordered me egg fried rice from the lodge, as there was no immediate prospect of lunch. In the meantime, I forced myself to eat a bar of chocolate and a foul tasting Power bar, and felt a little better. These things, which are absolutely brilliant for instant carbo-loading, come in three different flavours, none of which can disguise the fact that the basic components taste little better than yak shit.

"God knows when it'll come or what it'll taste like, but that's what they were cooking so that's what I asked for."

I was finding it hard to hold a conversation. Ray wanted to pick my brains about the terrain on the other side of the bridge before Phulong Karpa. But my brains were too scrambled to provide much helpful information, and I wondered whether I should reveal how I felt to my doctor. I decided that I would see how I felt after lunch, and if I was no worse, I would somehow get up that hill to Lobuche, then try and scrounge something for my headache.

Next to me sat John the vicar and John the Buddhist who appeared to be engaged in a quiet and profound exchange of views on the theological disciplines of each other's religion. Two Scotsmen talking philosophy in Duglha. Or they could equally well be talking about the last time Patrick Thistle won the cup.

Wish was the last to arrive, and made a beeline for the lodge where, with hands together, he bowed and warmly greeted the proprietor, who appeared to recognise him, or perhaps just recognised the fact that to feign recognition made sound commercial sense.

"Welcome, O hallowed one!" mocked Annabel from the terrace. I smiled, and felt better for the realisation that if I could still laugh at Wish, I could, in all probability get up that hill.

\*

Reaching the ridge at the top of the moraine at Upper Duglha represented a milestone which was both psychological and physical.

Shaking off the lassitude after an extremely edible bowl of egg fried rice, followed by the rather less appetising fare prepared by our cooks, was a supreme test of will. The lethargy I felt made the prospect of putting one foot in front of the other as appealing as the anticipation which preceded dessert each night at supper. For this reason, Bill Tilman once described the apathy induced by the onset of mountain sickness as Mountaineer's Foot. I have also heard it described as being similar to a massive hangover. If I ever had a hangover like this, I doubted very much if I would ever drink again.

But as time slipped by and the gathering on the terrace reluctantly began to collect possessions and depart like cousins leaving a funeral, I knew I would have to summon whatever energy I could, or I would sit here forever. And, when all was said and done, there wasn't much to keep me in Duglha.

Getting started is always the worst bit, I told myself unconvincingly and, besides, I felt no worse than when I had arrived.

An hour and a half later, after innumerable stops, I had somehow dragged myself sweating, head bursting and panting for breath to the top of the boulder-strewn hill. It had seemed interminable, but at last I was rewarded with a spectacular view beyond Duglha, now far below, along the Pheriche Valley over which Ama Dablam, Kang Taiga and Thamserku dominated the eastern skyline.

For some reason, which owed little to logic, I felt that this was a major turning point, a significant landmark which had been achieved, a test of resolve which I had passed. I had assailed this barrier which had appeared almost unassailable in my mind. I now felt certain that I would get to the start. If I got to the start, I would get to the finish.

I was considerably heartened by this positive line of thinking which had replaced my negativity at Duglha, although my head still ached ferociously. Sitting on a rock trying to restore some semblance of order within my cardiovascular system, it occurred to me that descending this moraine in the race was going to be as hard as getting up it. I searched for any obvious line of descent which would have been obscured from the bottom, but there was none. Attempting to run down this nine hundred foot switchback of rock would be to invite disaster, but there would be those that would do it. Like the descent from Tengboche, here it would be necessary to exercise extreme caution.

Beyond the ridge that announces the end of the long climb, there are physical landmarks which are both beautiful and moving. They serve as a poignant reminder that no one is immune from the wrathful toll that the mountains can wrest from those who dare to challenge them. For it is here, on the level ground beneath the watchful gaze of the distant Pumo Ri, the first of the attendant peaks in the Everest cluster to reveal itself, that twenty or so piles of neatly stacked rocks form gravestones, erected as memorials to the Sherpas who died carrying the white man's burden. A fitting place and a fitting tribute to the brave men who gave everything in the service of those whose dreams drove them to the pinnacle of the world.

It is an eerie place, where the wind whistles a low litany, as if echoing sutras of the spirits of the departed. The atmosphere reminded me of the American War cemetery in Normandy where the whistle of the wind whispers to the souls of the thousands of young men who gave their lives to gain our freedom from oppression. There is an unquestionable air of peaceful solemnity which abides in each transcending the tragedy of the sacrifice. Everything has a price, but perhaps brave deeds and noble pursuits reflect the intrinsic good not always obvious in mankind.

I paid my respects, and moved on.

\*

There was once again a definite path to follow. It led over loose rocks and contoured the upper part of the moraine beneath the glacier. On either side of the ablation valley, great peaks spiked the blueness of the afternoon sky. Awi Peak, Lobuche East, Lobuche West, Pokalde, and Mehra; none of them giants, but all of them with a price on their head.

The valley had been eroded by the shallow but rapidly flowing Khumbu Khola, whose origin, not far distant, sprung from the icemelt of the glacier. To reach Lobuche, I knew I would have to cross the stream. I saw a path on the western bank, and crossed the stream by way of stepping stones, which would be hard to find in the race. To make matters worse, the path on the west bank continued on down the valley, but as the stream was shallow, the worst that would probably happen was that I would get wet feet.

The path led gently upwards, and before long I was relieved to see the distant buildings of Lobuche, our penultimate destination.

Lobuche, at almost 16,500 feet above sea level is the summer *kharka* belonging to Khunde, a large village in the hills above Namche Bazaar. In summer it is a temperate pasture but in winter it is a barren wilderness where the temperature reputedly can fall to as low as minus fifty degrees. It has the world's highest village stores, three very basic lodges and has an uninterrupted view of the first of the real giants which surround Everest. Nuptse, at 7,855 metres, is the colossal shark-toothed wall of rock and ice which joins Lhotse and Everest itself in the most imposing mountain citadel on earth. Although the baby of the trio, Nuptse dominates the eastern skyline and dwarfs Kongma Tse and Pokalde in the foreground.

I stopped at the first of the three lodges, where the Gurkhas sunned themselves on the benches in its little courtyard. I had not seen them since my arrival at Dingboche, and was relieved to see that they had not come to a sticky end at the hands of the mad axe-woman. I was equally relieved that they did not appear to have brought her with them.

"Where's your friend?" I asked Charlie.

"Mrs P.? We won't see her for a while," he replied with relief. "She's headed back to Namche. I expect she'll be there to make a nuisance of herself on the finish line."

It went without saying that this lodge was the most comfortable of the three, and that the Gurkhas had taken all the available accommodation. I bought and drank two litres of water, and wandered off to find our tents. They were not difficult to find. We were camped on a flat terrace outside the higher of the three lodges overlooking the rocky valley where the stream was just a trickle.

I deposited my belongings in tent Fourteen, and went in search of accommodation. It was starting to get cold, and at three thirty the day came to an abrupt end as the sun dipped below the rocky hill behind Lobuche. Suddenly, it was very cold indeed. The lodge above the tents was warm but crowded and there was no room at the inn. However, in the third lodge I was more fortunate. The reason that there was no shortage of room was soon evident. It was bloody cold. The dormitory was separated from the kitchen and family living quarters by a thick stone wall, and therefore did not benefit from the heat generated from cooking. The sleeping accommodation consisted of two tiers of wooden slats, which ran the length of the building. And that was it, take it or leave it. Not even a token flea-infested mattress.

I took it. Despite the fading daylight, which filtered through the gaps where the walls joined the roof, the building was solidly constructed and had glass, however dirty, in the windows. I decided that the roof provided better shelter from the bitter cold than the thin blue canvas of tent Fourteen, and returned to collect my belongings. Simon had arrived, and I scrounged another of the miniature rugby ball shaped pills which last night had eventually kicked my headache into touch. He had decided to endure another night in the tent, but wandered with me back up to the lodge, in search of something to eat.

Inside were Adrienne and Dave Blakeney, who had also opted for the relative comfort afforded by the lodge. Dave, who believed that long trousers were for sissies even at eighteen thousand feet, had wimped out, thus tarnishing somewhat his super-tough-guy image. Talking to Adrienne was a girl who I didn't recognise. I joined them at the little table and Adrienne introduced me to Dr Liz Harding, who was working at the Khunde hospital and had trekked up to join us for the race. Liz was a New Zealander, whose running experience was limited, but she had the considerable advantage that her training had been conducted entirely at over eleven thousand feet, on and around the trails over which the lower part of the race would be run.

Richard and Al Hughes from the film crew had taken 'bunks' on the upper tier, and a beneficial spin-off of this was the light which they had fixed over the window above the sitting area. Not only did this illuminate the room as darkness fell, but it also caused a barely perceptible, but not insignificant, rise in temperature. A less beneficial spin-off, however, was that the generator which provided this comfort, triggering faint memories of a distant civilisation, was on the other side of the window, and would drone on all through the night. As it was also charging the batteries for my video camera, it was a noise that I could live with.

We were joined by several others, including Ray, who declined my offer of a slat in the dormitory, being curiously attached to his tent. Eventually the *didi* entered, and lit the stove. She was a reticent woman of indeterminable age, who had very recently given birth. Distance from her noisy offspring was the one positive feature of the dormitory being separated from the family's living quarters.

The lighting of the stove was something of a performance. Gradually the thing was coaxed into life, devouring great chunks of yak shit. Satisfied that she had fulfilled her side of the bargain, the *didi* slammed shut the ventilator at the bottom of the stove which tempered the thing's hunger to consume fuel and regulated the output of heat, dusted her hands and left, leaving the door open. Although some of the smoke managed to find its way up the chimney and into the freezing evening air, most of it saturated the room with a smog of foul smelling fumes.

"Don't these people feel the cold?" asked Joy, who clearly did.

"They just don't want us to die from bloody smoke inhalation before they get paid," replied Ray.

Word of a lit stove travels fast, and before long the lodge was crowded. I resented the intrusion, particularly as it was my lodge. I had found it, and I was staying here. I resented it even more when Wish entered, and parked his bum squarely in front of the stove. This was something which Wish had done throughout the trip wherever stoves had been lit, and something which intensely annoyed Ray. In the more temperate regions, it had mattered little, but now it contributed to tensions magnified a hundredfold by the cold and the altitude.

"Wish, when your bloody arse is sufficiently toasted, don't feel shy about lettin' the rest of us see the stove."

"All right, Ray, all right. Keep your fucking hair on man!" replied Wish, temporarily forgetting his guise of revered mentor and guru of all things cultural, and lowering himself to our level.

Wish moved away from the stove, and the fragile warmth began to filter through. Soon it was sufficiently warm for the removal of balaclava, fleecy mitts and down jacket. But both layers of Buffalo stayed firmly on.

*

The mess tent was no longer crowded.

At least a third of our group, for one reason or another, had decided to give supper a miss. Many were suffering from the altitude. Some had climbed into the warmth of their sleeping bags and refused to emerge until the sun had once again thawed this frozen wilderness.

And some were just plain knackered. It had been a tiring day, and the climb to Upper Duglha had not been achieved without a price. Young or old, reasonably fit or super fit, that climb had hit everybody, and most of us were glad that tomorrow was a rest day.

Ramon and Jordi, the two Spaniards, with Armando, the Italian, and Gobet, had trekked right up to Gorak Shep from Dingboche, climbed Kala Pattar, and returned to Lobuche in time for supper. That impressed everybody.

We were advised that tomorrow would be the better day to climb Kala Pattar for those who wished to do so. Kala Pattar is the small (a mere 5,545 metres) trekking peak whose summit affords the best views of Everest that it is possible to obtain. It is a podium which offers a peerless sensation of rubbing shoulders with the mountains at the top of the world. It also is an admirable venue for the typical British eccentric to indulge himself in whatever bizarre act of self-expression he may wish to perform. One Scottish nutter, on a previous Everest Marathon Expedition, ferried his bagpipes all the way up and played them at the summit.

Those who wished to make the excursion would breakfast at six and leave by seven, so that they could complete the eight hour round trip, allowing for time at the summit, and be back before the sun slipped beneath the hill and the world froze.

Ray and I were not tempted to join them. Despite my altitude headache having greatly receded, I knew that it was being kept at bay by medication and that I hadn't felt the last of it. If the sickness that had resulted from my physical excesses on the previous rest day had taught me anything, it was that a rest day should be exactly that – a rest day.

Ray and I had therefore ruled Kala Pattar out of our itinerary. Something which before departure had for me been an integral and important part of the trip now seemed an unnecessary encumbrance which would eat into vital reserves of energy. I had any number of pictures of Everest from Kala Pattar. What would it matter that I myself had not stood on top of that little cairn? I had not anticipated that I would think this way. If we did not climb it tomorrow, we would certainly not climb it on the day before the race. That was out of the question. Dieter had made that mistake two years ago, although, by his own admission, his pre-race preparation had been less than ideal.

No, tomorrow we would sit around the place. We would eat, we would drink, we would admire Nuptse and the lesser peaks, and pray that with each passing minute our bodies would grow more immune to the ravages of this hostile environment.

At least, that was the plan.

Supper, that night, resembled an international dragons' convention, as the kerosene lamps glowed through the practically freezing billows of our exhaled breath, filling the tent with a gentle but ghostly luminescence. Our head-torches cut through the mist like search lights in the blitz, scouring the inner recesses of serving pots for anything edible which remained unconsumed. The last of the drinking chocolate had long since disappeared, coffee was in short supply, and the tea resembled the colour of my urine. Which reminded me to drink more of it.

Most of us had by now developed the renowned Khumbu Cough, and there was as much coughing in the mess tent as in the Crucible in Sheffield during the World Snooker Championships. My cough, as coughs tend to be when I get them, was chesty, and I prayed that an infection would not set in. Others had dry, sharp barks. All were caused by the altitude and the cold, dry air. A few people had developed bronchitis and were on antibiotics, their condition closely monitored by the doctors.

So far we had been lucky. Only one runner one had been evacuated and, if we could just survive another day, then there was every chance that we could all make the start. In around thirty-six hours time, the doctors would assess our fitness to proceed to Gorak Shep and, if passed fit, we would be issued with our race numbers.

But now it was night-time. And night-time, like in all good horror movies, was when the demons of the mountains descended to do battle with our weakened and defenceless bodies.

The stove in the lodge had long since died, and it was pitch dark. Ice formed on the inside of the windows. As I climbed fully dressed into the thinner of my two combined sleeping bags between the comatose shapes of Dave Blakeney and Adrienne, the generator outside the window, like Eckart, droned on and on. Unlike Eckart, however, it was a purposeful and reassuring drone, and soon I drifted into a dream-filled sleep.

*

They say at altitude you dream. You dream with almost hallucinatory clarity, as the thin air plays tricks upon a mind stripped of whatever lucidity its normal waking state may possess. It is not uncommon for people to pee in their sleeping bags, as a combination of the increased fluid intake and dreams of what they desire most, a decent toilet, conspire to trigger the water works. I had not thus far slept long enough to venture far into the land of dreams.

Until now.

I was on a boat. A small boat; an inexpensive one. I was lying on the deck in the sun beside a dark-haired girl whose face I could not see. There was something familiar about her. The sea was dead calm, and the sun danced dizzily on the silvery ripples, as the little boat apologetically displaced the water.

There was no one at the helm, but I didn't care. I knew that I couldn't possibly turn the rudder in any case. I was too weak; I was too tired. I was also aware that we were moving slowly and inexorably towards the edge of the world. But that was a long way away and I didn't care about that either. I was not in control of my destiny.

Time passed. There was no urgency. The boat phut-phutted lugubriously towards the horizon, over which we would soon fall. I sat up, half intending to tell the girl, but she had gone. A black dog sat in her place, with its back to me. It had one ear raised and the other half-cocked. There was also something familiar about it. Beside the dog was a very old television. I turned it on, and a picture crackled onto the screen. The camera panned across a busy street, where traffic rushed headlong by. On the pavement stood a little girl in a maroon overcoat with her back to me. There was something familiar about her. She turned and waved to me, smiling, and called "Daddy!"

And then I saw a bus approaching rapidly from the left. She must have seen it. She must have, surely. But something on the far pavement drew her attention. A tall man in a blue coat wearing a balaclava. The bus was close now. The figure beckoned to her with a long bony finger. The little girl looked at me, and smiled again, then she turned and stepped into the road. The brakes of the bus screeched and time seemed to stand still.

Suddenly, the figure in the blue coat pulled off the balaclava to reveal a skull draped in taut yellow skin from which a pair of mad, cruel eyes bulged, laughing hysterically and mercilessly.

Angrily I shoved the television over the side of the boat, at the moment we reached the horizon. And then we were falling, spinning uncontrollably into a black void. The blackest night I had ever known. And all the while the brakes of the bus echoed, and the hollow faced man screamed hysterical laughter, and the boat droned on. And on.

Suddenly I was being sucked into a vortex, some sort of black hole where stars twinkled on the periphery of my vision. Debris rained on me all around, from the boat, from the bus, and the television hit me on the head and I winced with the pain. 'It's only a dream,' I thought. 'It isn't pain, it isn't real.'

Then the stars faded, and there was only darkness.

I was sitting up in my bunk rubbing my head. I was sweating profusely and my heart was pounding from the vividness of my dream. But the pain was real enough. This was no altitude headache, I thought, feeling the lump on my forehead.

It was then I realised that my journey back to reality had been precipitated by a violent collision between my head and the upper tier of bunks as I sat up.

"For Christ sake, Rich," came a voice from above. "We're trying to sleep up here. What the fuck are you up to?"

*

Dawn was approaching.

I flitted in and out of fitful sleep, fearful of the images and demons that my mind could unleash until the first faint light of a new day crept into the sky and I knew there would be no more dreams.

Not for now, anyhow.

# "We All Have Wings, but Some of Us Don't Know Why" [1]

## Wednesday 24th November

I was wide awake.

Through the frosted and filthy windows of the little lodge I witnessed a truly spectacular scene. The sun was rising behind the towering Nuptse, fringing its ridges with an orange glow like a halo and peeping from behind its steeply rising northern flank, as its first rays kissed the glacier and the valley below.

It was eight o'clock. The cold dormitory was deserted except for Liz Harding and myself, as the others had risen early for the trip to Kala Pattar. Breakfast for those remaining was not until nine o'clock, and as it had been described as a buffet breakfast, there was likely to be even less worth getting up for than usual. Content that today was a rest day, I snuggled deep into my sleeping bags and turned on my Walkman.

It was time to reflect on the trip. Here we were at sixteen thousand, five hundred feet or so, little more than forty-eight hours away from the toughest race of my life, amongst the majesty and devastating beauty of the mightiest mountains in the world, and I couldn't help feeling that I wasn't getting the most out of it.

The constant fear of injury or illness that could jeopardise the race was a worry which stood between me and the full appreciation of my surroundings.

And so, despite my resolve of the previous evening to conserve energy, I decided to do something about it.

After breakfast, which consisted of three fried eggs, tea and chapattis from the lodge, plus a packet of my dehydrated beans and

---

[1] INXS

sausage which I persuaded the *didi* to boil in the bag, I found Ray. Like me, he was feeling better, and the warm sunshine made our outlook on life a whole heap more positive.

"Fancy a walk?" I asked.

"What d'you have in mind?"

Behind Lobuche rose a long stony ridge-backed hill which separated our valley from the valley which ultimately leads to the 5,690 metre Chola La Pass. Above the hill were the twin peaks of Lobuche East and Lobuche West. The former is a Group A trekking peak for which one would require a permit, while the latter was free.

Not that it mattered. The term 'trekking peak' is a misnomer, as virtually all of them are well beyond the experience or ability of the average trekker. Most require specialist equipment and snow and ice expertise.

But in the foreground, overlooking Lobuche, there was a ridge of rock which ran to the north connecting three little peaks, the highest of which, my map told me, was 5,365 metres. It would not be necessary to go right to the top to be rewarded with an unrivalled view of the mountains at the head of the valley and the Khumbu Glacier beneath whose western lip we were camped.

It didn't look very far away, particularly as it was dwarfed by two rather larger pillars of rock and ice, standing like protective big brothers in the background.

"Up there," I said to Ray, pointing to the ridge above us. The idea appealed to Ray but for different reasons. My motives were largely aesthetic: to feel close to the mountains which had been a backdrop to the journey, hitherto observed en passant from the isolation of the path. I wanted to be a physical part of this wonderful scenery; to touch it; to feel it against my skin.

Ray's motives were more pragmatic and were performance related: to gain height during the day and sleep at a lower level is supposed to greatly assist acclimatisation. And here was an opportunity to do so without the hassle of the long trek to Kala Pattar.

I collected my cameras and we set off.

Climbing the hill was a good deal harder than I had imagined. But we paced ourselves, mindful of the consequences of pushing too hard. With frequent stops to chat and for me to photograph the mountains and the receding camp beneath us, it took us almost an hour to attain the ridge of the hill. But it was already worth the climb. From here was a superb view of both valleys, with the mountains to the west revealing their true majesty. Tawoche, Cholatse, and Awi Peak, the latter of which was almost at eye level. It came as no great surprise to learn that Ray had forgotten his camera, his mind was now preoccupied with the race.

We climbed higher, and soon reached the rock and scree slopes leading to the ridge. We stopped, and Ray surprised me by displaying an interest in our surroundings to the extent of taking out his map and trying to identify the peaks around us.

"That's ah... that one's Nuptse," he said a little uncertainly, pointing to the craggy giant across the valley. "Everest's stuck over behind it. You can't see it from here."

"What's the one that looks like an ice cream ahead of us?" I asked.

"That would be... ah... I think that's Pumo Ri." It was. Pumo Ri, meaning 'Bride's Peak', was named by Hillary. From a distance, the snow and ice covered smoothly symmetrical slopes which rise steeply from rocky shoulders to a rounded summit resemble a white veil hiding the facial features of the rugged south face. Or the hatchet face of the bride. Or an ice cream. At 7,161 metres, it stands on the west flank of the Everest cluster. It's a good job I hadn't been in Hillary's boots, or it would have been named 'Cornetto'.

"The next one is Lingtren." He paused, and pointed at the huge pyramidal rock face. "Next to it is Khumbutse. It's about the same height as Lingtren, over six-six. Then you drop down to Lho La Pass – that's 6,606 metres," he read. Lho La is one of the high passes over which thousands of Tibetans fled from the Chinese Invasion, and over which an estimated thousand refugees a year still flee from Chinese brutality. It is a precarious and arduous trek, and many seasoned mountaineers have experienced extreme difficulties crossing it. It was a measure of how much the repressive Chinese regime repulses these people that they were willing to risk their lives to move from one area of profound hardship to another.

"Behind Lho La is Chantse. It's actually stuck way behind Everest, so it looks smaller, but it's still over seven-five."

"Ever thought of becoming a guide?" I asked. Ray was well into his stride.

"Then next to it..."

"That one?" I asked pointing at the mountain between Chantse and Nuptse.

"Yea... y'see that one doesn't have a name. Shit! Over seven-two, and it doesn't even have a bloody name!"

"Who gives these things names?" I asked.

"Christ knows."

Fifty million years of growing pains, then fifty years of anonymity in the shadow of Everest, whose name the world knows. It didn't seem fair.

"I reckon we should give it one, then."

"What do you suggest?"

"Well, let's see. It's between Khumbutse, Chantse and Nuptse. When I was a kid I used to have a dog called Floppsie. What about that?"

"Naw. You can't name it after a bloody dog!"

"It's better than some of the names I've seen on the map. There's a peak east of Namche behind Thamserku called 'Hunk'. It sounds as if it was named by a frustrated female Australian backpacker!"

"What's bloody wrong with frustrated female Australian backpackers?"

Closer inspection of the map revealed that it was in all probability Everest's west shoulder, but all things considered, we thought that it had every right to a name of its own at almost 24,000 feet.

"Go on. You think of one then," I prompted.

"Well, if it's where we think it is..." of that there was no guarantee, "it's above Gorak Shep. Probably right over where the bloody race starts. I reckon we could call it 'Marathon Peak'.

"Wonder what the Nepali is for that. We'll have to ask Wish!"

Ray snorted in disgust at my suggestion, and we set about the scramble over scree and boulders towards the first small outcrop of rock. It was further away than it had appeared, and it took us almost a further hour to reach it. It was a precarious clamber, and I slipped frequently, painfully affecting my desire to experience physical contact with the land.

But it felt good to be up amongst the mountains, pioneering explorers naming peaks. We may have entered the realms of fantasy, but it felt good anyway. Hell, we were almost mountaineers, and by the time we had attained the second small peak, we were actually climbing. The hand and footholds may have been plentiful, but as the degree of ascent approached the vertical, the hump-backed hill up which we had walked laboriously receded into the distance, and Lobuche was only perceptible by the tiny blue and green specks of our canvas city, far beneath us.

"Should we be doing this?" I asked Ray, as we crossed a small ridge leading to a narrow and exposed rock ledge extending from the sheer rock face, below which there was a lot of daylight between rock and land.

Ray was already traversing the ledge when I slipped. Paying more attention to filming than to where I was poised on the ridge, I placed rather more faith than proved justified in my new Rockys. Suddenly the ground disappeared from beneath my feet, and I viewed the world from an unexpected and unwelcome angle. Although my slide was checked well before I came close to the ledge, and I was shaken rather than hurt, it provided an answer to my question.

"Probably not," Ray replied.

Not deterred, we continued. Neither of us were climbers, but there was something compelling and thrilling about what we were engaged in. What we were doing was dangerous, and I began to be aware that getting down was likely to be equally hazardous. I remembered reading somewhere that when you reach the summit of a mountain, you are only halfway there. And we weren't even anywhere near the summit of anything.

Beyond the ledge was an easy stretch which seemed to confirm that we had been right to continue. It was tiring, and I had to stop frequently with lungs screaming in air as thin as the veil of intent in a politician's promise. Ray, who was clearly much better acclimatised, was finding the going easier. He was as relaxed as I had seen him and, as we climbed higher above our camp, our tensions melted like ice on the morning mess tent canvas, as we became engulfed in the grandeur of our environment and the pleasure of a physical pursuit that was at once both different and challenging.

Ahead of us was what appeared to be the third outcrop, but when we reached it we realised that the terrain rose sharply to the west, leading ultimately to the summit of Lobuche East. That was almost one thousand metres above us, and one glance at the wall of rock to our left confirmed it would be foolhardy to climb higher. Besides, where we stood was as good a place as any to savour the mountains which surrounded us. We found ourselves in a small sheltered hollow like a bomb crater. To the east was a short ridge leading to a rock buttress which supported a huge and tempting but unsteady-looking boulder. Ray was drawn to the boulder, like Wish's bottom to a stove. He straddled the ridge leading to the buttress, and in a flash he was sitting on top of the boulder, smiling nonchalantly. The north end of the rock overhung the buttress by some distance, and beneath it was an alarming drop of several hundred feet. I supposed Ray knew what he was doing.

"Is that thing safe?" I asked.

He laughed. "Is anything up here safe?" He surveyed the magnificence of the scene before him. "I tell you what, though: you can throw away the rest of your bloody photos, mate," he called.

"It's a good job you haven't taken any then," I said, pointing my video camera towards Ray, silhouetted against the almost tangible Nuptse behind him. I suddenly realised that the record button on the camera must have been engaged when I fell. Once more, with shades of Mallory, I had involuntarily filmed fifteen minutes with the lens pointing in the direction of my feet. But this time I had unwittingly captured some of the most dramatic footage of the entire trip.

I reclined in the bunker while Ray perched precariously on his hazardous-looking vantage point. Each of us was abandoned to our own thoughts, a world away from the pressures of the trek and the uncertainties of the race, a universe away from home. Silence reigned, save only for the whistle of the wind punctuated by our coughs.

Even if nothing else were achieved from the trip, it would forever stay with me for this moment alone. And if I never again saw Ray after a week next Friday, our friendship would remain closer than the comfortable informality of a whole host of people whose familiarity I had mistaken for intimacy. For we had shared a wealth of memories, enough to fill the vacant shelves of the libraries deep in our minds, and gather cobwebs long after less notable volumes had been consigned to the out-tray. And, for now, it felt as though we were the only two people in the world.

I resisted the urge to say something utterly crass, such as "Why don't you and the family come and visit us sometime?" There was, in fact, no need to say anything.

It was Ray who broke the silence.

"This is bloody magic!"

"That Ama Dablam looks fantastic from any angle," I said.

"Yea, she's a beauty."

Again we lost each other in silence, together and alone in our wonderment at the splendour of this strange land.

"D'you see the frozen lakes on the glacier?"

Far beneath us, the Khumbu Glacier, some ten kilometres in length, runs from the feet of Lingtren and Khumbutse down the ablation valley to the moraine above Duglha. From high above, it resembled some huge unfinished motorway, silently awaiting completion by constructors on a twenty-five million year tea break. The glacial lakes, some a hundred metres or more in width, resembled frozen puddles in the potholes, which reflected the sun like a mirror beneath a child's model garden.

We changed places so that he could take a photograph of me, using my camera with the same stunning backdrop. But despite the euphoria which we both felt, I lingered on the boulder no longer than necessary, experiencing more than a touch of vertigo.

And then we both lay in the shallow sheltered hollow, savouring the warmth of the sun and the tranquillity of the stadium from which we enjoyed this unbelievable panorama. It was incredible to think that this was made by the same construction firm that made the Grand Canyon, the Victoria Falls and the Giant's Causeway – Nature PLC. I was moved. Perhaps God, or god, had had a hand in it.

"Do you feel something... something sort of omnipotent out there?" I asked.

Ray hesitated before answering.

"D'you mean, some sort of spiritual force behind all of this, that controls nature and drives our destiny?"

"Yea, something like that."

Again he hesitated.

"Naw. Why, do you?"

"No," I replied, then thought. "I just wanted to be sure I wasn't missing anything."

Again we lapsed into silence. Ray hadn't mentioned the race since we had left Lobuche. This was something of a record. But all records must be broken.

"All we have to bloody do now..." he said, pulling the rim of his hat over his eyes and lying back against the rock, "...is to run a bloody marathon."

I sighed, and thought of the words of the last song I had heard through my Walkman, which had been banging about my mind all day:

> *I told that you,*
> *That we could fly.*
> *For we all have wings,*
> *But some of us*
> *Don't know why.*[1]

\*

Hunger drove us down.

It took much less time than anticipated to retrace our steps to Lobuche, and we arrived to find that lunch had long since ended. It was hardly surprising; for we had lost all track of time, and it was after three o'clock. We resorted to our boil in the bag meals which the cook boys willingly prepared for us. Preparing a meal which took one minute and was palatable was probably a new experience for them.

We spent the remainder of the short afternoon writing dairies and consuming gallons of the seemingly endless supply of hot Lemsip which the eager cook boys fetched for us. 'Hot' was a notional conception, as water now boiled at around seventy degrees.

As the sun began to dip below the hill up which we had begun our side trip, I chased its last rays by climbing over the rocks above the path that tomorrow we would take to Gorak Shep.

But then it was gone, the warmth suddenly drained from the afternoon, and, at three forty-five, the quest to survive the night began once again.

My lodge was now full. The experience of a bitterly cold night had driven most of our group indoors, although a few hardy or parsimonious souls still preferred the familiarity of their blue tents. I had a new neighbour. To my left was Joy, and next to her was Simon. Somehow, I had a feeling that I wouldn't get much sleep tonight. We were also joined by a guy named John, from Birmingham. He had been made redundant and his wife had left him. So he had sold

---

[1] INXS 'Never Tear Us Apart' from the album *Kick*.

everything he owned, apart from his stereo, and was travelling the world.

I felt my headache proclaim its return, but this time I was ready for it. With the deviousness of an addict, I had scrounged a variety of painkillers, sufficient, I hoped, to keep it at bay until the race. By approaching different doctors, I had hoped not to attract too much attention.

But they had more to concern themselves with than my relatively mild symptoms of mountain sickness.

Around four thirty, we received some devastating news. Kathy Crilley, who had been struggling since the early stages, had become seriously ill and had been evacuated to Pheriche on a stretcher carried by four porters. I didn't envy her the journey down the steep moraine from upper Duglha, particularly as darkness crept up the valley. The news badly affected everyone's morale. We had hoped that we would all make it to the start, however unlikely that may have been. As several people had been evacuated prior to the start of the previous race, we knew the chances of everyone starting were not good. Poor Kathy; whatever optimism had driven her to return to Nepal to erase the nightmare memories of her previous trip now lay in tatters. All that mattered now was survival.

*

There was an air of hopeful expectancy that the stove was about to be lit, with the entrance of the *didi*. However, these hopes were not well founded, and despite some not too subtle prompting from Ray and me, she collected a bowl of potatoes from one of the sacks in a corner of the dormitory where they were stored, and left.

It was now very cold indeed, and tonight there was no generator to supply light and to give the illusion of increasing the temperature by a degree or two. My hands and feet felt like blocks of ice.

Suddenly, I remembered a clever little gadget in my rucksack which I had bought for just such an eventuality. Proudly I took out my solid fuel hand warmer and read the instructions. Joy had one of these little devices also, and between us we set about trying to coax the things to provide some warmth. First you light one end of a solid fuel charcoal rod. Then you gently blow until at least one centimetre of the rod is evenly glowing. Finally, you place it in to the middle of the glass wool padding, inside the velvet coated metal casing, which sits neatly in the palm of the hand. The idea is simple enough, and no doubt the thing will prove its worth on a miserable February afternoon on the Rugby touchline. But in Lobuche, all it proved was that I had wasted my money and effort carting the thing up here.

What the instructions didn't tell you was that, at over sixteen thousand, five hundred feet where there is a distinct lack of oxygen in the atmosphere, these things burnt with all the efficiency of a stack of soggy yak shit.

We tried lighting both ends. We even tried breaking them into smaller pieces and lighting both ends. But as soon they were placed in the casket and the lid closed, they went out, like damp squibs. Up here, they were about as much use as a solar powered car in the British climate.

The cold and the interminable wait for food was getting to all of us.

"How can these people live like this?" asked Jerri Lee who, despite her absurd-looking white fluffy ears, was clearly feeling the extreme temperature worse than most.

"They don't bloody live like this," replied Ray. "It's us who have to live like this. They're all snug in the kitchen, huddled around a hot bloody stove!"

It was a combination of frustration, cold and perhaps even anger that drove Ray and I out into the sub-zero temperature in the fading twilight world beneath the shadow of the glacier to search for fuel.

"I am going out now," I paused at the door, quoting the words of Captain Scott. "I may be some time."

"Aye, but were 'e goin' out to look for yak shit?" replied John Dunging.

We soon found what we were looking for stacked against the gable wall at the kitchen end of the lodge. We sneaked furtively around the building with arms full of dried cakes of the precious fuel. With a final glance around the front of the building to check that the coast was clear, we scurried back inside the dormitory, quietly closing the door to a rapturous heroes welcome. We would, of course, be discovered, but once the stove was lit and the valuable supply of fuel secreted away, it would matter little.

"Well done, lads!"

"Did you pick it up with your bare hands?" asked Jerri Lee, whose morbid fascination in just how low we could sink in order to keep warm had overcome her absorption with being cold.

Ray studied his hands, and shot Jerri Lee a look which conveyed both disbelief and pity.

We needed paper. Procuring the fuel was one thing, but lighting the stove was another. There was, of course, no available wood. Eventually we managed to persuade various people to reluctantly tear from their note books or diaries sufficient paper to kindle the fire, and Ray set about trying to light it.

At first there was elation as flames leapt high, casting flickering shafts of light around the darkened room, and billows of the vile smelling, but welcome, smoke poured into the dormitory through the open top.

But then the flames died, and hope faded. There was even a murmur or two of disappointment as the smoke dissipated, leaving the stove as dormant as it had been before. Suddenly I remembered the charcoal fuel rods for my hand warmer. In an environment with a hint of oxygen, they just might smoulder away long enough to coax the yak shit into life.

I lit both ends of three of them and blew on them gently, until each radiated a warm glow, then hopefully buried them amongst the still smouldering dung cakes in the stove. Then Ray took over, blowing desperately in an attempt to fan the feeble radiance into a flame.

Mike had entered the dormitory and momentarily observed from a distance this extraordinary scene, until curiosity defeated him.

"What are we doing here?" he asked.

"They're burning yak manure, dear." replied Jerri Lee, with a thinly veiled hint of disgust.

"Bloody smoking it more like," said Ray, his blackened face grinning hideously as he emerged from the bowels of the stove. "It's just like hash, man!"

"You're bloody enjoying this!" I said.

"What we need's some bellows," suggested Dunging.

"What's wrong with my bloody lungs?" retorted Ray. "Everything I do there's something bloody wrong with it!"

"All right, all right. Get on with it, then. You've got enough spare puff for bellows."

"Here, let me try something." Mike, who had carefully assessed the situation in the objective and clinical manner with which he practised in the distant world of a cardiac consultant, stepped forward, paperback in hand. Fussily, he flapped the book a dozen or so times over the aperture at the top of the stove, then looked cautiously but expectantly inside. Nothing happened. He tried again, flicking his wrists a little more vigorously, but still nothing happened. The patient was not responding to treatment.

Ray wasn't impressed.

"Ah shit..."

"No. His lungs are better than the book," adjudged Dunging, the referee. "If you chuck the book in, it might burn!"

Mike had no intention of chucking his book in. He shrugged his shoulders and sat down, defeated.

"Have you come across this phenomenon in California, Mike" I asked. I had switched on my video camera in order to provide Ray with a more powerful source of light than our feeble head-torches. I might as well record this farce, I thought, and pressed the record button.

"We do this all the time in California", he replied, "but we usually use cows, as yaks aren't happy in California."

"Are you taking pictures of your home away from home Richard?" asked Jerri.

"Yea, that's right," I replied, panning the camera around the darkened upper recesses of the dormitory. "The Lobuche Hilton."

Funny, I could have sworn that the light from my camera reflected two minute pricks of light, like a tiny pair of eyes, followed by the fleeting movement of a small black shadow retreating into the gloom. But in this uncertain world, I could no longer be sure of what was real and what was imagined.

Ray had given up with the stove. He attributed his heroic failure to sub-standard yak shit. But in our toil we had forgotten the bitter cold, and with the blood-curdling cry inviting us to supper ringing in our ears, came the realisation that we had occupied ourselves for well over an hour.

We were one step closer to the start. Once we had endured tonight, there would be only one more night to survive. We could count down the hours to the start of the race and tick each off with a sigh of relief and growing confidence in our chances of reaching the start in a relatively healthy physical state.

And then, with the race behind us, there was Namche to took forward to. Beyond that was still too distant to contemplate.

"Well", I said to Ray, as we prepared for the fifty yard dash to the mess tent, "nothing's perfect. As Plato once said: 'There is this, and there is what we would like it to be.'"

"Sounds more like bloody Pluto if you ask me!"

\*

The family who owned the lodge regarded us with a curious sense of detachment. They had made us neither welcome nor unwelcome. We were simply there, occupying the dormitory which was an annex or appendage to their own dwelling space, and doubled as a storeroom for their potatoes.

When we asked for food, we received it; eventually. If we asked for hot water in which to wash, or boiling water in which to reconstitute our dehydrated food, these requests were granted impassively.

They got on with their frugal lives in one end of the building, which was warm, and we existed equally frugally in the other end of the building, which was not. At sixteen thousand, five hundred feet, customer satisfaction did not appear to be high on the agenda. There was no guests' comments and suggestion book, and the *laissez faire* attitude of the management did much to suggest that they were not relying on us booking up for our next visit on our departure. In fact, a herd of *Dzopkyo* might even have considered looking for alternative accommodation had they been subjected to the lack of attention accorded to us.

But while the *didi* and her family had not gone out of their way to ensure that we enjoyed our stay, they had not unnecessarily intruded upon it either. Until now.

With the lack of deference accorded us, it should have come as no surprise that, at around 11 p.m. the door was flung open like a raid by the IRS. Into the room came two noisy little men, one carrying a kerosene lamp, who had either not been told, or did not care, that there were twenty-five or so people inside, who, in around forty-eight hours time would be about to embark on the toughest race of their lives and would appreciate a little peace. One by one, they set about carrying the sacks of potatoes noisily from the room, colliding with anything between them and the door, only to return them minutes later with similar panache.

Why, amid a packed dormitory of exhausted and frozen bodies, some of whom were laid low by the ravages of their hostile environment, and all simply praying for an undisturbed night's steep, it was necessary to carry out the annual potato audit at this hour of the night, God only knew.

Was this some sort of bizarre ceremonial ritual triggered by the reading of the signs amongst the tea leaves in the blackened pot on the stove, or were they simply checking that none of their potatoes had been stolen? If we could sink so low as to help ourselves to their supply of yak shit, was anything really safe?

An hour or so later, they had finished. As they left the dormitory potatoless, the kerosene lamp went with them, and we knew there would be no more potato counting tonight.

The door slammed shut, and I snuggled down to sleep only to be thwarted by the realisation that I was in desperate need for a pee. That morning, I had noted several sleeping bags hanging out to 'air' in the sun, a probable testament to those foolhardy souls who had chosen to ignore the warnings of their bladder.

'Better not chance it,' I thought, reluctantly prising myself from my bags, and preparing for the mad dash to the back of the building, the unofficially designated pee spot. No peeing at the front of the building was the unspoken rule, for when it froze the resultant skating rink would have potentially lethal consequences.

I collided heavily with the table both on the way out and way back, causing cries of anguish from those at last drifting into welcome sleep.

At last, there was peace, and I settled down once more between the inert shapes of Joy and Simon.

"Good night, ladies, good night, sweet ladies, good night, good night."

"Shut up and go to sleep!"

# "There's a Rat in the Kitchen, What Am I Gonna Do?"

## Thursday 25th November

There is, up here, no definitive line between one day and the next. Darkness and light reign supreme in their respective territories, and the ticking clock by which our normal lives are governed is as irrelevant as a stove that refuses to light.

When the sun ceases to provide the fragile heat that makes outdoor life just about possible for around six hours each day, you go inside, in search of warmth. Darkness falls and, when you have eaten, there is nothing else to do, and so you go to bed. Then there are the distractions that the middle hours of darkness send to disturb you. Ultimately, they cease, and you try to sleep. When nothing has happened for a long period of time, you make the assumption that it is night-time. And when things start to happen once more, you make the assumption that the dawn of a new day will shortly follow.

The potato men had been bad, very bad. But what followed them was worse. Much worse. And to make things worse still, there was a lot of darkness left between the next intruders and the dawn.

\*

I was dreaming. It was dark, like the darkness in my dream of the previous night. In the blacker than dead of night vortex at the edge of the world I was spinning, falling inexorably towards the nothingness that awaited me in infinity. But something had changed. Something, I felt sure, was missing.

The noise had gone, that was it! The droning noise was absent from my dream tonight. I listened carefully. No, it had definitely gone. But, wait... there was something else. A different noise. A sort of scuffling noise coming from somewhere above my head. And there were other noises too. The stertorous breathing sounds of people deep in sleep.

I was not dreaming, I was awake. So what then, was the scuffling noise above me? It seemed to be getting closer.

Someone else had noticed it too. Suddenly the night was once more alive as the beam of a torch not far from me cut through the blackness. It was Simon.

"What is it?" I asked.

"Ssssshh!" he replied. "Look!"

I lent over Joy who awoke with a yelp of surprise.

"What's the heck's going on?" she asked, not expecting to be awakened by a strange man crawling uninvited over her.

"Ssssshh!" I said, "there's something up there!"

All three of us lay still, frozen by both horror and the thrill of expectancy at the secret concealed in the upper tier.

Simon altered the angle of the torch beam, and the shaft of light picked out something long and white dangling from a hole in the wooden slatting above his head.

"That's my toilet paper!" announced Joy, sitting up and groping through the pocket of her down jacket. "It's been taken from my pocket!"

The white tissue twitched, then slowly disappeared through the hole. There was more scuffling, followed by the unmistakable sound of the patter of tiny feet. Then nothing. Simon switched off the torch, and we lay still, straining for the sounds of movement from above, fervently hoping that we had imagined it. Perhaps someone was playing a joke, or maybe the tissue had fallen through the hole, and its owner had reclaimed it to blow his nose. But people who need to blow their nose do not make the noise of small feet upon wood and, with fear in our hearts, our suspicions simply needed confirmation.

We didn't have long to wait.

Simon switched on his torch again and shone it at the hole. It was no longer empty. Two bright eyes, dazzled by the light, shone back. A black-tipped quivering snout and long thin whiskers announced the unmistakable facial features of a rat, beyond which lurked the shadow of a body the size of a small cat.

Joy shrieked. "It's a rat!"

"Christ! It's massive," I remarked, with growing fascination. "What the hell does it feed on?"

"Potatoes," deduced Simon, equally fascinated. "I'll bet they disturbed its nest when they moved the potatoes." And now it was building another one above our heads.

Simon sat up suddenly and bashed the wooden bunk above his head with his fist. The rat instantly disappeared, and Simon was rewarded for his heroics by being immersed in a shower of rat's droppings.

"What the hell's going on? We're trying to sleep up here!" Upstairs they were clearly unaware with whom they were sharing their bunks.

"We've just seen a rat head your way," I called. "But don't worry, 'Ratbusters' are on the job."

"It's been in my pocket! Look!" Joy spoke slowly, as if in shock. During her time as a WPC, she must have seen many horrific and harrowing scenes, and witnessed the grisly aftermath of many a grim road traffic accident. But this was personal. And there was nothing any of us could do about it.

Trailing from her pocket was the remnants of a shredded toilet roll. Further investigation revealed what was left of a bar of a chocolate, still in its wrapper and gnawed into fragments.

"The thing's been in my pocket!" she repeated, as if in shock.

"Something must have disturbed it," said Simon. "I wonder if there are any more?"

Joy tossed the remains of the chocolate bar towards the corner of the room, as if to banish in disgust the culprit which had attracted the intruder.

Simon's torch followed the flight of the chocolate as it first bounced on the table and landed on the end bunk, close to Dave Blakeney, who had slept soundly through everything. He turned his torch off and we lay still, paralysed in the blackness of night with sleeping bags drawn tightly to us, waiting for the noises to begin again. Sleep was impossible. I had no idea what time it was, but I feared that dawn was still some way off.

It wasn't long before it began again. The noises were more distant than before, as if the rat was trying to conceal its whereabouts. But it was there. Somewhere. And then the scuffling noises grew louder.

"Are you awake Simon?" I asked.

He replied by turning on his torch.

"It's over there, by Dave", I said, "where the chocolate landed."

Simon shone his torch in the direction I had indicated. At first it only picked out the prostrate shapes of sleeping bodies. Then it reflected the glint of silver paper, and attached to it was the mouth of a rat, the sinister beady eyes as stony and lifeless as those of a shark. Sensing danger, it darted into the shadows and was gone. But seconds later, the sweep of the torch exposed something else.

At first I thought the movement was Dave stirring in his sleep, but then the light from the torch captured them. Three of them. All built like brick shit-houses, sniffing and twitching around the bottom of Dave's sleeping bag. And they were bold. They were not going to be deterred from sniffing out the abandoned chocolate by a tittle bit of light.

"Oh God! There's three more of the things." Everyone has a nightmare; something which they hope will never happen. This was Joy's. And now she was living it.

"We'd better get them away from Dave!" Simon warned.

"Well, if I was a rat", I replied, trying to make light of a situation which I was relishing little more than Joy, "I wouldn't hang about there too long. Have you smelt Blakeney's feet recently?"

I groped towards the bottom of the bunk and found what I was looking for.

"Simon, keep the torch on the bastards and lean back. This could go anywhere." I sat up and took careful aim, not wishing to hit our sleeping leader full force with one of my Rockys, which now doubled as a rat-seeking missile. The skills honed in many an illicit Prep. school slipper fight came to my aid and although my Rocky lacked the aerodynamic qualities of the sponge-soled, tartan velvet-uppered Woolworth's specials of my youth, it did the job. The boot flew into the midriff of the nearest rodent with a satisfying thud and subsequent squeak, and the startled rats, suddenly fearful, took flight.

Unfortunately the sudden and unprovoked attack had left them disorientated, and while two of them fled across the floor, the third, doubtless boosted by the carbo-loading from the potatoes, did a very passable impersonation of Sally Gunnell over our sleeping bags before disappearing beneath the lower tier at the far end of the dormitory.

Dave rolled over and grunted in his sleep, oblivious to the drama.

"Ungrateful blighter," I said. "That's all the thanks we get for saving his life!"

I switched on my torch, and looked at my watch. It was three thirty. I needed a pee, but a walk across that rat infested floor appealed about as much as a swim in the South China Sea.

Mercifully, that was the last we saw of the rats. They were still there, of course, and every so often one of them would run across the floor, just to let us know they were still there. If they were back amongst the potatoes that was not our problem. They could be squatting there amid their dumbbells, munching fistfuls of steroids to supplement their potato diet, for all I cared. In a few hours time we would leave this hellish building never to return.

But until the horrors of the night were banished by the first streaks of dawn across the sky, we drew the draw cords of our sleeping bags very tight indeed. Lying intensely still, intensely awake, each of us had long abandoned any notion of sleep.

*

The only compensation of a sleepless night is the prospect of a better night to follow. I hoped that my body would simply switch off tonight, my need for sleep was now so great. However, with the increased altitude at Gorak Shep, and temperatures possibly as low as minus thirty degrees, the prospects of sleep were not good. I did not consider it all that likely that I would arise refreshed and ready for anything tomorrow morning, with all the zest for life of those enviable but surrealistic people in the breakfast cereal adverts.

Gorak 'get down' Shep, as Bryan English had christened it, was a place to 'do' in a day, according to the guide book. An overnight stay was not recommended and should be avoided if possible, due, not least, to the sparsity of the accommodation. But for us, it was not possible. We had no choice. Gorak Shep was journey's end.

With this in mind, and Dieter's insistence that it was essential to stay in a lodge on the night before the race, I had asked the Gurkhas, who had visited Gorak Shep yesterday to book ten slabs in the best joint in town, which they assured me they had done. Of this I was sceptical.

Most people in the dormitory had slept reasonably well after the departure of the potato men, and many of those in tents claimed, fairly unconvincingly, also to have slept well.

In the early morning light there was no visible evidence of the rats, other than the droppings, and Dave accused us of making the whole thing up. I wished I had been a little less circumspect with the aim of my Rocky.

"Probably mice," he said dismissively, upon examination of the droppings. "Can't see what all the fuss is about."

"Fucking big mice, then," I said, concealing my annoyance with difficulty. I was also beginning to wish that Joy's chocolate had bounced rather nearer to the top of his bag. He would by now have been on first name terms with them. "If those were mice, then this lodge needs a cat the size of a bloody Rottweiler!"

I was feeling irritable. Under normal circumstances, lack of sleep makes me irritable, but the anticipation of another miserable night to look forward to made my sullen mood all the more pronounced.

I breakfasted on my own, on the stone ledge outside the lodge. But I had little enthusiasm for the fried eggs, chapattis and tea which supplemented my last packet of sausage and beans. A solitary figure, I was in no mood either for the humour around the breakfast table, and considered it best to stay clear of the inevitable fuss and jostling which could easily lead to a flashpoint. I couldn't even be bothered to renew the usual piss-taking banter with the Gurkhas sitting outside the lodge below. Besides which, at eight it was still bloody cold.

After breakfast, came the moment of truth: our medicals. Once declared fit by the doctors, we would be issued with our race numbers. That meant that, barring catastrophe, we had been cleared to stand on the start line at 7 a.m. on the following morning. There was, of course, still a considerable chance that the final leg of the trek and the last night in these extreme conditions would cruelly conspire to prevent this, but with numbers safely in our rucksacks, our confidence would be buoyed up.

It was my turn. Simon called me over in the brusque manner of the specialist with a busy round who wanted to be on the first tee by 9 a.m.

"Good morning doctor, thank you for seeing me."

"How're you feeling?"

"Oh... so so, can't complain really."

"Any headaches, vomiting, insomnia, loss of appetite, dizziness, loss of balance or disorientation?"

"Intermittent headache and insomnia. But I don't think that the insomnia has too much to do with the altitude, do you? What about yourself," I asked.

"Oh, pretty much the same," replied Simon. "Now I want you to walk ten paces in a straight line."

"Come on, I'd have a job doing that at home," I said and staggered off uncertainly towards the lodge.

"Hmmm," murmured Simon, doubtfully. "Okay. Now I want you to answer three very simple questions. What's your name, where are you, and what are your children called?"

"Christ, Simon, I thought you said simple questions! Let's see... I think I'm okay on the first two: my name is Richard, I'm at present in Lobuche, which is beneath the Khumbu Glacier, approximately three miles south west of Gorak Shep... but I'm buggered if I can answer the third one. Would you settle for dogs, or can I consult my diary?"

"Stop pissing about. There's nothing wrong with you. Shove off and get your numbers."

\*

The numbers were allocated in alphabetical order. I was number seventeen. That was one behind Pierre André, and that, I sensed, was as close as I was likely to get to him.

With my three numbers proudly and carefully stored in my rucksack, I paid a visit to the shop to replenish my supply of water and chocolate before departing.

The Highland Grocery Store, Lobuche is the highest retail outlet in the world, and would shame many an 'open all hours' corner shop back home. At a glance the ramshackle chaos that places Red Cow powdered milk next to Beck's beer implies that the proprietor is not fully cognisant of exactly what it is he is selling. But upon closer inspection, climbing ropes, ice axes and down jackets are all to be found in more or less the same pile, and are offered for sale with no less aforethought than places dog food next to cat food in Sainsbury's.

This incredible emporium sells anything that it can get its hands on which well-endowed expeditions retreating to civilisation have no further need for. And these, at sixteen and a half thousand feet, are largely what could be termed as luxuries. Duracell batteries, a vast selection of chocolate bars and other confectionery, rum, beer,

Nescafé coffee, strawberry cordial, and a variety of soaps and even towels packed the flimsy shelves. I wouldn't have been surprised to find a chest freezer full of ice lollies and Findus frozen single TV dinners for the lost and the lonely.

I even half expected to see Reg Holdsworth grimacing somewhere behind the climbing gear ready to bleed me of every last rupee for a bag of frozen peas.

There was no Reg Holdsworth, but the ultimate corner shop in the world charged the ultimate prices, reflecting its elevated aspect.

We left Lobuche in dribs and drabs, Early and Late Birds intermingled and at last united in this, the final push to our destination. I set off with Ray, but lacked the motivation to trek at his pace, particularly as my headache began to return. There was no hurry, I told myself, to arrive at Gorak Shep and, with each step becoming more arduous, I resigned myself to a steady crawl. There was no path, simply an intricate network of trails along the valley floor, and the increase in altitude was barely perceptible by anything other than the increase in effort required to walk it. I tried to imagine myself running down through this wilderness tomorrow. I couldn't. It was a desolate and uninspiring trek and, as we neared the head of the valley, so the feeling of being hemmed in became more acute. Huge brown hills of stone and scree towered above and denied us the majesty of the scenery that they obscured.

Two of these hills had to be climbed and, as with the climb from Duglha, there is no true line of ascent. Instead, a precarious and exhausting scramble over loose boulders eventually led to the next level. I paused at the crest of the first climb, the hammering of my heart painfully echoing through my head, and looked for the logical line down which I should descend. There was none and, to make matters worse, it was not possible to see the bottom of the hill. It would be important not to go too far to the left, as that would mean descending into the wrong side of the valley or, worse still, taking a detour onto the glacier itself!

The second climb was a moraine hill of around five hundred feet at the side of the Changri Shar Glacier. Beyond this the path led over rocks to the unannounced crossroads of three glaciers: the Changri Shar, the Changri Nup and, of course, the Khumbu, until it became impossible to follow. I was now walking on glacier, although the rocks and sand under my feet concealed the geological contortions of the millions of years that lay beneath.

I suddenly became totally disorientated, and gradually the realisation dawned that I was lost. I also realised that I had not seen another soul for some time. Great walls of rock rose in every direction. There was nothing else; just rock and sun. To judge by the position of the sun, I must have drifted off the path to the left and was heading north west up the Changri Shar Glacier.

Panic set in, as first I walked in one direction, and when that yielded no way out of this stony prison, I tried another. There was no clear rationale behind my efforts, but if I could get above this basin, perhaps I could see the path beneath me. Or better still, instead of contouring the moraine mountain, perhaps I could traverse it, and drop down into Gorak Shep which must be on the other side. I walked and I scrambled until I felt exhausted, worry and frustration adding to the toll demanded by the physical effort. I was like a spider in the bath, I thought, only how many spiders have to run a bloody marathon as a reward for escape?

And then I became convinced that I could see a path below me to my right. With almost joyful relief, I abandoned my attempted traverse and descended into the rock basin. There were no landmarks, no points of reference to mark it so, taking great care not to take my eye off the path, I carefully clambered down over the rocks to the sandy floor of the glacier.

But somehow, by the time I had descended and reached the point where I had seen a clear path, it had disappeared without a trace, vanished like a mirage. There was only sand and rock. Rock and sand.

I sat down on a rock, utterly dispirited, and drank some water. They would come looking for me, I supposed, but that was little consolation. I would probably not be missed until evening, as my reputation for straying from the flock would not suggest that anything was amiss. Also, the fundamental principle with which Ray and I had kept faith throughout the trip, was that we would do as we pleased as long as it did not inconvenience others or interfere with their plans. I tried to think how I would have felt on the evening before the race, had I been asked to join the search for some idiot who had failed to turn up in camp. Ray might wonder where I was, but would probably assume that I had decided to climb Kala Pattar or take some other detour. Well I had. Some bloody detour.

"Shit, I said to myself. "This is worse than Cornwall. This is even worse than bloody Dartmoor. Why the *hell* don't I ever learn? *What the bloody hell am I doing here?*" I wanted to scream, but I felt too defeated, too empty. On Dartmoor, no one can hear you scream. At seventeen thousand feet, you don't have the breath to scream. I sat, head in hands, until I could bear the smell that emanated from them no longer. I studied my hands, with some interest. They were virtually black. God knows what the rest of me must look like. It was over five days since my last decent wash. It would be weeks before the last of the grime would be removed.

And it was perhaps then that I realised the truth about the Everest Marathon, and why it is unparalleled as a test of endurance which is not only physical, but also mental and perhaps even spiritual. The term Marathon owes its existence to a feat of endurance made famous by a Greek messenger who ran the 26.2 miles from Marathon to Athens to convey the news of a decisive battle. History, or mythology, does not relate what this stoic messenger had been engaged in immediately prior to his mad dash from Marathon. He may have been peeling potatoes. He might even have been washing his general's chariot, or weeding his garden.

But had he spent the previous sixteen days and seven hours edging ever closer to the point where the human body simply refuses to tolerate any more deprivation of oxygen, sanitation, sleep and eat food as appetising as silage, let alone function with any degree of athletic performance, he would have invented the field telephone instead.

There are longer races. There may be even tougher races. But the paradox was that the 26.2 miles which I had to took forward to tomorrow, if I ever found my way out of this basin, was a skip and a jump compared to what we had just done to get to the start. And there would be no thoughts of withdrawal, for there was no other way to get down, unless one was very, very ill indeed.

Yet in the last sixteen days I had learnt much about myself and this bewildering but beautiful and often savage wonderland. This land which seemed so totally at odds with anything I had previously encountered on the planet earth as to challenge many of the values by which I had lived my hitherto normal life. For the first time in my thirty-seven years of reasonably predictable and safe progressions through life, I had done something that was different. Really different. And for the first time I looked at my life from outside the parameters of its everyday experience. Right now, I felt that owning a shiny piece of machinery that could do the standing quarter mile in a shade over fifteen seconds seemed just a little unimportant.

And here was another paradox. After sixteen days of trekking to get within spitting distance of the top of the world, tomorrow morning we would be running away from it. But that had its compensations. Tomorrow we would be running towards a shower of sorts, a decent meal, a cold beer and softish bed in a lodge where the only rats were trekkers who didn't pay their bills. Tomorrow we would be running back towards the reassuring comforts of the consumer world to which we belonged.

And that was what I had to took forward to once I figured out how to get out of this desolate quarry.

I got to my feet in time to see Fergie and Liz Harding wave at me from fifty yards away on the path, and the crisis was over. Together we clambered over the remaining half eternity of moonscape which was familiar to Fergie, having trekked it yesterday, and half an hour later were greeted by the first sight of Gorak Shep.

\*

If ever a place had an appropriate epithet, it is Gorak Shep. Literally translated as 'Graveyard of Crows', I wondered why whoever it was that accorded it this name had stopped at crows.

There is an air of finality here which makes it a good place to end the journey; the full stop at the end of the sixteen day sentence which had begun so long ago at Jiri.

Although there is a trail of sorts which leads north to Everest Base Camp, around a two hour walk from Gorak, there is little point in making the journey. Base Camp was once described by John Hunt as: "A lifeless wilderness, which had the effect of lowering everyone's morale." From Base Camp there is no view of Everest, and the icefall of the Western Cwm leading ultimately to the South Col, which is also obscured, is scant reward for the effort. I had heard a rumour that Base Camp had become so crowded during the pre-monsoon climbing season that fights had broken out amongst climbers from different expeditions waiting for their crack at the mountain. Similar to other rumours I had heard about the litter along the Everest Highway, and the sheer volume of trekkers on the trail, I imagined that it was a gross exaggeration.

For most people, Gorak Shep is journey's end, the top of the escalator, and Kala Pattar is the pinnacle from which the world's highest mountain finally and spectacularly reveals its true glory.

The last thing I expected to see at seventeen thousand, five hundred feet was a sandy beach. But rounding the final shoulder of the moraine, this is one of three bizarre features of Gorak Shep which stops you in your tracks.

The second is the frozen lake which lies beyond the beach. So unexpected is this meeting of sand and water, albeit frozen, that it seems impossible that man, with his passion for the ludicrous, did not play a part in the creation of this surreal setting. Perhaps it was an unfinished project by Center Parks and there was a nine hole golf course beyond the lake.

The third distinctly odd physical feature of Gorak Shep is Kala Pattar itself. With a name meaning 'Black Rock' one would naturally assume that it would be black. Other than its tiny apex, it is not. In fact, it is a gently sloping green, grassy-looking knoll whose insignificance is accentuated by the fact that it is situated directly beneath the striking grandeur of Pumo Ri.

Descending from the moraine through loose gravel, we came to the upper two of the three lodges, situated on either side of a flat sandy plain above the beach. We had already spotted the familiar blue jackets worn by the Gurkhas from afar, and joined them on the sunny terrace outside the lodge. Behind the lodge, the Late Bird tents were being erected. This, I assumed correctly, must be the best of the three lodges, and therefore unlikely to be the one wherein Charlie had booked my ten slabs.

"Is this it?" I asked.

"Sorry mate", replied Charlie, "this one's virtually full so I booked you ten cots in that one." He pointed at the dilapidated building across the plateau. It was difficult to tell whether the sorry-looking structure was in the process of being built or falling down. "It seems quite nice in there, and there's plenty of room."

"I'll bet there is," I replied.

I ordered a tea from inside the Gurkha lodge, and used this as an excuse to check surreptitiously on the availability of accommodation. The proprietor confirmed that there was only one space available, but there would be plenty of room tomorrow night. Big deal. Inside a relatively cosy-looking dormitory, where a warm stove already pumped smoke and warmth into the room, there was little evidence of occupation of the sleeping spaces. I could only assume that the lads in blue had come to a mutually agreeable arrangement with the owner, and had bagged the entire place for themselves to prevent external intervention denying them a good night's sleep before the big day. To avoid adverse publicity and accusations of a lack of public-spiritedness, they had perhaps left one or two cots for the general public, in the hope that the general public could be gently dissuaded from their occupancy.

Or perhaps it was just me being cynical.

The proprietor of the second lodge greeted me with as much reticence as one might expect from a proprietor whose ramshackle lodge at the top of the world had barely been accorded 'commended' status in the Gurkha 'Good Lodge Guide'.

However he confirmed that ten spaces had been reserved, and that I would pay for them now, he demanded. I would not, I told him.

From the inside, it looked even worse. There was no discernible lounge, but an ante room leading to the dormitory contained a table, a couple of broken chairs and a wooden bench fixed to one wall. It also had a huge hole in the roof, through which there was an excellent view of the massive western flank of Nuptse.

The earthen floor of the dormitory, and wooden slatted cots supported unevenly by large flattish stones, did little to enhance the ambience. There were windows which contained glass, but there were also spacious gaps between the windows and the walls which contained nothing. Not surprisingly, there were no signs of other 'guests'. If Mary and Joseph had come across this empty inn in Bethlehem, they would have asked if there was a stable in the vicinity.

But I was cold and hungry and, with the lack of mental clarity which altitude induces, I found it hard to make a coherent decision. I laid out my belongings on the slab, and dried the sweat that felt like ice on my back. Dressed in my Buffalo suit, I sat down to consider the situation. There was no stove anywhere near the dormitory. In fact, I had seen nothing to suggest that there was a stove at all. It would be freezing in here tonight and I would be no better off than in my tent. What about the third lodge? It had to be better than this. I was on the verge of repacking my gear and leaving, when the thought struck me that it may also be full. But what if I was the only one in here? Well, at least there wouldn't be any rats tonight, I thought, looking mournfully at the holes in the roof and walls. Too bloody cold.

Just then someone entered and spoke to the proprietor. I went out to the lounge to see who it was. It was Shigi. He was looking for accommodation.

"No room!" announced the owner abruptly. By comparison, his demeanour when I had arrived would have won him Forte's 'Manager of the Month' award.

Shigi walked through the lounge and stood at the entrance to the dormitory surveying the twenty empty slabs unbelievingly.

The owner stood behind him.

"No room, I tell you! People come. You go!"

I suddenly realised that he hated the Japanese even more than he hated financial loss.

Shigi looked at me appealingly. I shrugged. I was staying out of this. Then I remembered his capacity for snoring and I also remembered the empty cot in the Gurkha lodge, and an idea occurred to me. A devilishly good idea.

"There's a bed free in the lodge over there." I pointed through the gap by the window to the building outside which the Gurkhas relaxed in the sun. "At least there was a few moments ago. It's nice and warm in there. If you're quick you'll get it."

Shigi thanked me and left, and I imagined I caught a barely perceptible nod from the proprietor. I shouldered my camera belt and, leaving the remainder of my belongings on the slab, set off to see what the lower lodge had to offer.

Out in the warm sunshine I looked across to where the Gurkhas reclined in the sun as Shigi disappeared through the door leading to the dormitory.

'You poor bastards,' I thought. 'You've no idea what you're in for.' With a chuckle, I set off towards the beach.

Ahead of me towered Nuptse's vast pillar of rock and fluted seracs over which the dark and final pyramid of Everest's summit loomed. Where I slept suddenly became unimportant. I had less than six hours to savour the intimacy of this audience with Mount Everest. With hands thrust deep into pockets, I whistled as I strolled down the rocky path onto the beach where the breeze blew sand into my face.

Fifty yards later I stopped, gasping for breath. I could probably manage any two of the three, but walking, whistling and breathing at the same time was definitely out of the question.

*

The blue and green tents identified the Early Bird headquarters which was adjacent to the third lodge. Outside in the walled courtyard my brothers in arms sat or reclined as the ritual of lunch went through the final throes of preparation. The performance was enacted with the same obsequious deference from the cook boys as from a hotel waiter on the last day of your stay.

For this, in effect, was the last lunch. Tomorrow was race day. On Saturday we would be either dead, or spend the day in an alcoholic haze on the balcony of the Tawa lodge, which would amount to about the same thing. This, all being well, would be repeated on Sunday. Then on Monday we would trek back to Lukla, and any further beyond that was still too distant too contemplate. Particularly the flight back to Kathmandu.

I looked at the cook boy who shone bright teeth at me and proffered a plateful of coleslaw, cold baked beans and spam. No, you're going to have to give me something better than this if you want my Thin Lizzy T-shirt. I smiled back.

"Daal Bhaat?" I asked hopefully. His smile broadened.

"Ah, daal Bhaat," he shook his head and, still wearing a smile that conveyed pity as well as deference, he told me, "No daal Bhaat."

I took the plate and thanked him.

Conversation was now exclusively focused on the race. Nervously, each expressed their own anxieties and shared worries now building like gathering storm clouds, rolling inexorably towards the final dawn. These, and softly spoken aspirations. Just to finish, was the simple understated ambition that bounced around the courtyard like an echo in a disused quarry. But many of our group had deteriorated since leaving Lobuche, and the increase in altitude had been acutely felt by all of us. John Webster was now very ill, and Joy was not much better. Even as recently as yesterday, the race had still seemed remote and distant. But now 'just to finish' would represent a considerable achievement for the scores of runners who had sacrificed everything during the months of gruelling training. And for what? To witness the unrelenting deterioration of their bodies by the unremitting grind of the tortuous journey to the start. I was lucky. I just felt tired. More exhausted than I had ever felt before. I slumped down on a bench beside Ray. I wanted to sleep, but somehow had to summon sufficient energy to eat this unappetising meal.

"Not eating?" I asked him.

"Not that bloody rubbish," he replied and told me that he had ordered *dhal bhaat* from the lodge.

"So what's the game plan for tomorrow?" I asked.

"What still bloody concerns me the most", Ray confided quietly, "is bloody getting lost." This, of course, I knew. "So I figure if I sit in behind Gobo and the Gurkhas, certainly until well beyond the glacial moraines, and quite possibly Tengboche, then I might have a reasonable bloody chance of drawing them out over the last third."

Ray was also concerned about what to wear and, although the temperature might still be around minus twenty degrees at 7 a.m., he had more or less decided to start in shorts, rather than waste time stripping off later.

He had enlisted Nat's assistance, and had given him instructions to prepare a revolting sounding concoction of grated Power Bar and Staminade which he would present him with at Pheriche. Many of the medical crew and marshals had left to make their way down the course and take up their race positions. Bryan English had stayed at Lobuche, Liz and Adrienne were at Dughla, Nat and Annabel had returned to Pheriche and Sue had gone back to Pangboche. Most of the Late Birds were responsible for the lower reaches of the course, apart from John Dunning who had manfully offered to hike all the way back to Namche then out to Thamo to give aid at the furthest extremity of the course.

Ray had planned every last detail with the scrutiny and method of someone who had come with serious aspirations of winning the race. He confided that his kit was already neatly arranged in his tent. Not only this, he had also already assembled his minimum gear, and was proud of the fact that it would fit neatly into a bumbag, with room to spare. As such, he would be the only runner who would not run with a rucksack.

"What about you?" he asked.

"Oh, I don't really know," I replied vaguely. I hadn't really given it much detailed thought, but knew it would be important to keep my strong competitive urges in check, or I could run into trouble in the early stages and blow everything. "But I'll tell you one thing – I won't be sitting in behind Gobo and the Gurkhas, that's for sure!" I went on to say that, if my walk across the beach was anything to go by, the early stages of the race would present me with a straightforward choice between running and breathing. And on the whole, I preferred breathing.

"What time d'you reckon you're looking at?"

"I'd say about six and a half. Six at very best. At least, that's roughly what I'd worked out. But if I'm feeling anything like this tomorrow, that could be days, not hours."

"Naw, you'll do it in a lot less than that," Ray predicted. "It shouldn't take you more than five and a half. Say, five and three quarters at most."

"I wish I had your confidence," I told him. I wasn't sure quite what he based his optimism on. I felt the tingle of nervous anticipation as we spent the next fifteen minutes discussing how best various difficult parts of the course should be approached. We had, of course, discussed them a hundred times before.

We lapsed into silence, and listened to the buzz of the conversation around us. Pierre André was entertaining a small attentive audience with his account of the Mount Cameroon race which he had once won, and in which he had once recorded a DNF (did not finish). In many ways it sounded more fearsome than the Everest, though incomparable, as it lacked the basic ingredient which made tomorrow's little jaunt quite unique – a sixteen day walk in which guaranteed that runners were virtually 'Dead On Arrival' by the time they reached the start line.

"You would enjoy it," he said to me, with a broad grin.

"Why?" I asked.

He laughed and shrugged his shoulders. "Why not? For sure, you like crazy things, *n'est-ce pas*?"

This indeed was a compliment, coming from a man who made my lunacy look like a quiet night in front of the telly.

"I'm rapidly going off them," I replied.

Someone asked him if he would be back again in two years' time. No, he replied, win or lose this would be his final Everest Marathon. In fact, it may well be his last marathon. He now wanted to turn his attention to mountaineering.

Well, that was another thing we had in common. Win or lose, I doubted if I would be back in two years' time. But I wanted to turn my attention to more mundane matters, such as my family.

I wanted to change the subject, and asked Pierre André what he did for a living.

"Sometimes, I work," he told me with a smile. And at what did he work, I enquired? He worked for a Swiss company that made and marketed baby food, he informed me.

"It is good?" I asked.

"Yah. It is good." He paused and thought. "You know", he sighed, "baby food is like life itself. There is more to baby food, than just baby food."

"You mean", I said thoughtfully, "that there is more to life than just existence."

*"Mais oui, naturellement,"* he said with a broad grin.

\*

I had to get away. There was a tension around the lodge that crackled and rumbled with more electricity than a dark and pregnant sky before a thunder storm. It was still too far from the race to become immersed with the stomach-knotting, bowel-moving jittering which had preceded every race in which I had taken part since the age of six. I didn't want a gutful of adrenalin right now. Not until five to seven tomorrow morning, thank you very much.

I picked up my camera belt, and set off slowly across the beach. There was a group of Late Birds playing with a frisbee at the upper end.

Kala Pattar looked much bigger from our end of the beach. I aimlessly scrambled over a short rocky outcrop rising sharply from the beach and began to follow a path which contoured the hill towards Pumo Ri, gaining height gently but significantly.

I had no intention of going right to the top, which was reckoned to be a climb of about an hour and a half. All I wanted was a bit of privacy and a good view of Everest. Moreover, dressed in my only clothes which were dry, I had no desire to find them soaked in sweat. I walked slowly. The effort required was immense.

At first I took thirty steps before I had to stop and rest. Then it became twenty, and ultimately ten. The path was easy to follow, in fact it was like a motorway when compared with sections of the coastal path at home. Unlike the scrambling and climbing which Ray and I had enjoyed yesterday, this was a stroll. But a breathless stroll. Whereas we had been restricted by a lack of mountaineering acumen, I was now restricted by a distinct lack of oxygen. The difference in altitude may have been minimal, but the effect was incredible.

Gradually I realised that the rate at which I was gaining height had reduced, and the path which I was following in all probability led to one of the high passes into Tibet rather than anywhere near the summit of Kala Pattar. This was confirmed as I laboriously approached the final set of ten steps before the extended rest which I had promised myself; another path which clearly led up to the summit joined mine.

Despite my earlier resolve, it was tempting to follow this path to the summit. I could quite clearly see two people standing on the little summit, and although it was too distant to recognise them, I couldn't see how it would take me more than half an hour to reach it. Forty five minutes at the most. But then I remembered that Dave had instructed us to attend a dress rehearsal for the start of the race so that we would get away smoothly in the morning, which would take place at 3 p.m. It was now past one thirty, and I would need to allow at least an hour to get down. That would make it very tight, and I could end up pushing myself hard and paying the penalty tomorrow.

With a last wistful look towards the summit, I sat down on a conveniently placed boulder, close to where the two paths met. From here I had a magnificent view of Everest's summit and South West Face which dominated the skyline between the West Shoulder, or Marathon Peak" as Ray and I had christened it, and the spiky finger of Nuptse's ice-capped pinnacle which pierced the deep blue of the early afternoon sky like a Manhattan skyscraper. This would do, the view was doubtless better from the top, but this was a good compromise. My heart wanted to go to the summit, but my head, once again pounding with the exertion in the thin air, told me that I should not have even come this far.

I was again well above the Khumbu Glacier. Towards Base Camp, the glacier resembled a mountain range in miniature, with craggy slate-grey peaks jutting above the walls of the ruts worn deep by the tracks of the giant caterpillar plant that in my imagination had laid level this most perplexing of nature's dead end streets. Then, looking south, there was the frozen lake, beyond which was the boulder from whence we would hopefully set off in around seventeen hours' time. And then the beach rising to the moraine where the path was now plainly visible running parallel to the glacier. Now the glacier resembled a ghostly white ice-encrusted sea, shimmering with the heat from the sun and the dust driven on mischievously by the wind as it gathered momentum on its daily journey up the valley. And finally the lakes, the frozen crystalline lakes sparkling in the afternoon sun.

And then, of course, there were the mountains. There was too much for the eye to take in, and too little time to appreciate it. If Tengboche had been the grandstand for the world's finest mountain scenery, half way up Kala Pattar I was shaking hands with Luciano, having a beer with Will Carling with the French well and truly routed, and getting off with Lois Lane after Superman had revived her. It was like comparing a Ferrari to a Lada: it is possible to buy them both in red, and they have four wheels and an engine, but that is where the similarities end. I was like the schoolboy who had been given the keys to the tuck shop, but I only had half an hour to gorge myself.

With the notable exception of Everest which had been concealed behind Nuptse, I was amongst the same mountains as yesterday. Only today, they were much closer; somehow they looked different. So different that, overwhelmed by the emotion of the moment, I unwisely accompanied my visual record on video with a commentary which subsequently proved to be wildly inaccurate.

"From where I stand on Kala Pattar, I have the most remarkable view of Mount Everest, the highest point on earth, flanked by the lesser giants, Nuptse and Lhotse..." True, to a degree, but not possible from where I stood. What I had described was the view from the south. Somehow I had confused Lhotse with the West Shoulder, our Marathon Peak. Lhotse is not visible from where I stood. In fact neither is it anywhere near where I stood, nor does it in any way resemble the West Shoulder, other than by the facts that it is big, has a peak, and wears snow for a coat when it gets cold in winter. Fancy not recognising the mountain you had named twenty-four hours ago. No wonder Mallory had problems. Had I been standing on the summit of Kala Pattar, I would have had a terrific view of the Lhotse face where Lowe and Ang Nyima performed their heroic step cutting, which sweeps down to the South Col. But I wasn't.

It got worse.

"...and the South Col, leading to the South East Ridge, by which the summit was finally gained." What I was identifying was a ridge of rock or col which joined the West Shoulder with the West Ridge, a massive four mile barrier of rock separating the North and South West faces. This had been largely unnoteworthy until Hornbein and Unsoeld successfully climbed it and reached the summit in 1963, descending by the South East Ridge, thus achieving the first traverse of the mountain.

The South Col is not visible from where I stood either. From the summit of Kala Pattar, the South Col, described by Hunt: "...as dreary and desolate a place as ever I expect to see, where a constant wind adds to the dread that possesses it," can be clearly seen.

But it is easy to be wise after the event, and all that mattered was that I was privileged to be sat amongst the most stupendous mountains in the world and, not only that, I felt I had achieved something by just getting there.

Through the viewfinder of my video camera I noticed today's date. It was 25th November, and it suddenly occurred to me that in exactly a month's time it would be Christmas Day. Christmas Day! We would probably be in Wales with Kirsty's family, in the luxury of her brother's large bungalow with a choice of three toilets and two bathrooms. We would probably be about to sit down in the softly lit dining room at the huge mahogany table with the high backed antique chairs. Nel would be carving the turkey and Andy and I reflecting over our third pint of home brew, upon an enjoyable run over twelve miles of South Pembrokeshire coast path. Granddad would be semi-comatose in the armchair after his second can of Carlsberg Super Strength Lager, as the children, under cover of the chaos, tore the place apart.

And I would be boring anyone who would listen about being *there*. But that was a world away, and what was important right now was being here. In any case, I could never describe what being here was truly like. No video, no slides however good the quality, could adequately describe what was in front of me and lay all around me now. Perhaps accentuated by the time it had taken to get here, the deprivation, the mental and physical endurance, I now understood better than ever before about the mystical qualities of these formidable mountains. Perhaps this was what Mallory had in mind when he responded to the questioner demanding why he wanted to climb Mount Everest, with the enigmatic reply: "Because it is there."

If only I could bottle one moment of being 'there' and take it home and say "Look, this is what it was really like!" The crunching and shifting of the constantly moving earth beneath the frozen waste of the creaking glacier, the whoosh of small avalanches dropping off the mountains, the crackle of collapsing ice bridges in the giant meringues of the ice field leading to the Western Cwm, where climbers of stature and rare brilliance and brave and loyal porters fell to lonely, frozen deaths imprisoned in the silent vault alongside undeserving novices. The silent echoes of the cries of anguish from the ghosts of the departed, the frozen bodies and the debris that lie hidden from the photographic eye that sees everything yet understands nothing; nothing but the brutal romance of the spindrift and the snowy cornice. They too, who had not come here to die, but had risked all, and for what? To lie heroically entombed in an icy crevasse where night will never fall, and day will never dawn.

The waste of a life, of one hundred lives.

The unimportance of it all.

If only I could bottle just a part of this and take it back, I could uncork the bottle and see where it stood alongside little Jimmy's lost sock, Caspar's confiscated comics, or little Tommy's terrible table manners.

The trivial, unimportance of it all.

I knew that I could neither bring it back for others to understand, nor could I put the cork back into the bottle and toss it away, toss it out to sea, to drift away and be forgotten. Another holiday. Another memory.

With the same unsafe, disconcerting certainty that, no matter what happened tomorrow, I knew I could never again find importance in little Jimmy's lost sock, Caspar's confiscated comics, or little Tommy's terrible table manners. Yet, that was where I belonged. I was a part of that world. And I would have to deal with the same dull monotony of that distant life once again. And soon. That no pain, no risk, cotton wool-wrapped, litigation-freely-available, disposable-sweet-wrapper of a life that is called civilisation. That world, where there is always someone or something to blame, where we drink freely from the fountain of triviality and where the god of Image smiles sublimely as we flock to prostrate ourselves at his altar beneath the neon billboard.

And then my thoughts went to home. Of baby Cameron mewling and puking in his mother's arms. And boy, could he mewl and puke. Of Rosanna, my Rosanna of whom I am so proud, and in whom I see both great things and that same impetuous headstrong independence which both my mother and I possess, and which scared me half to death in the lonely hours of a waking nightmare.

I could picture Rosanna announcing to her nursery teacher, Mrs Sutherland: "Daddy's shivering in Shivilaya!" And I could also picture Mrs Sutherland asking Rosanna, as she had asked me: "How's he getting there then, by Sherpa van?" Ah, a little knowledge is a wonderful but dangerous thing.

And then Jake, who at seven has an understanding of life that goes no further than pain and comfort, hunger and contentment, and for whom all the knowledge of the universe is less important than why he is not allowed to suck his thumb all day.

And Kirsty, who selflessly and lovingly attends the very vocal demands of two small children, and two equally vocal but less demanding dogs, and reads the needs of one child who is so severely handicapped as to be totally dependent upon her for a lifeline. I wondered how she was coping, a month was a long time. And how I could repay her for what she had sacrificed to allow me to be here. For now, she was 'there', and was probably finding the mystical properties of me being 'here' were wearing a bit thin.

I suddenly missed them more than I had done over the previous three weeks. I felt guilty for abandoning them, and then my mind returned to the race. It was important that I did well tomorrow, I desperately wanted them to feel proud of me. It was all well and good looking at the mountains and feeling uplifted and inspired, but that was not exclusively what I had come here to do. If I could return home with my head held high, knowing that I had done my best, and achieved my goals, then it would have been worthwhile. If I failed, I would want to forget the whole thing, and that would trivialise the sacrifice, hardship and deprivation which Kirsty had willingly undertaken to allow me to be here. I would have not only let myself down, I would have let her down.

My eyes were stinging, and I realised that I had been crying. Well, sort of crying, because real men don't cry. I looked at my watch, it was almost two thirty. The wind had increased, and already it was becoming bitterly cold.

I had had my audience, my private sixty minutes with Mount Everest, and it was time to go.

\*

Coming down was considerably easier than going up.

The blue and green canvas of our tents again caught my eye. At the upper end of the beach, there appeared to be a full complement of Late Bird tents, whereas at the lower end, only five blue tents had been erected, presumably as everyone else had opted for the lodge.

I realised that I had had my last night under canvas, unless of course I had a complete mental aberration and opted for a tent tonight. Slumming it in a tent in either Namche or Lukla was not on my agenda. I also realised that tomorrow morning I would pay my final visit to that hideous green latrine tent. At six fifty tomorrow, it would be farewell to the last latrine. Farewell to The Last Latrine... that would be a good name for a book, I mused, and a tiny acorn of an idea plopped into my mind which would grow into a sort of lacquered veneer flat-pack of an oak tree that was to entirely occupy my waking thoughts for the subsequent eighteen months.

With an end to these deprivations in sight, my spirits rose considerably as I descended the hill. A song popularised by Bryan Ferry, which I had included in my *Desert Island Discs* tape and could never get quite out of my mind throughout the trip, mystically acquired some new words:

> ...*And still those little things remain,*
> *that bring me happiness or pain...*
>
> *Those green latrine tents*
> *And the smell of faeces,*
> *Athletic cling-ons*
> *In perplexing places,*
> *Oh how the ghost of you clings*
> *These foolish things*
> *Remind me of you.*

*A snoring Jap*
*Who's in the next compartment.*
*Those urgent words*
*That told you what my fart meant.*
*The tea the cook-boy brings,*
*These foolish things*
*Remind me of you.*

*The smell of porters*
*As we hold our noses.*
*The Sirdar whistling*
*As the mess tent closes.*
*The song that Blakeney sings,*
*These foolish things*
*Remind me of you.*

*The scent of sweat*
*That lingers on my pillow,*
*Wild popcorn only seven rups a kilo,*
*And still my guts have wings,*
*These foolish things*
*Remind me of you.*

*I know that this was bound to be.*
*These things have haunted me*
*For you've entirely enchanted me...*

I was both pleased and alarmed that nostalgia had already set in. Pleased, because if I could already laugh about my reminiscences of the past three weeks, they must be fond memories in the making. Alarmed, because here I was at eighteen thousand feet, absolutely knackered and at the limit of my physical tolerance, with the small matter of a marathon to run in the morning. Also, in my experience, nostalgia is a land which is best visited but fleetingly, and I had no intention of adjourning there. Certainly not yet.

\*

Dave's three o'clock dress rehearsal took place at around three thirty. Most of the Early Birds were on time, but there was a distinct lack of Late Birds which was greeted with a growing irritation by our leader and prompted less than sympathetic comments such as: "Why can't the bastards get here on time. Are they bloody incapable of following simple instructions or what?"

At last, everyone appeared to be present. The first thing that had to be done was to ensure that no one was missing by numbering off. This is a straightforward process which I frequently use to see how many children are present in a class, or to divide the class into groups. It is a simple process which even eight year olds, with brains that would scarcely rival those found in the common or garden worm, can take in their stride.

But somehow, at seventeen thousand, five hundred feet it became as wildly impossible a task as defining Einstein's theory of relativity and then coming up with a better one of your own. The runner in possession of the number previously defined as 'one' called out his number, this was followed by the runner in possession of the number 'two', and so on until all of the seventy-two runners were accounted for.

To begin with it had been mildly amusing when someone forgot their number despite wearing it on their shirt, or when someone else had replied with his name instead of his number. But after twenty minutes the tension and frustration had risen to boiling point, and there was a goodly chance that the next person to screw it up would be lynched. Dave spoke for most of us when he said that if we wanted to spend twenty minutes doing what should take approximately a minute and a half at six fifty-five tomorrow morning at around minus twenty-five degrees, that was our prerogative, but we might get a little cold. Only he didn't phrase it quite like that.

Next was the seeding procedure. So that no one would be held back sprinting up the three hundred yards of beach at minus twenty-something degrees at seventeen and a half thousand feet tomorrow morning, we were asked to divide ourselves into three groups.

The first stood at the start line, and was for the elite runners. Those who had a good chance, or thought they had a good chance of finishing in the top twenty. To give us an idea, if you could run a normal marathon in less than two hours thirty, this was where you should stand.

The second group was for those whose 'normal' marathon time, or predicted marathon time, was under three hours. I had never run a 'normal' marathon, but adjudged this to be the group for me, particularly as it contained one or two people whom I had resolved to beat, especially the rumbustious water-swigging little man who had cast aspersions on my lager drinking so long ago at Heathrow.

The third group was, diplomatically, for those who were intent on taking it easy over the first part of the course, or those whose ambitions were more modest. Or those who were just too damned ill to care any more. This was the 'just to finish' group. I noticed some good runners in this group, and I predicted that many of them should finish in front of runners in the group ahead of them. It was symptomatic of how the trek or illness had sapped their morale that they placed themselves at the back.

The procedure served little purpose other than to provide an opportunity for the puffing out of chests, and a staking of claims which stamina, commitment and, above all, luck over the 26.2 miles would either substantiate or shatter.

Finally, Dave ran through the procedure for tomorrow morning. We would be awakened (which was largely irrelevant as it was unlikely that anyone would be asleep) at 6 a.m. by the first whistle. This was the cue to get moving. The second whistle would be blown at six fifteen, and this would herald the arrival of rice pudding, porridge and tea. The third whistle, some fifteen minutes later, would be to warn us that the race would commence in exactly half an hour. At six forty-five, the final whistle would invite us to place our kit bags, which would not reach Namche until Saturday morning, on a pile to the left of the wall outside our lodge, and sleeping bags, which would reach Namche that evening by express delivery, to the right.

We had the rest of the day to ourselves. It was four o'clock and, as the sun dipped behind the first of the mountains, the temperature began to plummet.

My thoughts again turned to the pressing question of accommodation and the continued quest for food.

The lower lodge which was adjacent to where our tents had been erected, appeared to be, from the outside, a slightly more substantial affair than the second of the upper lodges wherein I had left my kit. Also, inside the building, there was genuine warmth, which not only emanated from the little stove which pushed heat into the kitchen and sitting area of the building, but also from the atmosphere. In the small kitchen, an effort had been made to insulate the room. Something resembling cling film had been placed over the window, and something resembling silver foil was plastered over the walls.

The *didi* was a smiling girl of around twenty, wearing once blue jeans so filthy that no self-respecting coal miner would have been seen dead in them. She was undeniably pretty despite being in obvious need of a good wash. The space on the benches fixed to the walls of the small kitchen was occupied by Pierre André, Valeri, Ramon, Armando, Jordi and several of the Sherpa lads who would be running tomorrow, and had come inside to share a joke and a tea. The middle part of the lodge doubled as a lounge and dormitory, and here three or four old codgers sat at the table engaged in a game and consuming the local rum. I had no idea where they had come from, or what they were doing here, and it struck me as absurd that any hostelry in this remote wilderness could have its own local clientele. Particularly as no one appeared to live up here.

Beyond this little group was a continuous row of cots, not dissimilar to those in the upper lodge. I suddenly noticed that one of the sleeping bags placed on the cots to reserve the space contained a body. Closer inspection revealed that it was Joy. She was awake.

"Are you all right?" I asked. She obviously wasn't.

"No", she replied, "I feel terrible."

There was nothing I could do. But Simon was looking after her, and had gone to fetch his medical kit.

There were no spare cots in this, the warmest part of the dormitory, so I went through to the annex of the L-shaped building, where rather less effort had gone into insulation, and where the temperature was several degrees lower. Again, there appeared to be no room, and I was about to turn away despondently, when I thought I heard a strange noise from the far end of the room, where it was already dark. I heard the noise again, slightly louder this time.

It was like someone trying to speak. Eventually I could make out the shape of someone lying on a bunk.

"Who's that?" I asked, moving closer.

"Me," replied a Scottish accent.

"John?"

"Aye." It was John the Vicar.

"How are you?"

"Och, no too good. I'll be all right though." He coughed violently for several minutes which seemed to contradict his previous statement. "There's a bed over there that's no been taken."

He appeared to be right. I thanked him and, having made sure that he was being looked after, I slung my jacket on it and set off to retrieve my kit.

\*

The Japanese-hating proprietor of the lodge where I had taken a cot was not happy.

For one thing, no one had materialised to claim any of the remaining cots which had been reserved. In fact, no one else had materialised at all.

For another, I had just told him that I was leaving.

"You pay for beds!" he demanded. "Two hundred rupee!"

"All right, I'll pay for my bed," I conceded. That was fair enough.

"You take ten beds, you pay for ten beds. Two hundred rupee!" he repeated.

"I took one bed, I'll pay for one bed. Twenty rupees, take it or leave it," I said, peeling off four five rupee notes from my much diminished wad.

He was furious. Beneath the grime of his leathery brown face, a deep puce had set in. He took the notes, screwed them into a ball and stamped on them. He was not having a good day.

"Ten beds you take. Two hundred rupee!"

The cold, my headache and the fact that I hadn't come all this way for a pointless argument, increased my irritability.

"If you want to be paid for ten beds in a shack with walls like a sieve that people wouldn't sleep in if you paid them, then why don't you go and ask the person who booked the ten beds. He's over there in that lodge. The one with a stove and no holes in the walls." I pointed through the window. "But I'll warn you, he's a Gurkha officer and might not take too kindly to the suggestion!"

With that I shouldered my rucksack, into which I had rapidly stuffed my bedding during the altercation and, praying that I hadn't left anything behind, stamped out of the door and onto the beach where the temperature had dropped another few degrees in the gathering gloom.

*

John the Vicar was a sick man. It was really nothing more than a bad cold. But a bad cold in these extreme conditions was a hop and a step away from pneumonia. And that could quickly become life threatening. To be suffering so badly with no more than twelve hours until the race was bad news. A lesser man might perhaps have asked to be evacuated, and a lesser doctor might perhaps have insisted on it. But Simon knew how much completing the race meant to John, and was going to give him every chance of achieving it. And so under the caring and vigilant eyes of Simon and Jerri Lee, a nurse by profession, John's condition was closely monitored, and oxygen was administered when necessary.

It was now bitterly cold in the dormitory annex. Closer inspection of the walls and windows revealed that our end of the building had about as many perforations as a Tetley teabag. However, John steadfastly refused the offer of a bed in the warmer end of the lodge, but finally I managed to persuade him to take my lightweight sleeping bag.

The good news was that Joy was feeling a little better and joined us on the bench in the kitchen where a dozen of us sat huddled together for warmth, awaiting food and the beginning of the longest night.

Gorak Shep is home to the world's highest slow food outlet. The *didi* was a willing if ponderous worker, and each plate of fried potatoes took forever to appear. Valeri got himself onto my Christmas card list for life by offering me one of his chips, but others were not so lucky.

As Dave, Bryan, Zvoni and Simon received their plates, we learned that a panful served four portions, and my order was two panfuls behind. It seemed to speed things up a little if we peeled and sliced the potatoes ourselves, and it also helped to pass the time. I had a feeling that my order of chips would coincide with the *didi* announcing that it was the end of her shift and the outstanding orders being muddled so that I would go to the back of the queue once more.

But just when things were getting quite desperate, another woman appeared. She was somewhat older, but her years of experience had taught her to cook Vegetable Fried Rice and soup concurrently and, as such, was to this lodge what Betty Turpin was to the Rovers Return. This was an unexpected bonus, and I quickly placed an order for both.

By the time the bloodcurdling summons to the mess tent heralded the last supper, my food had still not materialised, and so I decided to stay in the lodge. It was also passably warm, and the sudden exodus meant that I could move into pole position by the stove.

A few minutes later, Ray returned, looking more animated than he had hitherto been upon discovering what gastronomic delights the cooks had prepared for us.

"Come and have a look at this, mate!"

"No, I'm staying in here. It's warm, and my food's nearly ready."

"You'll regret it. It's good!"

I vacillated.

"If this is a bloody wind up to get my seat and my food I'll bloody kill you, Brown!"

"It's no bloody wind up. But if you don't want your Irish Stew, just say so and I'll have yours!"

Irish Stew is my favourite meal in the entire universe. I knew it wouldn't be as good as the Irish Stew my Nana cooks in the red pot on the wood-burning Esse in Ireland, but I just had to try it. The *didi* motioned that my potatoes were ready, and Betty pointed to the soup and the Vegetable Fried Rice which she was about to serve.

"Keep it hot. I'll be back in a minute."

Ray was right. It was magnificent. The pleasure of eating it was only slightly dulled by the fact that it was so cold in the tent that my face had lost all sensation. I had three helpings in quick succession, and darted back into the lodge where I wolfed down the food which had been waiting for me.

Not long after, I was again summoned to the mess tent for pudding. Normally I would not have given the sludge served for us the time of day, but tonight the cooks had baked a cake which bore the simple message: "Good Luck!" It was a touching and heart-warming gesture, and to a man we felt guilty about slating them for their culinary incompetence. In fact it was so moving that, with a diminished clarity of thought and judgement caused by the altitude, in time-honoured British tradition, we gave them three cheers, much to the amusement of our foreign friends.

\*

Later that night, shortly before we turned in, we had a visitation. Martin Stone, beside whom I had sat on the flight from Heathrow, would be attempting to break the three day ten hour world record between Base Camp and Kathmandu, starting on the day after the race. Martin, who had spent the previous sixteen days filming with the Late Birds, had walked up the glacier to Base Camp to make contact with a Japanese climbing team, the only one presently staying at Base Camp. The team were waiting for 1st December to arrive to commence a Winter attempt on the hazardous South West Face, first climbed by Scott and Haston, in 1975. This route had yet to be climbed in winter, and the Japanese attempt was a high profile affair containing several notable climbers, some of whom had previously reached the summit.

Martin had been warmly welcomed by the climbing party. Once they had recovered sufficiently from the shock that this well-spoken, modest and distinctly sane-looking young Englishman was about to attempt something that made their stroll up the South West Face resemble an easy day for a lady, they agreed to let him stay the night before his attempt and provide food and warm clothing.

When they learnt from Martin that there were a further seventy-two nutters staying at Gorak Shep, who were about to embark on something equally ludicrous, if not quite as extreme, they just had to see for themselves.

And so, at around 8 p.m., we were honoured by a visit from the esteemed Japanese party, including their leader, a wizened little man who smoked continually, and we chatted for some time as they depleted the lodge's entire stock of rum before setting out to return to their canvas home by moonlight. They were thrilled to learn that there were Japanese runners in our party, and someone suggested that they might like to meet Shigi. I managed to persuade them that Shigi had turned in already, anxious to get a good night's sleep. I had no intention of allowing the very satisfactory domestic arrangements which I had engineered to be interrupted. Besides, for all I knew, the Gurkhas could already be in the process of disembowelling him.

It was time for bed. Outside, as I took my last pee against the courtyard wall under a bright moon illuminating Kata Pattar and Pumo Ri and casting shadows of the mountains across the beach, I felt strangely sad. This was the beginning of the end of the adventure. I stood and listened to the sounds of the massive force of nature on the move that spoke to me in the dead of night, warning of the dangers of this desolate but beautiful land. Warning, but beckoning me to return.

By a curious coincidence, my 'bed' saw me placed in alphabetical order between Pierre André and Al Hughes, the cameraman who would be running with his camera tomorrow. I pointed this out to Pierre André.

"For sure. We have rearranged things so that we sleep in numerical order. That way we can number off in our sleep!"

It was so cold that I had to wear my down jacket in my sleeping bag, and vowed that if I ever returned I would bring three sleeping bags. Throughout the night, Simon attended to John, and seemed to be with him each time I awoke from what passed for sleep. My mind refused to switch off, with fears about what the night may still hold, both for myself and others, and anxieties about what tomorrow would bring. I had dreaded this night, perhaps more than anything else, for so long now. And now I was living it.

I prayed for the dawn, and somehow felt lonely, crushed, together but alone amongst a mass of sweaty, snoring bodies whose humour, anxieties and friendship I had shared and treasured in this adventure.

*...tonight I miss my girl... tonight I miss my home...*[1]

---

[1] Bruce Springsteen

# The Race: "If You Fail, Whatever You Do Don't Blame the Weather"

### Friday 26th November, 6 a.m.

The first whistle went to announce the end of the longest night. I was amazed to find that I had slept reasonably well. People stirred as I shuffled out of the relative warmth of my four-season pit and staggered stiff-legged towards the agony of the frozen latrine tent. God, what wouldn't I give for a brick shit-house, a Twyford's porcelain bowl and a mug of steaming coffee with a copy of *The Times*!

Ray was up and dressed. He looked almost dapper.

"How're you feeling?" I asked.

"Good. I didn't have too bad a night." He had been one of the hardy few lunatics who had slept in his tent. Most of the others looked as if they had gone five rounds with Mike Tyson.

It was cold, bloody cold. So cold, in fact, that the contents of my water bottle were frozen despite storing it deep inside my rucksack. But there was little wind, and that was what in 1991 had lowered the temperature to minus twenty-two degrees. I was relieved to learn from Joy, who still looked very ill, that it was as warm as minus fifteen.

### 6.15 a.m.

The second whistle echoed through the lodge, announcing the arrival of porridge, rice pudding and tea. It wasn't much of a breakfast for a condemned man. Particularly if you don't like either rice pudding or porridge.

"Half an hour to go. Get up and get packed!" yelled Dave.

I declined the food but had several cups of tea to accompany my last bar of Cadbury's Dairy Milk, whose wrapper had mysteriously disappeared and so had acquired a liberal coating of the grime that was in the bottom of my pocket. I gave up trying to eat my frozen Power Bar when my teeth threatened to part company with my gums.

I had more or less decided what to wear. I was too much of a wimp to start in shorts, and so had opted for easily removable layers. I applied the cold Vaseline to protect the parts of the body where sweat rashes can make movement almost unbearably painful, not only during a race, but for days afterwards. It was hard to concentrate, the cold and the nervous anticipation conspired to make every movement sluggish and uncertain.

Over my shorts, T-shirt and vest, upon which I had painstakingly pinned my numbers the previous evening, I dressed in my long thermal bottoms, thermal top, and Buffalo jacket. Lastly I put on two pairs of socks, and fastened the laces of my running shoes looking hopefully at the unconvincing repairs effected by the Tibetan. I was dressed, apart from my thermal gloves, fleecy mitts and balaclava which I would put on at the last moment. Like a good Boy Scout, I had now worn everything I had brought with me.

## 6.30 a.m.

The third whistle sounded.

"You have ten minutes," Dave informed us. "Kit bags to the left of the wall, sleeping bags to the right!" I felt a rising surge of panic as I surveyed my kit. Christ, how the hell was I going to get all this together in ten minutes? Most people seemed to be almost ready. Nerves tingling with anticipation helped dispel some of the numbness caused by the cold. God, it must have felt something like this before the Battle of the Somme. In ten minutes time we were going over the top. Literally! I had to get moving.

Then I noticed Pierre André was still in his sack. He had snored all night, voluminously, and had the nerve to complain about my feet smelling! I told him that snoring and noticing the smell of someone's feet were incompatible. Suddenly, he was up, ready and wishing me "Bonjour. 'Ave aye nayce day!" while I was still struggling to distinguish my stuff-sack from my rucksack.

Then he was gone, and that was the last I saw of him until Namche.

John the Vicar and I were the only ones left in the lodge. His condition had not deteriorated during the night, thanks to Simon and Jerri Lee's selfless efforts. But he was in no shape to run a marathon, and he knew it. If he could just make the cut-off times, then he could complete the course somehow. I didn't feel optimistic, and in his heart I did not think he did either. But he was going to give it a go. Having somehow completed my packing, I helped John to get his kit together. He had mislaid his gloves which, apart from anything else, were demanded as part of the minimum kit requirement. I gave him my thermal gloves and we set off across the beach.

## 6.55 a.m.

We stood at the start line, alongside the thin blue line of the Reebok Everest Marathon banners. I had said my farewells to the last latrine, and prayed that my guts would not be too volatile over the coming hours, as I carried no toilet paper and I would have to "go native."

We numbered off without incident, and shuffled around nervously and aimlessly in the bitter cold, hugging, shaking hands and wishing each other good luck. There were so few of us that again I felt the strange sensation of loneliness. We were barely five rows deep, making a mockery of the seeding process.

I wandered over to Charlie, who was standing at the front with the other Gurkhas.

"Did you lads steep all right last night?" I asked, hopefully.

"Yea, no problem, Rich. We slept like logs," he replied. "Why, was there any reason why we shouldn't have?"

"Oooph, ah... no," I said. "Not that I can think of, Charlie."

"Well, best of luck mate," he said, shaking my hand. "I suppose I'll be on my third beer by the time you finish!"

Ray came over, and we shook hands.

"Get a cold beer in for me," I said. "And don't use all the bloody hot water!" We had done a lot together, but this, I knew we would do apart.

Dave called us to our starting places. I felt the adrenalin pumping.

"It's six fifty-five, the temperature is minus fifteen degrees, have a good race – GO!"

At last.

We were off and running...

*...Nor law nor duty made me run,*
*Nor public men, nor cheering crowds,*
*A lonely impulse of delight*
*Drove to this tumult in the clouds...*

Well, walking to be more precise. Like most people, I sprinted away only to be reined back in, as if attached to a length of elastic approaching its limit, after fifty yards. And like most people, I was reduced to a stuttering, gasping, agonisingly slow crawl as I reached the end of the beach and the first small climb onto the moraine. Each breath seemed to carry a knife as it tore into my throat and lungs in the cold morning air.

At last I slipped into a jog as my body grew accustomed to the bitterly cold, thin air. It was difficult to get any rhythm, as at the merest hint of uphill, running became impossible. I stole a final glance back at the mountains with a curious mix of emotions which, like the trip itself, was too paradoxical to merit the energy required for comprehension.

Descending the two moraine hills that led to the ablation valley above Lobuche were as every bit as precipitous as I had anticipated. However, once I had reached the floor of the valley, I was relieved to see that I had picked the right line and was making better progress than those who had held the high ground and descended too far to the left of the valley.

Once I was running over relatively flat ground I felt much better. The drop in altitude was significant and, although the sun had not yet cleared the mountains ahead of me, it was considerably warmer. I cursed myself for starting the race in too many clothes, and whipped off my balaclava.

## 7.40 a.m.

I reached Lobuche and the first of the aid posts. I almost took a wrong turning which would have taken me down the valley below the *Kharha*. I was warmly greeted by Bryan, and Pierre André's girlfriend, Jeanne, who helped me to strip off.

"What are you doing after the race?" I asked, and got a playful slap across the cheek as a reward. I gulped down chocolate, tea and water and, putting on my Oakleys, thanked them and set off. My pit stop had taken around five minutes, but it had been worth it. I had ditched my heavy gear, which would be brought down later, and could complete the race without another major hold-up.

The path ran slightly downwards following the shallow flowing Khumbu Khola, which I knew I would have to cross at some point. I was caught by two of the Late Birds and, as I had been running on my own since Lobuche, I was quite relieved that I hadn't missed the crossing, which was little more than a collection of stones. My relief was shortlived.

"Any idea where we cross the river?" one of them asked me.

"Somewhere around here, I think," I replied.

"It's somewhere before Dughla isn't it?" said the other runner, uncertainly. Christ, that's helpful. Had he walked all the way up with his eyes closed, I wondered? Something on the far side of the stream caught my eye. It was someone running in a white peaked cap. It looked like Valeri. Then I saw the crossing, as I ran past it. I stopped abruptly, causing my two companions considerable consternation.

They followed me across the river, where the path climbed slightly, and I began to draw away from them, pleased that I was feeling stronger. I ran on my own through the Sherpa memorial at upper Dughla, where the little piles of stones looked all the more poignant as the sun rose higher above Ama Dablam, Kang Tiaga and Thamserku, whose great ridges and spires cast long shadows down the Pheriche Valley on a perfect Khumbu morning.

Descending the moraine at the end of the glacier to Dughla was agonisingly slow and almost fatal on one occasion, when I lost my footing and only just managed to regain my balance, averting a fall that could have had serious consequences. I could only watch in frustration as the two Late Birds whizzed past me. It occurred to me that another paradox of the trip was that I had entered a predominantly downhill race in the knowledge that I am a poor downhill runner.

At last I reached the bottom, and was cheered by the enthusiastic encouragement I received from Liz and Adrienne.

Approaching the bridge at lower Dughla, I picked out the path to Pheriche, and felt confident in my navigation. I also noticed that the two Late Birds, who had flown past me on the hill were now heading up the higher path towards Dingboche. I called to them, and they somewhat reluctantly retraced their steps and joined the lower path just in front of me without a word of thanks. Following the course of my previous run, I took the short cut through the tumbledown walls of Phalong Karpo, and arrived in Pheriche before them.

## 8.20 a.m.

I had reached the seven and a half mile mark almost an hour and a half after setting out. That, I calculated, was about 11.5 minute miles. I was pleased, for although it compared badly to the eight minute miles I run over mountainous terrain at home, this wasn't home. I had a vague notion that if I could average overall something less than fourteen minute miles, I could finish in around six hours. But, although the terrain had been difficult, I realised that it had been pretty well downhill so far, and the toughest climbs were in the last half of the race.

I got another warm welcome, this time from Nat and Annabel.

"Well done, Marvin, you're not quite last. Actually, you're doing much better than I'd expected – you're thirtieth at the moment." Annabel was in charge of one of the cameras and, doubtless under the guise of authenticity, filmed me having a pee.

"Bugger off!" I said.

"There's something wrong with this zoom lens I think," she replied. "Everything looks very small!"

"The way you handle that thing, it's a good job you stayed away from surgery."

I was familiar with the stretch between Pheriche and Tsura, which sloped gently downwards until it reached the bridge. Beyond the bridge, I took the higher of the three paths, and was rewarded for the hard slog with a good view of the path that followed the valley of the Imja Khola to Tsura. Below me I saw two other runners, again Late Birds, who appeared to be lost. I wondered where all my group were, they must be either ahead of me or behind me.

"Are you guys lost?" I called.

"Do you know where you're going?" one of them replied, non-committally.

"I think so," I replied. They climbed up to the path which I was following, and we ran together for some time.

It was now a quite beautiful morning, and beyond Tsura the path, although narrow, improved, and I began to relax and enjoy the run. I grew in confidence as each step I took brought me closer to the finish and my goal.

At Pangboche, I was greeted by Sue and, snatching a cup of water, ran through, reluctant to destroy the rhythm I was at last beginning to find. Leaving Pangboche, I remembered Tom's mark on the stone, and the typically Irish logic behind his method reminded me to take the lower of the two paths. I had now lost my two recent companions, who had stopped for refreshment.

The next thing I had to look for was the path that led down to that remarkable bridge that crossed the Imja Khola before the path began the climb to Tengboche. But that was still some time away and, enjoying a rare of stretch of path that was both wide and level, I started to stretch out. Unfortunately, I was also intent on enjoying the scenery, in particular the trees which clothed the steeply rising hill on the opposite side of the valley. I had not seen trees for almost a week, and the greenery was a refreshing change. Ahead of me, I noticed the long sloping roof and the upper tiers of the Tengboche monastery far in the distance. I looked at my watch and felt a surge of optimism as I realised that I was well up on my predicted split.

What I failed to notice was the thin slick of clear ice on the path which had resiliently resisted the best efforts of the early morning sun. My right foot had no trouble finding it, however, precipitating the first of my three falls. Suddenly I was in the air, my feet above my head. Then I came back to earth. Heavily. Before I slammed into the path, I had the presence of mind to turn my head and place my right hand beneath my right hip. What this achieved was to protect my face, and my Oakleys, from a direct confrontation with the path, the outcome of which would have had little beneficial effect on either of them.

As a result of my quick thinking, I merely landed on the back of my head and my right hand. At first I thought I had broken my leg, as I couldn't move it. Then, as the fuzziness in my head began to clear, the pain in my hand hit me, and I found I could move my leg sufficiently to release my hand. I suddenly felt very weak and very sick, and thought that I was going to vomit. I tried to breathe deeply and keep calm and, after what seemed like an eternity, the nausea passed. The two Late Birds whom I had run with to Pangboche appeared and helped me to my feet.

"Anything broken?" asked one of them.

My hip was agony, but at least I could now move my leg and it seemed capable of bearing some of my weight. I tried to hobble a few steps, and again I came close to vomiting as the pain hit me. I also came close to tottering off the path, and down to the river, as I lurched close to the edge before collapsing. They got me back to my feet and I tried again. This time the pain was tolerable, and I knew that I would eventually be able to continue.

And then I noticed my fingers. The middle knuckles of my middle and fourth fingers had already doubled in size and refused to bend. My hands were so black from the dirt and dust that it was impossible to see how much bruising there was, but I knew that they were broken. I had broken both of these fingers twice before; once beneath the 'careless' boot of a Pontypridd forward, and once on a similar fall on the Cornwall coast path.

"No," I replied. "Nothing serious. I've smashed my fingers, but I'll be all right."

"That's okay, then," said the other, understandably anxious not to waste any more time. "You don't need your fingers to run."

I agreed that I didn't, and thanked them for their help and concern. As they set off, I hobbled painfully behind in their wake. A few moments later, I saw the path which led down to the bridge, and consoled myself with the fact that I would probably would have missed it had I continued at the speed at which I was moving.

Some fifteen minutes later, just in time for the climb to Tengboche, the pain in my hip had eased enough to allow relatively good freedom of movement in the joint.

## 9.57 a.m.

After a tortuous climb of what was only around three hundred feet, but could easily have been twice that, I arrived at Tengboche, and the fourteen mile mark. Halfway up the final stretch leading to the saddle of the hill where Ray had done his Canary impersonation, I caught Wish, who was also suffering. He told me that his legs "had gone", and that he was badly dehydrated – so badly that his urine had turned a dark, blood red colour.

We both stopped for refreshment before tackling the drop to Phunki Teng and the much feared Sarnassa Hill. It had taken me three hours and two minutes to reach Tengboche, which I would have settled for before the race began, but before my fall I was beginning to entertain hopes of reaching Tengboche at around two hours forty-five. One compensation was that I hadn't been able to overstretch myself, and felt relatively fresh to tackle Sarnassa Hill. I ate some fruit, some chocolate, and had several cups of water, tea and Staminade. I had decided not to carry any water, so it was important to have a good soak at every opportunity, even if it meant wobbling along like a fish tank on legs for the next twenty minutes.

Once around the corner and past the pagoda that resembled a car wash, I stopped to relieve myself, which was also filmed for posterity by Stephen Isles.

"There's going to be a hell of a lot of shots of people peeing in this documentary, you know," I said. He looked embarrassed and turned the camera off. I was pleased to note that my urine was still a reassuringly clear colour.

From here you can see Chorkhung, which is above Namche, and the end is almost in sight. Almost, but not quite, because concealed from view are the two most notorious and testing parts of the race, Sarnassa Hill and the loop, lurking in deep valleys or behind mountains, waiting to drain every last ounce of energy from tired and ravished bodies.

At Tengboche, I learned that Pierre André had a nine minute lead over Hari Roka, and Ray, who had gone through in two hours eight was in fourth position behind one of the Gurkhas. Gobet had reached the fourteen mile mark in one hour fifty-seven, over an hour before me, which was a bit depressing and meant that I didn't have a very good chance of catching him. There was little between the first four, and I was delighted to learn that Ray was near the front, running strong and hard on Gobet's heels. Eleven minutes was a lot to make up, but I knew that Ray would be strong on the hills. However, Pierre André was five minutes ahead of Maitland's split, and had not disguised the fact that he wanted his record.

The descent to the river at Phunki Teng was as agonising and treacherous as it was frustrating. Good downhillers can make up time over this section, and I was passed by runners I thought I had left for dead at Pangboche. Fall number two was not of my own making, and mercifully left me unhurt but absolutely seething. One of the Late Birds whom I had rescued from a side trip to Dingboche at Dughla, shot down an almost vertical bank above me, no doubt high on

Diamox, causing an avalanche which precipitated my unscheduled descent down a thirty foot drop. He had obviously taken Dave's advice to look for shortcuts literally, but why anyone should want to risk their neck, or anyone else's, to shave a couple of seconds from their time was beyond me. Particularly when they hadn't bothered to check the route in the first place. I was less than impressed with his nimble footwork and, if I were to repeat what I said, the words would probably burn a hole in the page. However, I survived with minor cuts and scratches. I was more annoyed to discover that the lenses of my Oakleys were badly scratched.

At last, I reached the bottom of the hill and crossed the latticed wooden bridge. Although angry and frustrated by my slow descent, I was mindful that Sarnassa Hill had crippled many a good runner over the years. However, my speed trekking with Ray paid dividends and, by marching the steepest parts and running economically, I had the satisfaction of catching all those who had whizzed past me after Tengboche, and several others. Passing my friend who had sent me hurtling over the edge gave me particular satisfaction, as I had decided that I would rather die than finish behind him. I resisted the temptation to say anything.

The rush of adrenalin made me feel good, and I actually wondered why everyone was going so slowly. Even so, I was staggered by the sheer length of the climb. Just when you think it is safe to come out of the closet and run again, you are presented with the second half of the hill, where the path is so inconsistent that it is impossible to achieve any rhythm. Some sections are so boulder strewn, that both hands and feet are needed to clamber over the huge rocks which form the path.

## 10.55 a.m.

At last I reached the feeding station at Sarnassa, which is the seventeen mile mark. Here I received two pieces of information, one of which was welcome, and one which was not. The good news was that I was now in twenty-third place. The bad news, imparted by Graham Webster, John the Vicar's cousin, was that Scotland had been well and truly routed by the All Blacks at Murrayfield on the previous Saturday. This information, which he had learned from the short wave radio belonging to one of the doctors, did not bode well for the confrontation at Twickenham tomorrow. If England lost, Annabel would be unbearable.

I drank a vast amount of water and set off, confident that I had now cracked the hardest part. I had climbed the hill in under half an hour; less time than it had taken me to descend from Tengboche. However, after Sarnassa Hill, with trembling legs, any slight ascent is brutally punishing, and I was surprised to find that the next three miles were considerably more uphill than down.

I was now entirely on my own, and managed to run lightly over the level and downhill stretches, jogging or marching the uphill. Long stretches without a glimpse of another human ahead or behind inspired the notion that I might yet achieve a better than predicted position of twenty-third. I might even catch someone on the loop. But ahead of me were the elite runners, and I was unlikely to make much of an impression on them. These would be, I imagined, the Gurkhas, top mountain runners like Pierre André, the Kiwi ultra-distance runners, the sub two hours twenty marathoners, and wiry, grizzly, wizened little men who bounced down mountains like rubber balls. And of course, the Sherpas, the Nepali runners whose backyard we were running through.

The stretch to Chorkhung seemed to take an eternity. Each time I rounded a bend or followed a promontory where the path swung out to expose a sheer drop to the Dudh Kosi far below, I expected to see Chorkhung, but it was never there. My watch told me that I must have been going much slower than I had thought, and I suddenly felt tired. It was half an hour already since I had left Sarnassa, and I had hoped to complete the two and a half miles in around twenty minutes. My heart sank as I began to realise that my dream of finishing in less than six hours was slipping away. If only there had been someone to push me, I would have concentrated harder, I thought. Even worse, the tiredness brought another unwelcome visitor – that old familiar lassitude, and I began to lose the will to achieve anything other than finishing. After all, who cares, I asked myself, what difference will half an hour make?

Once again, the words of Yeats came to mind, which, slightly altered, perfectly expressed my present crisis, frequently referred to as 'hitting the wall':

*...I balanced all, brought all to mind,*

> *The miles to come seemed waste of breath,*
> *A waste of breath the miles behind*
> *In balance with this life, this death.*

At last I rounded the final bend and saw Chorkhung ahead.

## 11.28 a.m.

Beneath Chorkhung lies Namche. I tried not to imagine Pierre André whistling in the shower, or lowering his second beer, but it was difficult. Leaving Chorkhung, you can see your lodge, you can hear the applause for the early finishers, you can virtually smell the finish. But this is only the twenty mile mark, and the inventors of this lunacy applied the final twist of the knife in the form of the Thamo loop. But at Chorkhung my motivation had returned, and I wanted to get the remaining six miles over as quickly as possible.

Having gulped down water, tea and chocolate I set off for Thamo knowing that I would have to push myself hard to complete the loop in anything less than the eighty-seven minutes I now had to achieve my target.

Dot Coates, the physiotherapist who helped to marshal the Chorkhung aid post, expressed concern at the state of my fingers, and that seemed to trigger the pain. Until then, I had completely forgotten about them.

Running along the path that contoured the hill above Namche, I heard a great cheer, which I knew was for me, and propelled my aching limbs forwards. I listened for further cheering as I ran which would tell me that I was not alone. None came. I relaxed and concentrated on the path which, though familiar, was as vague as any thus far. I cursed myself for swinging too wide around the *chorten* above Namche which meant running fifty yards further than was necessary.

Beyond Namche I was reminded that the path to Thamo is a switchback of hills. I decided to try to jog the flat stretches, run flat out down the hills and march up the slopes. The most demoralising part of this stretch was passing those running in the other direction on their way back to the finish. I was surprised to see two of the Nepali Gurkhas go by. I thought they would have finished by now. Next was New Zealander Russell Prince, then two of the locals and, close to

Thamo, came Fergie, Valeri and Dave English, looking absolutely shattered.

On the last downhill wooded section before Thamo I had my third enforced lie down. Thankfully, bizarre as it was, it caused considerably less physical pain and mental anguish than the previous two. Shortly before it happened it occurred to me that one of the hazards which we had expected had been notable only by their absence. For me, at least, thus far the race had been yak free.

But belting headlong down a narrow section of path, I rounded a bend fully expecting to see the path continue uninterrupted to the bottom of the next hill where it would begin to climb again. It didn't occur to me that I might encounter other road users. It probably didn't occur to the yak at the tail of the train just around the bend either, that she would encounter some lunatic who would be unable to stop and would be forced to take evasive action which would result in his lying beneath her staring at her underbelly. Mindful of my previous close encounter with recalcitrant yaks, I tried to climb the bank on the inside of the path, and squeeze past the train, thus avoiding a possibly lengthy delay. I would probably have managed it had my foot not discovered the only piece of mud on the entire subcontinent. Losing my footing, I slipped down the bank and under a somewhat confused-looking yak, or nak, as I soon discovered. Thankfully the beast was too stunned to move, and I managed to extricate myself, and squeeze to the front of the train.

## 12.08 p.m.

I collected my orange band, which proved that I had visited Thamo, from John Dunging.

"Nearly there, Rich," he encouraged. "'Ave you managed to do it wi'out steppin' in anythin' nasty?" I tried to laugh, and took the cup of water he offered me.

The water was warm and tasted foul, but it was important to drink plenty as there was still the final three undulating miles to tackle.

Suddenly I saw Charlie Moores sitting on the wall opposite the aid station. In my confused mental state, I thought he had completed the race, and had come back out to Thamo.

"What are you doing?" I asked him.

"I've had it, mate. I'm knackered." He was severely suffering from the Sarnassa Hill blues, and was going through what I had undergone before Chorkhung. Only much worse.

"Come on, let's help each other," I said, and we set off together. Gradually, as I had done on my previous run from Thamo, I began to feel stronger, and the knowledge that I was getting closer to an achievement in which I would take pride for the rest of my life spurred me on.

With a sudden and unexpected surge of energy, I increased my pace, leaving Charlie behind. I felt a little guilty, but I began to realise that if I pushed myself over the remaining mile and a half, I still had a chance of finishing inside six hours. The last mile was as uplifting as the three miles out to Thamo had been depressing. Instead of runners who were approaching the finish passing from the other direction, it was me who was now nearing the finish. It gave me particular satisfaction to pass the Late Bird who had sent me hurtling down the bank on the descent from Tengboche. Not far behind him came Tom, and behind him, Wish and John the Buddhist, to whom I gave words of encouragement. But now, each tired and painful step was carrying me closer to the end of this bizarre and wonderful ordeal.

The last uphill stretch was behind me. I knew that, because I had reached the flat, windy part of the path which was just before the *chorten* that was above Namche. Ahead of me, running very slowly was Dave English. I caught up with him, and he told me that he had had a torrid race, and had been suffering badly since Sarnassa Hill. His watch had stopped shortly after the start, and he had pushed too hard over the early part of the race. I told him we could finish inside six hours, and, with a spring in our steps, together we scrambled down the hill past the monastery and through the narrow and treacherous streets of Namche to the finish.

No words can describe the euphoric feeling of that final descent into Namche. It was exactly as I had imagined in my reverie before I left Namche, almost a week ago. Except that Dave and I were straining, not for victory, but simply to finish inside the six hours barrier. But there was no less cheering from the hoards of people that lined the streets and jostled for a space on the parapet outside the Thamserku, or hung precariously from every vantage point they could find. As far as they were concerned, we were the victors.

*Past the post office, past the bank, over the rough cobbles; we asked questions of each other that had not been asked before, and which mere words could not answer, fighting it out to the death like gladiators in this land of smiles above the cloud. With every last ounce of energy, willing to risk everything simply to get across the finish line.*

*And then, it was over.*

Or, to be more precise, I was over, for my fourth and final tumble. And within sight of the finish. Dave had run ahead of me, we were not racing each other, we were racing the clock. He crossed the finish line amid uproarious applause, as I hurtled down the stone steps leading to the field below the Thamserku where the blue banners and funnel announced the finish. There had hitherto been a temporary gate barring the entrance to the field, made from wooden planks which slotted into grooves on either side. These had now been removed to allow the runners to enter the field.

Well, sort of removed. I noticed too late that the bottom plank was still in place and, catching it with my foot, was sent sprawling headlong through the entrance and landed heavily on my aching hip. At least that solved the problem of what to do as I crossed the finish line, I thought, as I got to my feet unsteadily. I staggered over the finish line in twenty-second place, in 5 hours 56.59 minutes, twenty-one seconds behind Dave, to receive my medal and a kiss from Diana. It was a moment I will treasure as long as I live.

"Couldn't Reebok have sent over a dolly-bird for this?" I asked, and got a playful slap on the cheek.

Ray was standing at the finish wearing a white scarf, which I assumed must mean that he had a badly cut neck or had finished in the first three places. Beside him was a tall, slim elegant woman and two robust-looking lads of around nine and eleven years. He introduced me to Liz, his wife, and his two sons, Ross and Scott.

"What bloody kept you?" he asked me with a smile, handing me a cup of water.

"I did it..." I gasped breathlessly, "...inside six hours... that'll do me." My last fall had winded me badly. "What about you?"

"Oh not bad." He looked almost pleased. "I came third."

"Well done! What was your time?"

"Inside four and a half."

"Settle for that?" I asked, beginning to recover.

"Yea." There was no regret, no hunger behind his eyes. The look of want had departed. The pain and the drive were all behind him, left along the path that had led us back from the desolate frozen wastes of the highest start line of any race on earth, to this benign oasis. "I'll settle for that."

Ray Brown had not only finished third. In a time of 4 hours 28.38 minutes he had smashed the previous Vet's record of 5 hours 01.55 minutes which had been set by Ken Hirst of Canada in 1991. To better the record by over thirty-three minutes was a quite phenomenal feat. Pierre André had won, but was disappointed in that his time of 4 hours 03.29 was not fast enough to take Maitland's record. Stretching away from Roka who finished seventeen minutes behind in second place, Gobet had relaxed too much over the last phase of the race to take the record.

Dave English came over and shook my hand.

"Thanks, Rich," he said. His race had been disappointing, but in the end he was pleased to salvage something by finishing in under six hours. According to form, Dave should have finished in the top ten, but in this race the form book had gone out of the window.

I sat down on the parapet overlooking the finish. Suddenly an overwhelming feeling of relief that it was all over hit me, that and the fatigue of almost six hours of total concentration and taking my body to the physical limit, and I felt drained. Drained but elated. I had feared failure more than anything else and, as the trip progressed, my expectations of my own performance had became higher. Now, as I watched Charlie cross the finish line, it began to sink in that, tumbles, broken fingers and yaks apart, I had had a good race and achieved my goals.

I walked over to congratulate Charlie, who was also generous in his praise.

"Well, done, Rich, you did a lot better than I thought you would, mate. I take back everything I said. Well, nearly everything!" Then his eye fell on a familiar figure hovering around the desk where the results were being collated. "Oh bloody hell. What's she doing here? I thought we'd seen the last of her!"

It was the mad axe-woman of Dingboche.

"Shit, let's get out of here before she sees us," I said.

Inside the Thamserku, many of those who had finished ahead of us were tucking into the complimentary soup and tea which had been laid on by the lodge.

I slumped down beside Fergie.

"Where d'you come?"

"Seventeenth," he told me. "Not too bad, considering."

For the Gurkhas it had been a vastly disappointing morning's work. Despite the weeks of acclimatisation and high altitude training, the detailed logistical preparation and recce of the course and, of course, all the hype, they had failed to achieve a finisher in the first three places. Gyan Bahadur Limbu, Dharmabikram Sunwar and Birbahadur Balal had finished in fourth, fifth and sixth places respectively. Kev had finished ninth, and of course Charlie had suffered the ignominy of finishing behind me.

At least they could joke about it.

"Where I think you went wrong", I said, "was not drinking enough rum on the night before the race!"

Opposite me sat Mark Woodbridge. He had astounded everyone but me by finishing in tenth place. His time of 5 hours 14.52 was well within his target of five hours thirty minutes, and I could tell he was quietly delighted with his performance. And so he should have been.

The first Briton home had been Bob Worth, a thirty-seven year old ex-banker from Cumbria. In fourteenth place was Cath Procter, a thirty-five year old doctor from Yorkshire, who finished in 5 hours 32.43, breaking the ladies record by almost fifteen minutes. Behind her, in fifteenth place, was John Wagstaff, and apart from the Gurkhas, Dave and I were the next British runners to finish.

I borrowed Ray's towel, and had a tepid but welcome shower. I had no clean clothes to change into other than my minimum gear, so I bought a T-shirt and a pair of socks from one of the shops close to the lodge. Curiously, they didn't seem to sell underpants, so I went without. I was beyond caring.

Sitting on the parapet in the warm sunshine waiting for the runners to come in, I could have sworn that I noticed a smell that somehow seemed strangely out of place with the surroundings, coming from behind me. It smelt like Chanel perfume. It can't be, I told myself. I had to be imagining it. But the captivating scent grew closer and stronger. And more inviting. Then the smell spoke.

"Have you just run?" she spoke in an Australian accent.

I looked up to see who owned the voice, and to whom it was speaking.

"Hi, have you just been running?" she repeated. She appeared to be talking to me. My eyes fell on a smartly dressed shapely young woman, with golden blond hair, wearing make-up and nail varnish. I was either dead or dreaming. No one, not even Jerri Lee, dresses like that up here. If she was real, which I doubted very much, she must have been beamed down from a space ship.

"Y-Yes, I've just finished," I replied, prepared to go along with this dream, for the time being.

"How did you get on?" she asked.

I told her.

"That's very good, well done!" she replied. "I'm Kim, and this is Charlene. We're from Brisbane, Australia."

I hadn't noticed Charlene, who looked more like a trekker; dressed in practical but ethnic clothes, which were gratuitously grubby, and wearing a ridiculous hat. She had probably ferried Kim's ball gowns and make-up accessories up the hill from Lukla.

"What are you doing up here?" I asked. It wasn't an unreasonable question. She was overdressed for Kathmandu, let alone Namche. Thomas the Tank had just crossed the finish line.

"We've walked up from that little old airfield at Lukla."

"Are you going up to Tengboche?" I asked.

"Tengboche? No," she replied. "I think we've walked far enough. We'll kick around here for a couple of days, then head back down the hill again." Kim and Charlene had left their husbands and kids at home, and were having a girls' holiday. I hoped that my wife would never get wind of that idea.

"Are you guys having a big party tonight?" she asked.

I told her that I thought tomorrow night would be the big night, but I imagined there would be something going on this evening.

"Good," she said. "We'll catch you later." I very much doubted it. Although the combination of the Chanel, the make-up and the blond hair was a heady and racy concoction, I was beyond the lure of this illustrious Siren. But I knew one or two others who weren't.

John the Buddhist had just finished the race as the girls departed, and I went over to congratulate him. Despite the pain from his ankle, he had achieved a good time, completing the race in 6 hours 46 minutes.

As the afternoon wore on, friends and familiar faces came down the hill and along the cobbled streets to the finish line in various states of pain, fatigue and emotion. The deafening applause and warmth of the encouragement of those who had finished, and those who had simply been enthralled and captivated by the absurdity of the whole event, was moving.

Shortly before three o'clock, Joy crossed the finish line. This was a remarkable achievement, as she was still suffering badly from the illness that had laid her low the previous evening. Had she been at home, she wouldn't have considered getting out of bed to make a cup of tea, let alone running a marathon.

Another remarkable achievement was recorded by Al Hughes. Al ran with his video camera, stopping to film footage of the race for the documentary, and doubtless to satisfy his craving for roll-ups, and completed the course in thirty-eighth place in a time of 7 hours 29.08.

Forty-five minutes later, Lloyd Scott and Andrew Burgess crossed the line together. This was an even more remarkable achievement, as Lloyd had been unwell for several days, and had suffered on every step of the journey from Gorak Shep. He collapsed at the finish line, and it was several hours before he was well enough to get to his feet again. Thankfully, his recovery was progressive, and he suffered no lasting damage from the ordeal. Each of us would have a tale to tell; moments of self-doubt, perhaps moments of greatness, but few can have displayed the courage of Lloyd and Andrew to complete this tortuous event.

Almost unnoticed in the frenetic action that followed Lloyd and Andrew's arrival, I had the satisfaction of catching sight of my rumbustious little critic slip across the finish line. He later had, of course, an impressive array of excuses as to why he had not finished in the top twenty places.

The last runner to complete the race, in an appropriate sort of way, was Shigi. He strolled across the finish line waving majestically to his admiring public in the time of 10 hours 05.04. At least this time he completed it.

Almost an hour later, we all assembled on the parapet outside the lodge to welcome the back-up team of Dave Blakeney, Martin Campbell and Simon Petrides, who had completed the entire course, ensuring that no one or nothing had been left behind.

But they brought with them some sad news. Despite Simon's efforts and his own determination, John had collapsed at Pheriche, unable to take another step. Nat and a young porter had stayed with him and would help him down when he was well enough to travel. This news affected everyone, for this had been the only real disappointment in what had been by far the most successful event so far. Even Cathy Crilley, who had been evacuated to Pheriche, had been well enough to start her race from there, and had bravely completed the remainder of the course.

No one had had to be evacuated from Gorak Shep, and of the seventy-one runners that had started, all but one had completed the race. This was a remarkable achievement, and a credit to the organisation and dedication of Diana, the leaders, and their respective teams. And, of course, it could not have been achieved without the blessing of the gods of the mountains.

Even the weather, that stalking horse of so many failed Everest expeditions, had been kind to us. No one could heap the blame for their disappointment on the conditions, which, apart from the sub-zero temperature for the first few miles, had been excellent.

The race, as expected, threw up several curious anomalies. No one would have expected Eckart, at sixty-five years of age, to finish ahead of D.J. MacPhee, the thirty-six year old runner who had been successful in the highland Jura fell race. The New Zealanders, too, were a little disappointed with their results. Although Russell Prince finished in a creditable sixth position, his wife, Viv, missed out on the ladies' prize, and although she also broke the previous ladies' record, she finished not far ahead of me in eighteenth place. Only two places in front of me, was Alan Hall, who had been hampered by a back strain. Ray, of course, felt duly vindicated.

Mike Harper, the winner of the Annapurna half marathon, finished in sixty-seventh place. He had been unwell for a large part of the trip, and was just relieved that the race was over. One place behind him was Mike Silpa, who was well beaten by his wife Jerri Lee, who, despite a sleepless night attending John, managed a very dogged forty-seventh position.

As the sedation caused by the euphoria at completing the race began to wear off, the pain from my fingers returned steadily. Simon examined them and confirmed that they were probably broken, but there was nothing that could be done other than to isolate them with a splint. However, squeezing them together only made them more painful, and rendered my right hand completely useless, so in the end we gave up.

I was flattered when Richard, who had heard about my close encounter with the underbelly of the yak, put me in front of the camera and asked me to describe my experience. The size of my fingers also attracted media interest, but these interviews, like my previous ones, somehow ended up on the cutting room floor.

*

Later that evening, I joined Ray and his family for a meal in the subdued atmosphere of the Khumbu lodge.

We shared two bottles of beer, my first alcohol in almost three weeks. I felt light-headed as we toasted the realisation of our dreams and the achievement of our goals, and remembered absent friends.

Ray's race had been as eventful as mine. Later, he was to write his own account of the race for the official Everest marathon book:

"...I have only hazy memories of much of the race due to the natural mechanism for forgetting pain. I slotted in amongst the first four or five runners and found the pace quite sustainable but had difficulty with orientation. Those who had run the course before were certainly at an advantage. After a couple of excursions off the main trail, which is not well defined across the glacial moraines, I decided to sit in behind the Gurkha runners and rely on their guidance.

I arrived at Pheriche well inside my expected split and gulped down a special concoction of grated Power Bar and Staminade which Nat had painstakingly prepared for me. Just before Pangboche I rolled my ankle very badly and it took a kilometre before I could put full weight on it again. With ligaments stretched, I was to twist it a number of times and it really hampered my downhill running. Fortunately, there were a few ups and mostly gentle downs until Tengboche and I was managing to hold my position. I lost the Gurkhas on the steep track down to Phunki Teng and, in my frustration, took several spills which left me looking worse than I really was.

I had always regarded the steep ascent to Sarnassa as the main challenge of the race so I was elated to find that, at the top, I had made up most of the ground I had lost on the descent. I had a special advantage now: ahead at Chorkhung my family would be waiting, I hoped, as I had last seen them a month before when I left Perth. It was an emotional moment when they came into view ahead. A quick hug from Liz, my wife, and it was off to Thamo. The slightly downhill undulating nature of this trail draws the best out of spent bodies but leads to doubts about their capabilities for the return. At the turn around I had closed to within a few hundred metres of Hari Roka in second place, but was feeling very light-headed from the pain in my left ankle, and was worried that it would give out completely. My pace dropped off and my last split was very slow, but making sure of third place and breaking four hours thirty minutes was all that concerned me. The steep stony descent into Namche amid the hoots and whistles of the onlookers was made in dazed euphoria.

This was a once in a lifetime achievement and there was my family to share it with me."

Ray and his family had taken a room that you couldn't swing a cat in, should a suitable cat be available to be swung, on the top floor of the Khumbu. His language was equally vivid in the presence of his family.

"What happened to the Canary suit then?" I asked him. "I'd hoped you were going to run in that."

"Naw, that was just to wind up the bloody film crew. I gave it away to some bloody porter years ago. He thought it was bloody magic!"

It was a wonderful evening, and one I will treasure for ever. But I didn't want to intrude upon the family reunion, and so shortly after dinner I left to seek out my own accommodation for the night. Diana had booked beds for everyone in all the lodges in town, and unless we had made our own arrangements, which I soon wished that I had done, we were allocated a bed at random. I was told that I had a bed in a small dormitory on the first floor of the Traveller's Lodge, which was close to the old Tibetan's emporium. His repair on my shoe had lasted better than I had expected, although both shoes were now in a sorry state, with the fabric around the toes looking as if someone had poured acid on them.

At nine thirty, as I was about to set off to find my bed, our kit arrived. The sleeping bags, as promised, had arrived earlier in the evening. The porters had responded to the challenge and had excelled themselves by completing the twenty miles fully laden in under fourteen hours. And for not one rupee more.

I realised how tired I was, and despite the temptation to join the party who were headed for the Panorama lodge to help Pierre celebrate the retention of his crown, my body cried out for rest.

I found a free bed by the wall in the dormitory, which was more like a corridor, already occupied by a group of snoring Late Birds. I satisfied myself that I had beaten them all in the race, and this made me feel better.

I cheered up still further when I discovered across the landing, a room with two holes in the floor, which was probably the only en suite toilet in the Solu Khumbu.

A deep and dreamless sleep, for once, hit me like a sledgehammer.

## Saturday 27th November

Most of the day seemed to pass in a euphoric haze on the balcony of the Tawa lodge. I had promised myself that I would pig out on all the things which I had been deprived of, or not felt like, for so long. Beer, chocolate, cakes and all the other goodies that were on offer in this Garden of Eden.

But after a breakfast of chapattis, fried eggs and coffee, I was content simply to sit in the warm sun beneath the white capped mountains, and watch the pageantry and bustle of the busy market of another Namche Saturday morning. Beer could wait until the sun went down, and I had no more craving for chocolate than I had to run another marathon.

People came and went. I related the tale of the not totally repulsive female apparition who had greeted me shortly after I had finished the race. Knowing smiles and a prolific clearing of throats confirmed that one of our party, sitting not far from me, had done rather more than pass the time of day in genteel conversation with the young lady, thus confirming that she was flesh and blood and not a product of my fatigued mind.

Most of the Late Birds left to stroll down the hill to Monzo after lunch. There was nothing in Monzo, and no one could understand why they had opted for a night under canvas when they could have had another night of relative luxury in Namche and made the trek back to Lukla in one day.

The Gurkhas had gone. But that was different. They had been under orders to return to Kathmandu immediately after the race. Only instead of being feted as all-conquering heroes, presumably they would be confined to barracks, and given copious amounts of potato peeling and sentry duty as a reward for returning empty-handed. I was sorry to see them go, as I liked them and they certainly livened things up.

One of the beneficial by-products of the Late Bird exodus, was to create some space in the lodges. Mark Woodbridge had a spare bed in his twin room. Possibly because he liked me, or possibly because he was an accountant and as such had an eye for reducing estimated expenditure, he offered it to me. This was something he would live to regret. I gratefully accepted, and moved my belongings to the small room on the top floor of the Thamserku.

I arranged to have my washing done by a little tailor's shop which also claimed to do laundry, promising that it would be ready for collection by tomorrow morning. This transpired to be a mistake. To make a promise like this in these parts, you have to have a keen eye for weather forecasting, and they clearly did not.

My legs were stiff, and walking was a painful exercise. My fingers looked like burnt sausages, and my hip, which I had protected from the worst of the impact in my first fall, was very painful. These minor niggles apart, I felt fine, although understandably still very tired.

The rest of the day was passed quietly chilling out, soaking up the atmosphere and the warm sunshine until the long twilight drove us indoors.

*

It was Sue's birthday. We ate in the mess tent because the cooks had prepared food for us, and although we had been eating in lodges all through the day, we didn't have the heart to disappoint them.

We had acquired the Late Bird crew. Ours had presumably accompanied the Late Birds to Monzo, and although the food they served was equally uninspiring, the little men who served it were of a totally different breed. Whereas our cook boys and kitchen porters were by nature quiet, deferential, almost obsequious, the characters who replaced them were animated party animals, who wanted to make a game in which we were expected to participate with the serving of each course. They were disappointed when we showed little inclination to join in, preferring our own humour to infiltrating the jokes and repartee that had been established with the Late Birds. Which was presumably why they attempted to poison us with a pudding which defied all belief and made the sludge seem as attractive as Death By Chocolate to a chocoholic.

I produced my small bottle of rum, which I had been carrying in my washbag since Karikholi, and Bryan did an impersonation of our leader which had us rolling on the floor in laughter.

Back in the lodge of the Thamserku, John and Nat, accompanied by the young porter who had acquired Nat's cricket cap for his loyal assistance, had arrived. John was considerably better, and was in excellent spirits. Although he was obviously desperately disappointed by his failure to complete the race, he would not let that cast a shadow over the party atmosphere which pervaded those of us left in Namche. He even managed a joke about England's prospects against the All Blacks, in the light of his country's dismal showing.

"Your prediction?" I asked him.

"England three, New Zealand one hundred and thirty-three!" he replied, with a smile.

During the day, we had managed to locate a Late Bird doctor, Ian McPherson, who was staying an extra night in Namche and possessed a short wave radio. And so at 8 p.m. precisely, a small fanatical group of us huddled around a table in the lounge of the Thamserku as a feeble and intermittent signal brought us the commentary from Twickenham on the World Service.

As predicted, it was a tense and compelling match, played at a furious pace. With Nigel Redman, who had not been in my original selection, dominating the crucial area of the line-out, Jon Callard kicked the goals to keep England ahead in a tryless game. When Andrew dropped a goal with ten minutes remaining, a desperate All Black side mounted wave after wave of all out attack in a last ditch attempt to breach the English line. Each attack that was foiled, each knock-on, and each clearance kick was greeted with howls of delight, until at last, at the final whistle with the score fifteen to nine in England's favour, the place erupted. The *didi* and her family, who had probably thought that they had seen enough excesses of bizarre behaviour yesterday to last them a lifetime, could only survey the hysterical scene with mild amusement. It was one thing to run a marathon from nearly eighteen thousand feet, but it was quite another to go berserk because a little box on the table told you that a man on the other side of the world had managed to kick a leather bag of air over a bar and between two upright posts.

"Let's go and find some Kiwi's, and rub their noses in it!" suggested a Late Bird rugby enthusiast, uncharitably.

"Are you sure you're not a football supporter?" I asked.

But I had my own personal bit of nose rubbing to do. Before the others could spoil the surprise, I had raced up the steps to the Panorama lodge, where the party was in full swing. Annabel was sitting next to Pierre André.

"Oh hello, Marvin," she began. "Have you come to complain about the music being too loud, or have you just come to depress us all generally?"

It was my moment of greatness. No eternal footman was going to make this moment flicker. It was the nearest to revenge I would get for the weeks of jibes, the delight she had taken at my misfortunes, and the "Marvin, you're a real loser" which I had endured.

I sat down opposite her.

"No, Annabel", I said, "I've only come to depress you. I don't suppose you've heard the score from Twickenham."

"You're wasting your time Marvin. I can spot a wind up a mile off."

"It's no wind up, Annabel. The final score was New Zealand nine, England fifteen! And New Zealand were bloody lucky to get nine. It was a rout!" I was enjoying this.

"I don't believe you, Marvin. There's no way we'd lose to the Poms. I suppose this is one of your sad, pathetic little jokes."

"It's no joke, Annabel." With that the rest of the group entered, and for the next fifteen minutes *Swing Low, Sweet Chariot*, and *Jerusalem* drowned out the music from the ancient tape player belonging to the lodge.

"That's enough lads", I said, "after all we've got some Kiwis present, and we know how magnanimous they are in defeat!"

\*

The rest of the evening passed in a blur.

When the electricity went off at ten o'clock, Dave organised some extremely silly games which we were too tired or too inebriated to do anything other than go along with. Ray, who was still suffering a lot of pain from his ankle, had wisely stayed in the Khumbu with his family.

At last, we got down the hill and off to bed. I remember feeling slightly disappointed with myself for drinking more than I had intended to. I also remember feeling much worse than I usually do even after drinking considerably more.

But worse was to follow. Much worse.

# Dysentery and Descent:
# "Show Me the Way to Go Home"

## Sunday 28th November

I shall remember Sunday 28th November for ever. I will forever be able to recall exactly what I was doing on 28th November with the clarity that some people can recall with absolute certainty exactly what they were doing when JFK was assassinated or when Elvis died.

Because on Sunday 28th November, I was busy dying. While that might sound just a touch melodramatic, it was not far from the truth.

I awoke at seven o'clock, and felt ill. I had a headache, was shivering badly, and felt as if my stomach was about to explode. It was. I managed to struggle to the byre that passed for a toilet, and liquid poured from my bottom. I threw up. Then liquid poured from both ends. I got back to bed, beginning to realise this was more than a hangover, and suddenly the eruptions of fluid started all over again, only this time I was nowhere near the toilet.

Mark got Simon and Bryan, who managed to obtain a large metal washing bowl from downstairs, which I sat on virtually non-stop for the next six hours.

They also obtained a smaller bowl into which I vomited virtually non-stop for the next six hours. And all the while I stared at a packet of coconut biscuits which belonged to Mark sitting on the window ledge, and wondered if I would ever eat again.

They gave me pills to stop me dehydrating, which I threw up. They gave me pills to place under my tongue to stop me vomiting at the mere sight of water, and I threw those up as well. They would have given me pills which would have knocked on the head, in a very one-sided contest, what they had now diagnosed as dysentery. But unfortunately someone had already given those rather clever pills away to the Khunde hospital.

I have never been so ill in my life. Apparently most people thought it was a hangover, and had little sympathy. Certainly our leaders did. But by the time Simon had passed the lounge ferrying the tenth bowl of brown fluid to be disposed of, most people began to realise that it was more than a mere hangover.

I was exhausted but could not sleep. I was shivering with a fever and the fright at what was happening to my body. I could control nothing. I could think of nothing other than the fluid that was being sucked from my body. I was thirsty, but I could not drink.

Simon and Bryan talked in hushed voices, but I could make out the words saline drip and enema. There was no saline. One of them murmured, "Give him half an hour," and then they were gone, and I was alone; a weak and pathetic mess, shivering and shaking; suddenly terrified of dying alone and in a foreign land.

Mark had been fantastic. He had stayed with me from the beginning until I managed to tell him to clear out.

Some time later, when the waves of nausea and cramps were getting closer together, and reaching tidal proportions, Simon returned.

"I think we've found something that should do the trick. Once we've stopped you throwing up for twenty minutes, we'll give you one of these."

Somehow, with light at the end of the tunnel, I managed to keep the little pill which he gave me pressed under my tongue, and twenty minutes later, he gave me two different pills.

"Take these, and have a sip of water. Not too much."

I could now look at water without throwing up. I took the pills and swallowed them.

"These two should work pretty quickly together. You'll be feeling better soon."

I was feeling better already. Seven hours had passed since the illness had got hold of me. It had been the most utterly wretched seven hours of my life.

"Where did you manage to get these?" I asked feebly.

"Never mind that. Let's just say we managed to scrounge them back," he replied. "Try to get some sleep now. We've got to get you down the hill tomorrow somehow!"

I later realised just how concerned Simon and Bryan had become over my rapid deterioration. I had somehow contracted an unusual but extremely virulent strain of dysentery which, if unchecked, can lead to total dehydration, followed by death within twenty-four hours. I had been lucky.

Some hangover.

But Simon had quashed any lingering thoughts of my illness being caused by my own over-indulgence with the announcement that he had never, in his medical experience, seen anyone look so ill, who was probably not going to die.

*

A few hours later I awoke, and although extremely weak, felt much better. I knew that the worst was behind me. I had a steady stream of visitors. Mark sat and talked, and I listened. I loved listening to him talking. Everything he talked about had a quiet but earnest enthusiasm. I felt as if I had known him for years. Just to be with another human being and know that some day soon I would once again enjoy the simple pleasures of life and home that he talked about, made me happy.

John the Vicar, paid me several visits.

"Christ, Richard, you look worse than I felt two days ago!"

"Have you come to read me the last rites, John?" I asked.

"Och no, those are the other fellas who do that. The ones with the pointy hats and the incense. Anyway, I hear you're on the mend."

Next Ray put his head around the door.

"Well, took on the bright side mate, you haven't bloody missed anything today. The weather's been piss poor, and Dave made us play this bloody game of International Giants, Wizards and Dwarfs, so, all things considered, you've probably been better off bloody out of it."

Annabel paid a visit, and treated me with a good deal more sympathy than I deserved after my shortlived moment of glory last night.

"Have you ever thought of doing amateur dramatics, Marvin. You'd make a great corpse!"

Others followed. Dave English, who lent me a tape, then Zvoni, Tom and Valeri. They had spent the day trekking up to the Everest View to have lunch at Zvoni's invitation on his expense account. Unfortunately, they had a wasted journey as the hotel had mislaid its Visa processing machine and they would have had to carry sackloads of banknotes up the hill to cover the cost of the meal. Well, as Wish had often said, what would you expect? This *is* Nepal.

The lodge family were kind too. The *didi* brought me a hot water bottle, and a huge and warm yak fur rug. I didn't care that it was infested with every variety of termite known to man. One of the girls brought potato soup and plain toast at seven thirty. This was welcome, although I wasn't able to do justice to it all.

I was disappointed but not particularly surprised that neither of our leaders had bothered to see for themselves how ill I was. Doubtless they had other things on their minds.

The only important thing I missed was the bank, which, paradoxically, was open on Sundays and not Saturdays. I was very low on money, so I borrowed five hundred rupees from Ray, which I hoped would get me to Kathmandu. It didn't. Things now strangely started to seem to increase in price, or we were buying more. I had to borrow a further one thousand rupees from Simon, who was loaded.

## Monday 29th November
## Recovery in Namche, and Gentle Retreat to Lukla

There is probably no better feeling than waking up the morning after a day at death's doorstep, and feeling health return, strength in the limbs and even the hint of an appetite. I had been concerned about either having to be carried down to Lukla, or possibly staying and recovering in Namche and flying out on my own later. Also, I did not want to be cheated of the final three days in Kathmandu, which were now an almost tangible carrot at the end of a rapidly receding stick.

I packed slowly, finding things a real effort. I was still very weak from the dysentery, but the illness that had floored me had departed. Simon had given me his supply of pills, which would put the illness well and truly behind me. I told him that I hoped he didn't mean that too literally, as I had had enough of that yesterday!

The porters had left yesterday, as they would not do the trip to Lukla in one day, I therefore had all of my kit to carry. This was the one time I could have done with sharing my load with a porter. They had done pretty well out of me.

To make matters worse, when I went to collect my laundry, which I had been promised would be ready on Sunday morning, I found not only was it soaking wet, but it had clearly not even been wrung out.

"Come back this evening," said the owner when I demanded my clothes. I was furious – the weather on Sunday may not have been conducive to drying, but there had been virtually a full day's sunshine on Saturday.

I had been impressed with the work ethic and the eagerness to help of these fine proud people of the Solo Khumbu, and this was an exception.

I told him I would pay for the washing, but not the drying, so he could have one hundred and fifty rupees. I wasn't even sure that the clothes had been washed. I wrung out a T-shirt, and the water and the shirt looked filthy. They had probably slammed them into a bucket of water when he saw me coming.

He wasn't happy about my offer, pretending first not to understand and writing the price on a piece of paper. I was furious, and told him: "one hundred and fifty, take it or leave it!" The trouble was, I only had the five hundred rupee note, borrowed from Ray.

Eventually he agreed, and took my note to a nearby shop to change. I cursed myself for being stupid, as that was probably the last I would see of my money. Moments later, I felt guilty for my dark thoughts when he returned with my change and thanked me politely. Maybe I had been a bit harsh on him, I thought. However, the weight of my black bag full of sopping clothes soon dissuaded me of that thought.

I managed to persuade our *didi* to cook scrambled eggs, which were not on the menu. They were so good that John the Vicar had some too. You could almost feel the change in mood as the women of the lodge became visibly more relaxed as our numbers dwindled. They are not a greedy people, and I wondered whether our vast intrusion on either side of the marathon had been worth the disruption we had caused. After all, even during the height of the trekking season, they would not be engulfed with a group of our size, intensity and demands. I wondered if they felt it had been worth it.

We paid and left by ten thirty. Outside the sun shone brightly as Mark and I strolled leisurely through the near empty streets of Namche. In contrast to my first arrival in Namche, less than two weeks, but almost a lifetime ago, the clouds had gone, and the path seemed less foreboding, our goals achieved.

It was a pleasant walk down, but I had forgotten just how long and steep the descent to the Imja Khola and the magnificent suspension bridge at the foot of the climb was. In contrast, my trek in had been shrouded in mist, low cloud and depression brought on by constant dives into the undergrowth to appease my overactive bowel.

The trail was much less crowded than before, and it was a world apart from the feeling on the way up. We were veterans, in some way, survivors with a tale to tell. Soon, we would be home and we could tell it.

Mark was good company, and for the first time on the trek I actually enjoyed going at a pace that allowed conversation without busting a gut to get somewhere. I had been ill and, despite feeling stronger by the minute, I enjoyed the respite that that allowed. Besides, the sun shone, and it was uplifting to have access to the spectacular views denied us on our ascent.

We caught Ron Isles, who had also not been well the previous night, and carried on together to Phakding. We passed our lunch stop on the way up, where I had suffered with the shits, removed John Dunging's from my jacket, and played cricket, injuring my hip. It seemed a long, long time ago.

At Phakding, we stopped at a pleasant-looking lodge and joined the rest of the camera crew and the Gobet party. The clouds were beginning to gather, and I wrapped up against the approaching cool of the afternoon.

We ordered food. This was the first time on the trek I had stopped at a lodge for lunch, and was reminded of just how slow the service can be. Most of my order came in dribs and drabs after constant reminders. Eventually, I gave up waiting for my rice, paid and left, feeling irritated by the lengthy delay.

From the bottom of the valley, we began the long climb to Lukla. Once the back of the climb had been broken, the path was good and the walk into Lukla was a pleasant one. The path was actually wide enough and sufficiently obstacle free for a four-wheel-drive vehicle to travel about two miles. This prompted speculation between Mark and me as to how long it would be before the commercialisation of the Solo Khumbu would see a road all the way to Namche. Hopefully never, but it is probably inevitable.

We entered Lukla at around four o'clock, passing prosperous-looking lodges boasting Western-style facilities. One bore a sign opposite its entrance requesting passers-by: "Do not dirt here! A far cry from: Do not allow your dog to foul the pavement.

Past the last *chorten*, we walked down the high street, which was as muddy, dirty and smelly as I remembered it. Chickens scurried across the street, doubtless conscious of the approaching hour for dinner, and lazy dogs lay in entrances, scarcely bothering to watch the world go by.

We found the aptly named Panorama lodge with little problem. It had a garden with wooden benches and tables, and was entered by an ornate flower-festooned gate which served little purpose, as there was no fence on either side. For a moment the scene awakened memories of a scruffy pub on an English summer's day.

There were no single rooms left. Rob Haworth, the chief medical officer, had seen to that, reserving rooms for his chums still meandering along the trail. The Panorama was owned by someone connected to Highland Sherpa and, I believe, related to the Tenzing family who owned a considerable amount of property in Namche.

It was a solid comfortable building, with a French-style outside toilet, a shower and a spacious dormitory. The dormitory was warm and, at twenty rupees a night, there seemed little point in paying thirty-five dollars for a room in the Holiday Inn, sit down toilet or not. Simon had opted for this and it was tempting to join him, but in less than twenty-four hours we would have all the luxury we could handle.

That, or we would have crashed into the side of the mountain opposite the end of the runway.

A little discomfort would make it all the more special. There were some who took this ideal of deprivation to extremes, and were actually staying in tents. Not only that, they had opted, on some sort of nostalgic whim, to eat the trek food. Still, at least the trek crew were still functioning and keen to please, and I felt a little sorry that their efforts went largely unappreciated. Whether the food was barely digestible or not, the cheerful little men who prepared and served it had seemed to enjoy our company, and were so keen to be of service. It was almost an insult to shun them now that we were a whisker away from civilisation. I had no doubt they were used to it.

I showered and sat down in the comfortable cushioned wicker chairs in the lounge. There was a stove in the centre, which threw out more warmth than I had felt for what seemed like weeks. We were burning wood again and not yak shit. I suddenly noticed something on the floor which I had not seen since leaving home – a carpet.

Others entered, and food came and went in the usual sedate and erratic manner that is service in the Solo Khumbu. This was to be our base, and a meeting was scheduled for 6 p.m. to inform us of tomorrow's arrangements.

Two things of interest came to light this evening. First was the sad news that Martin Stone had failed in his bid to break the record from Base Camp to Kathmandu. Martin had passed through Namche on Sunday, having spent the previous night with our friends from the Japanese Winter climbing party eating sushi and drinking saki. They had provided him with a tent, down clothing and a sleeping bag.

At six thirty the next morning he had set off, and had run down through Namche ahead of schedule. Just before Lukla, he began to get painful twinges from his left knee. Continuing beyond Lukla, the twinges got considerably worse. With dwindling confidence, Martin began to realise that the chances of success were receding. He continued the painful descent to Surkhe before conceding defeat. The prospect of twelve hours in the dark, running unsupported with severe pain resulting from each step, both ascending and descending, was understandably too much.

Eventually he had limped back up the hill back to Lukla, and managed to locate us at around nine thirty. Unfortunately, it was impossible to get a message to Stephen Isles, who had left Kathmandu to meet him at Kirantichap.

We bought him beer and commiserated. He seemed pretty philosophical about it, and I wondered if I would have been so cheerful in his position. I also wondered if I would have had the sense to stop. It wasn't the kind of thing one was likely to get a second bite at.

Martin's failure was regarded with something approaching relief by certain members of the film crew. News of his success would have dulled media interest in the marathon and made the job of marketing the documentary all the more difficult.

The other item of interest which prompted a considerable amount of discussion, was news that two members of the Late Bird party, one male and the other female, had broken into the Lukla control tower the night before. They had been caught in the act, and had spent the night in Lukla jail. Rumours that they had been flown out on the first flight and faced immediate deportation and a lifetime ban from Nepal were rife. In fact it transpired that after several hours of grovelling and testimony to their previous good character by the leaders of the Late Birds, they were fined one hundred dollars each (which seems to be the general cost levied on everything) to repair the door, and were put on the first plane out this morning. This prompted speculation that if breaking into Lukla control tower guaranteed one a seat on the first plane, we all ought to be doing it.

The guilty pair had experienced the heats of passion in the Lukla disco bar, had got incredibly drunk and went looking for a secluded spot to do the wild thing. Why, God alone knows, did they choose Lukla control tower? There were any number of tents to pick from. It is probably the only place in Lukla, or indeed Nepal, which was patrolled by armed guards. They had forced open the door, and had barely exchanged exploratory drunken gropes when the Lukla militia had entered, and extinguished the fires of passion.

By ten o'clock, I was exhausted, and headed for bed. It was warm in the dormitory, and shortly after sorting out my pee bottle for the last time, and saying a prayer for good weather in the morning and to be spared a sudden violent collision with the mountain opposite, I went out like a light. This was the last night among the mountains, feeling the pulse of Nepal.

Only this time, the pulse was the rhythm of the beat from the disco bar across the street.

# Kathmandu Revisited, and the End of an Adventure

## Tuesday 30th November

There are few things in life I dread more than flying. And, there can be few flights, anywhere in the world, that can rival the journey in or out of Lukla airport. Of course, I knew all about this before I had committed myself to the trip. Westerners who have survived it share the Nepali sense of the macabre, and embellish their stories appropriately with nods of the head and knowing looks at each other.

In truth, like practically everything else in Nepal, apart from the risks of illness induced by either altitude or the lack of any sanitation, it is probably somewhat overstated.

For fear of the unknown is part of the charm of Nepal.

So, it was with a mixture of emotions that I looked out of the window at 6 a.m. and observed clear blue skies. The day that I had dreaded more than any other, had dawned bright and clear.

On the way up, I had passed some of my empty moments sorting and prioritising what was to come into a kind of 'brown trousers' order. First, appropriately, there had been using the 'toilets' without falling backwards into them or stepping in something. There had been the intense cold to worry about. Would my Buffalo gear be warm enough? Would I survive in a tent for three weeks? What would the lodges be like? Were the suspension bridges that bad? How dangerous was a yak on the charge? Then there was the worry of the altitude, my main fear. And then, of course, the race itself. One by one, I had ticked them off, and grew in confidence and strength as the end of the ordeal approached.

But always at the back of my mind were dark forebodings of the vast chasm that had to be crossed between Lukla and Kathmandu.

And now, as I had a gargantuan pee in the garden of the Panorama Lodge and watched the sun come up, spreading its mantle of light and warmth over the lower hills, I was glad the day had come.

A man can stand only so much deprivation, and the limit of my tolerance had approached faster than I had expected with the onset of dysentery. Now I would hang-glide off the hill if I had to. But there would be no need, as the fine weather should guarantee that the planes would get in and we would get out. I had requested a seat on the first plane, and this had been agreed.

My mammoth pee was the result of having only one pee during the night. This was due to throwing my pee bottle out of the window accidentally whilst emptying it.

I breakfasted on scrambled egg again, packed leisurely and sauntered over to the Sherpa Coffee House just about in time for our seven forty-five meeting. Planes could start arriving as early as eight, we were told, and we had to be ready. Inside, it was as warm as I had remembered it from last time. Now, however, there were no clothes to dry around the little stove in the centre of the room.

Our leader was extremely agitated.

"Right, now listen up," he began. "This airport is a fucking joke." No one was laughing. "I've never got out of here without somebody or something being left behind, so there's no reason to expect that today will be any different. Just because it's sunny here is no guarantee of planes taking off from Kathmandu. As you no doubt know, there's no radar in Kathmandu, so fog in the Kathmandu Valley means no flights." He was warming to his theme. "Also, these boarding passes which I am about to issue, are about as much a guarantee of a seat as a piece of toilet paper. As you can tell, I'm not in a very good mood this morning." We wouldn't have guessed!

Then we were left to our own devices. Planes might arrive at any moment, on the other hand they might not, with the worst scenario being that we would have to endure another night and try again tomorrow.

Simon had passed a comfortable and expensive night in the Holiday Inn, but had no desire to repeat the experience. Neither had the lunatics, including Mike and John Dunging, who had spent the night in tents. That really would be wallowing in nostalgia.

I was feeling pretty good, and not too nervous about the flight. I was amongst a good bunch of people, and that counted for a lot. I wandered down to the area where the planes turned, which was the only flat part of the airstrip. Here, a game of Frisbee was in progress, and I joined in, attempting to catch the Frisbee, listen to my Walkman, and take photographs at the same time. As I could never understand the aerodynamics of the Frisbee, I soon tired of the game and wandered down the airstrip to further inspect the wreckage on either side.

Eventually, I wandered back to the departure shed to find that everyone had been issued with their boarding cards and had gone through. There was considerable excitement as the arrival of planes was imminent.

We queued for the security check. Facing us were two curtain covered cubicles, one labelled men and one women. Toilets, we all thought. Not so. Eventually it was my turn and as the curtain was drawn behind me, I was greeted by a cheerful little man in military uniform who didn't speak a word of English.

He pointed to my large SLR camera:

"Camera," I said. He nodded.

We repeated the process with my small camera, then went through the contents of my rucksack. He came to my video camera and shook it violently, which annoyed me.

"Big bomb," I said, flippantly. He looked at me, and smiled.

Next was my palmtop computer: "Heroin," I said, beginning to enjoy myself. Again he smiled at me, and I smiled back. And so it went on. I had a grenade in my sunglasses case, cannabis in my toothpaste, and a remote control missile launcher in my Walkman.

On the other side of the hut, we stood around waiting for planes. Most people had climbed the muddy bank overlooking the runway, and there were more clicking cameras than greeted Lindberg after crossing the Atlantic. I joined them, and had just enough juice in the video's battery to capture the little Twin Otter picking its way unconvincingly between the mountains, and touching down half way along the runway. It was a smooth landing, but that was the last thing smooth about it. The little plane kicked up a huge plume of dust, stones and boulders and, like a Barnes Wallis creation, bounced and stuttered along the track until it reached the turning circle and came to rest.

Relieved-looking tourists emerged and walked unsteadily to the perimeter, hopeful of being reunited with their luggage. They had survived their ordeal. Generally it was considered that the flight into Lukla was more hair-raising than the flight out. Once over the mountain passes, our descent into the Kathmandu Valley should be relatively straightforward.

The plane was rapidly unloaded. Baggage handlers worldwide share the same contempt for their cargo, and the cases were slung to one side with little concern for their contents.

Then everything happened very quickly. We were called forward. As requested, I was on the first plane, but that was no guarantee that I would get aboard. There were sixteen seats, and fourteen of us plus an assortment of luggage and cameras. Last night there had been a fairly lively conversation about how the cameras and the camera crew would travel. Ron had insisted that the cameras and crew would travel together. There was a considerable amount of heavy equipment, and it might mean leaving someone behind to catch a later flight as a result. There was a fair amount of hostility to this. We had cooperated with the film crew every inch of the way, but now that the race was over there was no sound reason why the precious camera equipment should have priority over the paying members of the party. Everyone was happy with this except Ron. In the end it was decided that the crew and the equipment would be split between planes, and Martin Stone selflessly volunteered to wait behind if one of the planes was overloaded. At least we didn't have the generator. That had been donated to the Khunde hospital after our last night at Lobuche.

We walked across the dusty apron, which not long ago had been the scene of our Frisbee game. The sun shone brightly as I took one long last look at the snowy peaks beyond Lukla. The trip had outstripped my dreams. I felt the same sadness I had experienced on Kala Pattar before the race, and again on leaving Namche yesterday. It was all about arriving and departing. Coming and going. A trek is only a trek when you're going somewhere. And now we were going home. Hopefully.

A Royal Nepal Airlines official inspected my boarding pass suspiciously and I scrambled through the tiny entrance into the plane. To my surprise there was a well-dressed and relatively pretty hostess seated at the rear. This must be one of the most glamorous occupations open to Nepali women, and certainly, as it would transpire, one of the easiest. For all she did throughout the flight was to hand out sweets shortly before the take-off.

She greeted me with the inevitable *"Namaste,"* and a cheery smile, and I found a seat close to the front.

We were all aboard. My heart was thumping like a drum – like so many things that had happened over the last month, I couldn't believe I was doing it.

The door closed. That was it, there was no going back now. My palms were sweating as I sat hunched over my rucksack and fumbled with my Walkman.

Everyone knew how much I was looking forward to this.

"Why has the pilot got the instruction book out I wonder?" asked Wish.

"Hey Richie," said Bryan, "do you think that could be oil leaking from below the wing?"

Meantime, Tom, in his inimitable Roscommon brogue, was giving his account of what was about to happen. If I had heard it once, I had heard it fifty times.

"Well now, you see", he began, "they'll rev the engines right up. And then they'll let the thing go, like a catapult, you see, and it'll bounce a couple of times before it goes up. Then when we get to the end, they'll brake hard on the left, as we drop off the cliff, and that way we won't hit the mountain on the other side. We hope."

"Thank you, Tom."

"Have you flown from here before, then Tom?" asked John Dunging.

"No," came the reply.

"But he knows a man who has," I said.

There were two Nepali pilots, smartly dressed in black slacks and blue braided woollen pullovers. They didn't look much like pilots, but this didn't look much like a plane either.

The pilot who had been reading what Wish had correctly jested was the manual, closed it, surveyed us with a broad grin and turned his attention to the small array of dials before him. The average Lada had a more impressive-looking dashboard. The pilot on the right stole a glance at us, smiled at his partner, and went back to flicking switches above his head. I wondered if any of them worked, and if their preparation for take-off was as scientific as the method by which they arrived at deciding when the plane was full.

This, literally, had to be seen to be believed. A little man, holding a metal pole about four feet in length, had stood at the back of the plane. Every so often, as loading had progressed, he placed the pole on the ground, directly below the lowest point of the tail of the fuselage. When the top of the pole and the bottom of the plane met, the last occupant of the plane, animal, vegetable or mineral, was removed with the minimum of ceremony. This done, the door closed, and no amount of protestation or promises of goats, whisky or wives could open it again.

The engines revved so hard I thought they would surely fall off the wings. There was one on each side, roughly at eye level, presumably so that the pilots could see if anything went wrong with them.

The banter and joking continued, as we started to taxi towards the end of the runway. Runway? That was a joke. Well, whatever it was like we were going down it in a few seconds time, headlong. Towards certain death.

I looked around. We were a close group, I was amongst friends. If I had to die now, at least it would be with people whom I knew and cared for, not shaking and puking, alone and frightened in a dark and dank little room. That thought did little to calm my nerves.

For the last few months, I had been unable to cast my thoughts beyond these mountains. The excitement, the hardships, and the perils. Now this was about to end. One way or the other.

We came to a halt, awaiting final instructions, like 'GO', from the control tower. I wondered if they'd fixed their door yet.

I supposed they had to check there wasn't another plane about to land. With the mountains which surrounded the landing strip providing a formidable natural barrier, it wasn't possible to circle in a holding pattern, waiting to land, as in normal airports.

The little plane had two seats on the right hand side, and a single seat on the left. I had a last look at my fellow travellers. Wish and Al sat on the right at the front, talking Welsh, as usual. One minute they were talking English, then as soon as someone else joined them, they started to speak in Welsh. If we did crash, I supposed that part of the collective funeral service would have to be in Welsh.

Opposite them sat Shigi, the snoring Jap, scouring the paper for news of his financial investments.

Behind him sat the English lads, one behind the other. Bryan had offered to operate my video camera, and sat by the window. Bryan was the extrovert, the joker, the copier of Valeri's laugh, while Dave was the quiet one, the thinker.

Opposite them, and in front of me, were Simon and Sue. Sue had been one of the many characters in the group, with an infectious laugh and broad cockney accent, that endeared her to all of us. But like many of us, she had had her share of problems. At the end of the trip, she had a world tour to look forward to, for which she had taken two years off work. Right now I didn't envy her. After Kathmandu, I was ready for home.

Behind the English lads sat Annabel, and behind her sat Richard, the jester, the smooth television presenter, who had kept our spirits up in the darkest hours. Beside me was Joy, now, like me, almost recovered from illness.

The others sitting behind me were John and Mike, Tom and Zvoni, and the hostess sat at the very back. Since the race Tom had changed, and he was now almost unrecognisable from the dour and ultra-cautious man with the solemn face who had started the trek.

We sat for what seemed like ages, probably for no other reason than to build the tension.

"How're you feeling Marvin?" asked Annabel, implying the worse I felt the more entertaining it would be. Surprisingly, I wasn't feeling too bad, but played up a bit for Al's camera, by adopting the crash position with my head on my rucksack. This was bound to appear on the video, even if my earlier interviews didn't. It did. I was right. It was one of two shots in which I appeared on the final documentary. My head, or the colour of my hair, must have been mistaken for some rare Nepali bird of prey which attracted the fleeting interest of the camera. I later concluded that I must have been either too cynical or too anti-Welsh.

"Are we up yet?" I asked.

We weren't.

"Oh Goodness me no!" said Richard, "not another day like last Thursday!"

Suddenly we began to move. Slowly at first, then gathering speed, we rattled and bumped along the runway. Past the Buddha lodge, past the campsite, past the bigger of the crashed planes on our left. Surely the little plane couldn't take this buffeting much longer. Would we burst a tyre? Would the tail touch the ground? Would our world explode around us?

Then we were up. There was a cheer.

Then we were down. "Aaaaaagh!"

Then we were sort of half way up. We were neither up nor down.

Then we were up again. There was a massive cheer. This time we stayed up.

Then we were over the cliff.

And gaining height. Suddenly, everything was very smooth, but very noisy. I relaxed, and asked the hostess for another sweet, and we all had more sweets, apart from Shigi, who hadn't looked up from his paper. We finished the sweets, which made the hostess rather redundant.

Within minutes we had retraced the steps that it had taken us days to walk. Over Karikholi, then over the first of two high passes, Tragsindho, with its monastery which I had fleetingly visited.

Then we were looking down on Junbesi, the steep-sided valley with its pine and rhododendron forests, the entrance to Sherpa country and home to the brightly dressed and pretty young girls who had entertained us with their dancing, so long ago. The valley which I had run along, losing the toe of my shoe, sweeping down from Lamjura Pass and the gateway to the Kathmandu Valley.

We flew over Lamjura Pass with feet to spare. From the air, it didn't look as paint-scratchingly close as it had from the ground. Over the prayer flags and waving trekkers following the trail up from Sete. I wondered if the dead goat would still be on the roof of the Solu Khumku New Green View Blue Sky lodge if I came back in ten years' time.

The ground fell away beneath us, as we flew towards the fertile terraces of the foothills and away from the snow capped peaks, and our memories.

Gradually the land levelled out, and we began our approach to Kathmandu, to be greeted by the curious sight of the shroud of smog hanging at about five hundred feet over the city.

We landed smoothly and uneventfully and the ordeal which I had dreaded more than any other was over. Now the party could begin!

\*

We boarded an ancient bus outside the airport, which, in contrast to Lukla, appeared to be totally security-free, and were on our way to the city. It was as strange to see, once again all the vibrant sights of daily life in the city now as it had been three weeks ago.

Entering the hotel, the relative opulence was incredible. Simon and I again shared a room, this time on the fourth floor. It seemed grander than before, or perhaps it was just the deprivation that made it seem so. Everyone disappeared to drain the hotel of hot water, but I put off that luxury until I had attended to the rather pressing business of obtaining some money.

I was down to my last two hundred rupees, and had debts to repay. I was banking on being able to convert my Visa card into something more useful than a piece of plastic. To do this, what I needed was a bank and so, primed with the information provided by reception, that there was a large and substantial bank literally around the corner, I set off.

It was a large and substantial bank, but had not been made large and substantial for the purpose of issuing money to the likes of me. This was the State National Bank, Nepal's version of our Threadneedle Street. That was the first piece of duff information I had been given. The other was from Diana, who held our passports. I was sure that I would need my passport to carry out such a financial transaction, but she was adamant that a trekking permit would be sufficient. In the event I was right, and when I eventually found a commercial bank, some two miles away, I was told that I had had a wasted journey. No passport – no money. Despondently, I took a *tuk-tuk* back to the hotel having agreed a price with the driver that would be covered by the much diminished contents of my wallet.

Back in room 101, I set about adjusting to civilisation again. After all, there were one or two things in our room which I hadn't seen for three weeks. They all seemed to begin with the letter 'T'. First, there was the toilet. It was almost sheer luxury to sit on this small but significant manifestation of the technological progress of mankind. I say almost, because we were unlucky enough to have a toilet with a wobbly seat. Still, it was as near to decadence as I had experienced during the last three weeks, to sit on the toilet with my guide book and plan my sightseeing.

The other two items beginning with the letter 'T' I could actually have survived without. The first was the television. It's funny how it always happens. You want to fight it, but it always gets you in the end. You enter your rather smart hotel room, be it in Manchester or Madras. You turn on the television, satellite of course, and flick through the ten channels of rubbish. A golf tournament in the States, some obscure tennis championship in Taiwan, a history of the automotive industry in Chicago, a chat show featuring a little-known local spiritualist, the Third World's attempt at romantic comedy and, if you're lucky, the BBC World Service, with a grim and grey-looking John Major leaving Number 10 on a grim and grey English winter's day. And do you turn it off? No, you go back to the golf, because while the commentary is as dull and uninteresting as the action, at least it's a safe and familiar reminder of a world you had left behind almost a month ago.

The third 'T' was of more use but a cause of considerably greater frustration.

The telephone.

In Nepal, the presence of a telephone by one's bedside serves a more decorative function than a practical one.

In theory it is possible to call room service, order an alarm call, or arrange to have one's laundry collected and washed. Sometimes this even happens. But try making an international call!

Eventually, I was reunited with my suitcase, which I had left in safekeeping before the trek. However, I had lost the key to the padlock, and a maintenance man had to come and cut it off with a hacksaw.

Down in reception, Diana had at last received my passport. Another *tuk-tuk* ride, curiously cheaper than the last, took me back to the bank, and I was ready to draw my money on my Visa card. I had previously requested seven thousand rupees, but had decided that, after paying my debts, this might leave me a bit short. One can't change money back, so the trick is to get no more than you need. I could always pay the hotel bill by credit card.

I asked for another two thousand and the girl received this request with a certain measured frostiness, as this meant another verification phone call to Singapore. The bank was like any Western institution and exuded calm efficiency. The employees were well-dressed and there was an interesting contrast of smells. Opulent Western perfumes and colognes from behind the counter gave way to the stench of the peasants, of which I was one, waiting to change money.

Back at the hotel, having attended to my laundry and other mundane chores, I prepared to bathe. I had been putting this moment off, but now I could wait no longer. Even the offer to share John Webster's scotch was not sufficiently tempting. In any case, Simon had recommended I restrict myself to three beers, so three beers it was to be.

First, I had a shower to remove the worst of the grime and dirt and then a long, hot bath. To my surprise, the water was still warm. Next a shave, and the arduous and painful removal of almost three weeks' growth. Karikholi was the last time I had shaved, and that had been only to pass the time.

As the last of the superficial grime which had been unwillingly prized from my body finally yielded to the unfamiliar force of soap and water, and spiralled down the plughole to mingle with the city's water supply, the adventure of a lifetime came to an end.

I lay on my bed, and ate an entire box of Pringles, deciding what to do next.

## Wednesday 1st December

There is no shortage of things to do in Kathmandu, and the beauty of it is that none of it costs the earth.

We spent the next two days doing all the things we had talked about doing and dreamed of for the last three weeks. We did a bit of sightseeing, only because it was arranged for us. We did a lot of shopping, and I haggled until my heart was content. But mainly we did nothing, except lounge in the warm sun on the terraces of rooftop cafés, eating, drinking, and casting wistful glances at the distant foothills beyond which lay the snow-capped peaks of which we were now veterans, and which gave us the hard-earned right to do absolutely nothing.

The following morning, most of us joined the sightseeing tour which combined the cultural bit with a good opportunity to look for some bargains. On a relatively civilised bus with the same guide who had accompanied us on our earlier tour, our first port of call was Bodhnath, which is the largest stupa in Nepal and is the religious centre for the Tibetan population. The temple, our guide informed us, was built in the fifth century by the Hindu king using dew instead of water, a building method which is notable only for the fact that it failed to catch on. I celebrated this fact by buying a ridiculous waistcoat embroidered with elephants, and Simon bought a Tibetan tea urn which looked like a cross between a hatstand and a giant bicycle pump. The temple is surrounded by a circular street crammed to bursting point with monasteries and shops waiting to fleece the tourists, and crowded with hawkers who displayed their wares on the street.

Our next stop was Pashupatinath. This is the most sacred Hindu temple in Nepal, and one of the most significant Shiva temples on the entire subcontinent. The king always pays a visit here to receive a blessing before he embarks on an important journey. Westerners are not allowed to enter the temple, but there is plenty to look at, as there is always a cremation or two going on in one of the four burning ghats along the riverbank, designated for the common people.

However, it was what was going on behind the public toilets that held more interest for most of our group. A strange little man, wearing only a towel wrapped around his waist, prepared, for a negotiated and mutually acceptable fee, to perform a more bizarre ritual than any we had hitherto witnessed. Wish acted on our behalf as negotiator, and the price of twenty rupees per person was agreed for this curious little man to lift a large and extremely heavy-looking breeze-block using only his penis.

He thus began a build up to an act which he doubtless performed for incredulous tourists many times each day. However, we were sceptical as he struggled with both hands to wrestle the block into place and tie a length of cloth first around the weight, then to his person.

"Oh my god!" he uttered, as if the task were Herculean.

"Oh yea!" replied a cynic, "Shakespearean!"

"You try it!" he countered, angrily.

"I really think someone should test it first," suggested Ron Isles, the most sceptical of the disbelievers.

"Where's his beautiful assistant?"

Martin Stone was volunteered, and was pushed to the front of the gathering.

"One penis, I mean one hand, Martin!" said a voice from the throng.

He lifted the band tied around the block and the exertion showed on his face, confirming the weight of the load.

"It's well heavy!" he confirmed. That was good enough. We got our money out.

What followed was quite remarkable. If it had been David Copperfield, we would have, to a man, been less impressed. Even if he had had Claudia Schiffer for his beautiful assistant! For this was no illusion. This sweating, grunting little ethnic throwback appeared to go into a trance, repeating a curious litany which I could have sworn contained several decidedly non-ethnic swearwords, and then perform a strange dance which heightened our sense of anticipation.

"It's the Pashupatinath public toilets version of the Haka," I said.

The audience was transfixed. At this point the battery in my video camera annoyingly gave out. My back up had been, of course, with shades of Mallory, left on the bus.

Suddenly the dance and mantra abruptly ceased, and he stood very still. We inched forward. With his eyes tightly sealed as if deep in concentration, he tied the scarf around the end of his willy. Every vein on his neck stood out road map-like. He grabbed the end of his organ, straightened his knees, and the parcel of concrete rose from the ground slowly in front of the incredulous audience.

"Good... God!" said Ron Isles.

"That's incredible, man!" said Wish.

"And you kiddies who are watching, remember, don't try this one at home," came a voice from the back.

"You want more?" queried our host. "I lift more block for more rupee!"

We wanted more, and were prepared to pay for it.

The encore was even more unbelievable. This time he lifted three large blocks, a weight several times heavier than his previous load.

"I just hope his wife isn't expecting too much tonight," said Simon.

"Bloody good contraceptive," I said. "Perhaps if Kerry Packer got hold of the idea and offered big money contracts for a satellite TV Willy-Weight-Lifting-Super-League, it might reduce the population over here!"

The show had been all the more entertaining for the extremely seedy and slightly illicit feel to the open air auditorium in which it was held, behind the Pashupatinath public toilets. God only knew what the toilets were like inside, for where we stood there were faeces everywhere.

"I thought we'd left this all behind us," I remarked, as I cleaned my shoe on a relatively turd-free piece of grass.

"Well, whoever put it there certainly did as well," replied Simon.

"It was probably Dunging!"

"Hey, you bugger! I'm not bloody guilty. You'll give me a bad reputation!"

*

Outside in the street, I was instantly set upon by street hawkers selling jewellery, and after a prolonged and at times fairly heated haggling session, I bought two bracelets which took my fancy. Although I had managed to knock them down by fifty per cent, I was sure I was still being ripped off. But I didn't care. I was happy with my buys.

Back on the bus, John Dunging was also happy with his buy. He had bought a hat. John had worn his white floppy cricket hat, with the plastic name tag with which we had all been issued at Heathrow, throughout the entire trip. For him now to purchase a piece of headgear which was quite as absurd as that which he was wearing, was an indication of the effect that Nepal can have on even the most conservative of visitors.

"I mean, just look at that," he said, proudly justifying his purchase. "It's all embroidered. It's even got Nepal on it!" It suddenly became very clear how people who sold hats with Blackpool emblazoned on them managed to make a living.

"What do you think they'll say down your local at home?" I asked.

"Oh, I don't know." He paused. "I think they think I'm bloody barmy any road!"

"Where are the others?" asked Joy who had missed the side show. I told her as Simon joined us.

"What did he do?" asked Joy, interested.

"This aesthetic little man with dreadlocks, dressed in a nappy, for twenty rupees, lifted a breeze-block using only his willy."

"Did he manage it?" she asked.

"Easily," said Simon. "Then he grabbed three chunks of rock, approximately the weight of three or four breeze-blocks, wrapped them in a scarf, wrapped the scarf around his willy, and lifted the lot up."

"Wow!" said Joy, clearly impressed, but still foggy on a few details. "How did he actually get the willy to lift it?"

"He just wrapped it round the middle of the shaft of the willy and held the end with his hand, and lifted the rocks up."

"Did he have an erection?" asked Joy.

"No," Simon replied. "At least I don't think so. I certainly don't think I would have." He looked at me, "would you?"

"I very much doubt it. As a doctor", I asked, "would you consider that a medically sound thing to do?"

"Well, I tried it," said Simon, "But it didn't seem to make it any longer."

"Wish said he was going to do it around the back of the public toilets in Lampeter," said Ron Isles.

"He'd better not," Joy threatened. "If my squad car's anywhere near, I'll arrest him before he can do an encore!"

"I think you ought to arrest the bugger on suspicion anyway," I said.

*

Our next stop was Bhaktapur, the third major town of the trio which virtually run into each other in the Kathmandu Valley. It is also known as Bhadgaon, or the City of Devotees, our guide informed us, and still retains a medieval atmosphere.

"Was that a medieval car?" I asked, as an ancient jalopy almost removed the backs of my ankles and sped past hooting.

"Moaning again, Marvin?" asked Annabel.

This apart, there was unmistakably an air of timelessness which pervaded the narrow streets of Bhaktapur, overhung with intricately carved ornate wooden balconies. This is the clay pot capital of Nepal; indeed you can buy practically anything made from clay from elephants to miniature houses. Richard bought an elephant.

"We should have a sweep on how many pieces that arrives back at Heathrow in," I said.

Most of the larger shops accepted all major credit cards known to man, and Simon, Annabel and I found a shop which specialised in *Mandalas*. A *Mandala* is a hand-embroidered Buddhist prayer mat which depicts the geometrical and astrological representation of the world. There is no way of telling the value of these things, so in the end we agreed a good discount for buying three, and felt that we had got a bargain. Mine cost fifty dollars.

But our negotiations had been lengthy and we had missed the bus, so we hailed an ancient and battered taxi to return us to the hotel, having soaked up the atmosphere of Bhaktapur's Durbar Square.

That evening we enjoyed a tour of the bars of Thamel, ending up at the Mickey Mouse bar, where their cocktails were the speciality. There is no nightclub in Kathmandu, so this was the next best thing.

I became very tired at eleven o'clock, which reminded me that less than seventy-two hours before I had been practically on my deathbed. I managed to get a rickshaw to return me to the hotel and savoured the silence of the still night, as the little man pedalled me through a city asleep, where the dust lay still for a few short hours before the frenetic bustle of a million pairs of feet kicked it into life again.

## Thursday 2nd December

Tom and I spent the entire morning lounging on a Thamel rooftop café, watching the world go by, and speculating, amongst other things, as to why anyone would want to hang a mouldy potato from the trestled arch adjacent to us. We breakfasted, then had coffee, and before we knew it, it was time for lunch. We had arranged to meet Simon, Zvoni and Valeri in Durbar Square.

That afternoon, after an excellent lunch at a Bulgarian restaurant of Zvoni's recommendation, and on his expense account, Simon, Yom and I toured Thamel scouring the shops for something suitable to wear to the prize-giving ceremony that evening. Thamel is the T-shirt capital of the entire universe. In fact, there is so much going on in Thamel, that some would say that it is *the* centre of the entire universe. There are restaurants of every imaginable denomination, guest houses and hotels which range from the Spartan to the excessively opulent. But what holds the greatest fascination are the shops, in particular the little tailors' shops where they will run you up three hundred T-shirts overnight, embroidered with the entire contents of *War and Peace*, all for the price of half a pint of lager back home.

Simon had designed his own version of the Everest Marathon T-shirt, and Tom and I ordered one as well. Then we turned our attention to serious clothes buying. The little side street shops had a distinctly 60s ambience, and the off the peg garments were reminiscent of the trendy boutiques of the King's Road in its heyday. No one had told the good tailors of Thamel that the age of the hippy had come and gone. God knows what will happen if they ever hear about the punk era.

Two hours later, satisfied that we were the most absurdly dressed creatures on the entire subcontinent, we returned to the hotel, only to find that everyone else had had exactly the same idea, and looked equally ridiculous. There was more tie-dyed cotton in the tranquil, post-colonial lounge of the Blue Star than there had been at Woodstock. John Dunging's hat was a shrinking violet when compared with the voluptuous floppy velvet hats and the softer velvet flat caps of the sort that Tom had plumped for.

"What's happened Tom?" asked Annabel. "This is a bit of a transformation, to say the least."

I had to admit that, of all of us, Tom looked the most splendidly ridiculous. But that was probably due to his sober, if not sombre, outlook during the early stages of the trip. He was even smoking cigarettes now, something that he had never even done before.

Thankfully, generally he lost them and I stubbed them out, or they went out by themselves before he could put them to his lips.

"Well", he explained, with a broad grin, "at the beginning of the trip I had a hangover, and it took a long time to get over it!"

Some hangover.

\*

We assembled in the bar at 6 p.m. sharp for an Early Bird meeting. There were three reasons for this. The first, and principal, reason was to thank our sirdar and his assistant formally. They had looked after us superbly throughout the trip and, as a result of their unstinting devotion, everything that could run smoothly had run smoothly.

The second reason was because it was going to be a long, long evening, with lengthy speeches to endure, so it was important to start on the beer early.

But the third reason was the one which emphasised the *esprit de corps* which had made us such a good group, and showed that we were not above a bit of clandestine skulduggery. Browsing through one of the less significant backstreet tailors' emporiums, Jeanne, Pierre André's girlfriend, had accidentally unearthed a plot hatched by the Late Birds before they had departed for their respective rafting and National Park trips. They had commissioned the embroidery of a large number of T-shirts with the picture of a yak, bearing the legend: "Sambo Shafters eat Early Birds for Breakfast". Just why they daubed themselves with the somewhat unexotic and decidedly unflattering epithet of Sambo Shafters we never knew. But that mattered little.

Not to be outdone, Jeanne had designed a logo depicting a yak surprised in an act of gross indecency with another somewhat resigned-looking yak. Above the embroidery of the copulating yaks, were the words "Early Birds", and beneath it simply read "The Sambo Shafters". They could draw their own conclusions! Virtually to a man, we loyally placed our orders for a T-shirt. It was not the sort of thing you could wear out to the pub at home.

And now, as the T-shirts were surreptitiously distributed, it was necessary to formulate a plan whereby we would all appear in them together on a prearranged signal to maximise the impact, thus taking the wind out of the Late Bird sails.

I suggested the signal used by the British Lions on the ill-tempered South African tour of 1974. When the opposition resorted to foul play, the call of 'ninety-nine' was issued by skipper Willie John McBride, upon which the entire team would wade in, thus ensuring that the referee had a choice of either sending off the entire team or no one at all. And so, at an appropriate moment, 'ninety-nine' would be called and we would remove our outer garments to reveal the T-shirts. It would be the perfect retort.

We were ushered into the main conference room at seven thirty for the presentation.

On the stage was a long table covered in a white table cloth, beneath a huge banner which reminded us that we were at the Awards Distribution Ceremony of the Fourth Everest Marathon. This was largely for the benefit of the television cameras at the back of the room. Behind the table, a row of empty chairs waited for the visiting dignitaries to occupy them.

And then the lights went out. Another scheduled power cut reminded us of the fragility of our opulent setting. There was electricity in Kathmandu, but it was not our turn to have it. Nothing, it seems, not even the imminent arrival of three members of the Nepali cabinet, can defer the flick of a switch which plunges sections of the city into an arbitrary, but not interminable, period of darkness.

As porters scurried around in the well practised task of placing candles in their long-established positions, I noticed a smartly dressed man in a black suit, wearing a white shirt and black tie, arrive at the door. He looked familiar, but his disguise made him almost as unrecognisable to us as we must have been to him. Behind him was a tall, elegant woman, and two boys.

It was Ray Brown. I greeted him warmly.

"You'll find the corpse in the kitchen", I said, "please be discreet."

"What the bloody hell's going on?" he asked, as his eyes fell on the colourful sea of strangely dressed people before him. Even one or two of the Late Birds, who had returned that afternoon, had made an effort, but looked mundane in comparison to the excesses of clashing colours worn by Tom, Simon, myself and Dave English. The last time Ray had seen us, we had looked normal. Our clothes had clung to our tired and unkempt bodies with the adhesive qualities of the sweat and grime picked up along the trail. What on earth had happened in the last two days to induce us to buy a pair of trousers that you wouldn't use to change a spark plug on the lawn mower at home, or a hat that you wouldn't give the hamster to make a nest in?

"Colourful, isn't it?" I said.

"I didn't know it was bloody fancy dress!" he replied.

But it had been a colourful trip, through a colourful country, amongst colourful people. Tomorrow, and for most of the rest of our lives, we would return to sobriety and normality, and this lot would be buried at the bottom of a drawer, where even the moths would regard it with suspicion.

I sat with Ray and his family and they told me about their trek to Tengboche, which had been wonderful, and which Ray had found relaxing after the rigours and the growing tensions of the previous month, as we waited for the arrival of the guests.

We waited. And we waited. At last a message was received that they had been held up in traffic, but would shortly be here, and eventually, as the lights flickered into life once more, they arrived.

"It's a good job that this isn't the Savoy. The footman would never have let them in," I said to Simon, as three little men, dressed as if they had been living on the streets for several months, walked up the aisle to the platform, amid polite, uncertain applause. They were introduced by Diana as people with unpronounceable names, one of whom was the Minister of Tourism, another was the President of the Nepal Amateur Athletic Association. The third, and by a considerable margin the most important, an ancient little man wearing what appeared to be a woollen hat, was introduced to us as Ganesh Man

Singh. Mr Singh was the Supreme Leader of the Nepali Congress Party, a man of almost eighty years of age who had spent his life campaigning for democracy, human rights and civil liberties. Later that month, he travelled to New York where he was awarded the 1993 United Nations Human Rights Prize.

Perhaps it was understandable that he had never got round to kitting himself out with a decent wardrobe. After all, Michael Foot never did either.

The Rev. John Webster had been asked by Diana to speak on behalf of the runners:

"It is singularly inappropriate that I should reply on behalf of the runners, simply because I am the only runner who didn't run – the only runner who started but did not finish. But it seems to me important to participate to the best of your ability..." he addressed the guests. "...Your greatest asset, apart from your country, is your people. All of us who have participated in this venture have been deeply moved by the tremendously warm welcome we have received from the people of Nepal."

Zvoni had been asked by us to thank Diana, and he spoke briefly before presenting her flowers:

"I read, because I am quoting Goethe: 'Whatever you can do, or dream you can do, begin it! Boldness has genius, power and magic in it.' And many dreams became true here last week. We have this very fine lady, who had the vision and guts to organise such a beautiful event. I believe that you, like myself, will go home a better person."

It was an emotional evening. As the prizes were distributed, I looked around the room knowing that I was saying farewell to these people with whom I had shared so much, people for whom I had so much affection, and people whom I would probably never see again. Saying farewell to the last latrine had been sad in a curious sort of way, but saying farewell to flesh and blood memories was another. There had, of course, been talk of a reunion. But reunions seldom materialise, and even more seldom do they manage to recreate the atmosphere which had been so special.

Pierre got a playful slap from Jeanne for surreptitiously opening the envelope and counting the ten fifty pound notes which made up his winnings. As the guests departed to an impending cabinet meeting, the alternative award ceremony began.

That first night of the trek came back to haunt me as I was called on stage to receive the award for the person who had made the most effort to gain a cultural appreciation of Nepal throughout the trip. Or not. It was a T-shirt which read: "I love Nepali Culture", and was, appropriately, presented by Wish.

As we adjourned to the ballroom for the buffet and for the party to begin in earnest, I called the prearranged signal. The hideous T-shirts were revealed, Late Bird jaws dropped and hands froze midway between plate and mouth, as they realised that we had beaten them at their game and we had had the last laugh.

Annabel grabbed my arm. "What a bunch of losers, eh Marvin?"

Somewhere between the small hours beyond midnight and the dawn I got to bed, exhausted but elated. The party was still in full swing, but a combination of beer, tiredness and emotion told me to go while I could still walk. It had been a wonderful evening, and a fitting end to a magnificent, once in a lifetime adventure.

Proof positive, if any was needed, that adventure is not beyond the scope of any of us who have a dream and have the boldness to begin it!

> *Those green latrine tents*
> *And the smell of faeces,*
> *Athletic cling-ons*
> *In perplexing places,*
> *Oh how the ghost of you clings*
> *These foolish things*
> *Remind me of you...*
>
> *A cry at night for some more toilet tissue*
> *"Sod off," says Blakeney, "You have had your issue",*
> *Always, will the colour green*
> *Of that last latrine,*
> *Remind me of you.*
>
> *I know that this was bound to be.*
> *These things have haunted me*
> *For you've entirely enchanted me...*

## *Epilogue*
# "Great Four Weeks, but Great to Be Back"

### Saturday 4th December, 11.30 a.m.

Biman Bangladesh flight BG-704, unaffectionately nicknamed 'The Flying Tandoori' touched down at Heathrow after a cramped, smelly, alcohol-free, but largely uneventful flight some twenty-five hours after our departure from Kathmandu. This included the eight hour stopover in Dhaka which had, predictably, been hell.

Simon, Annabel and I had planned to escape from the airport, find a taxi that would take us to an international hotel, and bash the plastic for a decent meal and a few beers. But the plan never got off the ground. Our exit from the airport was barred by bored and trigger happy-looking guards who marched us to the 'restaurant' and insisted that we should eat the chicken and chips that had been provided for us. It was so rare, it could have walked off the plate.

Dejectedly, we whiled away the time in the lounge where the atmosphere was as feisty as the food. To make matters worse, I was rapidly sobering up from the beers I had enjoyed with John the Buddhist on a sunny Thamel balcony before departure, and the half bottle of Nepali whisky which I had shared with John the Vicar on the bus to the airport.

"What d'you think of this," I had asked him.

"I am..." he had thought, taking an enormous mouthful and slowly swallowing with the pained look of displeasure which a Scotsman reserves for drinking anything other than that which was distilled in his austere and desolate homeland "...slowly forming an opinion of it."

"Well, don't leave it too long. It's nearly all gone! By the way, why were you being dragged by your underpants down the corridor, screaming like a castrated yak, at six thirty this morning?"

"I was being ejected from my rightful residence by one Dr Carter." I never did find out what exactly happened but, on this occasion, the 'meddlesome priest' got his come-uppance. The carpet burns made him look as if he had suffered a crucifixion.

With stopovers in Dubai and Paris, the journey seemed to last forever, but the cool drizzle that wafted in from the open door as we stood on the apron at Orly was a welcome reminder that home was but a hop and a jump away.

The interminable wait for our baggage at Heathrow was pregnant with silent smiles and clumsy promises to keep in touch or even reunite. All of us wanted to be gone, but none of us wanted to say goodbye. It was unlikely that most of us would ever meet again.

Many of us wore the colourful, ethnic vestiges of our time in Kathmandu. What had looked fairly normal yesterday, now, under the bright strip lighting of the terminal three arrivals building, with stern, stiff-shirted, sober-suited officials surveying us suspiciously, looked absurd.

"You look ridiculous!" I said to Richard. "I dare you to read the news dressed like that."

"Well, when I get home I'll have a hot bath and consign these to the back of the wardrobe, probably never to be worn again. But it kind of gets you like that doesn't it? Anyway, you can talk, you looked a complete and utter twat yourself last night!"

I didn't disagree.

"What're you up to tonight?" I asked Bryan English.

"Well Rich, I reckon it'll be down to McDonald's. McChicken sandwich, large fries, then wash it down with a couple of pints of Stella."

"Glad to be back?"

"Yea, great four weeks, but great to be back!"

My luggage had arrived and I muttered a few goodbyes. Annabel surprised me by kissing me on the cheek, then predictably aimed a playful but nonetheless painful blow in the direction of my groin, and that was the last I saw of her.

There were hoards of people straining at the barriers beyond the customs, clamouring excitedly for the arrival of relatives and loved ones from a distant, far off world. Suddenly I picked out Kirsty and Rosanna in the crowd, and a tearful reunion ensued of kisses, arms everywhere and "Daddy, what have you brought me?"

And then I was back in civilisation, a subtly different civilisation, crawling along the M4 in three lanes of bumper to bumper traffic. Had it changed or was it me? It was a beautiful, bright, cold December morning. I noticed there was a thin covering of snow on the ground. It was almost like a Khumbu morning and I felt great.

In Number Twelve, Ivy Close, Windsor, Sally welcomed me in typical fashion: "Christ, Rich, you need a bath! Jenks has just popped out to the off-licence. You boys are going to the pub to watch the Rugby this afternoon, while the girls go Christmas shopping. Fair deal eh?"

"Count me in, I'm ready!" I replied enthusiastically, suddenly remembering that the All Blacks were playing the Barbarians in the final match of their tour. God, was it only a week since we were huddled around the tiny radio in the Thamserku Lodge, craning for every word that hissed and crackled through the metal grill, borne by the winds over the miles to one of the very few remaining true wildernesses on earth? Was it only a week ago that I was within a marathon's reach of the top of the world? Already it seemed like light years ago. In the last week, I had been dangerously ill with dysentery, flown in an aircraft that had less metal than a coat hanger, from a runway than had less tarmac than an Irish road. I had regained my strength and celebrated our survival or success in Kathmandu. And finally, I breathed the culture of that mystical city. Then at last, I had safely made the long journey, racing the sunrise over the barren Urals, to home.

"You're not going out dressed like that, are you?" Sally brought me back to earth.

I looked at what I was wearing. "No, I suppose not," I said sadly. I was definitely back.

"Besides which, you smell."

\*

And that is about all there is to tell.

The warmth of the third pint of Murphy's and the glow from the open fire in the packed and smoky public bar of the Admiral Nelson battled unevenly with the inevitable haze of fatigue that lengthy air journeys induce. Outside, tiny flakes of snow flicked against the window behind me, and a runner in a woolly hat jogged by on the wide muddy verge opposite. Cars rushed by, windscreen wipers swishing, tyres angrily hissing as the feeble snow that danced in the headlights fell fugitive to the warm earth and turned to slush.

This was the world to which I belonged. A world where people are constantly on the move – people to meet, people to talk to, deadlines to meet. A world where, to stand still and listen to the sound of millions of years of nature shifting beneath your feet is a sign of madness. A world where simply to stand still is seen as failure.

A mobile phone rang, and Tattoo Man at the bar talked loudly to someone called "Daz-mate" with a good deal of panache. No one took much notice. What would have drawn an excited crowd in Karikholi hardly raises an eyebrow in Windsor.

Somewhere, from far away, I caught the urgency of the half-time adverts that drew my mind back to the television in the corner. A nubile young woman in an extremely tight dress washed a red Lamborghini Diablo in the suggestive and Siren-like manner that tormented the chain gang in *Cool Hand Luke*. Christ knows what either was advertising, but it oozed opulence and greed and it drew me like a magnet.

I was beginning to realise how shortlived were the changes wrought by my recent experiences in Nepal.

"Nice, that," I motioned in the direction of the television.

"The car's not bad either," replied Jenks.

"That's what I meant. D'you know," I paused, "I could get over a hundred and sixty trips to Nepal for what that costs? In fact, for what that costs, I could probably buy half of Nepal."

"Yeah," replied Jenks, reflectively finishing his pint, "but which would you honestly rather have, if you had that much spare change?"

"Well, put it this way..." I said, searching in my reassuringly foul-smelling wallet, for something other than rupees to buy my round... "if I had a spare one hundred and thirty thousand pounds, I'd take the Lambo. But, if I ever have a spare eight hundred pounds, I'll be on the next plane to Nepal."

"But not to run a marathon!"

The Murphy's was obviously working.

"Who knows?"